Re-Presenting Feminist Methodologies

This book tracks the trajectory of gender in the social sciences and humanities through an exploration of the challenges and contradictions that confront contemporary feminist analysis as well as future directions. Drawing on research in India, the essays in the volume engage with the subject in imaginative ways, each one going beyond documenting the persistence of gender inequality, instead raising new questions and dilemmas while unravelling the complexities of the terrain. They also interrogate extant knowledge that has 'constructed' women as 'agentless' over the years, incapable of contesting or transforming social orders – by taking a close look at gendered decision-making processes and outcomes, sex for pleasure, health care practices, content and context of formal schooling or the developmental state that 'mainstreams' gender. Do existing feminist methodologies enable the understanding of emerging themes as online sexual politics, transnational surrogacy or masculinist 'anti-feminist' sensibilities? The feminist methodologies delineated here will provide readers with a toolkit to assess the criticality of gender as well as its nuances. The work foregrounds the importance of intersectionality and builds a case for context-specific articulations of gender and societies that destabilize binary universals.

This volume will be useful to scholars and researchers across the disciplines of the social sciences and humanities, especially gender studies, women's studies, feminism, research methodology, education, sociology, political science and public policy.

Kalpana Kannabiran is Professor and Director at the Council for Social Development, Hyderabad, India. Among her book publications are *Tools of Justice: Non-Discrimination and the Indian Constitution* (2012) and the edited volumes *The Violence of Normal Times: Essays on Women's Lived Realities* (2005), *Women and Law: Critical Feminist Perspectives* (2014) and *Violence Studies* (2016). She has taught at NALSAR University of Law and is co-founder of Asmita Resource Centre for Women. Kannabiran has written on gender, caste, tribe, violence, disability, law and free speech and is recipient of the VKRV Rao Prize for Social Science Research (2003) and the Amartya Sen Award for Distinguished Social Scientists (2012), both for her work in the field of law. She is on the editorial advisory committee of the Review of Women's Studies of *Economic and Political Weekly*.

Padmini Swaminathan is Professor and Chairperson of the School of Livelihoods and Development at the Tata Institute of Social Sciences, Hyderabad, India. A former Director at the Madras Institute of Development Studies, she also held the Reserve Bank of India Chair in Regional Studies at MIDS. Her research work covers industrial organization, labour, occupational health and skill development, all from a perspective of gender. Her recent publications include the edited volume *Women and Work* (2012). She currently serves on the editorial boards of several journals including *Gender, Technology and Development*, *Indian Journal of Gender Studies*, *Journal of Entrepreneurship* and the editorial advisory committee of the Review of Women's Studies of *Economic and Political Weekly*.

Re-Presenting Feminist Methodologies
Interdisciplinary Explorations

Edited by
Kalpana Kannabiran and
Padmini Swaminathan

LONDON AND NEW YORK

First published 2017
by Routledge

2 Park Square, Milton Park, Abingdon, Oxfordshire OX14 4RN
52 Vanderbilt Avenue, New York, NY 10017

Routledge is an imprint of the Taylor & Francis Group, an informa business

First issued in paperback 2019

Copyright © 2017 selection and editorial matter, Kalpana Kannabiran and Padmini Swaminathan; individual chapters, the contributors

The right of Kalpana Kannabiran and Padmini Swaminathan to be identified as the authors of the editorial material, and of the authors for their individual chapters, has been asserted in accordance with sections 77 and 78 of the Copyright, Designs and Patents Act 1988.

All rights reserved. No part of this book may be reprinted or reproduced or utilised in any form or by any electronic, mechanical, or other means, now known or hereafter invented, including photocopying and recording, or in any information storage or retrieval system, without permission in writing from the publishers.

Notice:
Product or corporate names may be trademarks or registered trademarks, and are used only for identification and explanation without intent to infringe.

British Library Cataloguing-in-Publication Data
A catalogue record for this book is available from the British Library

Library of Congress Cataloging in-Publication Data
A catalog record for this book has been requested

ISBN: 978-1-138-63379-7 (hbk)
ISBN: 978-0-367-27984-4 (pbk)

Typeset in Galliard
by Apex CoVantage, LLC

For

Maithreyi Krishna Raj

in solidarity

Contents

Contributors x
Acknowledgements xii

Introduction: re-presenting feminist methodologies 1
KALPANA KANNABIRAN AND PADMINI SWAMINATHAN

PART I
Mapping terrains 25

Section 1: Feminist journeys 27

1 Studying women and the women's movement in India: methods and impressions 29
JOAN P. MENCHER

2 'To bounce like a ball that has been hit': feminist reflections on the family 49
KALPANA KANNABIRAN

3 Masculinities in fieldwork: notes on feminist methodology 74
ROMIT CHOWDHURY

4 Real-life methods: feminist explorations of segregation in Delhi 91
GHAZALA JAMIL

Section 2: Unpacking disciplines — 113

5 Stories we tell: feminism, science, methodology — 115
BANU SUBRAMANIAM

6 Researching online worlds through a feminist lens: text, context and assemblages — 131
USHA RAMAN AND SAI AMULYA KOMARRAJU

7 The erotics of risk: feminism and the humanities in *flagrante delicto* — 158
BRINDA BOSE

8 Impractical topics, practical fields: notes on researching sexual violence in India — 179
PRATIKSHA BAXI

PART II
Exploring themes — 201

Section 3: Development — 203

9 Planning for modernization? feminist readings of plans and planned development in India — 205
PADMINI SWAMINATHAN

10 Unpacking 'win–win': how feminists interrogate microfinance — 229
K. KALPANA

11 Globalizations, mobility and agency: understanding women's lives through women's voices — 246
BHAVANI ARABANDI

12 'Ladkiyaan phir aage?' towards understanding the formal school system — 267
KUMKUM ROY

Section 4: Health 295

13 Researching assisted conception from a feminist lens 297
SAROJINI NADIMPALLY AND ANINDITA MAJUMDAR

14 RUWSEC Clinic: challenges faced by a grassroots
feminist clinic 313
SUBHA SRI B. AND T.K. SUNDARI RAVINDRAN

15 Feminist critical medical anthropology
methodologies: understanding gender and health care
in India 330
CECILIA VAN HOLLEN

Index 349

Contributors

Bhavani Arabandi is Postdoctoral Research Fellow at the Chao Center for Asian Studies, Rice University, Houston, USA. Her research explores how workers in emerging economies confront changes in labour, household and family arrangements.

Pratiksha Baxi is Associate Professor at the Centre for the Study of Law and Governance, Jawaharlal Nehru University, New Delhi, India. Also a founder of the Law and Social Sciences Research Network, she is the author of *Public Secrets of Law: Rape Trials in India* (2014).

Brinda Bose is Associate Professor at the Centre for English Studies, Jawaharlal Nehru University, New Delhi, India, and co-founder of Marg Humanities. She teaches, and researches in, literary modernisms, gender and sexualities, cinema, and the humanities.

Romit Chowdhury is a research scholar at the Department of Sociology, National University of Singapore, Singapore. His research is in the field of feminist studies (particularly masculinities), urban sociology, and ethnographic methods.

Ghazala Jamil is Assistant Professor at the Centre for the Study of Law and Governance at Jawaharlal Nehru University, New Delhi, India. Her research has focused on materiality and spatiality of culture, urban poverty and marginalization and urban governance.

K. Kalpana is Assistant Professor at the Humanities and Social Sciences Department at the Indian Institute of Technology Madras, Chennai, India. Her research area is development studies with a focus on the interface between gender and the development experience.

Sai Amulya Komarraju is a research scholar in the Department of Communication, University of Hyderabad, India. Her research interests include Feminist Media Studies, Feminist Cultural Studies, and Digital Culture.

Contributors xi

Anindita Majumdar is Assistant Professor, School of Liberal Arts, Indian Institute of Technology, Hyderabad. She has written extensively on commercial surrogacy and kinship.

Joan P. Mencher is retired Professor of Anthropology from the City University of New York's Graduate Center, and Lehman College, University of New York, USA. For over five decades, she has worked extensively in South India on issues of ecology, caste, land reform, agriculture, women and related issues.

Sarojini Nadimpally is a founder of Sama Resource Group for Women and Health, New Delhi, India. She is also a co-editor of *Reconfiguring Reproduction: Feminist Health Perspectives on Assisted Reproductive Technologies* (2014).

Usha Raman is Professor, Department of Communication, University of Hyderabad, India. Her research interests include cultural studies of science, health communication, children's media, social impact of digital media and cyberculture studies.

T.K. Sundari Ravindran is Professor at the Achutha Menon Centre for Health Science Studies, Sree Chitra Tirunal Institute for Medical Sciences and Technology, Thiruvananthapuram, India. She is also a founder member and currently Secretary of the Rural Women's Social Education Centre (RUWSEC), Tamil Nadu, established in 1981.

Kumkum Roy teaches Ancient Indian History at the Centre for Historical Studies, Jawaharlal Nehru University, New Delhi, India. Her publications include *The Power of Gender and the Gender of Power* (2010).

Subha Sri B. is an obstetrician with experience of working in tertiary and primary care settings. Since 2006, she has been working with Rural Women's Social Education Centre, Tamil Nadu, India.

Banu Subramaniam is Professor of Women, Gender, Sexuality Studies at the University of Massachusetts, Amherst, USA. She is the author of *Ghost Stories for Darwin: The Science of Variation and the Politics of Diversity* (2014).

Cecilia Van Hollen is Associate Professor of Anthropology at Maxwell School for Citizenship and Public Affairs, Syracuse University, Syracuse, New York, USA. She is the author of *Birth in the Age of AIDS: Women, Reproduction, and HIV/AIDS in India* (2013).

Acknowledgements

This idea of this volume took shape in the course of our conversations around the need for a text on the feminist methodology that draws on research in India and South Asia. The first step in this was to propose a special issue of the Review of Women's Studies (RWS), *Economic and Political Weekly* (*EPW*) – a proposal that was enthusiastically welcomed by the editorial advisory group, of which we are part. We are grateful to the members of the advisory group, and in particular to Lina Mathias of *EPW* for shepherding the special issue through and to the editor for permission to publish the *EPW* RWS collection in this volume. Even as we planned the special issue, it occurred to us that we could simultaneously work towards putting a text together that would enlarge the scope of the debate. We are extremely grateful to Shashank Shekhar Sinha, publishing director, Routledge, and his India team for their warm support of our proposal and for seeing this volume through press in a most painless manner.

Our contributors have been exceptional – we thank each of them for their diligence and patience. We are grateful to them for agreeing to be a part of this project. We have drawn upon the expertise of several scholars to review the chapters; we thank each of them profusely for their time, critical comments and suggestions that have led to, in some cases, rewriting of whole chapters, before being accepted for the volume. Our regret is that a couple of valuable contributors dropped out from this journey owing to personal commitments. We sorely miss the feminist historian's voice, especially on dalit worldviews, caste, gender, power and modern Indian historiography in this collection. But this is just a beginning, and we do hope it will trigger a nuanced and continuing conversation on critical questions of method and methodology in feminist research.

This volume is a tribute to Maithreyi Krishna Raj, pioneer in women's studies in India, and co-founder of the Review of Women's Studies, *Economic and Political Weekly*, along with Alice Thorner. This, along with Maithreyi's work over five decades as a feminist economist, and an architect of the Research Centre for Women's Studies with Neera Desai, has been extremely important in bringing academic rigour and activist engagements in women's studies together at a time when the field was still in a nascent stage. Her commitment to interdisciplinarity and her untiring pursuit of scholars and scholarship saw the Review of Women's Studies grow into perhaps *the* most important learning ground and forum for debate on women's studies and feminist research in South Asia. Feminist methodology and the interdisciplinary architecture of women's studies have been at the core of Maithreyi's concerns – as a teacher, a scholar and a pioneering feminist editor. We believe that the eclectic and plural collection of essays contained in this volume is an apt celebration of her life's work, and we offer her this tribute on our own behalf and on behalf of the contributors – with gratitude and affection, in sisterhood and friendship.

Finally, we acknowledge with thanks the support we have received from our colleagues and staff at the Council for Social Development, Hyderabad, and Tata Institute of Social Sciences, Hyderabad.

Introduction
Re-presenting feminist methodologies

*Kalpana Kannabiran and
Padmini Swaminathan*

This volume took shape in the 125th birth anniversary of Dr. B.R. Ambedkar, a milestone in our collective intellectual and political travels, which enables the tracing of 'different histories and futures of feminism and anti-caste politics in India' (Rege 2013: 56).

Binary gender to 'gender galaxy'[1]

It is extremely important to register that the moment we are poised at is one where women's studies, gender studies and feminism have been challenged in fundamental ways. We take note of Connell's concern that the deficit of recognition of scholarship from the global periphery is a 'structural problem of feminist thought on a world scale' (Connell 2015: 52). Intersecting with this is the fact that feminist scholarship even within the 'periphery' has very rarely, if at all, engaged with the ways in which gender is deeply embedded and implicated in social location and constituted by it. It is apposite to dwell for a moment on the nature of this 'structural problem' of feminist thought. While gender has been a useful category of analysis, the politics of history and intellectual production on a global level has resulted in the universal characterization of gender in binary terms of male–female, man–woman situated within heteronormativity to understand all cultures. The northwestern Europe–North American standard was applied to measure gender regimes and gender categories worldwide in feminist scholarship as 'the default understanding of gender', eliding the complex, culturally rooted ways in which gender takes shape. This forces questions related to the methodological implications of such flattening centre stage: 'what are the implications of making a particular conception of gender universal? What does it mean to extend a parochial, albeit familiar, understanding of gender to times and places other than those that gave rise to it in the first place?' (Sinha 2012: 356). More important, however, what exactly does the push beyond gender universals entail in these diverse locations across the globe? What are the ways in which these locations might prompt the feminist scholar to reconstitute the very category of gender, daring her to disengage gender from its entrapment in the uni-dimensional binary frame of sexual difference – to dislodge the default setting of man–woman as the proper referent of gender, as it were? For, as Sinha suggests, 'once gender is thus liberated from its unnecessary association with any one parochial history, it becomes newly available for a reinvigorated feminist theory and praxis' (Sinha 2012: 358).

Women have been the focus of policy, legislative reform, sociological research, economic thinking and, importantly, historiography – as a critical embodiment of inequality and asymmetries in power. Somewhere along the way, the focus shifted from women as subjects of academic attention to gender as a category of analysis, with gender standing in for a reference to women, not necessarily signalling a displacement of a binary logic. Gender inequality has been understood as male–female disparities, and gender-based forms of oppression have been understood as the oppression of women. 'Although gender, as a category in the law is nowhere defined as male and female, it has been *presumed* to be binary, a presumption that straddles the law and especially (quantitative) social research. For example, legislations have elaborated on the entitlements of men as distinct from women and on special protections, reservations and affirmative action for women; policy and databases have focused likewise on elaborating "sex/gender" in binary terms, in an attempt to aggregate measures of inequality or identify sources of discrimination' (Kannabiran 2015).

There has been some recognition in social research of the complex and intersectional character of gender orders, especially that gender orders are constantly constituted and reconstituted in multiple configurations with distinct patterns of hegemony among different masculinities and femininities (Connell 2012). However, in India, this recognition has not churned the terrain of gender to arrive at a new sensibility. Shah *et al.* (2015) provide us with a rich road map on how we might begin to plot the 'gender galaxy' – what does the ethnographic turn involve – in method, in conceptualization and in analysis? And how do we draw on historical/political erasures to trace the intellectual histories of sexual diversity – and context-specific articulations of gender? As Sinha (2012) argues, MSM (men who have sex with men) is one gender category that has emerged from strategic litigation for the repeal of Section 377. There is other work that suggests that *hijra/eunuch* is a distinct gender category – not 'men trapped in women's bodies', necessarily. This is a figure that crystallizes before us through the frames of law (Kannabiran 2015) and autobiographical narratives (Revathi 2010).

Much work remains to be done in India to actually dislodge gender from the captivity of binary frames that mask more than they explain. This volume on feminist methodology in large part focuses specifically on the experience of women and the creation of female subjects across disciplinary and thematic imaginings. It attempts to unpack and problematize the ways in which women/female subjects are positioned in social research and the humanities – which, rather than disintegrating into a gender galaxy in an extraordinarily affirming moment, is in fact getting crystallized into more rigid segregations and stereotypes, enforced through cumulative violence – caste, state, community and armies working in close concert.

Intersectionality, violence and discrimination

The relationship among sexuality, caste, tribe, race,[2] community, social location, violence, work and wages is complex, and each of these categories mutually constitutes each other, producing specific political economies of gender orders that are intersectional but also, importantly, co-constitutive and co-produced.

Arguing that intersectionality, far from being an analytical tool confined to the Global North, has in fact been used by people in the Global South without necessarily naming it as such, Collins and Bilge point to the example of Savitribai Phule, who 'confronted several axes of social division, namely caste, gender, religion, and economic disadvantage or class', addressing intersecting categories of social division in her political activism (Collins and Bilge 2016: 4). Of methodological import to us is their pertinent observation that since 'intersectionality provides a framework for explaining how social divisions of race, gender, age, and citizenship status, among others, positions people differently in the world' (Collins and Bilge 2016: 15), it is necessary to 'democratize the rich and growing literature of intersectionality' (Collins and Bilge 2016: 30), not limiting it to any one segment of population or, we would add, any one disciplinary, geographic or other location.

Critiquing the attribution of the term 'intersectionality' to Kimberle Crenshaw (Crenshaw 1991), widespread in the literature on this subject, Collins and Bilge see this view as reductionist of Crenshaw's work and stress instead the fact that she uses intersectionality as critical inquiry and critical praxis, building on the work of many who came before her. Working within the tenets of standpoint epistemology, Crenshaw identifies core ideas of intersectionality, demonstrates its use as an analytic tool and marks an important transitional moment in the history of intersectionality – from the period when it was deployed without being named to a point where it begins to be named: 'Crenshaw is clearly advocating for intersectionality as a social justice construct, not as a theory of truth disconnected from social justice concerns' (Collins and Bilge 2016: 84) – and her delineation of intersectionality goes far beyond the boundaries of law in particular geographic locales.

Most important, intersectionality as a tool can be (and has been) deployed to different uses by different struggles against oppression and structural violence. This is most evident, for instance, in the creative articulations of this concept that blossomed forth in the context of the Dalit mobilizations around the Durban conference, especially Dalit feminist mobilizations, which detailed the vulnerabilities and violence engendered by the organization of power around caste, religious fundamentalism, economic exploitation and the complicit state (see Kannabiran 2006).

Whether we take Savitribai Phule's writing as our point of departure for an understanding of the relationship among women, discrimination in society (especially on the grounds of caste) and the political order (as Collins and Bilge do too) (Collins and Bilge 2016: 3), or we mark the transitional moment that Crenshaw represents in the articulation of 'intersectionality', the theorizing of violence is central.

The startling rise in violence against young women and girls – sexual violence and death, as also the deep entrenchment of impunity for the perpetrators – triggers troubling debates on the shape of society post-violence and returns us to the very point where we began to interrogate the conditions of women's subordination. An important part of what we have tried to explore here is ways of countering amnesia and recovering voice through feminist research.

There is by now a large corpus of feminist writing that pushes for a nuanced and layered understanding of gendered violence and of the bases of impunity in our socio-political orders. In their recovery of the memory of the collective assault of women in Kunan Poshpora in Kashmir on the night of 23 February 1991, Essar, Ifrar, Samreena, Munaza and Natasha found the journey of the case to be just like the road to Kunan Poshpora: 'serpentine, full of uncertain turns, surrounded by hope, the destination constantly elusive' (Batool *et al.* 2016: 191). And yet, even while that night (24 years long) has held the story of grave violation, humiliation and treachery, it is importantly a long night of courage, bravery and truth. Chatterjee observes that 'the work of "writing Kashmir" (through documenting everyday lives and experiences of sustained violence) may constitute a feminist praxis, one that integrates critiques of gendered violence and attention to the complex labor of witnessing as intervention' (Chatterji 2012). The recovery of this and similar archives of struggles for dignity, justice and self-respect points to us the enduring, illimitable possibilities of feminist methodologies.

In her recent work on state violence, Geetha (2016) dwells on

> the implicit significance of recognition of suffering because in a fundamental sense, it is such recognition that challenges and illuminates the contours and details of State impunity. Further, it positions impunity as not merely a legal or political conundrum, but as a resolute refusal on the part of State personnel to be a part of shared humanity.
>
> (Geetha 2016: xxvii)

And impunity plays itself out along axes of caste, tribe, religion, region and nation in very specific ways. In speaking of the recognition of suffering, Geetha draws on experiences of sexual violence, which included torture, bodily humiliation of men and women, displacement and forced confinement in situations of conflict especially – Tamil Nadu during the hunt for Veerappan, in Kashmir and Manipur under Armed Forces (Special Powers) Act – and the persistence of hope in women's relentless pursuit of justice (Geetha 2016), echoed as we have seen in the recovery of the memory archives of the people of Kunan Poshpora.

The violence and impunity that we witness even as we speak crystallize around the folding together of Muslim and Dalit communities over the consumption of beef and accusations of cow slaughter. While the Dalit resistance culminating in Una on 15 August 2016 has been stunning in its reversal of the logic of caste – the collective refusal to lift animal (especially cattle) carcasses from villages by Dalits – there is a need to unpack the dense nesting of beliefs, social location and religious prescription/proscription around food (see Kannabiran 2012).

Patole provides a perspective on food and Dalit cuisine that draws on the historical experience of scarcity and hunger, where, often, salt is the only flavour in food. His book of recipes provides an account of the food his parents ate and their parents ate, and he, too, sometimes eats: 'It is an acquired taste, especially one that has been acquired due to centuries of discrimination.' He invites us to dip into the book, where we will discover that

> most of [the recipes] do not need oil. Why is that? Because, Dalits could not afford oil, and that is why we have dishes such as the steamed mutke, which is made out of jowar, garlic and coriander. Instead of oil we used beef fat. Then, there is the famous Maharashtrian dish, the rich puran poli, but the Mangs used to substitute ghee with buttermilk for obvious reasons.

Centuries of deprivation have made 'expert foragers' of Dalits – wild leafy vegetables, bee larvae and pumpkin leaves – and have led them to practise 'nose-to-tail eating' for the longest time (Patole 2016).

Most important for methodological purposes, a series of questions centre around food cultures, which require systematic attention of the feminist researcher: who can eat together; what can be eaten; and what shall not be eaten – by Dalit, Brahmin, Muslim, woman, widow, for instance? Within a family/community, who consumes which parts of an animal's body; what is the sequence in which people in a family eat – gender, generation and kinship/social status (Kannabiran 2012); and can the 'chuhri' dare to ask for fresh-cooked food from 'chowdhriji' – to recall Omprakash Valmiki's *Joothan* (2007)? What are the ways in which food is harnessed into the service of 'nationalism'? More pertinently, can food consumption be 'anti-national'? How would we begin to plot an Indian geography of food that is informed by diversity and the intersectionality of location, politics, choice, coercion and taste?

The changing contexts of feminist engagements

At the precise time when this volume was taking shape, universities and colleges across India witnessed an earth-shaking challenge to encrusted practices of caste, reductionist definitions of 'the nation', Hindutva and its constitutive violence and blatant derogation of life and liberty, in which university administrations have been complicit. This has also been a time of intense debates, disagreements and painful reflections on the meanings of discrimination, and the thin and ever-fading line between suicide and murder. At the centre of the churning is the interrogation of decay and institutional irresponsibility that has dropped deep roots into our university systems in particular and higher education in general. From the structure of the curriculum to allocation of research supervisors, due diligence by teachers, monitoring of student research and selection of areas for research, there is little doubt that dominant trends in teaching and research persist in being exclusionary and negligent of the diversity of life worlds and fundamental questions of human dignity.

At this moment of crisis, turbulence and rebirth (e.g. witnessed in the vibrant Dalit Bahujan interrogation of culture and politics, and also in the everyday resistance in practice, speech and writing especially from the Northeast and Kashmir), the question of feminist methods must be revisited and the feminist project reconstituted. We are witness to the shifting of the core of intellectual production, a moment that must be sustained, especially by feminist scholars if feminism is to be relevant for our futures. It is in this spirit that we urge new thinking on questions of method in feminist research. What are the new methodological departures feminism might signal? In order for feminist methodologies to nurture practices of self-reflexivity, they must move beyond marking identities to providing cogent accounts of the processes by which actors occupy standpoints in particular contexts. In caste society, for instance,

> the consciousness of caste is constitutive of the self . . . embedded in the fact of being, underwriting it in deep seated yet often unarticulated ways. It is also entrenched in the realities of class, which structure the experience of bare life itself. The caste-class nexus produces an array of articulations that tell stories of the complex contradictions between consciousness and survival, which are also stories of the caste system. This is not to argue that this consciousness cannot be ruptured or that the self cannot be reconstituted. It is necessary even while examining the ruptures, to delineate what elements of caste-class remain solid and unshaken, and what parts allow for a reconstitution. Even while there may be significant ruptures around you, in the normal course, these will have the status of folklore – of stories that you hear, of heroism that you see and believe but cannot 'know'. In order to know what the rupture of caste consciousness means, it is necessary to engage self-consciously in the politics of becoming, regulating notions of the self, deschooling and politicising the self in new ways that push you to belonging elsewhere.
>
> (Kannabiran 2008: 64)

1. Mapping terrains

Feminist journeys

This volume contains chapters in two parts. The first part explores the terrains of feminist engagements – tracing journeys through autoethnographic modes and life narratives, and pushing the boundaries of disciplines – testing the limits of disciplinary imagination with respect to the place of women in the gender galaxy.

The opening chapter – an autobiographical narrative – by Joan P. Mencher traces over six decades of experience as a public anthropologist and feminist researcher, looking at questions of caste (from an Ambedkarite perspective), matriliny and most recently sustainable agriculture and its social formations. Mencher's early essay 'The Caste System Upside Down or the Not-So-Mysterious-East' (1974) is an important contribution to the anthropology of anti-caste – perhaps the only one in the period that she was writing on this question.

The key feminist construct in the movements for women's rights beginning in the late 1970s in India was 'the personal is the political'. This assertion was at once universal and particular. While it drew on the experience of feminist movements in the West, it was turned inwards to look at the context-specific ways in which women were oppressed in India – class, caste, religion, tribe, region and political formation – providing distinctive refractions of the problem of women's subordination. A critical arena where the politics of belonging plays out, and indeed an arena where the feminist construct 'the personal is the political' makes most meaning, is *the family*. This is especially the case in India. Kalpana Kannabiran attempts in her chapter on the family to address questions of feminist methods through a close look at the family as an idea in India, through an examination of specific texts and histories to open out intersectional perspectives on the family – pointing to the different notations of 'the personal is the political'. She points to a small selection of texts – B.R. Ambedkar's castes in India, Ambedkarite, Dalit and Adivasi women's narratives, a *hijra*'s reflection on the idea and realities of the family, partition narratives – that situate our understanding of the history of this institution and its criticality to radical politics. Her attempt here is not to provide an account of the shifts and disjunctures in the family but to suggest different lenses through which we may begin to historicize the family. In tracing the ruptures in the personal, she traces the different notations of 'the personal is the political'.

One of the core areas where feminist engagements with the family are clustered is domestic violence. Romit Chowdhury enters the discussion on feminist methodology as a male researcher studying men and male positionalities within a homosocial, homophobic, heterosexual, patriarchal setting. The methodological implications of deploying feminist methods in research settings that are structured by the presumption of male privilege, anti-women worldviews and practices in the everyday, he argues, are complex and fraught with difficulties. How, for instance, might one open out the process of reciprocity in ethnographic research – a core feminist principle – when one is studying men's rights groups in India that challenge the feminist threat to the heterosexual family? In looking at men and masculinities in the context of men's organizing against feminist activism and advocacy, especially on the issue of domestic violence, Chowdhury reflects on the questions that threaten men, the solidarities of homosociality in this context, and the entrenchment of homophobia. Taking a close look at the resistance to feminism by men, what, he asks, may be the constituents of this resistance/antipathy and its internal (in)coherencies? Rather than dismiss it summarily, thus ousting it from the sphere of investigation, he argues for a more careful examination of the specificities of anti-feminist rhetoric and action, thereby pointing to the need to be attentive to 'a more subject-centred view of patriarchal formations.' This would perforce involve a re-invention of methods and tools and the daring to 'empathize with patriarchal impulses.'

This is followed by Ghazala Jamil who looks at practices of segregation – of Muslims in Delhi – defining her own location in relation to her research and unravelling for us the knots that tie the feminist researcher to her informant-collaborators on the field. Jamil attempts to disrupt dominant discourses on prejudice, discrimination and segregation of Muslims by looking at the microfoundations in everyday life that undergird macroexplanations with respect to inter-group dynamics and the play of power, class and gender, among other factors. She argues that an emancipatory impulse is critical and central to feminist methods – one that effectively counters a widespread fetishization of social science research where little attention is paid to the relationships of production of research findings and conclusions. Just as the women's movement and its political critique have impacted discourses that are not specifically about gender or sexual distinctions, the emancipatory impulse of feminist methods can also be deployed in enquiries that are not focused entirely on gendered accounts of social phenomena. Her experience as a feminist researcher studying segregation of Muslims in Delhi led to the discovery that her methods could not remain untouched by feminist politics even though her chosen theoretical frameworks were Marxist Urbanism and Critical Theory. She describes her use of methods as 'real-life methods', which were not structured or predetermined, and so could also be driven by the participants – allowing for co-creation of knowledge. In the end, she describes how this distinctive impulse of feminist methodology can produce accounts of life, which provide, in the words of Daniel Little, 'micro-foundations to macro-explanations' (Little 1986).

Unpacking disciplines

The second section of the volume examines disciplines and boundaries in knowledge production. If the point of feminist knowledge creation is not merely to unveil invisible categories, Banu Subramaniam argues, but rather to reinvent knowledge by resisting the very production of difference, how might this impact on science, scientific endeavour and the structures of scientific practice? She explores the implications of the rejection of the nature–culture binary for feminist science studies. What are the epistemological challenges of studying gender in the sciences and what methodological tools may be productively deployed for the purpose of understanding the relation between human and non-human, life and non-life?

Usha Raman and Sai Amulya Komarraju explore the field of cyberfeminist studies and set up a conversation between the offline world of feminist politics and online gender politics. Tracing the debate between Internet scholars from different disciplines on the nature of the relationship between the 'disembodied, anonymous medium' of cyberspace and the meanings of female subjecthood, they revisit old debates that remain relevant – Donna

Haraway's *Cyborg Manifesto* (1985) for instance – and new, emergent ones. Importantly, this essay travels through Indian cyberspace to open out the terrains of emerging online feminist activism in India. While there are stunning campaigns like the 'Pink Chaddi' campaign and Slutwalk, Raman and Komarraju urge us to examine the constitutive elements of cyberspaces, including cyberfeminism. How for instance are the gatekeeping functions performed, especially with respect to control over material resources and access to science and technology? What are the ways in which cyberfeminist routes provide opportunities for identity formation, community building and the cascading of resistance (as we witnessed in the Nirbhaya campaign)? At another level, they suggest that the effect of global capital flows on feminist politics may be extended to online spaces, which contain possibilities of both, the expansion of transversal politics as also its appropriation. How then, may we simultaneously address the rapid spread *and* sustained, measured deliberation over ideas? Finally, 'how do categories of class, caste, race and gender intersect and what kinds of technocorporealities get created?'

As we live through a historical moment of moral policing, violent stigmatization of 'the other', and moral panics, and witness a reining in of questions of sexuality into the discourse on rights as opposed to 'honour', Brinda Bose coaxes us to travel through humanities on 'an irrational wanton terrain away from the logics of rights, power and punishment via an engagement with praxis, form and situation into sharp materialist-hedonist possibilities of language, pleasure, profanation, the precarious and the tragic', using sexualities as a tool. Rather than stay within the narrow road of developmental formations that are limited, Bose argues for the exploration of the terrains of sexualities that might yield radically new visions for academic praxis. These visions would foreground and risk dissent, resistance, reflection, probing and thought, 'in infinitesimal opposition to the vanguardist.' What are the ways in which, humanities might, through a focus on sexualities, set up a conversation with the social sciences, interrogating the latter through the 'aesthetics of non-conformism and the non-conformism of aesthetics at once?' Arguing that the humanities method militates against the normative, against procedure and is at its core instinctive, unverifiable and transgressive, Bose suggests that it can, through sexualities, destabilise capitalist modernities and halt the march of the nation towards conservative globalism. Thinking of how we might effect this turn with respect to gender studies, she wanders through four territories of the humanities: 'language, madness and negation; pleasure, ethics and politics; profanation, labour and flânerie; pleasure, precarity, tragedy and revolution' – looking for ways of arousing gender studies into a politics of the erotic. In order for Indian feminism to resist the censoring realities of the everyday, she argues, it is important to invoke 'the borderlessness that attends to borders.'

Tracing the emergence of sexual violence as an object of anthropological research, Pratiksha Baxi argues that this is a product of historical, political and social processes that critique the constitution of rape as a public secret. Importantly, ethnographic writing about rape demands practices of transformative reading that inaugurate reading practices that displace horror, shame or voyeurism of any kind. Following the Delhi gang rape protests in 2012–13, there is increased attention to sexual violence as a legitimate field of research and subject of pedagogy. The social, political and historical peril of speaking against the trauma of sexual violence remains a public secret. Anthropologists who have experienced sexual violence while doing fieldwork have raised important questions about the risks of anthropological research and limits of ethnographic writing. Feminist autobiographical ethnographies of sexual violence interrogate the complicity of anthropological theory and research in the work of public secrecy. The emergence of sexual violence as an object of anthropological research is therefore equally a product of the historical, social and political processes that critique the constitution of rape as a public secret. In her chapter, Baxi reflects on the challenges of researching the everyday socio-legal processes that underlie the making of the public secrecy of rape trials and argues that the very process of conducting ethnographies of rape trials is complicit in the making of the public secret.

2. Exploring themes

The second part focuses on two themes – development and health – both of which have witnessed a burgeoning of studies on women. In the early decades of independence, a major scholarly exercise undertaken by Indian feminists across various disciplines was to address the issue of 'women's invisibility', historically and otherwise. This exercise found expression in terms such as 'the woman question', 'hidden from history' and 'relative visibility', which in turn led to efforts to rewrite our academic disciplines from the perspective of women. Chakravarti and Roy (1988), for example, who have been engaged in the task of retrieving women's history over a long time, sum up this effort as follows:

> It is evident that the process of evolving a historical analysis which takes sexuality, social reproduction and production into account may not be simple. Further, the usefulness or otherwise of each of these formulations needs to be tested through the analyses of specific bodies of evidence, and modifications may be required to suit the Indian context. In the ultimate analysis it is important that we are able to explain rather than explain away.
>
> (Ibid.: 337)

Development

Post-independence, the theme of development (economic and otherwise), centre staging the need to address the well-being of the population, has found multiple expressions: in the setting up of institutions such as the Planning Commission, in the passing of specialized legislations and laws and in periodically instituting commissions and committees to study and make appropriate recommendations; the latter have in turn spawned the setting of several bodies such as the National Commission for Women.

A signal contribution of Indian feminists in the field of development practice has been to engage with the Planning Commissions of the centre and states, as well with national and local data collecting bodies to (a) accord recognition to the economically productive nature of much of women's non-monetized activities; (b) conduct large-scale research that would immediately make clear how the economy was being subsidized by the unaccounted and undervalued work of the marginalized sections of society, including women; and (c) exert pressure on the governments of the day to redirect their budgets and expenditures to areas and sectors that would lessen the drudgery and thereby create conditions for gainful participation of large numbers of the marginalized sections in the economic life of the country. In other words, feminist explorations of the functioning of the economy have enabled the demonstration of the ways in which power embedded in socially constructed differences affects and is affected by the sexual division of labour in society, by the manner in which resources get distributed in the household, in the community and through the policies of the state.

Four chapters in this volume explore different but related aspects of 'development' using a feminist lens. Padmini Swaminathan's chapter examines the role played by Five-Year Plans in the economic life of the country. Given the fact that the political party that assumed power in 2014 has officially disbanded the Planning Commission and replaced it with the Niti Aayog, the chapter deems it important to document the journey of planning, the role played by feminists and feminist economists in particular to read and rewrite the plans from a feminist perspective. Methodologically, the exercise is situated within the larger feminist debate relating to 'transformation versus inclusion'; at the end of the day, the author is constrained to note that 60 odd years of planned development has not been 'inclusive' going by the Planning Commission's own admission in its subtitling of the 11th Five-year Plan, namely 'Towards Inclusive Growth'; the goal of transformation of society has systematically been relegated to the background, and/or all but forgotten. In other words, even as we bemoan the disbanding of institutions such as the Planning Commission, as feminists we cannot get away from asking certain hard questions: why did institutions such as the erstwhile Planning Commission fail so badly in their agenda of making economic development inclusive and gender just?

From the 1990s, 'empowerment' became the new liberation mantra. While feminists conceptualized empowerment as the transformation of power relations, the practice of empowerment policies on the ground, however, reduced the concept to individual economic empowerment; more specifically, it meant facilitating women's access to credit. Feminist critiques of the manner in which Indian policy makers have sought to integrate gender into development and thereby empower marginalized sections of the population, including women, are voluminous. Therefore, what are the questions that these critiques raise that need further engagement?

Using microfinance as her entry point, K. Kalpana begins by questioning the 'win–win' hypothesis of governments and funding agencies which claim that microfinance-centred development interventions alleviate poverty as well as empower women, even as they make lending to poor women not only viable but also profitable. Going further, Kalpana asks whether microfinance projects are able to 're-configure social relations and dominant ideologies of gender at play' within the domains of households, communities, markets and states. The tendency to view microfinance projects as converting women into 'successful' economic entrepreneurs has also come in for considerable criticism from several standpoints now adequately covered by feminist literature. Even so, as governments and funding agencies continue to push for more of the same, feminists have to continue asking questions (as Kalpana does), even at the pain of repetition, whether such programmes are able to challenge the oppressive structures of disadvantage that confine women petty commodity producers to the lower segments of the informal sector and whether these empowerment programmes have been able to modify intra-household gender relations and mitigate women's domestic responsibilities.

What are the other larger questions that the aforementioned manner of 'integrating gender in development' gives rise to? One, in the name of alleviating poverty and also empowering women, particularly rural women, a number of tasks are thrust on women, which makes them labour (in addition to their domestic tasks) but which does not fetch them the status of workers eligible for statutory benefits. Two, the pervasive spread of microcredit programmes and microfinance institutions in the countryside involving large numbers of women has not been interrogated from the labour studies angle. The disproportionate emphasis of these programmes and their evaluation on the aspect of how much and to what extent they have empowered women has masked the range of responsibilities (entrepreneurial and otherwise) thrust on rural women. In the process, the labour that women have been forced to expend because of these responsibilities not only continues to remain invisible; worse, these are designed and administered in such a way that they are outside the purview of protective labour legislation. Academically also, while feminist researchers have engaged considerably with the themes of invisibility and the unaccounted nature of much of women's work, including the theme of overburdening women in the name of economically empowering them, labour economics as a discipline has yet to frontally take on board the kind of issues raised earlier. In other words, what has continued (despite all attempts at integration) and even widened over the years is the polarization between feminists' concept of labour and what labour studies comprehends and officially captures as work – to the detriment of women.

In a refreshing departure, Bhavani Arabandi's chapter examines the manner in which opportunities created by economic liberalization have 'transformed' the lives of mostly urban-based, young English-educated and skilled professionals. Using feminist interpretive methodology, Arabandi's exercise provides a fascinating account of how these women are carving out a life for themselves in male-dominated establishments; in their zeal to conform to the capitalist construction of the ideal worker as one who works for long hours and is unencumbered by domestic responsibilities, these women end up being more male than the males themselves! Arabandi further demonstrates how these women resist the dominant framework of normative femininity; the messages from these narratives raise several important questions for feminists working towards transforming workplaces into gender-friendly organizations. At another level, while these narratives could be read as signalling the slow transformations taking place at the micro level, far more research of a longitudinal nature is required to decipher how long these women have been/will be able to hold their own at the workplace and in their homes – two patriarchal structures at the centre of almost all women's lives. An important challenge that Arabandi's chapter throws up for feminists is the manner in which Arabandi's urban, English-educated and skilled professionals distanced themselves from women workers in call centres asserting a distinctive class location and privilege, thereby calling for a more nuanced understanding of the category of modern 'global workers'.

Why does 'education' not only reinforce class and caste divisions but also heighten notions of respectability even as it enables entry to high-paying occupations? That education is key to empowerment and for attaining gender equality in households, communities and the wider society is a truism accepted at all levels. Considerable research has been done and continues to be carried out to address issues such as the persistence of gender gaps in educational attainment; the disproportionately more dropouts among girl children, among poor and in less developed countries; the disproportionately less number of girls and women teachers in institutions of higher learning and in intuitions aimed at imparting professional education, to name a few.

Increasingly, feminist explorations in the field of education have gone beyond grappling with issues of enrolment, dropouts, medium of instruction and so on, and have begun to raise troubling questions relating to the messages being imparted in the name of education, the experience of schooling for different sections of the population and in different organizational set-ups, the manner in which girls in particular imbibe and use the space and time provided in schools to socialize with other children from possibly diverse backgrounds, and so on. Micro-level field studies attempting to explore some of these issues have come up with startling information that in turn have severe implications for the continuation of girls' education.

Clarinda Still (2011) examines female education, marriage and honour among upwardly mobile Dalits. Using data collected during 15 months of ethnographic fieldwork (2004–5) in a Dalit community in rural Andhra Pradesh, the author describes how families who constitute the upper strata of Dalits are educating their daughters in order to marry them 'upwards' within their caste to a groom with prospects of employment. Education allows these girls to become housewives – a term that signals an escape from a life of demeaning agricultural labour that involves 'hard work in the hot sun' (ibid.: 1119). As educated wives married into salaried households, the anxiety is to acquire middle-class virtues that set them apart from their labouring counterparts: 'their language, dress, movement and manners must convey shame and modesty. As their responsibility for maintaining family honour increases, they are progressively more scrutinised and controlled' (ibid.: 1119, 1126).

This heightened emphasis on honour among traditionally egalitarian Dalits signals for Still the increasing concern about female sexuality. *Education for girls is seen as a particularly risky business*: on the one hand, she notes, education provides opportunities for sexual encounters, but on the other hand, it holds the promise of hypergamy. Given their already-precarious circumstance, many Dalits choose to cut short the education of their daughters rather than take the risk. While received literature views education of girls as a positive phenomenon, Still's ethnographic research shows how education can be a 'contradictory resource'.

From a feminist point of view, upwardly mobile Dalit women are turned from valuable workers into sedentary-status producers. But quoting Patricia Jeffery's ethnographic study of *pirzada* women (custodians of a Muslim shrine in Delhi) who live in strict *purdah* near a Sufi shrine in Delhi, Still emphasizes the need to examine how women themselves logically assess their situation within a particular economic and social framework. And therefore she concludes:

> This reminds us to look at the values that underpin Dalit women's active participation in the pursuit of honour and strategies of upward mobility, even when they seem detrimental overall. And while Dalits may not be using education in the way that liberals, feminists and policymakers expect, they are eager to educate their daughters nonetheless.
> (p. 1146)

Biswajit Ghosh (2011) combines field exploration and macro-data from census in an attempt to explain 'the enormous and escalating magnitude of child marriage in West Bengal in recent years'. According to the 2001 Census, 37.16 per cent of girls in the state of West Bengal married before 18 years, while the corresponding figure for the country, as a whole, is only 32.10 per cent. Further, among the 19 districts of West Bengal, Malda (the study area of the chapter) had the second-highest percentage of child marriage in the state after Murshidabad in 2001.

In Ghosh's view, the perceptions of daughters about the reasons for child marriages differ strikingly from those of parents and other elders:

> Both fathers and elders have identified 'poverty' as the major reason for fixing marriage of girls early. But a close scrutiny of their behavior in real life reveals that patriarchal values and institutions influence this pattern greatly. This is because parents with sound economic condition in Malda also fixed their daughter's marriage before they were eighteen. . . . In peasant families across Malda, notions of a girl's virginity and chastity are strongly linked to honour and status of a family or clan. Hence, there is tremendous pressure to minimise the risk of any untoward incidence or improper sexual activity through early marriage. The conservative peasant society of Malda does not normally report harassment cases of girls to the police, because such harassment may mean that she has lost her chastity. The community and religious leaders, who very often enjoy moral sanction to control life beyond religion, typically support such value structure and norms.
> (Ibid.: 50)

As in the case of Clarinda Still, Ghosh's study also emphasizes first the aspect of family status and honour that parents and community members strongly feel could be jeopardized because of girls having to step out for educational purposes. Second, while expenses connected with conduct of marriage are deemed inevitable, whatever may be the economic status of households, expending money on girls' higher education in particular is deemed unnecessary, avoidable since it is seen as not only not benefitting the natal family but also a huge risk (social and economic) that families, given their position and dependence on the community in their immediate vicinity, are not prepared to shoulder. Third, the earlier the marriage of a girl is settled, the lesser the dowry that parents perceive they need to pay for the same – a point flagged by both authors: families lower down the economic ladder argue that imparting higher education to their daughters would require them to look for even more highly educated grooms; the latter would translate into higher dowry demands that such parents can ill-afford.

Kumkum Roy's chapter on education in this volume adds one more layer to those already raised in the works of Arabandi, Still and Ghosh discussed earlier. Roy examines the ways in which the 'hidden curriculum and the examination system converge and diverge in shaping understandings of intersecting identities in terms of gender, caste, class, region, community and disability'. Conversations with university students, who traced their memories of formal schooling, enable Roy to demonstrate how class and caste differences played out in school on a routine basis – in seating arrangements in class, in the allotment of specific chores to students belonging to specific castes and so on. The teaching of gender is bereft of any context – caste, class or regional. While students are exposed to accounts of achievers (e.g. women astronauts), narratives about less privileged women are conspicuous by their absence. Roy raises the very pertinent issue of what constitutes 'success' in examinations based on textbooks whose world view is that of homogeneous middle or upper classes and with which students from underprivileged backgrounds cannot relate.

In a nutshell, while much of mainstream research on education is largely caught up in issues of access, enrolment, dropouts and so on, feminist research on education has moved way beyond to capture the manner in which patriarchal structures of the household, community and schools combine to constrain girl children in particular and children from non-privileged backgrounds in general from experiencing education as a liberating and empowering force.

Health

At various stages in the development history of the country, it is possible to identify certain themes/issues that have brought the 'women's movement' into direct confrontation with the state, even as the feminist movement has always looked to the state for resolution of many of its problems. For example, the period of the 1970s to the late 1980s/early 1990 saw heightened activity that (a) in policy discourse was labelled as family planning and (b) in the academia as the study of demographic transition, but which on the ground was translated into control of women's wombs.

On the assumption that economic development would be thwarted by uncontrolled growth in population, and on further assumption that the poor breed more coupled with socially and culturally regressive norms that was quick to 'penalize' women who either did not conceive or conceived only girl children, a veritable mayhem was let loose in the name of achieving the goal of fertility decline.

Sustained protests from women's groups across the country changed the discourse from the control of wombs to enhancing women's agency that would in turn enable them (the women) to *decide to opt* for fewer children. While feminists struggled to come to grips with the concept of 'women's agency', policy makers aided by demographers suffered no such pangs. Reading correlated data as causation, it was 'established' that enhancing girls' schooling and increasing women's workforce participation (which gave 'statistically significant' results) would achieve the desired result of bringing down fertility. It was left to the feminists again to call off the bluff even as they were careful in emphasizing that education and work participation (progressive on their own terms) had to be delinked from their instrumental link with fertility rates. The discourse again changed into family welfare even as targets for sterilization were surreptitiously retained. To cut a long story short, while in the 2000s the obsession with fertility decline lessened (also since there has been a widespread decline in rates, even if variously, across the country), other more serious demographic facts have risen to the forefront, such as the decline in child sex ratios, making everyone scramble for credible explanations.

The emerging scenarios on the demographic front post-1980s include (a) growing childlessness among the reproductive-age population (captured by decadal census data), (b) the phenomenal growth of the 'assisted reproductive technology' (ART) industry even as public provision of universal health care still eludes us, (c) growing numbers of women being drawn into surrogacy to supplement their meagre household incomes and (d) the late entry and feeble attempts being made by the Indian state to address the as-yet-unresolved legal and other issues raised by the fast-growing assisted reproduction industry and surrogacy. It is left to feminists to once again grapple with the multiple fallouts emerging from this scenario. Astonishingly, very little public-funded research is being done to address the issue of why infertility/childlessness is increasing over time in India. While several such issues remain to be researched comprehensively on a wider scale, feminists have taken up the immediate tasks of 'making visible' the adverse impacts of this industry and the collusion of different actors, state and non-state, in projecting ARTs as *the* answer to the problem of childlessness, and surrogacy as a win–win situation that benefits the economically poor surrogate and the child-commissioning couple.

The chapter by Sarojini Nadimpally and Anindita Majumdar in this volume critically examines the positioning of ARTs as a technology aiming to 'alleviate' the 'suffering and stigma that infertile women endure in India'. It demonstrates how the medico-industrial system has converted a social imperative (the idea of motherhood linked to the need to have a biological child) into a lucrative venture with scant respect to the fairly well-known adverse health implications of such invasive technologies, whether performed on the 'infertile' woman or the surrogate. The feminist nature of the exploration throws up several other uncomfortable questions that the different sets of researchers encountered on the ground, questions that go beyond health issues – for example, notions of who constitutes the 'family' and is the present understanding of 'family' adequate to accommodate the situation created by the ART industry. The resolution of this question becomes important in a society that is premised largely on situating pregnancy and birthing in heterosexual families and within boundaries of marriage.

Equally significant are the several dilemmas that studies such as the aforementioned ones raise for feminist scholars. Are we as feminists comfortable with commercial surrogacy? If so, do we also support the move to grant parental status to the surrogate, as suggested by the authors? What are the legal and long-term implications of including the surrogate's name in birth certificate issued to children born through surrogacy? What is the feminist rationale for suggesting that both genetic and gestational surrogacy should be allowed? Cleary, there are no easy answers here; but as feminists, we need to articulate and grapple with these questions even if it means that for every two steps that we take, we are pushed back by not just one but often several steps (see Batliwala and Pittman 2010 for an elaboration of this theme).

At another level, the Indian women's health movement, while being engaged in confronting the state for its oppressive population control policies and hazardous contraceptive methods, also seized the opportunity (like its Western counterparts) to reflect on women's bodies and how it shaped women's lives and health in the Indian context. In an interesting chapter in this volume contextualizing the setting up and tracing the journey of a clinic built on 'feminist rights-based perspective', Subha Sri B. and Sundari Ravindran provide a fascinating account of what motivated the Rural Women's Social Education Centre (RUWSEC) to bring into being the RUWSEC Reproductive Health Clinic, the continual challenges faced in ensuring that the clinic adhered to its vision and principles and, most important, the learnings from the venture that had to be eventually closed down. Abiding by feminist principles that required transparency in functioning, equal and active participation in decision-making by stakeholders in matters concerning their health and of delivery of health care, very soon brought the clinic into conflict with the medical establishment.

Elsewhere, and increasingly, feminists have begun building a body of knowledge that is simultaneously exploring existing practices and methods of teaching in medical establishments, as well as attempting to work closely with these establishments to impart feminist perspectives to their curriculum. Reflecting on her experiences – as a medical student and as a practising medical professional – Subha Sri B. (2010) unravels the insensitivity that characterizes the teaching and practice of some medical establishments she was closely associated with before joining RUWSEC Clinic. The insensitivity begins with the language that teaches students to view women in labour as 'cases' with 'dirty' bodies; these women are not only talked down to but also dealt with physically even when their screaming during labour is occasioned by pain, non-attendance or insufficient attendance by medical personnel. Among other observations, Subha Sri B. notes:

> While my experience of working with rural women in Maharashtra and Tamil Nadu revealed that knowledge of the body can be empowering and liberating, the way in which the same knowledge was imparted in medical college was extremely oppressive and disempowering.
>
> (Ibid.: 57)

Feminist organizations such as the Centre for Enquiry into Health and Allied Themes (CEHAT) have taken a lead in reorienting medical education to include 'gender' in the instruction and training of medical students. In a significant move captured in a comprehensive document (John *et al.* 2015) published by CEHAT, personnel from seven medical colleges have been part of a collaborative study aimed at examining existing medical curriculum and working towards sensitizing the same from a gender perspective. The document, among other things, captures the perceptions of medical personnel on several dimensions: on teaching, pedagogy, views about the different types of patients that visit the hospital and so on. What comes out starkly is the perception that gender as a concept or category is irrelevant to medical education; further,

> gender was understood by the respondents as [a] a demographic category; [b] health issues of women; [c] increased violence against women; [d] increased presence of women in the workforce. . . . The understanding was at best limited and at worst harmful.
>
> (Ibid.: xv)

Clearly, the hiatus between academic advancements that feminist researchers have thus far made (in this case, in the field of health and heath care) and their practice on the ground is still huge, despite attempts to bridge this gulf being continually made by feminist organizations such as Sama, RUWSEC and CEHAT, discussed earlier. How deep is this hiatus becomes clear from Cecilia Van Hollen's chapter in this volume, which takes us through her journey where she began as an anthropologist but now characterizes herself and her work as drawing upon 'methodologies as a *feminist critical medical anthropologist*' (emphasis ours).

Van Hollen's methodological attention to both structure and agency has enabled her to demonstrate how, for example, women's management of their reproductive health serves to reaffirm pre-existing gender norms even as it provides a space for its potential transformation. And, therefore, Van Hollen argues, the common global perception that poor, lower-caste women have little or no control over their reproductive health decision-making is erroneous for its inability to perceive the manner in which women exercise agency. It requires a feminist methodological lens to draw out the complex negotiations that poor women constantly engage on a day-to-day basis to decide on issues such as these: in which setting they want to give birth to their child (home or hospital), whether or not to continue with a pregnancy after an HIV-positive diagnosis and whether to breast-feed or bottle-feed their babies. For Van Hollen, these spaces and moments constitute the manner in which poor women challenge gender norms implicit in the management of reproductive health.

Conclusion

The idea of this collection of chapters focusing on feminist methodologies crystallized around our discussions on pedagogic practice and experience in classrooms across disciplines – economics, sociology, development studies, gender studies, disability studies and law, among others – and our learnings from feminist research and writing in other disciplines and locales. While we could recall a rich array of published works, the challenge of teaching feminist methodologies remained. Specifically, we are interested in exploring how scholars have approached questions of method in feminist research in India. If we argue, as we do, that feminist research is at its core a political project, what are the concrete processes through which methods take shape at the intersections of politics and location, to produce knowledge of a different order? The chapters in this volume, in our opinion, bear testimony to the production of knowledge of a different order that our contributors have made in their chosen field – knowledge production made possible by the explicit feminist nature of their research enquiry.

Notes

1 We borrow the term 'gender galaxy' from the title of Shah *et al.* (2015).
2 We draw attention especially to the resurgence of racial violence against people from African countries in India in the recent past and the targeted violence against people from the north-eastern states in various parts of north India and south India. Race as skin colour folds into deep-seated prejudice and discrimination at the core of caste ideology. Related to this is the articulation of caste discrimination as racism and racial discrimination in a post-Durban context.

References

Batliwala, Srilatha and Alexandra Pittman. 2010. *Capturing Change in Women's Realities: A Critical Overview of Current Monitoring and Evaluation Frameworks and Approaches*. Toronto, Canada: AWID (Association for Women's Rights in Development).

Batool, Essar, Ifrar Butt, Samreena Mushtaq, Munaza Rashid and Natasha Rather. 2016. *Do You Remember Kunan Poshpora?* New Delhi: Zubaan.

Chakravarti, Uma and Kumkum Roy. 1988. "Breaking Out of Invisibility: Rewriting the History of Women in Ancient India." In J. S. Kleinberg (ed.). *Retrieving Women's History: Changing Perceptions of the Role of Women in Politics and Society*. Oxford: Berg Publishers, pp. 319–337.

Chatterji, Angana P. 2012. "Witnessing as Feminist Intervention in India-Administered Kashmir." In Ania Loomba and Ritty A. Lukose (eds). *South Asian Feminisms*. Durham, NC, and London: Duke University Press (e-book).

Collins, Patricia Hill and Sirma Bilge. 2016. *Intersectionality*. Cambridge: Polity Press.

Connell, Raewyn. 2012. "Transsexual Women and Feminist Thought: Toward New Understanding and New Politics," *Signs*, Vol. 37, No. 4, Sex: A Thematic Issue (Summer 2012), pp. 857–881.

———. 2015. "Meeting at the Edge of Fear: Theory on a World Scale," *Feminist Theory*, Vol. 16, No. 1, pp. 49–66.

Crenshaw, Kimberle Williams. 1991. "Mapping the Margins: Intersectionality, Identity Politics, and Violence against Women of Color," *Stanford Law Review*, Vol. 43, pp. 1241–1299.

Geetha, V. 2016. *Undoing Violence: Speech after Sexual Violence*. New Delhi: Zubaan.

Ghosh, Biswajit. 2011. "Early Marriage of Girls in Contemporary Bengal: A Field View," *Social Change*, Vol. 41, No. 1, pp. 41–61.

John, Priya, Amruta Bavadekar, Ameerah Hasnain and Asilata Karandikar. 2015. *Gender in Medical Education: Perceptions of Medical Educators*. Mumbai: CEHAT.

Kannabiran, Kalpana. 2006. "A Cartography of Resistance: The National Federation of Dalit Women." In Nira Yuval-Davis, Kalpana Kannabiran and Ulrike Vieten (eds). *The Situated Politics of Belonging*. London: Sage, pp. 54–71.

———. 2008. "Making the Forked Tongue Speak: An Ethnography of the Self," *Economic and Political Weekly*, Vol. 43, No. 16, April 19–April 25, pp. 63–70.
———. 2012. "Regulating Cultures through Food Policing," *The Hindu*, 1 May.
———. 2015. "The Complexities of the Genderscape in India," *Seminar*, No. 672 (August), pp. 46–50.
Little, Daniel. 1986. *The Scientific Marx*. Minneapolis: University of Minnesota Press.
Mencher, Joan P. 1974. "The Caste System Upside Down or the Not-So-Mysterious-East," *Current Anthropology*, Vol. 15, No. 4 (December), pp. 469–493.
Patole, Shahu. 2016. "Why I Wrote a Book on Dalit Food," *Express Foodie*, 8 September. http://www.expressfoodie.com/main-course/why-i-wrote-a-book-on-dalit-food/ (accessed 11 September 2016).
Rege, Sharmila. 2013. "Introduction: Towards a Feminist Reclamation of Dr. Bhimrao Ramji Ambedkar." In Sharmila Rege (ed.). *Against the Madness of Manu: B.R. Ambedkar's Writings on Brahmanical Patriarchy*. New Delhi: Navayana, pp. 13–56.
Revathi, A. 2010. *The Truth about Me: A Hijra Life Story*. Translated from Tamil by V. Geetha. New Delhi: Penguin Books.
Shah, Chayanika, Raj Merchant, Shals Mahajan and Smriti Nevatia. 2015. *No Outlaws in the Gender Galaxy*. New Delhi: Zubaan (e-book).
Sinha, Mrinalini. 2012. "A Global Perspective on Gender: What Has South Asia Got to Do with It?" In Ania Loomba and Ritty Lukose (eds). *South Asian Feminisms*. Durham, NC; London: Duke University Press, pp. 356–373.
Still, Clarinda. 2011. "Spoiled Brides and the Fear of Education: Honour and Social Mobility among Dalits in South India," *Modern Asian Studies*, Vol. 45, No. 5 (September), pp. 1119–1146.
Subha Sri, B. 2010. "Women's Bodies and the Medical Profession," *Economic and Political Weekly*, Vol. XLV, No. 17 (April), pp. 52–57.
Valmiki, Omprakash. 2007. *Joothan*. Translated from Hindi by Arun Prabha Mukherjee. Calcutta: Samya.

Part I
Mapping terrains

Section 1
Feminist journeys

1 Studying women and the women's movement in India
Methods and impressions[1]

Joan P. Mencher

1. Introduction

One of the reasons I was asked to write for this volume is that I have been working on women's issues since 1958, long before the women's movement started either in the United States (where it only began in the 1970s) or in India. One thing that does stand out is that even before any movement existed, women working on women's issues were basically using the methods and ways of thinking that originated in the academic disciplines they were trained in. These methods were all theoretically gender-neutral, although in practice, male anthropologists often talked only to men. This was partly because access to women was difficult for them in some societies and also partly because males were seen as more powerful by some anthropologists. To the extent that women had been working in anthropology as the field itself developed, at least in the United States – starting with Ruth Benedict, a prize student of Boas – the field was slightly different.

To me, basically the feminist lens includes looking at all of the issues that concern social scientists, workers in the humanities and in the legal and health professions and political activists, making use of methods already developed (by women as well as men) – but now including a crucial women's approach. In addition, as opposed to the male approach that has been dominant until fairly recently (despite the pressure early on from Dr. Ambedkar), a wide range of feminist approaches have come to include, since independence, the effects of caste and class on women's lives.[2] When I first started work in India, especially in rural India, very few scholars were interested in the work I was doing, or in my perspective – not only as a scholar, but also as a woman, who also had the handicap of being a foreigner (though some were also interested in me as an American – perhaps because they had known few, if any, before me). However, it would have made more sense to them if I had been a male scholar, or even a mere wife, focusing on people's felt experience rather than just seeing people as 'subjects'. Today this has changed somewhat, though even now economists generally command more attention than anthropologists.

2. Feminism and anthropology

I cannot say how feminism became a part of my life, because I was less than six years old when I first noticed people giving less value to what a female child said, in contrast to how they listened to a male child. Even when I was in elementary school, I was aware that female lawyers (my mother had two friends who were lawyers) had either inferior positions or no serious legal role, compared to my father's lawyer friends. Thus, thinking about feminist issues predated my high school and college education. Though my classes were mixed before high school, I attended an all-girls' high school for grades 10–12, and then (after a single year at Hunter College in the Bronx, a new co-educational college) I transferred to an all-women's college (Smith College) for the remaining three years. Both in high school and at Smith, I was in an institution where it was taken for granted that women are entitled to receive a complete education and to become working professionals.

I decided to go into anthropology for graduate studies instead of continuing in physics for numerous reasons, which included reading Margaret Mead's and Ruth Benedict's writings for pleasure while taking physics, mathematics and philosophy courses. Furthermore, I had heard through the grapevine when I was in New York that the head of the physics department at Columbia had said that he would never give a PhD to a female student. This had a very negative influence on my thinking and led to my applying to Columbia for entrance into its anthropology department. At that time there were several women involved with the anthropology department at Columbia, including Margaret Mead, Ruth Bunzel and Gene Weltfish (whose class I attended during my first year).

As both Mead and Benedict had begun to show in their research based in diverse societies and in different socio-cultural contexts, gender roles were often different from what existed in the United States or even in Europe. This appeared very clearly in Mead's work in both Samoa and Bali, and to some extent in hunting and gathering societies like those found in New Guinea. Also, even though neither of them was given tenure at Columbia, Mead primarily was a strong influence on my thinking through her writing – and later also in person, especially after she became one of my dissertation advisors. Mead and Bunzel, along with other Columbia women, made me feel accepted there.

With the male students I often felt that I was fighting or struggling against them, even though they were older than I was – perhaps partly because I felt that my words were not heard. This was similar to the arguments I had often had with my father as a child, which covered almost every subject imaginable. But it was just assumed by (at least some) people at Columbia that the words of women also counted, especially to the women anthropologists I came to know as mentors and as teachers and by reading their books. From the very beginning of my anthropology graduate school experience, at least the female graduate students knew that they needed to talk with women as well as men in order to fully understand another culture.

In addition, before I arrived in India, I was aware of how political and social philosophies affect how women function, and of the important use of a feminist lens to look at just about anything and everything in human life. I had been aware of gender inequality from childhood and later on had learned from what people told me about how to fight for women and how important this fighting was.

During my graduate studies I became more aware of a gender perspective whenever I did any type of research, even for a class exercise. I was fascinated by what I read about the female suffragettes and how they fought not only for the right to vote but also for the right to hold office and all that entailed. I remember being often told I was too militant by some of my father's friends when I would venture an opinion. I wanted to be a strong woman because standing up for women's rights was an important part of my life, and I wanted to show that I was aware that women's words were often ignored or twisted. Thus, even as a young girl I made my opinions known forcefully, though not always tactfully.

I had applied to Columbia's doctoral programme in anthropology while I was finishing up my BA in physics. Early in my graduate studies I wanted to go to India and in fact had studied some Hindi to satisfy one of my language requirements, though I ended up doing my doctoral research as part of a large-scale study of Puerto Rican immigrants in East Harlem (part of New York City), which taught me a great deal that turned out to be useful in doing fieldwork in India. In this research project, which was based at a small health clinic in New York, my responsibility was to work with women, mothers of young children and elementary-school students. I was able to get to know the women quite well, using what has been called Spanglish (a mixture of Puerto Rican Spanish and English). I found the women I met in East Harlem, especially those who had come from Puerto Rico, quite open and friendly to me, especially when they found out that I was interested in their own lives, not only their children's, and in understanding their relationships with their husbands or boyfriends. As I spent more and more time with them, I came to know about their lives up to when we met and also their current lives – how they managed people, how they manipulated both their biological families and the other males in their lives and how they handled their finances. Life histories, which I had already learned about in my anthropology courses (building on my earlier experiences of talking with the women in my life), became an important part of my toolkit, both in this study and later in much of my fieldwork in India (see Mencher 1958).

By the time I arrived in India I had been exposed to many diverse methodologies for doing research, including standard personality tests such as the Thematic Apperception Test, ways of interviewing children about their perceptions of gender roles and interviews of both women and men on a wide variety of topics, including their life histories. I had also been exposed to poverty and family issues in the United States during my doctoral research, along with the often-complex ways in which government policies dealt with the needs of women (as well as men) in terms of housing, children's schooling and such issues.

3. My first trip to India

While I was writing my thesis, I applied for two research grants to go to India after receiving my degree in the summer of 1958. The first of these, a postdoctoral grant from the American Association of University Women, covered my research and some travel expenses, and was predicated on my completing my PhD before starting the work. The second, a Fulbright-Hayes pre-doctoral grant, paid for my travel to and from India as well as some travel within India, and required me to have an affiliation with the University of Baroda in Gujarat.[3] Because I was fascinated by matrilineal societies for a number of reasons, I applied to go to Malabar District (formerly a part of Madras Presidency), which had become a part of Kerala State by the time I reached India, though up to that time it had been part of Madras Presidency, and people in Malabar still retained close ties to the city of Madras. Malabar, along with Cochin and Travancore, constituted the main matrilineal (and to some extent matriarchal) area of India.

I was particularly interested in the Malabar region, because in the north there were matrilineal Muslims as well as Thiyyas (a semi-untouchable caste) and Nayars, and also because I had already made contacts with people from this area when I was in Delhi, Baroda and Madras City (now Chennai). Just before I left for India, I was fortunate in being visited in New York by Dr. Kathleen Gough, who was on the way to the United Kingdom with her small son. She had worked in Malabar in the very first years after independence and brought along a copy of her doctoral thesis on 'The Traditional Kinship System of the Nayars of Malabar' (Gough 1954; see also Schneider and Gough 1961), which I was able to go through at night while she slept, so I was able to take notes and read it before she left for the United

Kingdom. She also suggested that I stay at first in the village where she had worked in North Malabar, which I ended up doing before switching to work in South Malabar later. One of her comments always stayed with me: she mentioned that she was not able to learn much from women, and most of her conversations and discussions were with the men. She found the women less interesting, and I could understand that when I first spoke to the middle-class Nayar women, but later when talking to their daughters, and also to the Ezhava/Thiyya (lower-caste) women, my understanding changed a great deal because women of both groups were freer than the older high-caste women in telling me about their lives and personal issues. I became aware first in North Malabar, and then later when I moved to Kottakal in South Malabar, of the importance of crossing class lines and of working with both women and men.

3.1 Cheriamma's *family*

In addition, even before leaving for India, I was fortunate in obtaining an introductory letter to a woman member of Parliament (MP) who came from Malabar, Mrs. Ammu Swaminadhan, whom I met after reaching Delhi. She had already heard from several people that I was coming to India to study *marumakkathayam* (matriliny). She asked me to address her as Cheriamma (the Malayalam word for mother's younger sister). Through her, I had the opportunity to meet other female parliamentarians, including Lakshmi S. Menon, who was working with other MPs on special laws to perpetuate the rights of women belonging to matrilineal traditions – rights that were then being threatened by proposed new all-India uniform marriage and inheritance laws for women. I also met some of Mrs. Swaminadhan's relatives living in Delhi, in Madras City and in Malabar, and later on some who came to New York after my return.

During my first two trips to India I was unmarried and as such was welcomed into homes, looked after and also taught how young women were supposed to behave, in a way that would not have been possible if I had been travelling with a husband. I noticed the difference later on when I travelled in India with my husband.

My first stop in India, six days after arriving in Bombay (now Mumbai), was Baroda, where I was to be affiliated with the Department of Sociology at the University of Baroda, where Dr. M.N. Srinivas was a professor.[4] While in Baroda I had the opportunity to meet one of the first Nayar social anthropologists, Professor Raman Unni, who was affiliated to the University of Baroda and who had done fieldwork in Malabar. Once I reached Kerala in the fall of 1958, he helped me to visit several lower-middle-class *taravads* (traditional matrilineal households), which were still in the process of partitioning, and, in 1962, to visit some of the best-known Nambudiri Brahmin households along with several middle-class Nayar *taravads*.[5]

In Baroda in 1958 I became acquainted with several people indirectly related to Cheriamma. This included the brother of her second daughter's husband and his wife, who worked in Baroda. I also had the opportunity to get to know Professor M.N. Srinivas, who was officially my supervisor – even though I already had a PhD. I was happy to get to know him and really enjoyed meeting some of his friends, the Amins, who invited me along with Dr. Srinivas for a weekend at their farm outside of Baroda. I had an unusual experience there. As we were talking the first evening before dinner, I felt that some assumptions were being made about me because they had mostly known British scholars and very few Americans. When I mentioned in passing that my mother had been born in Czarist Russia and that I was of Jewish background, it was as if a curtain suddenly dropped from Dr. Srinivas's face, and he smiled at me warmly. From then on he treated me almost as if I was Indian and no longer a foreigner. I had never had such an experience before, certainly not in the United States, and it was unforgettable, as I was from then on treated as someone they could all be freer with. It added a kind of openness that I never expected.

Through Cheriamma, I had the great privilege of meeting numerous other women who had fought for independence, and a few who were coming into important positions under Nehru, along with others involved with the new laws being added to the Constitution and serving in government agencies and departments. While their numbers were small, they were quite outspoken in Parliament and in dealing with constitutional issues affecting women. The women coming from matrilineal families were especially concerned that they not lose their traditional privileges relating to the making and breaking of marriages, the inheritance of familial property and related issues. Even though they were fewer in number than the male parliamentarians by comparison with the US Senate and Congress, they were quite outstanding women. All of them had been freedom fighters.

I also had the opportunity of meeting some of Cheriamma's family members even before I went to the south, including one whose husband was also in Parliament and whose daughter and small children were all living in Delhi at that time, along with other family members, some of whom were passing through and others who lived in Delhi. Even in Delhi, before beginning my research, I felt that I had entered a totally different world from that of the other students who had come on Fulbright-Hayes fellowships, first because I already knew so much more about India than they did and was being welcomed into families, and also because they seemed to have a much more Westernized view of India.

4. Women and the Indian freedom struggle

This was all before the women's movement had started in the United States, and certainly before it started in India. Yet, because of women's participation in India's freedom struggle, in many ways I found many of the women I met when I first arrived, and even later on, to be stronger feminists than most of those I had known in New York – apart from those at Columbia, and in my undergraduate days at Smith College.

Later on, when Cheriamma took me around in Kerala (both Malabar and the former state of Cochin), I was also introduced to numerous older women who had been extremely active in the independence movement and who came across to me as exceptionally strong and knowledgeable and also concerned with women's issues in a different way than women I knew in the United States, as well as other women I met elsewhere in India. What I perceived was a sense of presence and entitlement that we see in many young women today, but that was different from what I had experienced in the United States or among non-Malayali women in India, especially middle-class women as differentiated from the small cadres of elite women from highly Western-educated households. Despite this, I was struck by how kind many of the older women I met were to me wherever I was.

Because I was coming to India with a fascination not only with matrilineal descent but also with the related issues of matrilocal residence and inheritance of family property, I was especially sensitive to all of the direct and indirect things I observed, such as the difference it made for a woman to be living in a house that belonged to her biological family instead of her husband's and not having to deal with in-laws very much. This made a big difference for the younger women, even though their older female relatives could at times be strict in keeping with their generational roles. The Nayars on the whole were rather conservative (apart from the Marxists and the extremely Left-leaning members of Congress), despite the transitions going on and the gradual impact of Western ideas of male and female behaviour stemming from both the older British norms and the newer US influences starting in the 1950s on these educated families.

One thing I had to put into action very fast after getting to India was to keep redrawing and revising, as I went along, my genealogical chart of this amazing family who in many ways not only influenced my research but also made me realize how different a view of India I was getting because of my early connections with matrilineal households, though even in those households males were fairly dominant.

The formation of Kerala State, and the push by some of the Kerala males to be respected by the more conservative Tamilians, especially Tamil

Brahmins and others they came in contact with in the large cities like Mumbai and Delhi and when they travelled abroad, also led to some of the Westernized Malayalis becoming more conservative than their grandparents. For example, a Nayar woman who worked as my assistant much later on (1972–84) told me that her grandmother had had two husbands and was quite a free woman, but she herself had to observe greater propriety.

When I first went to Madras City and was introduced to many Malayalis living there who came from northern and central Kerala, along with their high school and college-going children, I could easily see a difference between these matrilineal women and girls and the Tamil ones, especially in the early 1960s. And this helped me to focus on how the rules of inheritance and descent of a group of related and very distant or related people could affect women's roles (see Mencher 1962, 1963, 1965, 1966a, 1966b, 1966c).

5. My second trip to India (1962–64)

During my second trip to India, I also had the chance to meet some of the matrilineal Nambudiri Brahmins in the extreme north of Kerala, and also the only (to my knowledge) matrilineal Muslims in India. This has been noted to be extremely rare among Muslims worldwide, and there was at least among some of them a sense of pride in being different. During my first two weeks in Kerala in 1962, I stayed at the home of a well-known lawyer, Parappil Madhava Menon, who was helping various large and famous *taravads* partition their property. He took the time to show me a number of books written by earlier British legal experts and government servants who were concerned about preserving knowledge about matrilineal traditions. While staying there, I also learned a lot from his wife about her own life. She was a strong Congress leader at that time. (This family already had relatives in New York at the United Nations.) He was one of the main advocates involved in the partitioning of the Kovilakam in Kottakal which took many years, and was still going on when I lived there first in 1959–60 and later in 1962. Kottakal was the home of one of the main branches of the royal family of the Zamorin (ruler) of Kozhikode, the ruling family of this area prior to the arrival of the British. According to their rules for becoming the Zamorin (ruler), which went by age, often the Zamorin was appointed from the Kottakal Kovilakam (palace).

My interests changed somewhat during this visit, as I came to be more aware of just how different Kerala was from the rest of India. I also kept hearing the poorer women (especially those who worked as agricultural labourers) over and over again asking me one question: 'So what are you going to do for us?' Since I did not have money or goods to give them, the one thing I could offer was to write about them and try to publicize their situation, especially that of the poorer Thiyyas/Ezhavas) in North Malabar where they are matrilineal, and when I moved to South Malabar, the Ezhavas and other Pulayar and Paraiyar caste women. During the time I was collecting life histories and related data, I took histories not only from middle-class women but also from low-caste poor women, who worked as day labourers in someone's house or in the fields transplanting paddy and so on. I also became quite aware of how the better-off tended to moralize about the behaviour of the poor. This was especially true among the Thiyyas in North Malabar, and both Ezhavas and Pulayas/Paraiyas in South Malabar.

Following that earlier visit I had changed my focus, and the proposal I drafted when I got back was a comparative study of agroecology, settlement patterns, agriculture, women and farmers, which I sent to the National Science Foundation (NSF) for funding. It was the beginning of my awareness of how important a role women played in food production, especially agriculture, and how the ecological setting in which they worked related to family structure. Prior to starting work on my NSF grant, I did a small piece of research on the Nambudiri Brahmins because I had come to understand that I needed to know more about them – especially their women, but also the males (which included the head of the then united Communist Party of India, E.M.S. Namboodiripad).

In 1962 (for five months mid-July through half of December) I worked on a study of Nambudiri Brahmins in Kerala while also working on agriculture. I divided my interests in this way because I had come to realize that I could not fully understand how the matrilineal groups in Kerala functioned without looking at the traditional elites. It was quite striking to compare the Nambudiris with the other much more prominent matrilineal groups in the state, such as Nayars and Ezhava/Thiyyas. Among the Nambudiris, I came to really understand how this elite group of people mistreated their wives and daughters, and the tremendous efforts women had to make in order to get educated. Even among Nambudiri boys there was often a struggle to be allowed to get what they called Western education, and there was even greater opposition to education of daughters – though they had always been literate in Malayalam and they all read sacred texts in Malayalam. Indeed, in traditional Kerala, there was an important ceremony for each child's first writing, which was performed on a special sacred day in their lunar calendar. It was performed for all Brahmins, Nayars and other uppercaste boys and girls even traditionally, and stood in sharp contrast to the rest of India. Yet the Nambudiri girls did not learn the Vedas, though they did learn to read various scriptures. Many of them were jealous when they saw all the Nayar girls getting the Western-style education. In one village where I lived in 1962, young Nambudiri girls figured out how they could go to the temple, and then sneak out to go to Communist Party meetings, then go back to the temple and return home without their fathers' knowledge. This was a time of real rebellion, and they were very proud of their ability to do this.

From Kerala, I then went to work for about eight months in Tamil Nadu and then for about six months in West Bengal. After completing my fieldwork in villages in these other states, I then went to London and worked with archival material, focusing primarily on Kerala and Tamil Nadu in the early days of British contact. I have used that material in many publications; unfortunately, it contained very little information about women (see e.g. Mencher 1966c).

Following my first two research periods in India, when I was working without an affiliation with any Indian scholars except for official purposes, for my next two studies I was affiliated with male scholars: first Professor K. Raman Unni of the School of Planning and Architecture in New Delhi in 1970–72 (see Mencher 1974, 1978a, 1978b) and then Dr. P.G.K. Panikar, who was then the director of the Centre for Development Studies in Trivandrum in 1972–75. While I always had closer relationships with the women I met in the villages I lived in, especially in Kerala, because both studies were focusing on agriculture, I was not able to devote as much time to women's lives.

6. Methodologies

Although nobody had formally developed methods for studying women, their roles, their attitudes, their spirit and so on, just before I settled down in the first village I lived in, it was clear that all the methods of anthropology were as applicable to females as they were to males. When I first started to work in India, I hired a female interpreter-cum-assistant (who was older and more experienced than I was), and she was a great help in working in the first two villages where I worked in 1958 and 1959–60. By then I understood enough Malayalam that I could tell if my assistant was leaving things out or perhaps not correctly translating the questions I was asking. We took life histories both from women and men and from a variety of castes. I also did formal interviews, both of women and of their children.

Because of my earlier commitment, I administered some psychological tests (the data remains unpublished) and recorded many observations and overheard conversations. I also came to understand the difference between the Kerala women who primarily lived in the houses that were theirs by matrilineal inheritance – which were always in their own names in the land records – and the Kerala women whose husbands bought the houses they lived in, and certainly the houses of Tamil and Bengali village women whose homes belonged to their husbands. In the former case, there was a sense of independence for the women in their own homes by inheritance in how they felt about this ownership, and as one woman explained to me, a feeling that no matter what happened in her life, she had a home. Also, even when they were younger, they did not have to deal with in-laws.

The varied approaches I learned during my early years in rural India, along with my experiences in Tamil Nadu and even (though time was shorter) in West Bengal in 1963, led me to begin to formulate a research proposal for a large-scale study of women's roles in rice cultivation, to be conducted in three of the major rice-producing states – Kerala, West Bengal and Tamil Nadu. I was looking for a collaborator, and Dr. Vina Mazumdar, knowing it was hard for me to work with senior male social scientists, especially economists like Dr. Panicker, and also that it left me little chance to really explore my interest in gender studies, helped me forge a link with Dr. K. Saradamoni of the Indian Statistical Institute in Delhi.

This project, involving ten villages each in Kerala and Tamil Nadu and eight in West Bengal, required many assistants. The villages in Kerala stretched from the northern region near Cannanore all the way south to Trivandrum District. (Where possible, we selected two villages in each of five districts in each state.) We hired a local educated research assistant to supervise data collection in each state. Then in each village we hired village assistants to work for us, each from a different section of the village where possible. These local assistants were in turn taught how to collect data in their village or locality. They were expected to visit each household in the sample at least once a week. I devised charts to help some of the semi-literate women make marks on to record what they did each day. In a few places women managed to do it daily, while in others the visiting state coordinator had to help out. For many of the women, seeing how much they could do on pieces of paper was revelatory to them – in at least a few cases, it actually helped with their self-esteem. In other places, they found it too hard to follow. These records and the notes taken by the more literate village assistants were kept from about seven to eight months up to a full year. It led to a tremendous amount of data, which had to be coded and entered into a computer – a long, boring process (this was still early in the development of computers).[6]

6.1 Some methods used

One of the new and important aspects of this research was using local people, even semi-educated people, in direct data collection on a daily or weekly basis, and looking at any effects this might have on their thinking. It was made easier because of the extent of education of even the Dalit women and men in Kerala and Tamil Nadu. In West Bengal it was much harder to find Dalit people with any education, since schooling was less available there among the poor. One of the charts required noting how much money was contributed to the household by the husband and wife individually on each day. We used lines of different length to show how much each was contributing. In a few instances in Kerala, husbands were actually shamed into increasing what they gave to their wives, as they saw the different lengths of the lines on the charts. Though only a few were so influenced, it was an eye-opener to those men and women (Mencher, Saradamoni and Panicker 1979). Though some of the project data has been published (see Mencher and Saradamoni 1982, 1984a, 1984b), there still is considerable data that remains to be analysed from our bulk of materials.[7]

While the project was going on, I was often asked by economists (in India) why we restricted the study to three states and did not try to get a broader picture. In my own discipline, anthropology (normally called sociology in the United Kingdom, and by extension in India social anthropology, to distinguish it from physical anthropology), I often was asked why we were trying to collect data from so many regions. The reason I was motivated to design such a large study was that I hoped to be able to come out with conclusions that might have some policy implications, regardless of whether or not they were used by policy makers.

I restricted the study to (a) states where I had had some fieldwork experience before doing this study and (b) some of the states where rice was the main crop grown, as well as being one of the main items of people's daily diet (we could not include all of the rice-growing states).

The reason why so many villages were included in the study was that I had become acutely aware of the enormous regional and subregional differences in agrarian relations and ecology, as well as the sexual division of labour. Thus, more villages were included, and we only looked at a sample of households in each village – rather than surveying all of the households in each village, as a more intensive piece of research would have required. I tried to visit all of the villages in the study. Nine of the villages were ones where I had lived during previous field trips, and two others I lived in for longer periods during this study; others I visited for shorter periods. In rice areas of India, depending on the region, somewhere between one-third and three-quarters of the labour time spent in cultivating a given acre of paddy land was female. We made the decision to do our best to use local females if possible to help with data collection, using males from the village only where necessary. Wherever possible, we hired semi-educated (or in one or two rare cases in Kerala, educated) girls to help with the work (see Mencher 1982, 1985a, 1985b, Mencher and Saradamoni 1984a).

Many of these women, especially the landless labourers, decided then and there to get their children educated enough so that they could do something other than agricultural labour, whereas among those owning land, many decided to hold onto their land and develop it more. Towards the end of work in each village, the state assistant along with that village's assistant interviewed each of the women and their husbands to learn more about their future plans, what they expected from this experience and so on.

In the mid-1990s I hired an assistant to return to a few of the Kerala villages we had studied, to collect data on the women's reaction to the striking decrease in the availability of work in each season. Many were desperate for more work. I was told the same thing when visiting some of the villages in Tamil Nadu during the next few years, while going around with my former Tamil Nadu assistant each time I visited India after 1997.

7. The 'feminization of agriculture'

It is important to discuss the popular phrase the 'feminization of agriculture' – a phrase I have never heard used by any female who does agriculture – either as a landowner, as a landowner-cum-labourer or as a simple labourer. Nowadays this comment is being made by development officers, and senior males in charge of research or trying to influence policy. It is usually stated as something negative. Sometimes this comes out of the automatic assumption that India will follow the US model and its development – that is that people, especially males, will leave agriculture for urban jobs, even though the urban situation they enter is often quite difficult in terms of housing and job availability. Yet what intrigues me even today is whether this is something negative or something positive. What is really meant by the feminization of agriculture, and why are some of the women fighting to keep it? Since about 2011, whenever I was in India, I have heard even quite progressive male administrators and scholars use this phrase when talking about the situation where women are left in charge of their household farming as males from their households (husbands or sons) migrate to urban areas. Yet this is only considered a problem where females are not allowed to use implements (that might ease their work).

According to the 2011 Census of India, several scholars have noted that rural males appear to be moving more to nearby towns and cities, not necessarily to faraway cities. In some cases, that may mean that they wish to keep themselves available to help their families in the village, at least during the harvest seasons; this question requires more research and region-wise breakdowns. Often these males spend their weekends back with their village family or even do a little work on their own farm. It can be a small amount of work, but it means being with their wives and children and sometimes their parents. If they are needed to help with ploughing – still not considered something women should do (see Mencher 1993) – they can take a few days off from work (at the right time) or engage someone else for the work. In general, they are not quite ready to teach their wives to plough, though the situation may be different in Telangana (see Uphoff 2015). While I have often heard male administrators as well as research investigators, and even established social scientists, talk disparagingly about this 'feminization' phenomenon, the views of village women are often different. When I have made short visits to the rural areas I knew from before, many women expressed satisfaction with their taking care of and working on their family farms – even though they did not appear to broadcast this attitude. Clearly more research remains to be done on this shift. Looking at agriculture, the critical question has to do with land ownership. If they have to work as landless or even semi-landless labourers, then many women still want as many days of work as possible to bring in more money. At least this often holds in areas where female labourers have access to both primary health centres and ration shops along with food from employers, but if they own the land they work on or participate in exchange labour, then, of course, they prefer the least arduous work they can find.

Ignoring women in agriculture as the phrase the 'feminization of agriculture' is being used seems to be framing small-scale (even organic) agriculture as not 'modern'. Yet being forced off their land can be undesirable for both women and men. It can also be extremely unhealthy for the poor. In many parts of the world, the so-called feminization of agriculture can be something women like because it gives them autonomy. In fact, it is now growing at a time when people are fighting corporate agriculture in the United States.

One piece missing from some of the discussions of the feminization of agriculture always was how it gave the landless women a sense of autonomy. Also, it is important to understand the details of the roles of women in agriculture – from the work they do on their own land to supervising labourers to making decisions about which crops to plant – and how the women feel about these tasks. Questions about how the women who themselves do fieldwork view their present situation need to be further explored. Clearly, the answers to these questions will depend on the following variables, among others: (a) the availability of health care to deal with the health problems of women who do hard work for long hours in the fields; (b) cultural customs about the allocation of food, that is who gets to eat enough and who does not – as well as the availability and effectiveness of various state government policies like ration shops and the general availability of low-cost basic food supplies for agricultural labourers; and

(c) the degree to which the Dalit women agricultural labourers have been politicized to speak out and have joined together to support one another.[8]

With conventional practices, women working in agriculture perform what can be backbreaking tasks like seedling removal, transplanting and weeding in bent posture and under wet conditions for more than 1,000 hours per hectare. In addition, in areas where green revolution approaches are used, they are exposed to toxic chemicals.

New questions have always been coming up, and some do involve new methodologies. The System of Rice Intensification (SRI), especially as it was officially introduced in Tamil Nadu, Kerala and also Andhra Pradesh,[9] is really quite innovative and offers some relief from arduous work for women who work on their own or their family's land, however small. Over the past 30-odd years, I have become more and more convinced of the crucial importance of small-scale agriculture, especially since I first saw SRI at a non-governmental organization (NGO) called RASTA in Kerala in 2005.[10] But SRI enables farmers to work under healthier conditions, with little or no exposure to chemical fertilizers or pesticides, while creating various other physical and social benefits. In addition, there are far fewer seedlings transplanted, because in many instances only one or at most two seedlings are placed together in a hole and that too at larger intervals, so that planting takes less time once the women have learned how to measure the distance between mounds. The consequences are significant, as we learn from women in India, Malaysia and Cambodia (see Tiki 2015, Tiki, Chun and Savann 2015). Women from small and marginal farming families doing SRI have been making the news in India for their adoption of this new approach, which challenges the conventional beliefs and practices of rice farming. However, one rarely comes across any discussion of the impact of SRI on the labourers' physical well-being.

With SRI practices women spend less time in stressful postures carrying out repetitive movements, and they handle lighter materials compared to standard cultivation practices (see Uphoff 2015). SRI fundamentally changes the conditions under which women have to work. Conventionally, women working in bent or sitting postures in flooded fields for long hours come into contact with various disease-causing vectors, exposing them to multiple health risks like intestinal to skin diseases and female urinary and genital ailments. This affects their ability to work and earn money, and furthermore, it drains out their money on health care (especially in states that do not have good primary health centres) and makes them indebted for health care. With SRI practices, rice fields are no longer kept continuously flooded, thus reducing women's prolonged exposure to these water-borne disease vectors. Furthermore, where organic SRI is being practised, women do not face problems from chemical fertilizers and pesticides.

As women are the producers of our food, we cannot afford to ignore their well-being. When they thrive, our agriculture thrives and vice versa. The eco-logic of SRI has a body and gender-logic too, which need to be paid attention to and invested in if we are seriously concerned about our toiling women.

I had the opportunity to observe a very striking difference between Odisha and the south Indian states where I worked, Tamil Nadu and Kerala. At a meeting I was taken to in Bhubaneswar in February 2015, just looking at the Dalit and Adivasi women, it was striking to me how much harder life was for these women who ate less and lacked any kind of medical care.

8. Conclusion

What new generations of scholars can learn from the work I did and what I observed include the following:

1. Having access to historically older documents, which help us to see whether or how much many things have changed over time. This kind of information can also provide some perspective on current battles for women. Today in rural areas, at least some of the poorest women are in danger of losing their land, through struggles with outsiders, including (mostly male) 'developers' who seem to be doing their utmost to make the Indian countryside look like the United States or China or to be 'modern'.
2. The importance of going to a number of villages and never stopping with one village, as was traditional earlier on in anthropology.
3. Involving villagers in the research itself, and looking at both female and male leaders; also including both small- and medium-sized landowning farming households, as well as landless labourers of all castes and religious groups.
4. Talking to and including all castes, which often means working with people, especially women belonging to the so-called backward classes, as well as Dalits, and if found in the villages, scheduled tribe women as well as the diverse Muslim groups.
5. The importance of hiring assistants from the entire range of castes from Brahmins to Dalits, because doing this enabled me to get a clearer picture of the diverse ways in which each person viewed her or his world (and in addition actually living day by day with an assistant gives one insight that asking questions or even observing can do). This is because of the many things that come out accidentally as a result of just being with someone day after day.

6   The importance of both caste and class, and how a full picture has to include the full range, and only really close human relationships would help with this understanding.
7   Reading from the recent flowering of Dalit women's voices, especially from Tamil Nadu, where I had worked before, Andhra Pradesh and Telangana. I have had the opportunity of reading English translations from Telugu of Dalit women as directly translated as possible. Their English has been for me no harder to understand than the English of the Puerto Rican women I worked with in the 1950s, and in many places much easier to read. Their stories tell us better than any other research what needs to be done to make a difference for Dalit and tribal women.

Many women and their families are in danger of losing their land as they struggle with local city, town and state governments, along with the central government trying to move them to urban slums. Yet, having worked in the slums of New York City, I worry about what this will do to both adult males and females as well as their adolescent and younger children. This again takes me back to the work I did before going to India, among Puerto Rican women in New York City, and how they longed for the villages they had grown up in.

Notes

1   This chapter was published in the *Economic and Political Weekly*, Review of Women's Studies, vol. 51, no. 18, 30 April 2016, pp. 39–47. We are grateful to the editor, *EPW*, for permission to republish this chapter in this volume.
2   Only recently, a group of Dalit women activists came to New York from India and gave a fascinating discussion and performance about how they are doubly discriminated against in India. While they were mostly north Indian women, whose backgrounds were somewhat different from the Dalit women I had known in South India, they clearly had the same reaction to their situation. What was particularly striking was the reaction of some of the black US students in the room, who made it clear how they totally understood this combination of forms of discrimination (gender and race in their own case).
3   Though my main desire was to study people living in matrilineal households in Malabar, both my grant applications focused more on child rearing since that was a principal subject of my doctoral thesis. During my time in Kerala, I worked on both subjects, though I have published more on matrilineality and other things I became interested in as a result of living in Kerala villages.
4   As a side note, it was on the train to Baroda that I met a young woman, Sukumari, whose brother was married to a relative of Cheriamma. Interestingly,

during my first 30-odd years of travelling around in India, I experienced one after another such coincidences involving members of this family.
5 In 1970–72, I worked with Professor K. Raman Unni and assistants on a comparative study in Tamil Nadu and Kerala on a related but different set of issues.
6 I managed to get a fairly large grant from The Smithsonian Institution in Washington, using PL480 funds (rupee funds that were part of the official payback for US wheat exported to India during the mid-1970s under President Johnson), which enabled us to pay all of our village assistants what was then a decent salary – for many of them, the first salary they had ever earned. At the time, I did not fully understand all of the issues involved in using these funds but do appreciate how they helped us to carry out this large-scale study, which at least benefitted the poor village women (and a few men) who worked for us in Kerala, Tamil Nadu and West Bengal.
7 I would be glad to hear from anyone who might be interested to participate in this work.
8 I mention all of this because of recent work by Sabarmatee Tiki, the head of Sambhav (an NGO that runs a large organic and training farm outside of Bhubaneswar). She is the only scholar I know of who has studied the effects of hard manual labour on the bodies of women and men who work in rice cultivation. Her data clearly shows that SRI is less arduous and painful for the women who do transplanting and weeding. However, all of her data comes from a state where the nutrition of women, especially those who do fieldwork, is poor and where they do not have the primary health centre protections found in Tamil Nadu and Kerala. Thus, the situation is especially dire for poorer women in Odisha. I do not know if they indulge in any of the pleasurable activities like those mentioned to me by Tamil and Malayali women, such as singing together and gossiping and laughing, and the sense of comradery.
9 SRI has in recent years been adapted to other crops, giving rise to such terms as System of Wheat Intensification, System of Sugarcane Intensification and, more generally, System of Crop Intensification (SCI). This was accomplished mainly through the work of the Centre for Sustainable Agriculture in Hyderabad.
10 I have written several articles about SRI/SCI and given numerous talks about it, along with reading the work of many others, including Professor Norman Uphoff from Cornell University, whose latest book (Uphoff 2015) is the best summary of current knowledge on the subject.

References

Gough, E. Kathleen. 1954. The Traditional Kinship System of the Nayars of Malabar. PhD Thesis, Cambridge University.
Mencher, Joan P. 1958. Child Rearing and Family Organization among Puerto Ricans in Eastville: El Barrio de Nueva York. PhD dissertation, Columbia University.
———. 1962. "Changing Familial Roles among South Malabar Nayars," *Southwestern Journal of Anthropology*, Vol. 18, pp. 230–245.
———. 1963. "Growing Up in South Malabar," *Human Organization*, Vol. 22, pp. 54–65.

———. 1965. "The Nayars of South Malabar." In M.F. Nimkoff (ed.). *Comparative Family Systems*. New York: Houghton Mifflin Co., pp. 163–191.

———. 1966a. "The Namboodiri Brahmans of Kerala," *Natural History Magazine*, May 1966.

———. 1966b. "Namboodiri Brahmans: An Analysis of a Traditional Elite in Kerala," *Journal of Asian and African Studies*, Vol. I, pp. 7–20.

———. 1966c. "Kerala and Madras: A Comparative Study of Ecology and Social Structure," *Ethnology*, Vol. V, pp. 135–171.

———. 1974. "Problems in Analyzing Rural Class Structure," *Economic and Political Weekly*, Vol. 9, No. 35 (31 August), pp. 1495–1503.

———. 1978a. "Agrarian Relations in Two Rice Regions of Kerala," *Economic and Political Weekly*, Vol. 13, No. 6–7 (1 February), pp. 349–366.

———. 1978b. "Why Grow More Food – An Analysis of Some Contradictions in the Green Revolution in Kerala," *Economic and Political Weekly*, Review of Agriculture, Vol. 13, No. 51–52 (23 December), pp. A98–A104.

———. 1985a. "The Forgotten Ones: Female Landless Labourers in Southern India." In *Women Creating Wealth: Transforming Economic Development*. Washington, DC: JT&A, Inc., for the Association for Women Development.

———. 1985b. "Landless Women Agricultural Labourers in India: Some Observations from Tamil Nadu, Kerala and West Bengal." In *Women in Rice Farming: Proceedings of a Conference on Rice Farming Systems*. Brookfield, Vermont: Gower Publishing Co. (for the International Rice Research Institute, Los Banos, Philippines), pp. 351–372.

———. 1993. "Women, Agriculture and the Sexual Division of Labour: A Three State Comparison." In Deipica Bagchi and Saraswati Raju (eds). *Women and Work in South Asia: Regional Patterns and Perspectives*. London and New York: Routledge, pp. 99–117.

Mencher, Joan P. and K. Saradamoni. 1982. "Muddy Feet, Dirty Hands: Rice Production and Female Agricultural Labour," *Economic and Political Weekly*, Vol. 17, No. 52 (25 December), pp. A149–A167.

———. 1984a. "Landless Agricultural Women Labourers in Three Rice Regions of India: Their Work and Income," *Current Sociological Perspectives*, Calcutta, Vol. 3, pp. 67–82.

———. 1984b. "The Invisible Hand behind Agriculture: Landowning Women in Supervision and Management," *Current Sociological Perspectives*, Vol. 3, pp. 16–23.

Mencher, Joan P., K. Saradamoni and J. Panicker. 1979. "Women in Rice Cultivation: Some Research Tools," *Studies in Family Planning*, special issue edited by Sondra Zeidenstein, Vol. 10, No. 11/12 (November/December), pp. 406–408.

Schneider, David and E. Kathleen Gough (eds). 1961. *Matrilineal Kinship*. Berkeley: University of California Press.

Tiki, Sabarmatee. 2015. "SRI: A Practice That Transforms the Lives of Women," *Leisa India: Magazine of Low External Input Sustainable Agriculture*, Vol. 17, No. 4, pp. 18–20. https://issuu.com/leisaindia/docs/dec_2015-pages_1-36 (accessed 18 March 2016).

Tiki, Sabarmatee, Lim Liang Chun and Oeurm Savann. 2015. "Sri Cultivates Well-Being for Women," *Farming Matters*, Vol. 31, No. 4 (December 2015), http://www.agriculturesnetwork.org/magazines/global/women-agroecology/sri-cultivates-well-being-for-women. Accessed on 17 December 2016.

Uphoff, Norman. 2015. *The System of Rice Intensification (SRI): Responses to Frequently Asked Questions*. Ithaca, NY: Cornell University. http://sri.cals.cornell.edu/aboutsri/SRI_FAQs_Uphoff_2016.pdf. Accessed on 17 December 2016.

2 'To bounce like a ball that has been hit'
Feminist reflections on the family

Kalpana Kannabiran

> *To bounce like a ball that has been hit became my deepest desire, and not to curl up and collapse because of the blow.*
>
> (Bama, *Sangati*, vii)

1. Introduction

The key feminist construct in the movements for women's rights beginning in the late 1970s in India was 'the personal is the political'. This assertion was at once universal and particular. While it drew on the experience of feminist movements in the West, it was turned inwards to look at the context-specific ways in which women were oppressed in India – class, caste, religion, tribe, region and political formation – providing distinctive refractions of the problem of women's subordination. Although feminist writing of this period did not necessarily grasp the complexity of belonging and subjectivities in the experience of oppression, nor the realities of gender diversities, the particularities of each moment spoke of the specific ways in which power was deployed by the state, by communities, by families and by parties – a deployment that pointed to intersecting locations of the women concerned.

We have argued elsewhere that we can only understand the way people and groups relate to each other, if we look at the politics of belonging, which 'encompass and relate both citizenship and identity, adding an emotional dimension, which is central to notions of belonging' (Yuval-Davis, Kannabiran and Vieten 2006: 1). The politics of belonging, we argued, is situated in three different but complementary ways: *temporally* (specific historical conjunctures construct belonging in specific ways), *spatially* (the effects of, say, neoliberal markets are not the same across the world, each region experiencing cataclysmic changes in specific ways to specific effects) and *intersectionally* (intersecting and intermeshing social locations – class, caste, tribe, religion, disability, for instance – although unstable, determine access to power, resources and decision-making and are constitutive of gender) (Yuval-Davis, Kannabiran and Vieten 2006: 7–8).[1]

Gender orders are at the core of the politics of belonging and play out in distinct yet interlocking ways across temporality, spatiality and social location. If on the Indian subcontinent we see the specificities of caste, community, conflict and historical moments/processes like colonization, partition and neoliberal globalization leading to specific ontological commitments and epistemological standpoints about the place of women in the emergent social imaginary, there is over the same period a gender order that is not binary (male–female), with an active and visible presence of persons outside this binary. While there is some historical writing on gender diversities, what is most eloquent is the inadvertent unmasking of the transsexual woman, the *hijra*, through a punitive legislation, which, among other things, points to older practices of sex reassignment through the use of terms like 'emasculation' (Kannabiran 2015). The figure of the *hijra* encapsulates the intransigence of gender as a historical fact on the subcontinent, while also marking this presence in terms of class and social location (at the bottom of the social order) and the state in stigmatizing, criminalizing measures subject always to surveillance, policing and illegal detention.[2] The effects of 'contradictory embodiment', to echo Connell, on gender orders are complex and cannot be contained within identity discourses. The moment of recognition marks a situated politics of belonging that springs from 'the knowledge of gender arrangements, one's place in them, and how to proceed with everyday life' (Connell 2012: 868).

A critical arena where the politics of belonging plays out, and indeed an arena where the feminist construct 'the personal is the political' makes most meaning, is *the family*. This is especially the case in India. I will attempt in this chapter to address questions of feminist methods through a close look at family as an idea in India, through an examination of specific texts and histories to open out intersectional perspectives on the family – pointing to the different notations of 'the personal is the political'.[3]

The Indian family's 'oscillation between the scriptural and the actual' (Patel 2005: 21) in early sociological writing settled into more organized studies on inheritance, kinship, marriage, joint family systems and so on – all focused on the heterosexual family. Within this,

> Indian sociology and social anthropology of the family has . . . been dodging the study of crises such as bride burning, divorce, broken family, remarriage and the ensuing family organization, and the complications of families resulting from inter-caste and inter-religious marriages. . . . These developments have messed up the neat categories of endogamy

and exogamy, as well as the agnatic, cognatic and affinal structures and organizational principles.

(Patel 2005: 31)

But were the categories of endogamy and exogamy ever neat? And what factors really are 'messing up' familial spaces and relationships?

The rise of neoliberal marketplaces and neoliberal governance has had specific effects on the family and culture. The tumultuous changes in the ways the state operates, the dismantling of welfare, increasing privatization of education and basic services and the accumulation of dispossession, to use Harvey's phrase (Harvey 2005), bear specific consequences for family survival and struggles, especially at the individual and family levels – in terms of employment, health care, educational opportunities, migration, housing, to name a few. Neoliberalism as a form of governance depends on inducing and proliferating precarity by dispossessing peoples and communities, in order to satiate rapacious corporate hunger for land and profits. Criminalization and punitive rule then become methods of government that percolate down to the level of the locality and are enforced through the muzzling of dissent and free speech (by murder and grave assault).

In India, as elsewhere, neoliberalism has tied in neatly with the rise of a strident, violent majoritarian nationalism – Hindutva – in mainstream politics and government. The enforcement of narrow definitions of patriotism, of endogamy (religious and caste), the resurgence of hate crimes and 'recovering' women through the perpetration of violence and 'honour' crimes mark this moment, as we witness the new war cry of the nation, 'Bharat Mata ki Jai' (victory to Mother India). Gangs patrol streets in villages, towns and cities, policing food cultures in the name of Hindu religion and enforcing 'ghar wapsi' (returning home) and 'love jihad' on Hindu girls marrying outside caste and community if necessary through murder on the streets. Families are under siege in the age of Hindutva.

Feminist sociology of the family is yet to take stock of the realities of family violence against queer persons, and sexual economies of gender plurality and their impact on the family. As Shah *et al.* observe,

> One of the major sources of despair [among queer persons] . . . is the inability to find adequate support from natal families, their inability to comprehend the lives and choices of their children or their active violence towards the children in their care. The hopelessness of this loss spills over into other parts of their adult lives when they begin to enter other intimacies and enter systems of care.
>
> (Shah *et al.* 2015: Chapter 4)

Are these crises, or are they constitutive of the family/families at specific social, historical conjunctures? What are the conceptual disruptions forced on a feminist exploration of the family? We can scarcely forget that gender orders are constituted through systematic and pervasive practices of violence at the levels of the family, community and state spanning the local, regional and global (see Connell 2015). Which, then, are the texts that should form the foundational corpus for the study of the family in India that will adequately explain the intractability of caste and gender, and that will help us interrogate fundamentalist and majoritarian enforcement of family forms, violent proscription on choice marriages and the persistent problems of gender-based violence in stridently nationalist, neoliberal, caste society?

This chapter points to a small selection of texts that situate our understanding of the history of this institution and its criticality to radical politics. The idea is not to set out the fields of the family and investigate the shifts, crises and consolidation of power, decision-making and structure in specific forms or specific aspects of family life; instead, the attempt is to suggest different lenses through which we may begin to historicize the family. In tracing the ruptures in the personal as it is constituted at the intersections of social location, territoriality, politics and gender orders, I suggest a shift in the inarticulate premises that undergird studies of the family in contemporary Indian society. In doing this I follow the ruptures through to a more nuanced understanding of 'the personal is the political' and the mutually transformative potential of the personal and the political as also an acknowledgement of its limits.

Section 2 that follows this introduction presents Babasaheb Ambedkar's analysis of the relationship between caste and family as a foundational text for an understanding of the sociology of the family in India. Section 3 presents work on the late 19th and early 20th centuries that foreground the disjunctures in the family machine, even at the time that a new idea of a 'modern' family was being put in place. Section 4 presents voices from the Ambedkarite, Dalit and Adivasi movements that make a sharp departure from *savarna* (dominant [upper] class) ideologies of the family that are assumed to be normative in dominant discourse today. Section 5 presents a counterpoint to the heterosexual family through the voice of Revathi, a *hijra* activist. Section 6 provides fleeting glimpses of that most troubling moment – Partition of 1947 – which continues to resonate in our life-worlds in India today. Section 7 looks briefly at the spatiality of the family – the place called home. Section 8 provides the conclusion.

2. Babasaheb Ambedkar's *Castes in India*

Ambedkar's early work takes us to the heart of the matter: endogamy, exogamy, wife burning, intercaste marriage, organizational principles and the way they all must get 'messed up' through an annihilation of caste – in order for an egalitarian social order to emerge (Ambedkar 2002).[4] To start with his conclusion, a just social order – one that is just for women – can emerge only if caste is ousted, because caste is constituted by familial and kinship practices predicated on violence. Indian society is characterized by an elaborate custom of exogamy, which prohibits marriage between *sapindas* (blood kin) as well as *sagotras* (of the same class). The rules of exogamy are so rigid that any infringement or violation invites rigorous penalties. Over this exogamous society is overlaid the principle of endogamy. There is a difference between racial or tribal endogamy, where the universe is large and coterminus with cultural homogeneity, and caste endogamy, where a homogeneous population is split into mutually exclusive units within which the principles of both exogamy and endogamy operate in all their rigidity. This '*superimposition of endogamy on exogamy means the creation of caste*' (ibid.: 246, emphasis in original).

But clearly it is far from easy to reconcile the principle of endogamy with the principle of exogamy. For this to be possible, there must be in place complex rules of marriage that take account of the difficulties in maintaining an even sex ratio among persons of marriageable age from marriageable groups within a caste: '*The problem of caste, then ultimately resolves itself into one of repairing the disparity between the marriageable units of the two sexes within it*' (ibid.: 247, emphasis in original). Imbalances in the sex ratio arising from the death of a spouse within a caste – 'surplus women' and 'surplus men' – then are dealt with in one of three ways. A surplus woman may be burnt on her husband's funeral pyre. This is not a very easy proposition and not always possible. She may then be subjected to enforced widowhood. This is not easy either because she may still be attractive enough to threaten the morals of the group.

The second solution then lay in enforced widowhood, with the widow being stripped bare of anything that might be construed as a source of allurement (ibid.: 248). A surplus man could not be burnt on the funeral pyre of his wife 'simply because he is a man' (ibid.: 249) and a person who wields authority '*as a maker of injunctions*' (ibid.: 249, emphasis added). Nor could he be condemned to celibacy, because he is an asset to the group. The only way balance can be maintained with reference to a surplus man is to find him a wife from girls below marriageable age, so that the balance in the marriageable cohort is not disturbed. Sati, enforced widowhood and 'girl' marriage are the three mechanisms through which endogamy, and by extension caste, is preserved and perpetuated (ibid.: 250–252).[5]

Ambedkar provides for us a critical text that leads us back into a different past, one that has been sidestepped by historiographical projects that have addressed caste without grasping the epistemic import of transformational critiques of caste, and clears the continuing present of the encrustations of a conservative, *savarna* narration of India within which the representation of the family is firmly ensconced. What it also enables is a method of reading the politics of belonging and women's entanglement in webs of structural intersections, from the perspectives of women in plural locations, thereby grounding radically new practice on the 'ontoformativity of gender' (Connell 2012).

3. Intersecting histories of oppression and resistance

Feminist historiography in India has opened out a stunning array of methodological possibilities for exploring the place of women in Indian history in the colonial period – in relation to the many intersecting modes of power and hegemonies, subjectivities and interiorities. This historiography consists of at least two parts, with distinct voices, and divergent articulations of what constitutes women's history in colonial India. One part looks at *abrahmani*, non-Brahmin traditions, in different parts of the subcontinent and the ways in which the interrogation of caste was the pivot of social critique, with history being shaped around this critique by women who led the resistance against caste and shifted the terms of discourse around the position of women. Ambedkarite, Satyashodhak and Self Respect traditions constitute this part. The second part consists of feminist historiography that uncovered hitherto misrepresented struggles of *savarna* women against textual orthodoxy and oppressive conjugality. Caste and critiques of the caste order were not central to these accounts, and the voices of Ambedkarite women and women self-respecters were largely absent from this account. Both these historiographical projects traced women's journeys and moorings within the family very differently. This chapter focuses on *abrahmani* or anti-caste articulations of the family.

Recasting Women provided a cogent account of women's engagements with the family, using history writing, 'as a choice which cannot but undergird any attempt at a historical reconstruction which undertakes to demonstrate our sociality in the full sense' (Sangari and Vaid 1989a: 3). At a time when colonial writing laboured over presenting the 'peculiarities of Hindu civilization and the barbaric practices pertaining to women' (Chakravarti 1989: 34), the nationalist retort 'over whether a foreign government had a right to legislate for a people demanding the right to govern themselves' (Chakravarti 1989: 75–76) placed the image of womanhood above the experience of women on the ground – in disregard of the critiques of women's subjugation within the Hindu family by Pandita Ramabai and Rukhmabai (Chakravarti 1989: 78). While Ramabai raised the issue of female infanticide and Rukhmabai repudiated child marriage and critiqued the complicity of the colonial state with the Hindu orthodoxy, sati was perhaps the single practice that generated the biggest debate on the place of the woman vis-à-vis community (Mani 1989).

The voices of the women of this time are strident, and their critique of the patriarchal family is unparalleled. As the first moment in a lifetime then, female infanticide is irreplaceable. 'The census of 1870,' Pandita Ramabai wrote, 'revealed the curious fact that 300 children were stolen in one year by wolves from within the city of Umritzar, all the children being girls,' eliciting from her the ironic comment that 'even the wild animals are so intelligent and of such refined taste that they mock at British law, and almost always steal girls to satisfy their hunger' (Chakravarti 1989: 69). In 1887, Rukhmabai, an educated girl from the carpenter caste, refused to live with her uneducated, consumptive husband, challenging the validity of infant marriage and asserting her right to repudiate it in adulthood. She was threatened with imprisonment under Act XV of 1877 for non-restitution of conjugal rights (Chakravarti 1989: 73–74, Sarkar 2001: 194). Resisting the use of force, Rukhmabai interrogated the twin forces of religious orthodoxy and colonialism. Commenting wryly on the decision to force her to live with her husband, she wrote to Ramabai,

> The learned and civilized judges . . . are determined to enforce, in this enlightened age, the inhuman laws enacted in barbaric times, four thousand years ago. . . . There is no hope for women in India, whether they be under Hindu rule or British rule. . . . The hard hearted mothers-in-law will now be greatly strengthened and will induce their sons to sue the wives in British courts since they are now fully assured that under no circumstances can the British government act adversely to the Hindu Law.
> (Chakravarti 1989: 74)

Rukhmabai was not alone in questioning the permanence of unions contracted without the consent of women. Tarabai Shinde, writing in 1882, says,

> What does stridharma really mean? It means always obeying orders from your husband and doing everything he wants. He can kick you and swear at you, keep his whores, get drunk, gamble with dice and bawl he's lost all his money, steal, commit murder, be treacherous, slander people, rob peoples' treasures or squeeze them for bribes. He can do all this, but when he comes home, stridharma means women are meant to think, 'Oh, Who's this coming now but our little lord Krishna, who's just stolen the milkmaids' curds and milk and . . . then smile at him and offer their devotion, stand ready at his service as if he

was Paramatma himself. But how can people go on believing this idea of stridharma once they have begun to think about what's good and bad? They'd change their ideas straightaway, won't they?

(Shinde [1882] 1994: 79–80)

The early critique of Hinduism, specifically centred on the position of women in Hindu society – denoted by Aryan religion and Brahminism – was developed by Jotiba (Jotirao) Phule in Maharashtra. Writing on 'the most delicate subject of enforced widowhood upon Brahmin women', Phule says:

> The partial Aryan institution inconsiderately allows polygamy to males, which causes them to fall into new habits of wickedness. When his lust is satisfied with his legal wives, he for novelty's sake haunts the houses of public women. . . . In old age in order to obliterate the stigma upon his character, the shameless fellow becomes a religious man and hires public harlots to dance and sing in the temples with a view to venerate the stone idols, for his own satisfaction. After the death of this wicked man, his young and beautiful wife is not allowed by the same Aryan institution to remarry. She is stripped of her ornaments; she is forcibly shaved by her near relatives; she is not fed well; she is not properly clothed; she is not allowed to join pleasure parties, marriages or religious ceremonies. In fact she is bereaved of all the worldly enjoyments, nay she is considered lower than a culprit or a mean beast.
>
> (Phule [1884] 2002: 195)

Savitribai Phule shared Jotiba's zeal and acumen, as also the unflinching commitment to justice, speaking truth to power. Writing to Jotiba in 1868 in support of a Mahar woman who married a Brahmin man, now being stoned to death by the villagers, she says, 'When I got to know of this horrible incident, I rushed there and stopped the cruelty by scaring them with possible action by the British government. . . . I am sending the couple to you' (cited in Rege 2006: 36).

V. Geetha and Rajadurai raise the issue of emotion and structures of feeling in early modern Tamil Nadu and argue that the Non-Brahmin Movement led by Periyar tried primarily to displace the norm of a hierarchical conjugality by stressing mutuality and equality in conjugal relationships and rejecting rituals that denigrated women's position in the family (Geetha and Rajadurai 1998).

A close look at non-Brahmin traditions in politics points to a different intellectual history of family ideologies and family life – as also the place of the family in the larger social imaginary. There is recognition of the vulnerability of the woman within marriage and community; for Dalit women this is a vulnerability compounded by poverty, social violence and humiliation (grinding hunger with untouchability in food practices is a constant marker of everyday life). Yet, in their understanding of this vulnerability and their critique, women from the *abrahmani* traditions strike a stridently different path, which melds individual choices, collective action and the practice of politics transcending the *savarna* patriarchal trap. And it is Dalit women who are the artisans of this tradition.

While this spirit guides progressive legislation that seeks to improve the condition of women in the family, sociological data on kinship and marriage patterns that draw on the kinship of politics rather than or in addition to affinal/consanguineal kinship is scarce if at all. The result is that there is an idea of an alternative, without a systematic empirical documentation in the sociological mode. And the possibilities (tested in the here and now in numerous instances) of the 'alternative' progressive view not yielding a differently structured space for women remain unaddressed.

4. Dalit and Adivasi 'life narratives' as family ethnographies

While cracking open the family, the shapes that theoretical and epistemological frameworks take are determined by ideological/political/social standpoint and location. The politics of location and belonging that shapes individual, communal and collective actions is also constitutive of the acts of explanation. It is not without reason that Sharmila Rege has argued in the context of caste that 'the marginalisation of the non-brahmanical perspectives and experience in the institutionalised scholarship on caste has blurred our understanding of the relations between structural continuities and contemporary change in the social institution of caste' (Rege 2006: 2). We have already seen in the preceding sections that family, caste and religion are mutually constitutive and reinforcing, so that if it is *brahmani* frameworks that have been ascendant in the study of caste, the understanding of family, conjugality, parenting and relationship are determined by the same normative structures.

In the exploration of the family through the life narratives[6] of Dalit women, we witness the making of an *abrahmani* epistemological tradition that makes no distinction between private and public spheres – one that is based on a braiding together of the every day with the political and the conceptual, presenting an unparalled praxiological position that displaces existing pedagogical practice in relation to the family – bringing the politics of lived experience into the centre of a feminist sociological understanding of the institution of the family.

This tradition has its beginnings and indeed draws its grammar from the fusion of politics and conjugality in the lives of Dr. Ambedkar – Ramabai and Jotiba – Savitribai, lifetimes that crafted a new politics of the personal, in which, as Rege argues, there is a prioritization of community and politics over conjugality, which 'stands out from the middle-class discourse of the educated "companionate" conjugality that alienated women from the community without granting autonomy' (Rege 2006: 60). There is also, in this scheme, no disjuncture/contradiction between the protocols of the personal and the public. In the possibilities it held aloft, these were the ideals for the *abrahmani* traditions taking shape – realized to differing degrees.

In speaking about their lives, the accounts of home and family that comes through force us to recognize the shifts in the family as a spatial, emotional and cognitive entity – where the dominant rhetoric (*savarna* and state) on the 'gift' of education for the uplift of the oppressed classes is inverted. We see through the life narratives a reframing of the interiority of Dalit lives and a redefinition of the family in its arduous journey filled with hope towards a utopia in this life. Education is an aspiration that is wrested and appropriated as the new core of Dalit selfhood and the one certain tool to banish the figure of the brahman/*savarna* from their lifeworlds. Reflecting on the road travelled, the here and now presents a moment of truth, of celebration. And the family has been the vehicle in these travels – for each in a unique way, but for all stridently different from the *savarna* norm.

While a detailed consideration of these narratives is outside the scope of this exercise, a few glimpses will suffice to demonstrate the vast chasm between extant scholarship on the family and the view that emerges from the voices of these women.

The figure of the mother is distinctive in these Ambedkarite narratives, which range from lullabies to life narratives invoking Babasaheb:

> Sleep well O little one
> The whole world lies in the shadow of death, the lives of
> your parents were wasted,
> . . .
> I'll feed you doses of your Baba's courage,
> The dark night of the enemy has passed, it's dawn my dear child,
> In your baby talk sings the bird of equality
> (R.D. Gaikwad, cited in Rege 2006: 60)

How may we rethink the history of the family from a standpoint where the 'normal' travails of high-caste women – child marriage, enforced widowhood and sati in particular – did not account for the experiences of Dalit women? Urmila Pawar and Meenakshi Moon provide a valuable account of the struggles by the first generation of Dalit women in the Ambedkarite movement, who fought the violence of social exclusion – organizing against religious prostitution, denial of education, fair labour practices, among others – foregrounding the specificity of the struggles of Dalit women in a virulent caste order (Pawar and Moon 2008, see also Kannabiran 2006a).

Shantabai Dhanaji Dani's mother wanted this daughter to study. She took her to school – and although most Mahar children went to the Municipal Corporation School, Shantabai's mother believed the mission schools were better – they had better and more committed teachers. Therefore, she went to a mission school. She recalls her mother's oft-repeated statement: 'Listen girl, for the poor education is a ray of hope' (Rege 2006: 94–95). She loved studying. Her father taught her in the evenings and told her stories of the Varkari sants. When personal tragedy pushed him into alcoholism, the mother continued to work and support her and her siblings. When her stepsister escaped from an abusive husband, the parents brought her home. Poverty meant there was never enough food in the house; there were dreams and hopes and dignity and perseverance and tenderness that held the family together in a social environment that was violent in the extreme. The bonds within the family, between husband and wife, mother and daughter, father and daughter, siblings and extended family and community were sealed by a common experience of the routine and aggravated violence against Dalits and an intergenerational cascading resistance to caste violence.

From the time Mukta Sarvagod started her schooling at age five, she was made to sit at a distance from the teacher, drop her slate onto the teacher's table from a distance, have her slate slid across the floor to the back of the class where she was made to sit and have water sprinkled on her slate, since she was not permitted to touch the earthen pot that stored water to clean children's slates. There were other Dalit children who were beaten by teachers and withdrawn from school by parents unable to see their children suffer violence. Mukta's father, who worked in the railways, was haunted by memories of his people not being allowed to take wedding processions into the village; therefore, years later, when the Ganesh festival procession was taken out in Pune, he organized one under police protection in his town. He told her stories of how Mahars were given rotten grain as wages for a hard day's labour and how during the lean agricultural season they would make bhakris with greens and a pinch of flour – vegetable bhakris – that caused diarrhoea. Food, labour and hunger preoccupied Muktabai in her work with Dalit communities. There were kunbi families that were very poor too – like Lilu's family, which was a woman-headed household. Lilu's mother worked very hard and found different ways of making ends meet. While full of admiration for her capacity for hard work, much like the way

Mahar women worked, and her dire poverty, Muktabai observed that Lilu's mother's caste status ensured that she was never given stale food in return for her labour, and people extended cooperation in kind and labour when she needed it – something unimaginable for a Mahar woman in a similar situation. And Lilu's mother, poor as she was, struggle as she might, maintained her dignity in the village, providing a stark contrast to her own experiences of humiliation and anger that passed *between* father and daughter (not only *from* father *to* daughter).

'One of Shantabai Kamble's fondest memories is of her mother sitting outside their home on starlit nights with the children and talking of years gone by' (Rege 2006: 157). She told them stories of suffering and hardship – the plague, when the Mahars were so busy burying the dead that they had no time to eat. But each time she recounted her hardships and her struggles, she always ended it by telling Shantabai how she would see better days only if she studied well. She speaks of how her mother refused to send her niece to her husband's house because she was overworked, ill-treated and pushed to the edge of starvation by the husband and mother-in-law. Only after having the husband reprimanded publicly and threatened with ostracism if he dared to misbehave again did she send the young woman back with him. When Shantabai's husband married a second time without her consent and she returned to her parents' home in protest, neighbours tried convincing the father that it would be difficult for her to live by herself, to which her father retorted: 'If the girl stays on by herself, well and good – or else let her go wherever she wants to – we are not Brahmans you know' (cited in Rege 2006: 164). The dedication of her book reads: 'To Aaye-Appa (mother and father) who worked the entire day in the hot, glaring sun, hungry and without water, and through the drudgery of labour, with hunger pinching their stomach, educated me and brought me from darkness to light' (Rege 2006: 156–157).

What of other ties? Gorre Sathyavathi speaks of times when her mother was away and she would take her infant brother to a cousin who was also breastfeeding her child:

> She would feed my brother on one breast and her daughter on the other. When she went out to work on the land my mother would feed her child as well. Almost all of us in our family had fed at her breast and all the children in their family had fed at my mother's breast. So we were very close.
>
> (V. Kannabiran 2015: 14)

'In our adiyar community', says Janu, 'getting married has no great relevance . . . whether married or not, everyone had to work in the *jenmi*'s fields. Even so, to have a bellyful of food one had to go into the forest' (Janu 2004: 6–7). Madhusudhan and Ramdas (2016) point out that the growth and consolidation of patriarchy in Adivasi Koya and Konda Reddi families in Andhra Pradesh is ruptured by three critical factors: the *illarikam* marriage where conjugal residence is uxorilocal; women's responsibility and autonomy in the traditional economy for food, seeds and control over forest resources; and the *gotti* or village council that took collective decisions relating to family and community through a deliberative process. Increasingly, women have begun to participate in larger numbers and more actively in these public deliberations, which has also turned the tide of decision-making in their favour.

Illustrating the departures that an *illarikam* marriage enables, Ramdas and Madhusudhan cite the case of Kangala Satyavathi, who inherited 6 acres of the 15 acres of land from her mother – Satyavathi's was the third consecutive generative of *illarikam* marriage. When her marriage broke down with the husband's taking to alcohol and refusing to work on the land, she asked him to leave. Her mother attempted a negotiation through a meeting with elders, where the husband demanded transfer of land in his name as the condition for his return. Satyavathi and the elders refused and the marriage ended there.

Satyavathi worked the land, brought up her children – 'I will divide the land equally between my 3 children,' she says – and

> has taken the lead in her community to grow diverse food-crops – millets, cereals, pulses, oil-seeds, vegetables, greens, spices and fruits, along with re-establishing flocks of indigenous cattle, poultry, goats and pigs, all of which are critical for sustaining food sovereignty in her community and family.

Satyavathi is a respected leader of her village, the president of Tholakari, the women's wing of Girijana Deepika, which organizes women through principles of sharing and reciprocity which characterize Adivasi societies in this region: Sathyavathi says,

> We women hold on to our power and freedom through growing our food, asserting our knowledge, celebrating our festivals, singing and dancing, asserting our right to move freely in our territories. By doing this we are restoring equality and complementarity within our families and community.

Meena Dhanda's work on intercaste marriages in Punjab where one partner is Dalit points us in the way of a silent revolution where women, especially, persist in marrying outside caste, asserting their belief in a basic humanism and equality for all in the face of the ever-present threat of violence (Dhanda 2012). Kumud Pawde provides us with an account of her cousin, who eloped with a *savarna* girl. When the girl's parents filed a police complaint, the girl said to her mother in court:

> I have seen the disgust and hatred that you have for people of this caste. When I brought a mahar maidservant home you threw her out . . . and warned me 'Beware, never let the shadow of this caste fall, not even in our garden' . . . that's what decided things for me. If my mother feels so repelled by this caste, then I will marry a boy from this very caste.
> (Rege 2006: 248)

Neither the woman nor the man is a victim in these narratives. Nor is there a reification of motherhood and marriage. They tell the stories of their lives, lived in struggle, and create utopias in the everyday – fighting off poverty and hunger ('Hunger was a permanent guest in the household,' says Sathyavathi [V. Kannabiran 2015: 10]), persisting with school and with work; coping with domestic violence; calling abusive husbands to account, or leaving them when the going gets tough; keeping homes open to married daughters; refusing to be bound to the debilitating morality of brahmanical norms even while dealing with patriarchal authority and neglect; and, most important of all, sustaining a practice of politics that redefined community, solidarity, dignity and leadership. Creating spaces that are shared, or spaces of solitude (Sathyavathi), or affective families (Janu), in their independence and rootedness in community, these women turn their back on a social universe that speaks an unintelligible language – the family here is the space of resistance against a violent social order, and a space in which it is possible to wrest the possibility for negotiation and autonomy, and through this dignity and self-respect.

The consciousness of caste is constitutive of the self in caste society – embedded in the fact of being, underwriting it in multitudinous ways – inarticulate and/or articulate depending on location and politics. It is also entrenched in the realities of class, caste and community, which structure the experience of the everyday. The caste–class intersection produces an array of articulations that tell stories of the complex contradictions between consciousness and survival, which are also stories of the caste system. What are the ruptures in these narratives and lifeworlds? In order to know what the rupture of caste consciousness means, it is necessary to engage self-consciously in the politics of becoming, regulating notions of the self, deschooling and politicizing the self in new ways that push you to belonging elsewhere.[7] The family is a site of this struggle and its realization, as these narratives tell us.

5. 'Contradictory embodiment' and family orders

There has been some recognition in social research of the complex and intersectional character of gender orders, especially that gender orders are constantly constituted and reconstituted in multiple configurations with distinct patterns of hegemony among different masculinities and femininities (Connell 2012). Yet gender formation, notably gender transitions, continues to pose the biggest challenge to a theorizing of the family.

Although *hijras* have been recognized in the Indian subcontinent *as hijras/eunuchs*, the recognition was of stigmatized, criminalized practices of embodiment that were repressed by the state through mandatory registration, restrictions on mobility, obstruction of livelihoods based on performance, forced removal of children from transgender parents, arbitrary arrests and the criminalization of 'emasculation'. The transgender subaltern speaks powerfully through the repressive frame of the law – trapped and subjugated by heterosexual patriarchal power.

As an illustration of the methods of disciplining gender in families in India, I provide a brief account from Revathi's autobiography *The Truth about Me* (2010), which speaks eloquently about her life as someone who was 'born a male but wanted to live [her] life as a woman'. Gender saturates our social world completely, and gender identity is constructed simultaneously in many different ways, all together and in conversation with each other. Revathi's testimony provides insights into the ways in which the family as a disciplinary institution deploys biopower in order to extract gender conformity and subjugation to corporeal codes. This discipline has a specific context in caste, region, class, codes of conduct and work. Revathi's struggles are about personhood, identity and dignity, and about work, dress, gait, conduct, speech, likes, dislikes, affections and desires. The armoury of biopower, typically, is unsheathed only when the family is faced with a transgression of the heteropatriarchy.

Hailing from a small village in Tamil Nadu, she provides a moving testimony of her struggle with sexual identity, stigmatization and discrimination at home as much as in the world, and her extraordinary courage and persistence in making meaning of her life in a hostile world forces each of us to re-examine the truth about ourselves.

Her love for 'female work' and girls' games led to her being teased for being a 'girl boy' very early on in school, when she was still her parents' youngest son Doraisamy. The punitive corrective measures too started early on, with teachers caning her for 'not being brave like a boy'. But she behaved like a girl because that is the only way she knew – she did not know how to be a boy, and could not be a boy just because others asked her to. When she played female parts in plays, she was not playing a part. She was being her true self. When she donned her male clothes again, she felt she was going into disguise leaving her real self behind. As she came of age, more confusions – was it right for her to feel desire for other boys? Was she the only one who felt this way? Were there others like her? Where would she find them? As she got to class 10, she says, 'I experienced changes in my body and in my being. I experienced a growing sense of irrepressible femaleness, which haunted me, day in and day out. A woman trapped in a man's body was how I thought of myself' (Chapter 2).

Deeply troubled by her alienation from her own body and her self, she sought out people like herself, people who could understand where she was coming from, learnt a whole new cultural vocabulary and took on a female name that gave her a sense of rootedness she lacked at home. Returning home, getting battered by intolerant brothers and finding no support or sympathy, she runs away again and yet again – never fully able to sever her affection for her family and never able to live within its codes. Her community of belonging was not easy to negotiate either, although she found love and understanding there. Being vulnerable and stigmatized, although there were spheres of social intercourse with dignity, violence and extreme harassment stalked them on the streets – rape, molestation, sexual humiliation, physical attacks by men – known and unknown:

> At such moments, I felt despair, and wondered that people could be this way. . . . God has made us this way, I thought, we have no work of our own, our parents do not understand us and this world looks upon us with distaste. . . . Above all, we wanted to live as human beings do, with dignity.

Alongside the violence that marred her life, Revathi provides a fascinating account of the subcultures of the *hijra* world and the diversities therein – between Delhi, Mumbai, Bangalore – the joys, rituals, dress codes, hierarchies, relations of power, regulation of mobility between one house and another by the *jamaat* (congregation) of the community; and affections that built the bonds within this community. There were different livelihoods as well – asking money from shops, going for *badaai* (the custom where hijras sing, dance and confer blessings on auspicious occasions like the birth of a child or marriage) and sex work.

Being someone who valued independence and freedom, Revathi moves from place to place, one guru to another, one livelihood to another, disliking sex work intensely, craving for sexual happiness but finding she had no option but to treat sexual experience as work. She faces betrayal and dispossession from a father she supports through sex work, rejection from a man she loves and marries, returns to sex work after a spell of activism only to quit yet again.

Through it all, however, although alcohol is an escape, she finds comfort and solace in the *hijra* community: 'Only a pottai knows another's feelings, pain, loss, anguish. . . . We are, in a sense, like a flock of crows. We stick together' (last para of Chapter 9). And so she sets about talking to others like her, recording their stories of hurt and pain, of their suffering humiliation and social hatred – writing about them and about herself, so that we may learn the meanings of life, dignity, humanity, human diversity and humaneness.

6. Family scripts from partition and beyond

> Both men and women want children. To perpetuate family and race, both need a new human that springs from them. For this, a woman bears all the trouble. To agree to this union on the promise made by a pair of love-filled eyes is in her nature. If there is no companion, she will make do with the memory of one but if reflecting on the past is horrifying, how will she bear this great burden alone?
>
> (Kidwai 2011: 293)

The partition of the Indian subcontinent in 1947 witnessed one of the largest movements in world history. Approximately 8 million Hindus and Sikhs left Pakistan to settle in India, and 6–7 million Muslims from India left to settle in Pakistan between 1947 and 1951 (Hasan 2010: 246). Estimates of those killed in the violence of these times vary widely between conservative official estimates of 200,000 and 2 million. The violence was not sporadic – it was a flood that engulfed entire villages. It left corpses – dead and living (see Hasan [2002] 2013).

Reflecting on the situation of girls who had been recovered after abduction during the Partition of 1947, Begum Anis Kidwai recounts the girls saying of their children, 'Send these children off to their fathers. We don't want them.' The fear of society and shame lay behind these words,

> but the way they spoke did not indicate that an abiding love underlay it. They would wrap their arms around the child, weep, and push him at us, 'give him away. I can't keep him. Or you take him. He will survive, and when he grows up, he will meet me'.
>
> (Kidwai 2011: 293–294)

The partition discourse on patriarchal honour of the family and of community, which had disastrous consequences especially for women, finds new meaning today in the proscription of choice marriages and inter-community relationships through the coercion of *khap* (clan or cluster of related clans in north India) panchayats, ghar wapsi agents, moral policing and the cry of 'love jihad'. Prem Chowdhry, one the first feminist scholars to examine the enforcement of cultural codes on choice marriages, observes pertinently that [h]onour is enforced through the use of power – whether that of caste, class, gender or seniority with the family as the medium – and, finally, through violence. The more vocal opposition and acts of violence are traceable to the social groups, which stand to benefit the most by bolstering these cultural ideas (Chowdhry 1998: 333). Urvashi Butalia recalls the 'voluntary' deaths en masse of the women of Thoa Khalsa, while the men in their families stood witness in West Punjab. Reminiscent of the claim to 'voluntary sati,' honour killings such as this mask the realities of women in these situations. While some women might have acquiesced, the untold story is of those women (how many, we will never know) who were forced to die (Butalia 2000).

As a counterpoint to the power of the patriarchal order stands the Urdu writer Saadat Hasan Manto's story *Khol Do*, through Veena Das's interpretation, where the corpse-like body of Sarajjudin's daughter Sakina is brought into the hospital. To reduce the heat and suffocation in the room, the doctor says, 'khol do', pointing to the window. There is a faint movement and the near-dead Sakina struggles and loosens her salwar. The father is ecstatic – 'My daughter is alive!' while the doctor breaks into a sweat. Das's reading of this story is a departure that captures not just the essence of Manto but in so doing upstages the dominant rhetoric on honour in relation to collective sexual assault on women during conflict. At a time 'when ideas of purity and honour densely populated the literary narratives as well as family and political narratives, so that father willed their daughters to die for family honour', says Das, 'this father wills his daughter to live even as parts of her body can do nothing else but proclaim her brutal violation' (Das 2007: 47).

Parveena Ahangar's work as the founder of the Association of Parents of Disappeared Persons in Kashmir (APDP), following the disappearance of her son Javed Ahmad Ahangar after security forces took him away in 1990, provides us with another measure to understand the family. Javed was one of the estimated 8,000–10,000 Kashmiris who have been victims of enforced disappearances in Kashmir. The work of the APDP also points towards ways in which the very idea of the family is rent asunder by sexual assault of women (wives, sisters, daughters – women in the family) and the terror/anticipation of such assault by men in the valley. There are other uncontainable ruptures – the 1,500 'half widows' – women whose husbands (several of whom are civilians) have disappeared – who have an indeterminate status – both from the standpoint of the community and the state, and therefore precarious futures, in yet another expression of discourses of honour.[8] In providing support to families of the disappeared and in relentlessly searching for her missing son, 24 years after he was taken away, Parveena re-notates the home into a space that challenges the impunity of the militarized state, and the task of the mother to one that provides support to other families like hers in their collective pursuit for accountability, justice and recovery in a context of aggravated conflict, loss and grief.

7. The place called home

What are the spatial characteristics of this place called home? Feminist writing has looked at this space called home, reflecting with ambivalence on its centrality, especially when violence mars the contours of the home. Families have boundaries, and the home is that bounded space inhabited by the family – can we forget the judge in a constitutional court declaring that bringing the constitution into the family is like bringing a bull into a china shop? The family is imagined as a physical space with walls, doors and a threshold that permits entry and exit on clearly defined terms.

Babytai Kamble describes houses in the maharwada in the 1920s as being 'plastered with mud and decorated with eternal poverty': the *keli* or earthen vessel at the door with a coconut shell to drink water from, a wooden spoon and an iron *tawa* (griddle) for roasting bhakri, a couple of half-broken *chul* or hearths, a couple of earthen pots and a grinding stone. 'Above the chul hung the *valani* – the rope on which the skins of dead animals would be dried' – in her words the sacred thread of the Mahars, the marker of their caste (Rege 2006: 197).

Sathyavathi speaks of carrying her infant brother two and a half kilometres every day so that her mother who worked in a hospital there could breast-feed him. On the way, close to the culvert where she rested, there was a small hut with a well beside it.

> There was a neat fence around the hut. In the hut lived a bent old woman. The old woman kept her hut and the surroundings spotlessly clean. I would sit there with my brother and watch the old woman at work. I loved her cleanliness. I noticed that she lived alone. I thought, 'When I grow up I want to live like this. A small hut with a well, alone in a clean home.'
>
> (V. Kannabiran 2015: 13)

For C.K. Janu, leader of the landless Adivasi people of Kerala, the huts they lived in

> were merely protection from the wind and rain. Also against wild animals. The large common courtyard existed so that we could gather in groups or just relax and enjoy the breeze and the sunshine. And the forests, the streams and the fields existed all around it. Nature lay open for little ones to learn from. . . . The gurgling of water from the fields filled our nights . . . the winds blowing from forest to forest played rhythms on the skins of our backs.
>
> (Janu 2004: 51–52)

There were no lamps, no kerosene and no matchboxes. 'When it grew really dark outside, everyone would gather in the courtyard. Those who munched tobacco would do just that. We would sit for hours listening to what the forest mumbled' (Janu 2004: 3).

In rural Kashmir, from being a refuge in the quieter phases of militancy, the home 'became a virtual prison in the 1990s where militants could seek food and refuge and which could be searched by Indian security forces at any time'. The *midnight knock* was a metaphor of terror, vulnerability, fear, the anticipation of violence and impending loss and bereavement. The home was the place to which children may not return from school and men may not return from the fields after a day's work. The home was the place that did not belong to them anymore even while it was the only place that accommodated them.

Sumona DasGupta, writing about Jammu and Kashmir, reminds us that while the home swings in the feminist imaginary between being a site of extreme physical violence and being a refuge from physical violence outside it, 'sometimes the home can also emerge as a space of resistance which challenges the militarized might of the several "armed patriarchies" that surround it' (DasGupta 2011: 99).

8. Conclusion

I have attempted through this chapter to open out to view a small cluster of narratives that speak a different tongue and in fact constitute our intellectual history of family life. The life narratives excavate the basis of consciousness, peel off each layer of memory and see what lies beneath it, interrogating the location of the self on multiple axes carrying the narrator forward to a radically different site of belonging. Importantly, these are narratives outside the Hindu *savarna* experience and in opposition to it. The partition experience is immersed in the ideological frames of dominant religions. Begum Kidwai expresses her anguish at the predicament of young girls trampled in the stampede across borders. The post-partition experience of Jammu and Kashmir carries forward the troubling legacy of the partition – how do women rebuild family spaces and ties in the trauma of conflict, loss and bereavement? I have earlier explored the interiority of the family in an autoethnographic project that presented the internal ruptures and incoherences in a family history that militated against any monolithic/homogenizing narration (Kannabiran 2008). In this chapter as well, I have attempted to open up the ruptures amid the 'normal' to interrogate the premises of the normal in writing on the family.

I return in conclusion to the significance of intersectionality to feminist methodology, particularly in the study of the family. Rather than slide into the pitfalls of juxtaposing the West with the rest, the explorations of ideas, memories and theoretical constructions of the family and relationship presented in this chapter point to intersections between caste, the politics of location, education, the state and struggles against the dominance of different orders that produce distinct experiences of the family and women's specific locations within and in relation to it.

Challenging dominant narratives of bourgeois conjugality that spring from Hindu nationalism, we may extend Rege's concerns to explore the ways in which the seamless 'apolitical' terrain of the family in sociology, social anthropology and women's/gender studies especially may be ruptured through a different set of epistemic standpoints – opening ourselves 'to their turbulent processes of learning in order to challenge the manufacture of ignorance in which we are complicit through the privileges of class and education' (Bharucha, cited in Rege 2006: 4).

In interrogating domination, the women in these narratives are clearly mapping lines of solidarity and belonging outside their immediate contexts to a larger community of solidarity based on the kinship of politics, besides rejecting co-optation into a dominant discourse on the essentialized family. Material contexts (e.g. of poverty, hunger, displacement, armed conflict) constitute experience and memory, and determine shifts thereof. There are therefore larger interconnections between changes in the economy and polity that are immediately reflected in the shifts in crises as well as economic relations within and between families. Neither the intersections nor the resolutions, therefore, are fixed and unchanging, or even free of contradictions, but rather negotiated constantly and calibrated to an emergent consciousness of the ideal family for the realities taking shape – not the actual, necessarily, but a new horizon with the promise of a new, empowered future.

An important part of this challenge in the continuing present is the interrogation of discourses of family and caste honour and the violent enforcement of endogamy and untouchability practices against Dalits by other backward classes and dominant peasant castes. We also see a rise of conservatism in gender relations, especially within the 'employee' classes among the Adivasis, that Ramdas and Madhusudhan speak to, and among Muslim communities in areas under siege. Each of these has specificities of material and political context that needs close examination. But especially in the context of casteism driven by Hindutva politics, which fuels much of the contradiction and coercion we are witness to in the discourse around the family today, it is important not to lose sight of a fundamental, irreconcilable problem raised by Babasaheb Ambedkar: the annihilation of caste depends on the rejection of the philosophical foundations of caste and thereby a rejection of Hindu religion and 'Manu's madness'. The diligent commitment to intermarriage and interdining in personal and social life, and an ethical politics in conjugality and public life based on constitutional morality, was at the core of his imagination of social transformation.

Notes

1 Crenshaw (1991), Mohanty (2013), McKinnon (2013) and Connell (2015) provide a very stimulating discussion on intersectionality and southern theory.
2 Shah *et al.* observe that although there is discussion around queer concerns, 'the realities of persons assigned gender female at birth are often overlooked in the larger queer movement when issues of transgender persons are raised' (Shah *et al.* 2015, Introduction). Brinda Bose, in this volume, presents a fuller discussion of sexuality and its significance to feminist methods. For the limited purposes of this essay, I focus on the *eunuch/ hijra*, through one life narrative, while fully recognizing the 'gender galaxy' and its uncontainability as well as the specificities of violence, exclusion and discrimination based on gender.
3 For a feminist review of family studies across disciplines, see Kannabiran (2006b).
4 For a more detailed analysis of this essay, see Kannabiran (2009).
5 In the last decade of the century that began with these observations by Ambedkar, we witnessed *savarna* girls opposing the implementation of the Mandal Commission recommendations taking easy and spontaneous recourse to the justification that they will not be able to find 'educated' husbands – which, in fact, means that caste endogamy is thrown into crisis by opening out educational opportunities to disadvantaged castes – Dalit Bahujans – through reservations (see Rege 2006: 3).
6 Rege uses the term 'life narrative' as 'a wide-ranging term for exploring diverse modes around the autobiographical' (Rege 2006: 7, n. 1).
7 I have elsewhere examined the relevance of William Connolly's arguments on the politics of becoming and Martha Minow's response to an understanding of Dalit politics in India. See Kalpana Kannabiran (2006a).
8 http://www.jkccs.net/wp-content/uploads/2015/02/Half-Widow-Half-Wife-APDP-report.pdf (accessed 11 June 2016).

References

Ambedkar, B. R. 2002. "Castes in India." In Valerian Rodrigues (ed.). *The Essential Writings of BR Ambedkar.* New Delhi: Oxford.
Bama. 2005. *Sangati* (translated from Tamil by Lakshmi Holmström), New Delhi: Oxford University Press.
Butalia, Urvashi. 2000. *The Other Side of Silence: Voices from the Partition of India.* New Delhi: Penguin Books.
Chakravarti, Uma. 1989. "Whatever Happened to the Vedic Dasi? Orientalism, Nationalism, and a Script for the Past." In Kumkum Sangari and Sudesh Vaid (eds). *Recasting Women: Essays in Colonial History.* New Delhi: Kali for Women, pp. 27–87.
Chowdhry, Prem. 1998. "Enforcing Cultural Codes: Gender and Violence in Northern India." In Mary E. John and Janaki Nair (eds). *A Question of Silence? The Sexual Economies of Modern India.* New Delhi: Kali for Women, pp. 332–367.
Connell, Raewyn. 2012. "Transsexual Women and Feminist Thought: Toward New Understanding and New Politics," *Signs*, Vol. 37, No. 4 (Summer). Sex: A Thematic Issue, pp. 857–881.
Connell, Raewyn. 2015. "Meeting at the Edge of Fear: Theory on a World Scale," *Feminist Theory*, Vol. 16, No. 1, pp. 49–66.
Crenshaw, Kimberle. 1991. "Mapping the Margins: Intersectionality, Identity Politics and Violence against Women of Color," *Stanford Law Review*, Vol. 43, pp. 1241–1299.
Das, Veena. 2007. *Life and Words: Violence and the Descent into the Ordinary.* New Delhi: Oxford University Press.
DasGupta, Sumona. 2011. "Renegotiating Internal Boundaries by Women of Jammu and Kashmir." In Paula Banerjee and Anasua Basu Ray Chaudhury (eds). *Women in Indian Borderlands.* New Delhi: Sage, pp. 94–121.
Dhanda, Meena. 2012. "Runaway Marriages: A Silent Revolution?" *Economic and Political Weekly*, Vol. XLVII, No. 43 (27 October), pp. 100–108.
Geetha, V. and S. V. Rajadurai. 1998. *Towards a Non-Brahmin Millennium: From Iyothee Thass to Periyar.* Calcutta: Samya.
Harvey, David. 2005. *A Brief History of Neoliberalism.* Oxford: Oxford University Press.
Hasan, Mushirul. [2002] 2013. "Introduction: Partition Narratives." In David Page, Anita Inder Singh, Penderel Moon and G. D. Khosla (eds). *The Partition Omnibus.* New Delhi: Oxford University Press, pp. ix–xliii.
Kannabiran, Kalpana. 2006a. "A Cartography of Resistance: The National Federation of Dalit Women." In Nira Yuval-Davis, Kalpana Kannabiran and Ulrike Vieten (eds). *The Situated Politics of Belonging.* London: Sage, pp. 54–71.
Kannabiran, Kalpana. 2006b. "Three Dimensional Family: Remapping a Multidisciplinary Approach to Family Studies," *Economic and Political Weekly*, Vol. 41, No. 42 (21 October–27 October), pp. 4427–4433.
Kannabiran, Kalpana. 2008. "Making the Forked Tongue Speak: An Ethnography of the Self," *Economic and Political Weekly* (19 April), pp. 63–70.

Kannabiran, Kalpana. 2010. "In the Shadow of Partition." In *The Mushirul Hasan Omnibus*. New Delhi: Oxford University Press, pp. 245–278.

Kannabiran, Kalpana. 2015. "The Complexities of the Genderscape in India," *Seminar*, No. 672 (August), pp. 46–50.

Janu, C. K. (as told to Bhaskaran).2004. *Mother Forest: The Unfinished Story of C.K. Janu* (translated by N. Ravi Shankar). New Delhi: Kali for Women.

Kannabiran, Kalpana. 2009. "Sociology of Caste and the Crooked Mirror: Recovering BR Ambedkar's Legacy," *Economic and Political Weekly*, Vol. 44, No. 4 (24 January), pp. 35–39.

Kannabiran, Vasanth. 2015. *Sathyavathi: Confronting Caste, Class and Gender*. New Delhi: Women Unlimited.

Kidwai, Anis. 2011. *In Freedom's Shade*. Translated from Urdu by Ayesha Kidwai. New Delhi: Penguin Books.

Madhusudhan, N. and Sagari R. Ramdas. 2016. "The Family in Adivasi Society." In *Studies on the Family in India*. Secunderabad: Asmita, mimeo.

Mani, Lata. 1989. "Contentious Traditions: The Debate on Sati in Colonial India." In Kumkum Sangari and Sudesh Vaid (eds). *Recasting Women: Essays in Colonial History*. New Delhi: Kali for Women, pp. 88–126.

McKinnon, Catharine. 2013. "Intersectionality as Method: A Note," *Signs*, Vol. 38, No. 4, *Intersectionality: Theorizing Power, Empowering Theory* (Summer), pp. 1019–1030.

Mohanty, Chandra Talpade. 2013. "Transnational Feminist Crossings: On Neoliberalism and Radical Critique," *Signs*, Vol. 38, No. 4, *Intersectionality: Theorizing Power, Empowering Theory* (Summer), pp. 967–991.

Patel, Tulsi. 2005. *The Family in India: Structure and Practice*. New Delhi: Sage.

Pawar, Urmila and Meenakshi Moon. 2008. *We Also Made History: Women in the Ambedkarite Movement*. Translated and with an introduction by Wandana Sonalkar. New Delhi: Zubaan.

Phule, Jotirao. [1884] 2002. "Opinion from Jotteerao Govindrao Phulay on Note No. II, by Mr. B.M. Malabari on Enforced Widowhood." In G. P. Deshpande (ed.). *Selected Writings of Jotirao Phule*. New Delhi: LeftWord Books, pp. 195–197.

Rege, Sharmila. 2006. *Writing Caste/Writing Gender: Reading Dalit Women's Testimonios*. New Delhi: Zubaan.

Revathi, A. 2010. *The Truth about Me: A Hijra Life Story*. Translated from Tamil by V. Geetha. New Delhi: Penguin Books.

Sarkar, Tanika. 2001. *Hindu Wife, Hindu Nation: Community, Religion and Cultural Nationalism*. New Delhi: Permanent Black.

Shah, Chayanika, Raj Merchant, Shals Mahajan and Smriti Nevatia. 2015. *No Outlaws in the Gender Galaxy*. New Delhi: Zubaan (e-book).

Shinde, Tarabai. [1882] 1994. "A Comparison between Women and Men: An Essay to Show Who's Really Wicked and Immoral, Women or Men?" In Rosalind O'Hanlon (ed.). *A Comparison between Women and Men: Tarabai*

Shinde and the Critique of Gender Relations in Colonial India. New Delhi: Oxford University Press, pp. 73–134.

Yuval-Davis, Nira, Kalpana Kannabiran and Ulrike N. Veiten. 2006. "Introduction: Situating the Contemporary Politics of Belonging." In Nira Yuval-Davis, Kalpana Kannabiran and Ulrike N. Veiten (eds). *The Situated Politics of Belonging*. London: Sage, pp. 1–14.

3 Masculinities in fieldwork
Notes on feminist methodology[1]

Romit Chowdhury

1. Introduction

This chapter makes a small move at contributing to discussions on feminist research methodology in relation to the study of men and masculinities. It does so by drawing on field notes prepared in the course of an interview-based research project on men's rights activism in urban India. The chapter considers how gender sameness shapes the interview process and how hegemonic norms of masculinity inflect interactions between researcher and interviewee and, in turn, men's production of feminist knowledge. A male feminist researcher studying explicitly anti-feminist men encounters a number of dilemmas. How is the researcher to deal with the ready assumption of his respondents that because he is male, he will ally with anti-feminist initiatives? How may the researcher negotiate the ethical and the pragmatic when faced with abusive, anti-women attitudes in the field? In what ways do feminist principles pertaining to accountability and (mis)representation bear on studies of misogynist research subjects? A second set of concerns has to do with academic audiences to which the outcome of such research is likely to be presented. A male researcher studying men's rights groups risks being read as anti-feminist himself. What does the 'patriarchy baiting' (Kimmel 1998) that male feminist scholars are sometimes subjected to tell us about the practice of feminism and the status of masculinity studies in the academy?

A challenging critique that feminists have posed to social research has been that the sphere of knowledge production is itself a site of male privilege. The categories of thought that are used to understand society, what counts as knowledge, what methods of research are deemed valid and which voice is considered credible, far from being autonomous intellectual certitudes, are fundamentally gendered (Cook and Fonow 1986, Jaggar and Bordo 1989). Feminists' questioning of the epistemological assumptions of the knowing subject, which legitimize the subordination of women, impelled the task of making women's social worlds visible; this was envisioned as a partial corrective to masculinist knowledge claims. Any easy empiricism in pursuing this task, however, was soon complicated by questions about the epistemic value of experience and the politics of representation, and here, the debates between feminist standpoint theorists continue to be instructive (Rege 1998, Harding 2004). Among the array of concerns that energized these discussions, of particular methodological import to feminist studies that involve fieldwork has been the idea that the researcher and researched are framed in relationships of power. When women study other women in face-to-face research situations, how is access negotiated? Is being an 'insider' always advantageous to producing feminist knowledge? How do women researchers grapple with dilemmas of representation and the question of 'difference' in the practice of fieldwork? How do they handle the ethical/emotional burden of receiving sensitive information (DeVault 1999, Ramazanoglu and Holland 2002)? The awareness that ethnographic contact with less-powerful others is often exploitative makes feminist research prioritize ethical values of reciprocity, transparency, accountability and responsibility, with the objective of addressing hierarchical research relations (Skeggs 2001).

In contrast to this robust dialogue on methodology within feminist thought, the field of masculinity studies – certainly in South Asia, but also internationally – has seldom considered the implication of these debates for research projects which seek to understand men's lives. The anthropological literature on masculinities in India, for instance, does not include a sustained consideration of methodological issues involved in doing ethnography of gendered practices. The introduction to an anthology of essays on these concerns in Western contexts (Pini and Pease 2013) offers a set of reasons why methodological inquiries are important for men studying men and masculinities. To the extent that feminist research seeks to generate knowledge that will aid understanding and redressal of gender inequality, attention to methodological questions in examining masculinities helps maintain focus on hierarchical gender arrangements, at all stages of the research process. This is urgent because too often it has been possible for studies on men to focus exclusively on the trappings of masculine ideals without theorizing how these relate to male privilege and patriarchy (ibid.). It is, therefore, vital to consider the implications of feminist critiques of traditional research methods for men researching men. In addition, male researchers' adoption of feminist methods might require some negotiations with their own masculinity. Does the move from the traditional interview – which demands distance and objectivity – to the feminist interview – which involves reciprocity – require male researchers to re-examine their relationship to ideals of masculinity? For masculinity studies to yield feminist knowledge, the contributors to this volume suggest, researchers must address these methodological concerns.

I first encountered men's rights groups while searching the Internet for media reports on domestic violence in India. The earliest of these groups began their activities in the first few years of the 1990s but have grown steadily in number and scale of operation since the turn of the 21st century. Men's rights groups were formed with the objective of challenging what they see as a concerted effort by feminists and women's rights organizations to dismantle the 'Indian family' by inviting the law to enter the private domain. Their allegation is that mercenary women, on the strength of pro-women family laws and a new social climate that favours them, are exploiting men in a society that is steadily becoming anti-male. Indeed, to their way of thinking, gender social arrangements in the present day have made men into the true victims. Their proposed solutions, which prioritize legal safeguards for men, ideologically tie the issue of men's rights to saving the 'traditional Indian' social fabric from rupture.[2]

When I suggested the idea of examining the gender politics of these groups to some senior academics and peers, I was dissuaded from taking up such a project. This phenomenon, I was told, is simply a backlash against feminism and women's movements and men's rights activists are rabid women-haters with predictable, patriarchal views on gender and sexuality. What could an investigation of these attitudes possibly reveal that is not already known to social scientists? To my mind, there was also a methodological concern. The imperative of 'giving voice' to the unheard, particularly women, has seen feminisms turn to ethnography and interviews as tools suitable for this endeavour (Devault 1999). Is there any value for feminism in 'hearing' privileged groups' claims of subalternity? In attending to these questions, it seemed to me that an unavoidable fallout of the use of the word 'backlash' as an easy nostrum to characterize anti-feminist initiatives has been that it overlooks the value of both distinguishing between different kinds of reactionary political formations and examining any of them in some depth. Second, a number of feminist writings (see FitzGerald 1998, Hogeland 2004) that have theorized women's fear of feminist politics implicitly suggest that while women's rejection of feminism requires elaborate scrutiny, men's – particularly 'heterosexual' men's – opposition to feminist ideas is quite self-explanatory. Even as we summarily explain heterosexual men's resistance to feminism in terms of the patriarchal dividend, to understand the micropolitics of this resistance, it seemed important to me to ask why many men reject feminism. To the extent that invisibility is a cloak of the privileged, self-identified heterosexual men engaging in what can be described as a form of identity politics is a rather curious development. The formation of men's rights groups, I thought, provides occasion to partially examine men's relationship to feminist politics in the contemporary moment and unpack the ready answers that are considered sufficient explanations.

To this end, in 2011, I interviewed 14 men's rights activists and volunteers from across the country. I also participated in the Fourth Annual National Men's Rights Meet held in Kolkata on 15 August and 16 August that year. This meeting was attended by close to 100 members of men's rights groups. The pursuit of this research project, as a male feminist, gave rise to several methodological quandaries. In this chapter, I focus on the discursive contexts in which I conducted interviews with members of men's rights groups. In doing so, I demonstrate the gendered relations of power that operate in the interview process and why recognizing these is crucial to understanding both men's anti-feminism and pro-feminist men's conduct of research on men and masculinities.

2. Interviews and competing masculinities

It is important to note that men's rights groups have several women members. Some of the family laws that seek to provide safeguards to wives against injustices have the ancillary effect of bringing other women in the family unit, such as the mother and sisters of the husband, within the folds of criminality. To bolster their case against the alleged misuse of pro-women laws, men's rights activists claim that these provisions which are meant to offer women legal rights are, in fact, anti-women. Therefore, organizations such as Mothers and Sisters Initiative, All India Mothers-in-Law Protection Forum and Mothers and Sisters of Husbands against Abuse of Law have been formed to address this aspect of the problem. The annual meeting of men's rights groups which I attended had a number of women representatives from these organizations.

As I was interviewing Reena Gupta[3] (a 59-year-old, middle-class woman living in Bangalore, whose son was, at the time, embroiled in a case of alleged domestic violence), a male activist (Jignesh Tiwari, a middle-class man also in his late fifties) – who I had briefly spoken to earlier that day – joined us. Reena had initially been reluctant to share her experiences, saying that surely there were others present who could give me better information, but she relented to speak to me after some coaxing. Therefore, I was apprehensive that Jignesh's sudden presence would inhibit Reena. Indeed, as she resumed her narrative, she kept glancing at Jignesh to gauge his reaction. Neither of us was left in doubt about Jignesh's views for very long, as he began interrupting Reena by adding his own thoughts on the matter. Soon he picked up a thread in Reena's narrative and began holding forth. For a feminist researcher, moments such as these pose certain dilemmas.

On the one hand, every opinion that is voiced in the field is worth recording, and this man's interruptions could perhaps provide clues to power relations between men and women within men's rights groups. And yet, his repeatedly interrupting a woman respondent caused some annoyance in me, re-creating, as he was, the all-too-familiar pattern of opinionated men shouting down other – particularly women's – voices. This consciousness encouraged me to tell Jignesh that right then it was important for my research to hear Reena's views. Lest this exchange hinder my subsequent interaction with him – he seemed somewhat offended – I compensated for my firmness by taking his mobile number and assuring him that I would seek him out. Adopting such gestures of aggrandizement enables the researcher to avoid the problem of 'minimizing', that is, offended respondents becoming laconic and providing only terse replies to interview questions (Schwalbe and Wolkomir 2001). Jignesh hung around a while longer, in silence, before sauntering off. I was able to interview him at length later in the day.

It did not occur to me immediately that my irritation in that interview context had been about both imperious, older men cutting off women's speech and them not giving younger men a chance to express themselves. As a (male) researcher I expected to have control over the interview process, and hence, my annoyance with Jignesh in that situation was as much about competing masculinities, as it had to do with my training in feminist methods. Even as my pro-feminism alerted me to the silencing of a woman's voice in the field, it did not preclude my competing with another man for social power in the course of fieldwork. Thus, if being a female ethnographer often 'intervenes to block the process of knowing' in all-male spaces (Chopra 2004: 37), the temptation for the male researcher to contest with other men for hegemonic status in a fraternal field setting may equally inhibit the process of data generation. My experiential grasp of dominant cultures of masculinity, however, alerted me to the likely effect of this competition on a useful informant, and I was able to use codes of maleness to assuage his displeasure and retain access to him.

3. Questions threaten men

Indeed, as the provocateur of the interview, a researcher is the one who sets its direction. Semi-structured interviews certainly give much room for respondents to shape the course of this exchange, but the research questions guiding the larger project inevitably define the broad parameters of the interview (Presser 2005). The issue of control in the interview context works in a specific way in research on men and masculinities. To the extent that control is an index of masculinity, the position of an interviewee structurally demands that men relinquish some of this power. To this is added the unease of being questioned on many of the assumptions on which hegemonic masculinity is premised. Yet, in as much as interviews unsettle male respondents by probing the meanings they ascribe to masculinity, they simultaneously present interviewees an opportunity to engage in the work of signification by which a gendered sense of self is affirmed (Schwalbe and Wolkomir 2001). These power dynamics played out in a telling way in my interactions with a number of male men's rights activists. Since a significant component of my project was to understand these men's resentment of feminist views, in my interviews I intermittently posed questions that challenged their assumptions about men's and women's place in society. Consider these two excerpts from an interview exchange with Vikaas Wadhwani, a 36-year-old manager based in Hyderabad:

ME: Men's rights activists keep saying that men are the real victims in society today. But if you read the newspaper, you will see stories of women being raped, beaten, killed, molested every day. So what exactly makes men and not women victims?

VIKAAS (VISIBLY UPSET): What do you mean? Why are you believing all these news reports? National Crime Records Bureau shows that many more men commit suicide in a year for family problems compared to women. You have not done your research properly!

Farther on in the interview:

ME: You speak of the misuse of family laws. But are not all laws misused? Why blame women's groups for something that is true of the whole legal system in the country?

VIKAAS (IN EXASPERATION): Again you are asking these questions! Misuse of family laws is different because the family is special. If your family breaks up, is it the same as your business going bad? So how can misuse of domestic violence law be the same as corruption in business law?

Questions that appeared to doubt activists' narratives were experienced as threatening by several male respondents. While men's sense of being aggressed upon itself became important research data on masculinity, I had to be careful about not enraging anyone since I did not want to be asked to leave the meeting. There was a chance that if I upset an important person from these groups, all of them would refuse further inquiry and I would have to abandon this project. However, to pursue the intellectual queries that had provoked this study, it was crucial that I probe my respondents' narratives of gender.

If men's rights groups adopt the language of victimhood in their politics, this appears to sit uneasily with several group members and they resist acknowledging the emasculation that claiming to be a victim involves. Sooraj Rastogi, a 35-year-old hospital consultant in Madhya Pradesh, was fighting a case of dowry harassment and also had Section 377 filed against him by his wife, who had accused him of filming her naked and distributing the video to his friends without her consent. Sooraj appeared deeply uncomfortable when I asked him if he saw himself as a victim of pro-women family laws. He evaded this question a couple of times during the interview. Fumbling for words and angry that this question had been put to him a third time, he finally replied, 'These laws were misused against me. I see myself as an activist and I will fight against those who are doing this wrong to society till my last breath!' His voice gained in confidence as he evaded the victim word and self-identified as an active agent, in place of accepting the passivity that victimhood implies. Instances such as these demonstrate how the interview situation itself becomes an occasion for the identity work through which a masculine self is momentarily secured. For my interviews to successfully elicit narratives of masculinity, as a researcher I had to find a balance between pushing respondents towards an uncertain place and ensuring that this does not totally alienate them. Such exchanges emphasized the need for indirection on the part of the interviewer when asking potentially provocative questions. The pro-feminist male researcher's gender positioning vis-à-vis dominant cultures of masculinity, a position that has been described as 'outsider within' (Flood 2013), plays no small role in the exercise of such indirection during fieldwork.

4. Homophobia in the field

In the days leading up to the national annual meeting of men's rights groups, I experienced some apprehension about spending three full days in, what I assumed would be, a hypermasculine environment. My anxieties were very much about how my masculinity would be perceived by these much-older men – I was 26 years old at the time. I was worried that, as in middle school, I would be derided as 'soft' and would again have to deal with a blatant form of gender policing. These personal concerns also had a bearing on methodology. I had framed my research subjects as aggressive, potentially violent well before I had interacted with them. It was likely that this defensive stance would be noticed and I would fail to establish the rapport that aids self-disclosure. Like other male researchers in similar research settings (Flood 2013), I resolved these concerns by performing my heterosexuality in an overt way – referring to my girlfriend in our conversations, when I could well have not mentioned her – not only to facilitate homosocial bonding but also to allay my own anxieties about being perceived as unmanly. Social acceptance in this gathering would allow me to ask critical questions about the gender politics of men's rights groups, without seeming that I am 'against' them. As a cisgender man I was able to integrate myself into the culture of masculinity prevailing in the research environment by negotiating some aspects of my performance of masculinity; subsequently, this ensured access to rich data. In this research context, this is a privilege of the cisgender male researcher because, for many, such 'strategies of establishing masculine credibility are not really options, and "misfitting" becomes part of our routine experience of fieldwork' (Vanderbeck 2005: 398).

While my interjections about patriarchy occasioned some annoyance, questions about non-normative families variously disgusted and baffled several of my respondents. In response to their recurring complaint that the institution of family in India is under great threat, I asked group members for their thoughts on other kinds of family arrangements, such as those comprising two women or two men. One kind of reaction I got was like Suresh Rajamani's (a 51-year-old banking professional from Chennai), who responded in great puzzlement, 'Surely they can stay together as friends. But how does that become a family?' The other sort of response was voiced by Ajay Goswami, a 45-year-old management professional in Delhi, who cringed at the suggestion of a same-sex couple and said that men's rights groups have absolutely no connections with the gay movement in India. He did slip in the suggestion that heterosexual men often face sexual harassment from gay men in office spaces and that this needs immediate legal remedy.

Even as I noted his homophobic disgust of same-sex sexual/romantic intimacy, a particular situation in the meeting forced me to confront my own discomfort with physical proximity to other men. At the meeting two men were expected to share a double bed for the stay over. To my considerable surprise, I found, as I went to bed the first night, that my roommate (a Pune-based businessman in his early thirties) preferred to sleep just in his briefs! The prospect of sleeping next to a barely clothed man, that too a stranger, made me deeply uncomfortable. As I thought about my reaction, I became aware that my unease had much to do with the sex of my companion and was not simply about my notions of social inappropriateness. Despite this momentary awareness, I found myself recounting this episode to different groups of friends, in the months following this meeting, to great mirth and laughter. Again it occurred to me that this narration was as much about the pleasure of being humorous in a social gathering as it was about performing my heterosexuality. Such continuities between my and activists' practices of hegemonic masculinity made it impossible for me (as a researcher) to assume a superior ethical position over this group of men (researched) by adopting self-excepting 'critical distance'. In varying degrees, both the male researcher and his male respondents sought to accomplish the same expectations from hegemonic masculinity. Such encounters in the field underline the importance of consciousness-raising as a methodological tool in feminist research (Cook and Fonow 1986), which can prompt alertness to the likely influence of researchers' heteronormal notions about sexuality on both data generation and the interpretive procedures adopted by them.

5. Using homosociality as a resource

One evening in the annual meeting, I spent some time with three very active members of men's rights groups. Aakash Swarup – a 34-year-old, runs his father's car parts business in Gandhinagar – was mired in a messy divorce and domestic violence case. He later spoke to me angrily of his wife's 'unreasonable demands' of money when they were cohabiting, her animosity towards his parents and her repeated taunts about his unwillingness to 'do something of his own' instead of simply managing his father's business. That evening, Aakash, Jatin Saxena (38, advertising professional, Mumbai) and Leon Ritchie (42, management consultant, Delhi) were speaking admiringly about a man who had apparently shown great courage and determination in the face of false accusations about dowry from his wife and was now a 'free man'. As Aakash was expressing gratitude for the support that he has received from other group members in this difficult time, he suddenly became livid:

> You know what I feel like doing? I want to drag that bitch wife of mine to court and fuck her from behind in front of the bloody judge and lawyers. She said I've beaten her up, right? Then she will know what violence is!

Leon enthusiastically applauded this revenge fantasy, as Jatin submitted himself to a laughing fit; Aakash seemed pleased. Through this, they looked at me expecting my participation in and relish of this fantasy of rape as punishment. The kinds of conversations that are deemed permissible in the routines of sociability have much to do with how those present are perceived. The presence of the researcher, in many instances, prompts particular enactments of gender (Cowburn 2013). In the social setting of the meeting, rife with stories of beleaguered masculinity, perhaps Aakash felt the need to verbalize a sexually violent image in front of a male stranger as affirmation of male social power. The structure of homosocial heterosexuality often demands that men express intentions of sexual violence in all-male gatherings (Flood 2008).

The cisgender male feminist researcher, in being doubly inscribed – with the politics of feminism and interpellations of masculinity – is placed in a peculiar position when faced with such anti-women talk. Is he to protest against such verbal violence, or does he continue to record such narratives as ethnographic data? Does the researcher's silence in such moments imply a collusion with patriarchal attitudes, or a strategic suspension of feminist commitments in the service of the long-term goal of producing feminist knowledge? For me, there was no way to resolve this in a satisfactory way, but in that moment I decided, like other male researchers in misogynist settings (Schacht 1997), to 'play along' and use such anti-feminist camaraderie to establish joking relationships with informants for a project that sought to unveil the workings of male privilege. My complicity with their violent humour helped me gain some acceptance, and a little later, when the two other men had moved away, Aakash shared with me details of the evening he was picked up by the police:

> It was the worst night of my life, you know. I was watching TV in the drawing room. Mother was calling me for dinner from the kitchen. The door bell rang and next thing I know me and my parents are in the police station. Hawaldars laughing at me. I can't tell you how helpless and angry I felt that night in the lockup, my old parents sitting next to me. I could not look at them.

In stark contrast with his earlier expression, this narrative emphasized his vulnerability, the ignominy he experienced at the hands of law enforcers, as his parents and he spent the night behind bars and his despair at failing to protect his parents from this humiliation. This extra information allowed me to read Aakash's fantastical enactment of corrective rape in the courtroom as being simultaneously about the exercise of patriarchal control over his wife, brazen disregard of the reach of law and middle-class male notions of filial responsibility (Chowdhury 2014b). Methodologically, I was able to use sexist camaraderie as a resource in the fieldwork, in the sense that it allowed me access to two emotional states of an informant. This demonstrates how regimes of masculinity in research settings influence the data that is generated and the analyses that they enable.

Conceptualizations of the in-depth interview as a creative process that activates shared meanings emphasize mutual disclosure as a helpful strategy for facilitating understanding (Holstein and Gubrium 1995). Using friendship and conventional scripts of male homosociality to elicit good research data, however, is not without problem. I met Avik Mitra (28, software engineer, Kolkata) at one of the weekly meetings of a men's rights group in Kolkata. I saw him over three successive weeks. He was mostly quiet, hardly ever participating in the sociability of these group meetings, speaking only to ask clarificatory questions about some legal cases. It turned out that he and I lived nearby, so we would travel together after these meetings. Middle class, only a couple of years older than me, with shared tastes in the arts and culture, we struck up an easy friendship and began occasionally meeting over drinks. This rapport, however, complicated the research process.

My proximity to Avik tempted me to believe his assertion that he had been falsely accused of domestic violence by his estranged wife. This proved to be a problem because the purpose of my research was not to establish the veracity of either claims of violence or innocence. It was to examine the verbal strategies and cultural values that men mobilize to articulate their understandings of gender and the ideological function that these serve in preserving patriarchal social arrangements. To achieve this goal, I would have to treat interview material as narratives that construe gender relations in particular ways. My identification with my interviewee was, therefore, tending to compromise feminist methodological principles by deflecting research focus away from the gender asymmetry of social life. Revisiting this field experience in the light of related scholarship on face-to-face research situations (Presser 2005, Gottzen 2013), I tempered my eagerness to believe Avik by reminding myself that men accused of violence often use the interview setting as an opportunity to arouse sympathy, by variously performing victimhood, remorse and shame. Such situations alerted me to the additional responsibility of the feminist researcher to be aware of one's propensity to collude with dominant ideologies of gender. Interrogating how shared assumptions about masculinity might have affected my research data, thus, became a key task at the time of analysis.

6. Reciprocity in field relations and interpretive communities

A commitment to feminist methods requires addressing the relationship of power between the one who studies and those who are studied. In research with women, this has often meant enabling women participants in the project to have some control over how they are represented. As Richa Nagar (2013) argues, when research subjects are not given the opportunity to evaluate the ways in which they are rendered in writing, the exalted status of academic knowledge and the authority of the 'expert' remain unquestioned. Such a mode of knowledge production is masculinist. If allowing their subjects of research to 'talk back' has been a way for feminists to avoid exploitation in the research process (Oakley 1981), how do these precepts of reciprocity, collaboration and openness apply to studies of anti-feminist men? I navigated this question by shifting the emphasis from participatory values to those discussions on feminist methodology, which stress social transformation as a central goal of feminist knowledge production (Acker, Barry and Esseveld 1983). I reasoned that it is not incumbent upon feminist researchers to give further space to mainstream views on gender and sexuality because it is precisely against such framings of gender that feminist politics is directed. One of the struggles of producing feminist texts is, after all, wrenching from these traditional views on gender and sexuality, the right to speak and be heard. Hence, while it was important to represent the views of my respondents with accuracy and fairness, as a feminist researcher my interpretation of these views remained focused on unveiling their masculinist politics of gender.

Well before I began my interviews with men's rights activists, I considered the repercussions and necessity of disclosing to them my political stand as a feminist. I had thought that into each interview I would tell my respondent that I am a feminist researcher; his reactions to a self-identified male feminist, I had thought at the time, would add rich data to this project. However, while conducting the interviews I decided that the risk of jeopardizing the project was too great for me to take, and I did not publicly identify myself as a feminist. I justified this choice to myself by thinking that every act of self-presentation is always a partial, selective account. Moreover, relations in the field exerted no pressure on me to disclose my politics since the group I was interacting with immediately assumed me to be an insider.

Significantly, not just my research subjects but also several members of academic audiences to which I presented my analyses of men's rights activism readily assumed me to be politically sympathetic to their concerns. In every forum that I shared my thoughts on collective action around men's rights, I was told, 'We weren't sure which way you would go with this material.' What provokes this initial suspicion that studies on gender/sexuality conducted by cisgender men are likely to be exercises in patriarchal justification? Aware of feminist doubts about the political commitments of masculinity studies (Chopra 2009), as a male feminist researcher studying men's rights groups I felt obliged to convince two constituencies of scholars about the credentials of my research. For feminist scholars (mostly women) I had to preface my presentation with the assurance that this project, in the tradition of Critical Studies on Men and Masculinity, would be guided by feminist concerns. I considered, though, why this assurance still needs to be given. In spite of developments in thinking about the links between social location and knowledge claims (Alcoff 1991), in the everyday spaces of academic exchange, is there a tendency to reduce people's politics to their immediate subject position? Is feminism's criticality still thought to rest foundationally on the authority of women's experience? Or perhaps the need for assurance stems from the way in which men have studied men and masculinity in India, acknowledging feminist perspectives but seldom engaging centrally with feminist theories to make sense of their research problems? And second, I felt the need to speak to scholars outside of gender studies (mostly men), who were certain that such men and their politics are just laughable and do not merit academic attention. I was aware that for many such academics, despite the success with which feminisms have recast conceptions of the social, studies of women, gender and sexuality – especially by men on men – continue to be seen as soft issues. However, as a graduate student I felt the pressure of demonstrating to this scholarly community my project's 'value relevance' (Weber 1949).

In reflecting on the interpretive communities of men's pro-feminism and modes of social control in academic cultures, I was reminded of Sandra Bartky's remark that

> few men benefit professionally, not just in academia, but in most work environments, from too close an alliance with feminism; such alliances tend more to discredit a man than to advance his career. Coming out for feminism regularly earns a man not only the distrust of many feminist women but the scorn of so-called manly men who charge him with having been pussy-whipped.
>
> (Bartky 1998: xiii)

Perhaps when men conduct feminist research, what they want is not so much professional 'benefit' – how can pro-feminist men demand further professional rewards in a society that already favours them – but that the credibility of their research output as a feminist text will not be undermined simply by the fact of their advantageous relationship with patriarchy. Indeed as Avishai, Gerber and Randles (2012: 10) write,

> Rather than just being personally reflexive about our individual social locations vis-à-vis our subjects, we argue that we should be reflexive vis-à-vis the feminisms of the institutions within which we conduct research and develop our interpretive frameworks, the intellectual orthodoxies they may generate, and how they relate both to our research processes and the social spaces within which we conduct our research.

The emphasis on reflexivity in feminist and critical theories has sometimes tended to be in isolation from other aspects of the research process, such as research design, hermeneutics and politics of dissemination (Hopkins 2007). It seems to me, therefore, that discussions of feminist methodology, particularly around questions of ethics, must include critical conversations on professional gate-keeping practices, which influence topic selection, protocols of writing, funding, reception of research and hierarchical framing of subfields of academic disciplines. The place of male feminist researchers and that of masculinity studies in the academy would then need to be understood through these considerations as well.

7. Concluding thoughts

My larger research project on which this methodological reflection is based, as I have said earlier, sought to fine-graining existing ideas about 'backlashes' against feminism and contribute to understandings of male privilege in contemporary India. In concluding this chapter I suggest that adopting a more subject-centred view of masculinity is one way in which this task can be pursued. For evaluations of anti-feminism to add to existing understandings of men's relationship to patriarchal dividends, the feminist researcher must display the audacity to empathize with patriarchal impulses. One way of exposing the inner logic of anti-feminist articulations, I would argue, is to acknowledge misogynist expressions as 'feeling claims'. While these claims are likely untrue at the level of facts, they contain a grain of emotional 'truth'. This understanding demands treating interviews and participant observations not as mirror reflections of the lived realities of research subjects but as spoken discourse. The aim is to highlight the 'language above the sentence' (Cameron 2001) in interview transcripts and reach the processes of meaning-making through which men interpret their social situations. The key problematic for the feminist researcher in such undertakings is to then demonstrate the 'work' performed by such feelings (of disenfranchisement, anger, betrayal, responsibility and entitlement) in maintaining men's loyalty to patriarchal ideas. For me, the way to pursue this analytical task as a male researcher without losing sight of feminist concerns was to ask myself at each stage in the analysis – 'in whose interests?' (Skeggs 2001).

Acknowledging the axiomatic status of self-reflexivity in much of contemporary social research, particularly feminist studies, this chapter has sought to show how this self-analysis plays out in studies of men and masculinities and its implications for the knowledges we produce as male feminists. I have provided an account of how cultural expectations of masculinity affect relations between interviewer and respondent and, hence, the data that is generated. I have also attempted to briefly demonstrate how feminist knowledge projects are brought into relation with the subject positions of the researcher by the assumptions of academic audiences. Through this entire discussion, the effort has been to argue that men studying men need to be cognizant of elements in their shared experiences of masculinity in order to both use gender relations in the field as a resource for conducting feminist analysis and be aware of how these may inhibit such analysis.

Notes

1 I am indebted to Zaid Al Baset, Srimati Basu and Mary E. John for their comments on an earlier draft.
2 For a more detailed account of the demands and modes of functioning of men's rights groups in India, see Chowdhury (2014a).
3 Respondents have been anonymized to protect their identities.

References

Acker, J., K. Barry and J. Esseveld. 1983. "Objectivity and Truth: Problems in Doing Feminist Research," *Women's Studies International Forum*, Vol. 6, pp. 423–435.
Alcoff, L. 1991. "The Problem of Speaking for Others," *Cultural Critique*, Vol. 20, pp. 5–32.
Avishai, O., L. Gerber and J. Randles. 2012. "The Feminist Ethnographer's Dilemma: Reconciling Progressive Research Agendas with Fieldwork Realities," *Journal of Contemporary Ethnography*, Vol. 42, No. 4, pp. 1–33.
Bartky, S. 1998. "Foreword." In T. Digby (ed.). *Men Doing Feminism*. New York: Routledge, pp. 57–68.
Cameron, D. 2001. *Working with Spoken Discourse*. London: Sage.
Chopra, R. 2004. "Encountering Masculinity: An Ethnographer's Dilemma." In R. Chopra, C. Osella and F. Osella (eds). *South Asian Masculinities: Context of Change, Sites of Continuity*. New Delhi: Women Unlimited, pp. 36–59.
———. 2009. Book Review: Recreating Men by Bob Pease. http://www.xyonline.net/content/book-review-recreating-men-postmodern-masculinity-politics-bob-pease (accessed 5 September 2013).
Chowdhury, R. 2014a. "Conditions of Emergence: The Formations of Men's Rights Groups in Contemporary India," *Indian Journal of Gender Studies*, Vol. 21, No. 1, pp. 27–53.
———. 2014b. "Family, Femininity, Feminism: 'Structures of Feeling' in the Articulation of Men's Rights." In K. B. Nielsen and A. Waldrop Women (eds). *Women, Gender, and Everyday Social Transformation in India*. London: Anthem Press, pp. 189–202.
Cook, J. A. and M. M. Fonow. 1986. "Knowledge and Women's Interests: Issues of Epistemology and Methodology in Feminist Sociological Research," *Sociological Inquiry*, Vol. 56, No. 1, pp. 2–29.
Cowburn, M. 2013. "Men Researching Violent Men: Epistemologies, Ethics, and Emotions in Qualitative Research." In B. Pini and B. Pease (eds).

Men, Masculinities and Methodologies. Basingstoke: Palgrave Macmillan, pp. 183–196.
DeVault, M. 1999. *Liberating Methods: Feminism and Social Research*. Philadelphia: Temple University Press.
FitzGerald, I. 1998. "Feminist Glasses." In R. Else-Mitchell and N. Flutter (eds). *Talking Up: Young Women's Take on Feminism*. Spinifex: North Melbourne, pp. 3–14.
Flood, M. 2008. "Men, Sex and Homosociality: How Bonds between Men Shape Their Sexual Relations with Women," *Men and Masculinities*, Vol. 10, No. 3, pp. 339–359.
———. 2013. "Negotiating Gender in Men's Research among Men." In B. Pini and B. Pease (eds). *Men, Masculinities and Methodologies*. Basingstoke: Palgrave Macmillan, pp. 64–76.
Gottzen, L. 2013. "Encountering Violent Men: Strange and Familiar." In B. Pini and B. Pease (eds). *Men, Masculinities and Methodologies*. Basingstoke: Palgrave Macmillan, pp. 197–208.
Harding, S. (ed.). 2004. *The Feminist Standpoint Theory Reader: Intellectual and Political Controversies*. New York: Routledge.
Hogeland, L. M. 2004. "Fear of Feminism: Why Young Women Get the Willies." In S. M. Shaw and J. Lee (eds). *Women's Voices, Feminist Visions: Classic and Contemporary Readings*. New York: McGraw-Hill, pp. 565–568.
Holstein, J. A. and J. F. Gubrium (eds). 1995. *The Active Interview*. Thousand Oaks, CA: Sage.
Hopkins, P. E. 2007. "Positionalities and Knowledge: Negotiating Ethics in Practice," *ACME: An International E-Journal for Critical Geographies*, Vol. 6, No. 3, pp. 386–394.
Jaggar, A. M. and Susan R. Bordo (eds). 1989. *Gender/Body/Knowledge: Feminist Reconstructions of Being and Knowing*. New Brunswick: Rutgers University Press.
Kimmel, M. S. 1998. "Who's Afraid of Men Doing Feminism?" In T. Digby (ed.). *Men Doing Feminism*. New York: Routledge, pp. 57–68.
Nagar, R. 2013. "Storytelling and Co-authorship in Feminist Alliance Work: Reflections from a Journey," *Gender, Place & Culture: A Journal of Feminist Geography*, Vol. 20, No. 1, pp. 1–18.
Oakley, A. 1981. "Interviewing Women: A Contradiction in Terms." In H. Roberts (ed.). *Doing Feminist Research*. London: Routledge and Kegan Paul, pp. 30–61.
Pini, B. and B. Pease (eds). 2013. *Men, Masculinities and Methodologies*. Basingstoke: Palgrave Macmillan.
Presser, L. 2005. "Negotiating Power and Narrative in Research: Implications for Feminist Methodology," *Signs*, Vol. 30, No. 4. New Feminist Approaches to Social Science, Methodologies, special issue editors Sandra Harding and Kathryn Norberg (Summer), pp. 2067–2090.
Ramazanoglu, C. and J. Holland. 2002. *Feminist Methodology: Challenges and Choices*. Thousand Oaks, CA: Sage.

Rege, S. 1998. "A Dalit Feminist Standpoint," *Seminar*, Vol. 471, pp. 47–52.

Schacht, S. P. 1997. "Feminist Fieldwork in the Misogynist Setting of the Rugby Pitch: Becoming a Sylph to Survive and Personally Grow," *Journal of Contemporary Ethnography*, Vol. 26, pp. 332–363.

Schwalbe, M. and M. Wolkomir. 2001. "The Masculine Self as Problem and Resource in Interview Studies of Men," *Men and Masculinities*, Vol. 4, No. 1, pp. 90–103.

Skeggs, B. 2001. "Feminist Ethnography." In P. A. Atkinson, S. Delamont, A. Coffey, J. Lofland and L. H. Lofland (eds). *Handbook of Ethnography*. London: Sage, pp. 426–442.

Vanderbeck, R. M. 2005. "Masculinities and Fieldwork: Widening the Discussion," *Gender, Place & Culture*, Vol. 12, No. 4, pp. 387–402.

Weber, M. 1949. *The Methodology of the Social Sciences*. Translated by E. A. Shils and H. A. Finch. New York: The Free Press.

4 Real-life methods

Feminist explorations of segregation in Delhi[1]

Ghazala Jamil

1. Introduction

The 'add women and stir' approach does not produce what can be called feminist research. Nor can all methods deployed in a gendered enquiry be termed 'feminist methods'.

Admittedly, to talk of something specifically salient about certain methods deployed to create knowledge as 'feminist methods' is a tentative project, and there have been many claims and contestations on whether there is such a thing as feminist methodology. My aim in this chapter is not to essentialize certain methods as 'feminist' but rather to suggest that methods used by a researcher who is a feminist, in enquiries into phenomenon that throw up questions of hierarchies other than gender, would not remain uninfluenced by her feminist politics.

To look for elements in methods or a methodological approach that may be identified as feminist, one has to examine the feminist approach and see if it has applications beyond its immediate area of concern. Political and democratic rights of women have been one of the foundational concerns of feminist movements across the world and time. Discussions on fair representation in democracy by feminist scholars have greatly rejuvenated theory of democracy by indicating mechanisms for fuller participation of all members of a political community and by providing a nuanced normative account of citizenship and democracy (Jayal 1999, 2013), civil society and state practices (Chandhoke 1995, 2001) and identity-based contestations in Indian politics (Menon 1997, Menon and Nigam 2007). Feminist deliberations have, thus, contributed considerably to the discussion on democratization of representative political system per se. Feminist defence of biodiversity and indigenous knowledge (Shiva 1997, 2002) have contributed immensely in the critical understanding of globalization.

The feminist movement and feminist critique have affected discourses that are not specifically about gender or sexual distinctions. While such scholars in their works may or may not have exerted themselves on the question of methods, at the very least, this gestures towards the possibility that feminist methodology can also be deployed in enquiries that are not focused on gendered accounts of social and political phenomena. For this kind of wider applicability of feminist methodology, we need to delineate elements that would allow it to do so. What might be the nature of these qualifying elements? Discussing the narratives about specific/narrow concerns, various scholars contend that the narratives need to fulfil certain criteria to qualify as theory. A theory ought to be an abstract, symbolic and complex-enough representation of a social reality such that it comes across not only as a comprehensive system of ideas that describe and explain fundamental concerns of social life (Ritzer 1988) but also as a narrative that has effect outside the original site of theorization or original subject matter or discipline.[2] For this wide-ranging effect, a theory must include elements that are context-independent (Flyvbjerg 2001).

Despite existence of many and often conflicting accounts of feminisms, it can be claimed safely that feminism is a unifying narrative about the unequal nature of gender relationships. The discussions on feminist methodology also take place, with the ubiquitous gendered nature of social relationships and subjects of enquiry forming the background. In search of context-independent elements in feminist approach, I foreground shared concern among feminist researchers, namely attempting to overcome inequality in research relationships, valuing experience and emotion and aiming for consciousness-raising.

On the matter of context-independent substance of feminist theory, it bears quoting Menon from the introduction to her book *Seeing Like a Feminist*,

> A feminist perspective recognizes that the hierarchal organizing of the world around gender is key to maintaining social order; that to live lives marked male and female is to live different realities. But simultaneously, to be a feminist is to imagine occupying the marginal, relatively powerless position with reference to *every* dominant framework that swallows up the space at the centre.
>
> . . . When a feminist 'sees' from the position of marginality he or she has deliberately chosen to occupy, it is a gesture of subversion towards power; it disorganizes and disorders the settled field, resists homogenisation, and opens up multiple possibilities rather than closes them off.
>
> . . . To be a feminist is to recognise that apart from gender-based injustice, there are multiple structural inequalities that underlie the social order, and to believe that change is possible, and to work for it at whichever level possible.
>
> (2012: viii–ix; emphasis mine)

Alison Jaggar also insists that 'feminist enquiry is unusual in being explicit about its ethical and political stance, which motivates feminists to seek out and challenge the social biases lurking often unnoticed in existing knowledge claims' (2008: ix). Feminist enquiries have thrown up radical ideas regarding epistemology that have had a wide-ranging effect on all kinds of enquiries even though feminist researchers have not been overly concerned to claim these effects as feminist. In a definition of feminism that is not very commonly quoted, Hartsock (1975, cf. Hekman 1997) said, 'At bottom feminism is a mode of analysis, a method of approaching life and politics, rather than a set of political conclusions about the oppression of women.'

Therefore, we can ask, when feminists look at *any* social phenomenon and attempt to understand it in its entirety (not just its gendered nature), do they do research differently? In my experiences during my research on Segregation of Muslims in Delhi (Jamil 2014), I found that my choice of methods could not remain untouched by feminist politics even though my chosen theoretical frameworks were Marxist Urbanism and Critical Theory.

I describe my use of ethnography as an array of methods as a feminist researcher that I infused with Marxist ideas and bring together under the nomenclature of real-life methods. In the following sections, I gesture briefly towards the problems in scholarship on Muslims in India, before I mark out the contours of my study and detail my experiences during ethnographic fieldwork.

2. Ethnography as a feminist method

The original claim of ethnography was that it was an 'objective and scientific' method for the study of 'native' cultures by persons not from within those cultures. Since then it has had to contend with charges of colonial attitude and also of 'positivism' and 'naturalism'. The present debates on ethnography are more to do with the limits of representation and the power relations between the representer and the represented. Within this is also the matter of reflexivity of the ethnographer – the degree of her own awareness and acknowledgement of her subjectivity stemming from her position. The job that confronts ethnographers today is to 'struggle self-consciously to avoid portraying abstract ahistorical "others"' (Clifford 1988: 23).

But as Judith Stacey (1988) asked, 'Can there be a feminist ethnography?' In her discussion of this question while Stacey agrees that ethnography is a more suitable method for feminist enquiries than more positivistic methods because of its emphasis of the experiential, she points out what she considers an insufficient dialogue between feminism and *new ethnography*.[3] According to Stacey, feminists presume that feminist ethnography is undertaken by women researchers researching women, showing them to suffer from a 'delusion of alliance' (1988: 25). Her call is to further the dialogue between critical ethnographers and feminism on the representation of the other. Her response to her titular question is that there cannot be an ethnography that is fully feminist but 'there can be ethnographies that are partially feminist accounts of culture enhanced by the application of feminist perspectives'. She calls for acceptance of fallibility in ethnography's capacity to represent self and others but believes that 'the potential benefits of "partially" feminist ethnography seem worth the serious moral costs involved' (Stacey 1988: 26).

This chapter may be seen as part of the ongoing dialogue between feminism and ethnography, specifically in that it suffers no delusion of feminist researchers being concerned with an alliance only with women subjects. I am not entirely convinced of the distinction between partially and fully feminist ethnography, which is contingent only upon the identity of the participants in research. It is rather that a feminist ethnography must aim at constructing situated knowledge (which does not have to be branded incomplete and suffer from forced humility).

While epistemic privilege for the standpoint of the proletariat on questions of social and economic relations, and on history, is claimed, what is important to note is that in the Marxist scheme the epistemic privilege in not claimed as some natural and intrinsic quality of the members of the proletariat but as a viewpoint gained due to their material interactions within the capitalist structure of society and history (Marx 1964). In similar fashion, Marxist feminists argue that women's position in systems of care and reproduction (Hartsock 1983, Rose 1987) put them in a position to realize the problems of the patriarchal structure of society. Some allocate a superior epistemological position to women due to their position of oppression. This, by logic, privileges further the epistemological position of someone experiencing multiple oppressions.

A truly reflexive standpoint must not be caught in marking shared or different identities but must make available an account of how one came to occupy that standpoint. In this context, writing ethnography comes to occupy a central position in the practice of self-reflexivity.

In *The Predicament of Culture* (1988), James Clifford presents an optimist exploration of forms and manner of ethnographic writing that may escape the epistemological limits of ethnography's past as the Western colonial mode of representation of the colonized. This can be achieved by displacing the locus of ethnographic practice to forms that interrupt objectification and interpellation of people. For ethnographic researchers who reside in and belong to the culture they are studying, the problem of avoiding the binary of 'us' and 'them' is already taken care of to a certain extent (but not wholly, since, after all, identities are not singular). In an operational way, the issues of representation and power can be addressed partly by paying heed to Clifford's understanding of ethnography as a form of writing and, thus, ethnography as textual. Writing being an important part of ethnography and discourse analysis, I borrowed the conceptual framework provided by Clifford for the writing (and reading) of ethnography, which constitutes of 'language, rhetoric, power and history' (Clifford 1988: 25).

Thus, this study, which attempted to overcome the historical moorings of discourses that relate to the prejudice, discrimination and segregation experienced by Muslims in Delhi, found the perfect methodological accomplice in feminist ethnography. The thick descriptions in this work used language, rhetoric, power and history consciously to disrupt the dominant discourses from the position of those who are being studied. I make the claim that my use of ethnography was influenced by my feminist position, and of having permeated this ethnographic work with Marxism because of the stress I laid on the historicity of the subject as well as on the process.

The coming together of feminism and Marxism helps Marxism escape economic determinism while it helps feminism escape what I call the tyranny of micro-particularity. In this work, dominant ideology is not understood as entirely coherent, consistent and devoid of any contradiction. In fact, I follow the recognition among Marxist social scientists that '*macro-explanations* stand in need of *microfoundations*' (Little 1986: 127, emphasis original). In substantive terms, I drew from Daniel Little (1986) and especially tried to study material factors related to labour, land and so on, and non-material processes such as identity formation and culture for their ideological position within a system of production and control. I enquired into the class character of inter-group relationships of exploitation and structures of dominance that these require. But I did this through a close examination of everyday and lived experiences of people, including their resistance to and negotiations within the social experience. And conversely, throughout the examination of these everyday experiences, I attempted to demarcate stable and continuing structures through which people experience their everyday.

3. Feminist reading of scholarship on Muslims in India

In most sociological studies on the subject, Muslims are portrayed as a laggard community, loath to change its attitude in the race of demographic transition in India, in which other religious communities have reached milestones much ahead of them. One of the favourite flogging horses of Muslim detractors is the fertility rates of Muslims in India. Mistry (2005), for instance, reports on figures comparing fertility rates of various religions and concludes that decennial growth rates of Muslims have been higher than those of Hindus because of the relative backwardness of Muslim women. She fails to take cognizance that in many decades the Muslim fertility rate has been lower than Sikhs and Christians, as she also fails to note that for many decades, the infant and child mortality rates among Muslims have been lower than those among Hindus, because this fact does not fit into the framework of 'backwardness of Muslim Women', which has almost become a touchstone in the study of poverty and/or women's rights among Muslims. On matters of contraception use and relating fertility to education levels, Mistry continuously ascribes them to Muslim 'backwardness' – achieving no mean feat of establishing the existence of a phenomenon without defining it.

Mistry's failure to define what she means by 'backwardness' in a sound conceptual way is a problem that is symptomatic of subaltern nature of Muslims and the entire spectrum of these studies rather than a problem of her individual scholarship.

What unfolds in most such efforts is an essentialized identity tag, which pretends to have some operational basis but ends up only confirming the view of the hegemonic gaze. Research is often reduced only to the research findings that exist independent of the process, while the process through which the phenomenon being studied came to exist is not afforded any attention.

A recent study (Bhalotra, Valente and van Soest 2010), which has not received much attention, looked at the earlier-mentioned lower infant and child mortality rates among the Muslims compared to Hindus and commented that the figures are paradoxical within the frame of reference in which these figures have always been seen. Terming it 'puzzling', the study highlights and describes

> a hitherto neglected fact that . . . despite being, on average, less educated and poorer, Indian Muslims exhibit a substantial advantage in child survival over high-caste Hindus. This religion differential is much larger than the more widely recognised gender differential in child survival in India and it appears to have persisted for decades. (Bhalotra *et al.* 2010: 203)

The researchers conclude that in the closer-knit community due to various reasons such as its minority status and endogamous marriage, the expectant and new mothers as well as children are receiving better care. They add lower preference for male child and better girl child survival and sex ratio than the upper-caste Hindus to the explanation along with eating and hygiene practices related to their faith. Subjecting the already-available data to rigorous analysis and looking for possible explanations for the 'puzzle', they reach a conclusion that is indeed radical because it uses a vocabulary for Muslims that has almost never been used before.

In my opinion, reached not only on the basis of the preceding illustration but also after undertaking an extensive review of literature on Muslims in India, is that the most important question in front of Muslim scholarship is that of renewed rigour, creativity, shifting frames of reference and inventiveness in framing and asking questions.

4. Framing research on segregation of Muslims

While researching segregation of Muslim in Delhi, I began with a very broad view of the problems that I wanted to investigate. Study of Muslim localities or segregated Muslim enclaves in India is often clubbed into slums/ghetto studies in the city. While it is true that a majority of Muslims in India are poor, I also knew it to be true from my own experiences that Muslims of different classes are segregated *together* into many of these enclaves. The impulses of class-based divisions mix with communal logic to produce these geographies of discrimination that needed a nuanced enquiry looking into the impact of processes of globalization and neoliberalism on urban Muslims.

Approaching the issue from this point, I tried to overcome the implicit assumption in all studies of Muslims in India (and elsewhere, in the wake of global Islamophobia) that all observed and described phenomenon were ascribed to 'the difference' – the faith of Muslim people. Further, most studies commenting on the condition of Muslims in India also include subjects from other faiths (especially Hindus as significant 'others'), either for the purpose of some sort of comparison or to validate the assertions made by the Muslims. This is in line with the ideological situations in which Muslim experience is sought to be defined as seen through the Hindu-gaze. This knowledge allowed to me through feminist and Lacanian accounts of 'gaze' (Mulvey 1975, Krips 2010) enabled me to limit my study consciously given its theoretical framework and articulated emancipatory rationale.

4.1 Geographical markers of ethnography

Muslim population in Delhi is clustered in several large and small pockets. For my ethnographic fieldwork, I chose several areas from each of the three large clusters. In the first cluster, which I called Old Delhi for brevity, I limited my forays to some neighbourhoods like Beri Wallah Bagh, Hathi Khana, Ahata Kedara and Bara Hindu Rao, Qasab Pura in Old Delhi outside the precincts of Shahjahanabad, and Matia Mahal, Chitli Qabar, Daryaganj, Chandni Chowk, Bazar Sita Ram, Turkman Gate and Bawarchi

Khana inside the walled city. In the second (or Trans-Yamuna) cluster, I limited my fieldwork to New Seelampur, Chauhan Bangar, Jaffrabad and New Jaffrabad. From the third large cluster, Jamia Nagar, I covered Zakir Nagar, Joga Bai, Batla House, Abul Fazal Enclave and Shahin Bagh. From the smaller clusters I chose Nizamuddin, covering both the Nizamuddin West and Basti Hazrat Nizamuddin. And, finally, I conducted some interviews in Taj Enclave (also Trans-Yamuna) as an example of an elite Muslim housing society.

Evidently, these choices cover a lot of geographical ground, and the selection was made with conscious intent to cover a lot of ground in order to explore the spatial expression of the heterogeneity of Muslim population in Delhi in terms of class, occupational and cultural diversity. Temporality of the areas was also of significance in terms of change and developments within the areas. The historical significance and architectural continuity of history in everyday life of the walled city and Nizamuddin were important markers of selection. The centrality of Jamia Millia Islamia in the expression of (spatial) identity of Jamia Nagar is the main marker in selection of the area; and Trans-Yamuna as a closer extension to Old Delhi in post-partition Delhi and Delhi during constitutional emergency. These areas were chosen for intensive fieldwork also because Jama Masjid, Seelampur, Batla House and Nizamuddin are the nomenclatures of which the 'Muslim ghettos' narrative of popular discourses is made up of. The Taj Enclave is the newest in terms of chronology of settlements and was chosen to explore the otherwise unexplored construct of the elite Muslims and their viewpoint. However, even though fieldwork was not conducted in other areas, the participants often invoke their awareness of and connections with other Muslim settlements, and some of these areas are a significant presence in their narratives.

In the case of Old Delhi and Jamia Nagar, the choice was also influenced by my own familiarity with the localities – I spent my childhood in Ahata Kedara in Old Delhi and have lived in Zakir Nagar for over 25 years now. Nizamuddin was also a familiar location due to its proximity to Jamia Nagar and its location en route Central Delhi from there. The Trans-Yamuna cluster was completely an unfamiliar territory to me, thus the one where I did most rigorous fieldwork and spent disproportionately large amounts of time.

My attempt was to present a detailed descriptive record of various aspects of urban Muslim life in Delhi, employing micro-approaches that take real-life experiences of individuals into consideration and the macro-analysis of the social, cultural, economic and political positioning of Muslims on the urban tapestry of Delhi. I also tried to critically examine various representations of Muslims and Muslim areas of Delhi prevalent in the popular urban consciousness through analysis of popular and news media discourses.

5. Real-life methods

Multiple methods were adopted for data collection in the study. These – such as observation, walking, walking interviews, family interviews, individual interviews, focus group discussions and autoethnography – I club together into an umbrella term 'real-life methods'. Why do I call these methods real-life methods? Feminist thinkers have invoked the idea of 'reality' and its experience (as opposed to concepts) as the basis of establishing truth. Reality is considered as constructed by shared signs and meanings, and is thus processual and communicative in nature. Iris Young advocates that 'real social relations' be made the basis of a 'feminist historical materialism' (1980, cf. Hekman 1999). Haraway calls for methods that are accountable to patterns of reality which are not pre-existing, waiting to be discovered but depend on 'power-charged social relation of conversation' (1988: 593). For Marx (1993), reality *as seen* is both real and concrete. It is an externality to any acts of representation. When represented, it becomes knowledge based on real premises that is an abstraction of reality. But he insists that these too are rooted in and derived from real relations. Parts of this representation are then analysed – each taken as a whole and then understood in totality or as a unity. Marx's method claims to facilitate a comprehension of the real concrete that corrects the inversion of reality through ideology. For him this real whole is not 'chaotic' but an ensemble or unity of social relations. Clearly then, using this dialectic analysis in knowledge creation contributes to the efforts for transforming the reality.

It is in this regard that in this section of the article I describe my use of methods as real-life methods which were not structured or predetermined. They weave an element of serendipity into the research process and so could be driven by the participants as well – making it truly a process of co-creation of knowledge. The nomenclature is used to signify that knowledge production is a shared, communicative act; that focus is on actually existing material circumstances in the lives of participants (and amelioration of the same) rather than being driven by the need of conceptual or theoretical innovation; and, finally, that methods for knowledge creation must be close and familiar to the everyday life world of the participants and not seem alien and inaccessible to them. The use of this term is partially also in response to conventional and positivist social science research, which consists of vignettes of observations and conclusions about disjointed parts of, what is, in reality, the unified human experience. Like the tables showing migration statistics of people magically disappearing in one column/location and appearing in another, it constructs images of things and processes that do not actually exist. We get no idea of the experiences of the labouring bodies journeying to the hope of better lives. This kind of research loses much, if not all, of its emancipatory potential. Thus, the use of these methods also made me aware of, and able to avoid, the fragmentation of aspects of life for research purposes as if they did not have any connection with one another.

Because the real-life methods are not pre-structured, using them forced me to access additional methodological resources (visual methods, mapping, etc.) in order to understand further the experiences and references of my co-participants. This meant that I had to transcend disciplinary boundaries and ended up producing a better-rounded account of life. Many of these methods are already well known and widely used and do not need to be defined here. I merely note my own use of these as an ensemble in the study.

5.1 Home/family interviews

Semi-structured interviews of key participants often took place at their homes. I had not planned to interview several members of the same families, but because the interviews happened at home sometimes, a family member would be listening and would decide to contribute. Also, during some individual interviews there were references to another relative with an experience or profile that fulfilled the requirements at hand of theoretical sampling. I would request a reference and then contact this family member also for an interview. It became clear to me that interviewing families together at one site or separately was an extremely powerful method. I always found the narratives illuminated further in detail by supplementary information provided by family members. When family members were interviewed, especially parents and adult sons/daughters, there was often a clear difference in the analysis of the same life event, highlighting generational difference of opinion. In many instances, family members reported that some of the information they shared with me had never ever been discussed explicitly, especially losses incurred by the family during partition and other episodes of communal violence.

5.2 Autoethnography

While writing memos regarding my interviews or writing observational ethnographic field notes, I realized that my own life experiences sometimes threw in additional illustrations into the emerging theoretical narratives because of my own identity as a Muslim woman resident of Delhi. Using my 'lived experiences and personal history as a cultural site' (Alexander 2005: 422), I realized that autoethnography-internalized ethnographic practice can also be used intentionally to stretch the limits of individualized cultural identity and its presentation to audiences (Ellis and Bochner 2000). The feminist methodological underpinning in my work was also the reason why I decided to include autoethnography in my work such that I could practise self-reflexivity and analyse my own recollections also as anthropological data for the study.

5.3 Walking as a research device

Of all the other methods I used in my ethnography as an ensemble of methods, I think my use of 'walking' as a research device merits a more detailed description. Walking is a commonplace everyday practice. This construction of walking as a 'commonplace' unremarkable activity may have contributed to it being overlooked as a method of research. In urban cultural studies genre of research walking is beginning to gain recognition. Although seemingly commonplace, walking is a privilege that is contingent upon one's social and class standing. A landless labourer bonded to a landlord would never move beyond the limits of the village community. For an 'untouchable', walking was an activity that had to be undertaken in a strictly predefined way, any deviation from which could be fatal. While a trader could travel from the local *haat* (a regular local market or fair) to the town market or to wholesale *mandis* (agricultural or wholesale market), a woman's place was the *char-divari* (literally four walls). Mobility for women was often spoken of in terms of getting married and travelling to the in-laws' household in a *doli* (literally palanquin, ride in which brides travel from their natal to marital house after wedding) and then in a final journey upon death to the cremation ground in an *arthi* (bier). A woman loitering alone or a group of women hanging out at street corners may be judged of 'loose character', while the same activity is a routinized daily affair for men. Thus, you can become mobile only as the limits of your identities allow. In terms of sociological imagination, walking gives you the vantage point of being a participant and at the same time a detached observer. Benjamin (1999) talks of this 'flâneur', who is the product of modernity much as the 'tourist' is. Benjamin's fascination with the figure of flâneur, who rambles in the city 'taking in' his own perceptions, other people's behaviour and the physical space or environment, is because of flâneur's behaviour as a selective 'collector' of banal and novel sights that strike and amuse him. For Michel de Certeau (1984) walking in cities is an embodied method that can resist the discipline imposed by social space. It allows for a possibility of autonomous interpretation and an escape from being subjected to interpretation by it. The way the body relates to visuals while walking leads to a way of thinking about the space. Also, conversely, the way of relating to and being in the space leads to a style of walking or bodily negotiation with space. Rambling in the city or loitering, thus, has the potential of being constructed as conscious acts of resistance.

While walking as an ethnographic researcher, I experienced various emotions such as pleasure, awe and dismay at the sights that I witnessed, but I was constantly on the lookout for insights that could point out and challenge the very landscape of discrimination. As a researcher I delved into the everyday mobility patterns of people on the one hand, while, on the other, I myself broke the sluggish structured routes by walking on a meandering and random path within the sites that I was observing (and experiencing). Solitary walks (loitering) were easy for me in Jamia Nagar because of my familiarity with the place. Parts of Old Delhi and the walled city were also not difficult as I had lived here as a child and had continued the connection well into my late adolescence. My walks in these sites were akin to rediscovery. While the geographical distance between Okhla, Jamia Nagar and Nizamuddin is not much, the social distance is also not greatly felt. This helped my forays into Nizamuddin on my own. I live in Jamia Nagar, where a majority of the residents are middle class, educated and professionals. My appearance does not raise any eyebrows here. Nizamuddin and the walled city get a lot of outside visitors (e.g. tourists), so that covered my differences. In contrast, Seelampur – a hub of small manufacturing activity, its residents mostly the manufacturers and their labour employees – felt like a space of acute difference. As a result, throughout my ethnographic fieldwork I never grew into a completely independent walker in the Trans-Yamuna cluster. It was here that walking interviews helped the most. Walking with others also alters the script of narrative about a space in terms of visuals of things and goings-on that appear striking to the walker.

5.3.1 *Walking interviews*

Walking and talking with participants of the study was another rich experience, as it was accompanied by seeing and showing. The strength of this method was the opportunity available to me as a researcher to validate my interpretation. In case my interpretation of an observation did not fit the participant's interpretation, I could observe the dissonance and reflect on the causes of dissonance. These interviews gave me the great starting point of analysing how people experience outdoor spaces and built environments. It also provided more manoeuvring room to the participant in deciding where to take me, in what sequence and from which route. The participant-interviewee had enhanced power to steer the course of the interview compared with other kinds of interviews, including semi-structured ones. In a way, the participants edited my observations as a researcher like a montage of images that take on a special meaning because of their very organization and presentation. My interaction with the participants and simultaneously with the spaces that form their lived environment offered me insights that were much more valuable, especially in spaces with which I was not familiar.

During a walking interview, the participant and I would sometimes bump into someone the participant knew, who became curious as to the activity and its purpose. Metaphorically, this situation could turn the walk into an infinite number of directions, but literally, it was always a boon for the ethnographic project, and I learnt that even a trip on a tangent may prove to heighten the serendipitous element of fieldwork. The walks (solitary and interview walks) also helped me to develop a tacit knowledge of the spaces or tap into the tacit knowledge of the participants about the way spaces are organized. After the walk, I took notes of the routes and characteristics of different areas and linked with information on a phone GPS device during walks in order to be plotted on a map.

6. A self-reflexive account of immersion

I identify myself as a Muslim and have lived all my life in two Muslim localities in Delhi. It can safely be claimed that I have always been 'immersed' in the 'culture under study'. Even for formal purposes, my consciously aware registering of distinct realities of my surroundings as such began much before I began this study. Ethnography of this scale was possible only as I had access to the use of my identity as a heuristic attribute/device. The fact that I am an 'insider' made it possible that many ways of speaking make sense to me without the speakers having to make everything explicit – just as the participants in my study also knew that they could communicate to me simply about some of the experiential complexities of being a Muslim in Delhi (India). My identity of being a Muslim as a heuristic device enabled an understanding of, or knowledge concerning, my participants that would have been cognitively at a level of complexity that would be difficult to discern, at this scale in the given period of time for another researcher who did not have access to this device.

I must point out, though, that I did not begin with the full import or awareness of how I might put my identity to use for making my interactions richer. I did take care of the need to be sensitive to the sensibilities of my study participants in my dress and communication, but I also realized quickly that I needed to project myself as different – worthy of initiating and facilitating a discussion about Muslims and Muslim localities in Delhi. After all, people do not discuss these issues all the time, and they do not pursue these discussions with anybody and everybody. I perceived that the differences in my position as a researcher and differences in my demeanour needed to be downplayed, but I did not feel the need to exert myself too much to eliminate these entirely.

I found that my own apprehensions about my identity as a Muslim *woman* researcher were unfounded and definitely coloured by prevalent discourses of researching Muslim populations (despite my best efforts at cautious reading of these discourses). I have more often had difficult times communicating with some colleagues on university campuses and seminars, who find the mix of Muslimness and assertive feminism in my everyday demeanour, personal choices and political positions tough to decode. During my fieldwork, I often interacted with complete strangers with barely a reference and sometimes even made cold calls on people engaged in their day-to-day lives – at their shops, workshops, shopping for groceries, doctors seeing their patients and so on. Individuals and families welcomed me into their homes, extending warm hospitality and amenable to deep and sometimes disturbing discussions. I found myself also welcomed in institutions – madarsas, charitable organizations, coaching classes, occupational associations, informal groups of community leaders and office bearers of resident welfare associations (RWAs). As it turned out, a large portion of them were men. Many of these people may appear at face value eligible to be branded 'conservative', but after an initial few awkward moments they not only discussed many issues and experiences openly but also invited me for events they were organizing later. Some even sought my counsel on matters that they thought I could comment on as a social worker. Some of the elderly men decided that I needed more help with my endeavour and helped me to meet other people by inviting their friends to meet me or by walking with me around the locales that they thought would be of interest to me. With more than a hint of benevolent patriarchy, they pointed out that I was much younger and they were passing on their experiences and knowledge of the world to the generations to come through me.

Women participants (of all ages) tended to ask me a lot more questions than men participants regarding my personal experiences and my political stances, and the interviews with them were more conversational and dialogical. This was probably because they wished to know if, and how, I would judge them and whether they could be honest and open with me about their true opinions. Some were also curious about my life and asked me questions about my life choices as a married woman and as a mother and my everyday experiences.

For most of the participants, interacting with a Muslim woman researcher was a first-time experience. Many told me that they appreciated the work I did. Younger men also appeared to be enthusiastic about sharing their experiences and insights. They were aware that these were being registered in a formal research and were confident about their views. All in all, in most cases it appeared that my affiliation with the University of Delhi at the time, as a research scholar and a member of faculty, also somehow made the interaction important for them and threw open many sites of interactions that usually are not accessed by or accessible to Muslim women for a variety of reasons.

This discussion of my experiences as a researcher is not meant to indicate that the gender divide does not exist among Muslims. In fact, it is interesting to note that some interviews that could have been very rewarding – with educated men who were my contemporary in age and of comparable social standing – never materialized despite my most persistent efforts. This was possibly because research, like many other human interactions, is rarely a site for communication between equals. It probably made them uncomfortable that they would not be able to patronize me, but neither could they look up to me as a person of authority directing the interview as a researcher. What this does indicate is that the boundaries of the gender divide are not as airtight or straight as they are often made out to be even by Muslims themselves. It also means that my intuitive methodological tightrope act of balancing insider–outsider roles afforded to me a situated view that threw up insights and helped me access the complex and embedded knowledge of people about their own lives.

7. Writing feminist ethnography infused with Marxism

The narratives I wove and presented in the study of segregation of Muslims were sought to be poised as counternarratives – counter to the various mainstream narratives. The 'against-the-grain' approach of these counternarratives is especially suited for an attempted process of deliberate disruption by exposing the complexity and inherent contradiction of the 'official' and accepted discourses (Richardson and St. Pierre 2005). In my understanding, this was possible primarily due to my feminist approach to using ethnography infused with Marxism. It allowed me to present the subjects of study not in an exact replica of the actual communities since distortions are bound to occur in representation, but rather like an impressionist painting – brushing small dabs of paint rather than broad strokes. It also involves lot of broad outdoor impressions (*plien* painting) to catch a fleeting yet all-embracing impression of details and lighting. In a truly feminist fashion, the attempt was to emphasize the researcher's (artist's) perception of the subject as much as the depiction of the subject per se. The true challenge for this kind of writing is, apart from the validity of claims or conclusions, to also think of subaltern subjects of research as fellow participants of the study, even as co-authors. The test can be that, at the very least, the researchers may think of them as readers or audience of the research (and find ways to communicate research to them apart from the usual readers – research advisors, examiners, other academics, etc.). This might go a long way in ensuring one of the unambiguous characteristics of feminist methods, that is to make possible self-representation that empowers the participants to challenge dominant processes of representation.

8. On the theme of real estate and segregation in the city

As I have stated earlier, I was already alert to the framing of studies of segregation of Muslims as ghetto studies emphasizing social–psychological dimensions of discrimination. Communal discrimination is often described at the interpersonal rather than structural level. Sometimes benign neglect of the state in countering discrimination and providing civic amenities is also pointed out. In the course of my ethnographic fieldwork in Seelampur, I had also become alert to how this community of Muslim small manufacturers, far from being excluded, was actually well integrated in the global market and how its segregation aided capital accumulation in favour of other spaces in the city (Jamil 2014). In what follows, I describe a segment of my exploration and conclusions on the theme of segregation and real estate markets.

A friend, an urban planner by training who is originally from Munger, Bihar, mentioned to me:

> Members of my extended family who live in Zakir Nagar have moderately well paying jobs of technical sorts. They had nice houses in Munger, huge houses . . . and here when I came and visited them they were living in these small houses . . . which are architectural nightmare . . . but they are happy here because they think they are perusing their career and life goals, specially the women because they have freedom, they don't want to go back to Munger.

I shared this with one of my respondents, Mr. Moin, who is a software engineer living in Shaheen Bagh in Jamia Nagar. He responded:

(M): If they continued living in Munger, they won't get jobs in which they can bring home every month around a lakh. Even though you have expenses also – schools, transportation, just eating – everything is expensive. But there is also this thing that people have to show others that I am living in Delhi.

(G): Even though my living conditions have actually worsened?

(M): They don't think that . . . about living condition, they are happy that we are. . . . We are living here, its not a big house . . . okay, but rest of the things are better. We are in a big city – so nobody asks this question . . . its like . . . so what, we are in a big city, our children have more exposure than that small city, they go to malls and they do this, they know what is an escalator and elevator. . . . So they think that now they are better and they can be better still and some of them . . . their lives have actually become better. With some, what happens . . . parents were there and all children came here, now they don't have any option, either be alone or come here to this small flat to be with their children. They are living in rented house and they realise 'what we will do with property back home? Nobody is going back to live there'. So they sell a big house there and buy a 100 sq yard flat here, so this is also one of the stories.

These two interactions brought to my attention the fact that there was more to the issue of the segregation than just a combination of discrimination, security and poverty of Muslims. Why do even those Muslims who can afford to pay the market prices remain segregated in areas like the localities in Jamia Nagar. Some scholars have opined that this is a result of self-segregation being practised by elite Muslims (Gayer and Jaffrelot 2012).

In the early 2010s Jamia Nagar experienced intense construction activity, so clearly there was surplus capital for investment and there must have been buyers with capacity. I asked myself that if aspirations are at play, then there must be efforts to buy in localities that are not pejoratively labelled as 'ghetto' and can provide better environ and civic amenities. In a bid to capture the unity in the variety of mechanisms and processes of segregation, I focused on the nature of built spaces and real estate markets.

While walking in Shahjahanabad (the walled city), one of my respondents, Mr. Azeem Akhtar, had pointed out to me that for decades the eastern side of the Daryaganj has been exclusively Hindu. I asked him if it was because properties were more expensive because of better and spacious built environment. He said that is not the reason. He recounted the story of his neighbour, who was a well-to-do publisher and had made a higher offer (in the 1980s, Rs 2 lakh more than the next highest offer) to a home owner but was turned down.

There were numerous narratives (also in media) on stiff resistance not only by home owners to sell to Muslims but also by relatives and neighbours of home owners. I sought out a Jamia Nagar real estate developer to understand the mechanism. Mr. Shakeel pointed out to me Jungpura[4] and Nizamuddin West where such sales were beginning to take place. During my interviews with people in Bara and Beri Wala Bagh, people also spoke of their relatives in Model Basti near Filmistan, which in my experience had been an exclusive Hindu locality.

The two localities – Nizamuddin West and Model Basti – were already flanked by more dilapidated Muslim quarters. This brings down the desirability quotient of these neighbourhoods. A disproportionately high offer from a Muslim buyer can be persuasive for Hindu owners seeking a more posh address in town. The first few purchases in these localities are characterized by Mr. Shakeel as 'reckless purchases'. Thereafter, he said, speculation drives the prices even higher. With extreme profits, the readiness to 'leave the area to Muslims' also increases. There seems to exist an arbitrary but crucial threshold of tolerance of 'polluting' Muslim presence in the vicinity of a neighbourhood or inside it. In a site where maintenance of Hindu-exclusivity is important, neighbours and RWAs have strong opinions against sales to Muslims because it drives down the property prices and devalues their assets too.

9. Mechanisms driving segregation

The common-sense logic that market forces cannot be bothered about identity is so well entrenched that the studies on segregation of Muslims continue to be satisfied with restating the fact of segregation but do not venture to look into the mechanisms that drive it and bring them to the fore. This is true both of narrative/ethnographic studies and of studies with quasi-experimental designs. For example, Thorat *et al.* (2015) read discrimination in the rental market as 'failure of market' and entailing 'huge inefficiencies in the working of this market' (p. 53). In the vulgar, common-sense understanding of how markets work, finance capital should not be interested in whether a project/property is in a 'Muslim' or 'Hindu' area and what the identity of its investors are. But a harder look afforded me a view that these do matter in the market since identities have a material consequence – in that they seem to aide capital accumulation. I deduced that while some circuits of capital exist where Muslim investors can invest, it has to be done in a way that 'while the profits are maximised in the short run, the segregated topography of the city remains undisturbed' (Jamil 2014: 55).

10. Conclusion

Even though my enquiry was not a gendered enquiry, as a feminist researcher I was aware that while the research process is often expected to discover and present 'facts' as 'truths', this envisaging of research as unearthing social reality cannot be independent of the relationships of production of knowledge. In Marxist vocabulary, the tendency of reducing research to a commodity and concealing its real mechanisms amounts to fetishizing research. I was, thus, also aware that without being mindful of the history, ideology and relationships behind facts, research can fall into the trap of becoming a view from *within the existing order of things*. In selecting the methods for my study, I followed Marx's exhortation to conceptualize the experience of a social phenomenon and the processes in which the phenomenon is produced, together and simultaneously (Merrifield 2013).

At the heart of my claim of having used a feminist approach is my conviction that feminist politics can be simply performed as a challenge to the boundary between binaries – personal and political, philosophical and practical – and as a challenge to essentialized identities and erasure of experience. It can be performed by knowledge creation through sympathetic understanding and displaying reflexivity for situated standpoints. Finally, a feminist ethnography infused with Marxism can be performed through ethics of *care and emancipation*.[5]

As a result of the feminist and Marxist impulses, research does not remain just a moment of meaningless and/or mystifying interaction for research participants coming from subaltern or oppressed groups. It has the potential to become one that offers them an opportunity to express their humanity, or one of learning, just as it is for the researcher. It becomes a moment when the co-creation of knowledge is possible.

Notes

1 This chapter was published in the *Economic and Political Weekly*, Review of Women's Studies, vol. 51, no. 18, 30 April 2016, pp. 48–56. We are grateful to the editor, *EPW*, for permission to republish this chapter in this volume.
2 Consider psychoanalysis, which began as a therapeutic technique for relieving individuals from psychological ailments but has affected thinking about politics, society and art – arenas far beyond the clinical – to earn the nomenclature of psychoanalytical theory. Crucial to this extended, wide-ranging effect of psychoanalytical theory is a method informed by basic assumptions regarding, for example, the existence of the unconscious, which allowed the theory to find application beyond the original concern of the psychological well-being of individuals.
3 Postmodern or critical ethnography marked by a deeply self-conscious practice by ethnographer with regard to the intrusive and unequal research relationship (Stacey 1988).
4 Jangpura has a sizeable population of Muslim Kashmiri migrants and Afghan refugees living on rent but also now buying houses.
5 'Care' is understood as not just a moral concept but a political act performed with an understanding of human interdependency. It is capable of providing a space to the politically disenfranchised for democratic and pluralistic politics (Gilligan 1982, Benhabib 1986). 'Emancipation' is

understood here not just in terms of freedom from physical subjugation or amelioration in material conditions but also in terms of bringing out the role played by ideology and consciousness in creating and maintaining dominance (Horkheimer 1931).

References

Alexander, Bryant Keith. 2005. "Performance Ethnography: The Reenacting and Inciting of Culture." In N. K. Denzin and Y. S. Lincoln (eds). *The Sage Handbook of Qualitative Research.* Thousand Oaks, CA: Sage, pp. 411–441.

Benhabib, Seyla. 1986. "The Generalized and Concrete Other: The Kohlberg-Gilligan Controversy and Feminist Theory in Feminism as Critique," *Praxis International,* Vol. 5, No. 4, pp. 402–424.

Benjamin, Walter. 1999. *The Arcades Project.* Translated by Howard Eiland and Kevin McLaughlin. Cambridge, MA: Harvard University Press.

Bhalotra, Sonia, Christine Valente and Arthur van Soest. 2010. "The Puzzle of Muslim Advantage in Child Survival in India," *Journal of Health Economics,* Vol. 29, No. 2, pp. 191–204.

Chandhoke, Neera. 1995. *State and Civil Society: Explorations in Political Theory.* Thousand Oaks: Sage.

———. 2001. "The 'Civil' and the 'Political' in Civil Society," *Democratization,* Vol. 8, No. 2, pp. 1–24.

Clifford, James. 1988. *The Predicament of Culture: Twentieth-Century Ethnography, Literature, and Art.* Cambridge, MA: Harvard University Press.

de Certeau, Michel. 1984. *The Practice of Everyday Life.* Translated by Steven Rendall. Berkeley: University of California Press.

Ellis, Carolyn S. and Arthur Bochner. 2000. "Autoethnography, Personal Narrative, Reflexivity: Researcher as Subject." In N. K. Denzin and Y. S. Lincoln (eds). *Handbook of Qualitative Research.* Thousand Oaks, CA: Sage, pp. 733–768.

Flyvbjerg, Bent. 2001. *Making Social Science Matter: Why Social Inquiry Fails and How It Can Succeed Again.* Cambridge, UK: Cambridge University Press.

Gayer, Laurent and Christoff Jaffrelot (eds). 2012. *Muslims in Indian Cities: Trajectories of Marginalisation.* New York: Columbia University Press.

Gilligan, Carol. 1982. *In a Different Voice.* Cambridge, MA: Harvard University Press.

Haraway, Donna. 1988. "Situated Knowledges: The Science Question in Feminism and the Privilege of Partial Perspective," *Feminist Studies,* Vol. 14, No. 3, pp. 575–599.

Hartsock, Nancy. 1975. "Fundamental Feminism: Process and Perspective," *Quest: A Feminist Quarterly,* No. 2 (Fall), pp. 67–80.

———. 1983. "The Feminist Standpoint: Developing the Ground for a Specifically Feminist Historical Materialism." In Sandra Harding and Merrill Hintikka (eds). *Discovering Reality: Feminist Perspectives on Epistemology,*

Metaphysics, Methodology and Philosophy of Science. Dordrecht: Reidel/Kluwer, pp. 283–310.
Hekman, Susan. 1997. "Truth and Method: Feminist Standpoint Theory Revisited," *Signs*, Vol. 22, pp. 341–365.
———. 1999. *The Future of Differences: Truth and Method in Feminist Theory*. Cambridge: Polity Press.
Horkheimer, Max. 1931. "The Present Situation of Social Philosophy and the Tasks of an Institute for Social Research." In G. Hunter, M. Kramer and J. Torpey (trans.). *Between Philosophy and Social Science: Selected Early Writings*. Cambridge, MA: MIT Press, pp. 1–14.
Jaggar, Alison M. 2008. "Introduction: The Project of Feminist Methodology," In Alison M. Jaggar (ed.). *Just Methods: An Interdisciplinary Feminist Reader*. London: Paradigm Press, pp. 39–62.
Jamil, Ghazala. 2014. "The Capitalist Logic of Spatial Segregation," *Economic and Political Weekly*, Vol. 49, No. 3, pp. 52–58.
Jayal, Niraja G. 1999. *Democracy and the State: Welfare, Secularism and Development in Contemporary India*. New Delhi: Oxford University Press.
———. 2013. *Citizenship and Its Discontents: An Indian History*. New Delhi: Orient Blackswan.
Krips, Henry. 2010. "The Politics of the Gaze Foucault, Lacan and Zizek," *Culture Unbound: Journal of Current Cultural Research*, Vol. 2, pp. 91–102.
Little, Daniel. 1986. *The Scientific Marx*. Minneapolis: University of Minnesota Press.
Marx, Karl. 1964. *The Eighteenth Brumaire of Louis Bonaparte*. New York: International Publishers.
———. 1993. *Grundrisse*. London: Penguin Books.
Menon, Nivedita. 1997. "Reservations and Representation," *Seminar*, Vol. 457 (September), pp. 38–41.
———. 2012. *Seeing Like a Feminist*. New Delhi: Zubaan and Penguin Books.
Menon, Nivedita and Aditya Nigam. 2007. *Power and Contestation: India since 1989*. New Delhi: Orient Blackswan.
Merrifield, Andrew. 2013. *Metromarxism: A Marxist Tale of the City*. New York: Routledge.
Mistry, Malika B. 2005. "Muslims in India: A Demographic and Socio-Economic Profile," *Journal of Muslim Minority Affairs*, Vol. 25, No. 3, pp. 399–422.
Mulvey, Laura. 1975. "Visual Pleasure and Narrative Cinema," *Screen*, Vol. 16, No. 3 (Autumn), pp. 6–18.
Richardson, Laurel and Elizabeth A. St. Pierre. 2005. "Writing: A Method of Inquiry." In N. K. Denzin and Y. S. Lincoln (eds). *Handbook of Qualitative Research*. Thousand Oaks, CA: Sage, pp. 959–978.
Ritzer, George. 1988. *Contemporary Social Theory*. New York: McGraw-Hill.
Rose, Hilary. 1987. "Hand, Brain, and Heart: A Feminist Epistemology for the Natural Sciences," *Signs*, Vol. 9, No. 1, pp. 73–90.
Shiva, Vandana. 1997. *Biopiracy: The Plunder of Nature and Knowledge*. Cambridge, MA: South End Press.

———. 2002. *Water Wars: Privatization, Pollution and Profit.* New Delhi: India Research Press.

Stacey, Judith. 1988. "Can There Be a Feminist Ethnography?" *Women's Studies International Forum*, Vol. 11, No. 1, pp. 21–27.

Thorat, Sukhadeo, Anuradha Banerjee, Vinod K. Mishra and Firdaus Rizvi. 2015. "Urban Rental Housing Market," *Economic and Political Weekly*, Vol. L, Nos. 26 and 27 (27 June), pp. 47–53.

Section 2
Unpacking disciplines

5 Stories we tell
Feminism, science, methodology[1]
Banu Subramaniam

1. Introduction

'We tell ourselves stories in order to live,' the writer Joan Didion (1979) famously said. Stories are accounts we develop about objects – human, non-human, inanimate, non-material or imaginary. Academic disciplines develop accounts of the world – about the emergence of a nation, the development of cells, the rise in poverty, the extinction of species or the popularity of a political candidate. One of the central insights of women's studies has been to highlight the limitations of traditional configurations of academia, that is disciplines, in producing reliable accounts of the world. Academic disciplines, feminists have long contended, tend to produce accounts of the world that benefit the interests of power. Power and knowledge are inextricably interconnected (Foucault 1977). Three decades of feminist scholarship have taught us to carefully examine disciplinary knowledge claims and to develop new methodologies, epistemologies and methods to produce more reliable accounts of the world. But how do we do this? Disciplines are characterized both by the objects of their study (natural sciences study nature, social sciences study society and the humanities study the products of human culture) *and* by their methods of study (scientists tout the scientific method, humanists extol their ability to 'read' and interpret texts and social scientists pride their quantitative and qualitative methods that allow them to analyse the complexities of human society despite their inability to conduct controlled experiments). If the sciences do not offer us an unmediated study of the natural world removed from the culture or politics, and power and knowledge are inextricably interconnected as feminists contend, how then do we study the natural world?

The fields of women's studies and science and technology studies (STS) emerged from social movements and political struggles for a more just and inclusive world (Campbell 2009). Yet despite its commitment to gender and social justice, women's studies still remains firmly grounded in the humanities and social sciences. Similarly, gender remains marginal within scholarship in STS. Feminist science and technology studies (FSTS) bridges these two fields in recognizing the importance of the interconnections between studies of gender and science (Subamaniam 2009).

Why do we see gender everywhere? And when objects are imbued with sexed and racialized meanings, why are they inevitably organized in a hierarchy so that some are rendered superior over others? One of the central methodological insights of FSTS has been refuting the binary worlds of nature and culture. Defining the object of the biological sciences as 'nature' characterized by non-human life creates the illusion of a human-free world, a world removed from ideology, politics and culture. Conversely, human culture remains in the purview of the social sciences and humanities, a world removed from the natural. But what if we refuse this nature–culture binary? In coining the term 'naturecultures', Donna Haraway (1999) challenges us to reject the binaries of nature and culture and attend to the constant traffic of discourses, information and theories between the worlds of natures and cultures. There are no natures or cultures, only naturecultures.

If we recognize the interconnections of knowledge and power, how do we study naturecultures? How do we develop methodology and methods to study the natural world while recognizing that science and scientists are deeply embedded in their historical, cultural, political and economic contexts? This has been the fundamental focus of the field of FSTS. Bringing together (inter)disciplinary methodologies, philosophies, practices, assumptions, methods and languages of women's studies and the natural sciences, we see the emergence of new modes of knowledge production. This chapter explores the epistemological challenges of studying gender in the natural and physical sciences, and explores the methodological tools the field has developed to study the human, non-human, life and non-life. Here I briefly describe the field, explore the methodological innovations the field offers us in our understanding of the natural world and end with a vision of interdisciplinary women's studies that incorporate the natural sciences within its core commitments.

2. Feminism, method, methodology and epistemology

Feminist theorists of science have long recognized that it is difficult to decouple questions of method with those of methodology and epistemology. As Sandra Harding argues,

> Discussions of method (techniques for gathering evidence) and methodology (a theory and analysis of how research should proceed) have been intertwined with each other and with epistemological issues

(issues about an adequate theory of knowledge or justificatory strategy) in both the traditional and feminist discourses.

(1987: 2)

Early in the development of the field, scholars warned against any claims of a unique feminine way of studying the world (Harding 1987, Longino 1989, Hesse-Biber and Yaiser 2004). After all, the categories of woman, female or feminine are all caught up in the same binary logics as their corollary in the categories of man, male and masculine. The point of feminist knowledge production is not to merely extol the once-invisible categories of the feminine, and reestablish binary difference, but rather to uncover and resist the very production of difference. The production of difference shapes all aspects of science – scientific practitioners, scientific culture and scientific knowledge.

Sex, gender, race, sexuality, caste and nation are all categories of difference that emerged in particular political contexts. Science has been central to the emergence and development of these categories of difference, and thoroughly biologized by the sciences (Fausto-Sterling 1985, Schiebinger 1989, Hubbard 1990). In particular, recent work in post-colonial STS has shown that science is constitutive of colonialism. One cannot understand science without colonialism, nor colonialism without science. Science proved to be a potent civilizational tool for the colonial toolbox. The development of various bodily ontologies – sex, gender, race, caste, class and sexuality – was never independent but always steeped in the larger historical and political contexts in which they were deployed. Indeed, a central feature of the colonial enterprise was establishing 'a logic of biological difference' – the ideology that colonists were justified in colonizing and enslaving another people, and creating a hierarchy of bodily ontologies: men over women, rich over poor, black over white, upper caste over lower caste, heterosexuals over homosexuals (Schiebinger 1993, Hammonds 1999). Feminist analyses often ignore how central 'science' and scientific theories about bodies have been in shaping identity categories and their potentials. Indeed, science and technology have been 'the jewels in the crown of modernity', central to the expansion of empire and critical to the contemporary world (Harding 2012: 2). Sciences should therefore be understood as 'sciences of empire' (Schiebinger 2007), and almost all modern science should be understood as 'science in a colonial context' (Seth 2009). FSTS and post-colonial STS reveal that we should understand colonial power and policies as fundamentally biopolitical in nature, producing different bodies and keeping them in their 'proper' places (Grove 1995, McClintock 1995, Stoler 1999).

A key factor that has made this difficult is the status of mainstream Western science. While communities of women, marginalized communities in the West and those in non-Western worlds have long nurtured their own theories and practices of the body, and more generally about embodiment and materiality, these have largely rendered marginal, invisible or 'lesser' knowledges (Shiva 1988, Harding 2012). What is significant is how Western science has come to be the sole and best arbiter of truth despite the well-documented history of the Western science's appropriation of knowledge from across the world and the global travels and circulation of knowledges over the centuries (Goonatilake 1984, Arnold 1993, Fujimura 2000, Raina 2003, Raj 2013, Prasad 2014). Scientific knowledge continues to be privileged above all other forms of knowledges and understandings of the world.

A particular challenge of scientific methodology is its belief in objectivity and the scientific method – a methodology that produces a value-neutral account of the world, a 'view from nowhere' (Nagel 1986). Challenging such aperspectival views as a 'God trick' (Haraway 1988), feminist historians of science have revealed a history that is anything but value neutral. Exploring the world through the many eyes and viewpoints in the world produces not one 'science' but a world of sciences (Harding 2003). The idea of objectivity as a methodology that can produce a universal and ahistorical 'truth' needs to be rejected and replaced by alternate methodologies that recognize the social and political embeddedness of science, a location it can never escape. In reconceptualizing scientific objectivity, feminists have proposed alternate visions in strong objectivity (Harding 1991: 138), situated knowledges (Haraway 1988), science as social knowledge (Longino 1990) and agential realism (Barad 2007: 132), to name a few. We thus need to 'reconceptualize objectivity as a dialectic process so as to allow for the possibility of distinguishing the objective effort from the objective illusion' (Keller 1982: 593–594).

Feminists have also shied away from privileging any one methodology. Since the early years of feminist discussions of methods and methodologies, feminists have insisted that there is thus no distinctive feminist 'method'; rather, feminist analyses should be cognizant of the nexus of knowledge and power. A common theme that resonates across feminist analyses of science is that knowledge of the natural world is not out there to be discovered unmediated by human culture or politics. Rather, knowledge is an active engagement with the world. It comes 'to be' through complex processes, including the scientists and their objects of knowledge, both located in their material, historical, geopolitical, economic and political contexts (Longino 1990, Barad 2007, Stengers 2011).

3. The gendered worlds of science

Do computers have a gender? Lock and key? Do single-celled organisms? Insects? Reptiles? Mammals? Humans? The answer is inevitably 'yes'. A quick perusal of scientific knowledge reveals a world teeming with a variety of gendered objects (Keller 1985). Binary logics of science pervade science. Not only do we have men and women, and masculine and feminine, but we also have black/white, rich/poor, straight/gay and, especially, nature/culture. These binaries are replicated in our disciplinary formations. Emerging from a Christian clerical tradition, the development of Western science emerged as a 'world without women' (Noble 1992), just as women's studies emerged as a 'world without science' (Subramaniam 2009). Scientific culture, once a bastion of white male privilege, where women, people of colour or the poor were not seen as credible scientists or 'modest witnesses', continues to betray these roots in its contemporary practices (Haraway 1997). While science understands itself as a 'culture of no culture', a world immune from culture or politics, sociologists of science demonstrated a rich culture – teeming with the politics and ideologies of its historical and cultural locations (Traweek 1992, Knorr Cetina 1999, Reardon 2005). Who can do science, and where and how it is done, are all deeply interrelated and interconnected questions. Decades of work to increase the representation of marginalized groups have shown us that the structures of science, its cultures and its methods need to change if we are to truly produce a democratic institution for all. I explore the methodological insights of FSTS by examining three facets – scientific theories about women, and women's bodies; feminist insights into the production of scientific categories and methods; and finally innovative methodologies that imagine alternate configurations of science and knowledge production.

3.1 Making 'women': the scientific production of women's biology

Three decades of scholarship in the FSTS have tried to account for stories we tell about nature and, as a result, have revealed a powerful analysis of how power and science have been inextricably interconnected (Schiebinger 1993, Rose 1994, Haraway 1997, Birke 1999, Harding 2006, Fausto-Sterling 2012). Science and scientific theories of biological determinism were central to claims that denied women the right to rational thought and thus access to higher education, suffrage or a political/public life (Fausto-Sterling 1985, Schiebinger 1989, Hubbard 1990). Similarly scientists claimed the inferiority of non-white races, giving a scientific patina to the theories and practices of racism that provided the logic for slavery and colonialism (Gould 1981, Prakash 1999, Philip 2004). Homosexuality too was long pathologized as 'deviant' and perverse, criminalized and remained medicalized as a disorder in the Diagnostic and Statistical Manual of Mental Disorders until 1973 (Terry 1999). The logics of eugenics were the basis of the sterilization of countless individuals and the mass murder of still others. Historians of science remind us that the history of science is littered with the ghosts of scientific logic that deemed some lives worth living and others worth dying (Subramaniam 2014). It is the profound biopolitical power of science that has moved from once treating illness to now redefining and regulating normality. The bioscience today controls 'life itself' (Rose 2006) and death through an emergent necropolitics (Mbembe 2003).

Such profound biopolitical power over life and death can be understood only through recognizing that science is shaped by the political conditions of its times. Scientists 'produced' differences through scientific claims about bodies, the site of difference constantly shifting from anatomical and physiological differences to a genetic level in recent times. These biological differences are in turn invoked as grounds for claims of gender and racial differences in behaviour, temperament, intellect and human potentials (Bleier 1984, Schiebinger 1989, 1993, Hubbard 1990, Birke 1999, Rosser 2008, Fausto-Sterling 2012). These biological differences are then naturalized by culture. It is this tautological and circular logic that is rendered increasingly powerful as knowledge travels between natural and cultural worlds. Thus 'society writes biology/biological constructs gender' (Fausto-Sterling 1987). Cultural and social norms are rendered scientifically objective and biologically immutable, while scientific theories naturalize and biologize cultural mores and norms. As scholars have shown, just as gender was produced, so was race, sexuality, caste, nation, ability and other social and identity categories. These categories are never innocent but reinforce a logic of difference that shapes societies and their hierarchies (Hammonds and Herzig 2009, Fisher 2011).

It is important to acknowledge that these knowledges were not the result of 'bad' science by marginal scientists. Rather, as Nancy Stepan (1982) reminds us,

> the scientists who gave scientific racism its credibility and respectability were often first-rate scientists struggling to understand what appeared to them to be deeply puzzling problems of biology and human society. To dismiss their work as merely 'pseudoscientific' would mean missing an opportunity to explore something important about the nature of scientific inquiry itself.
>
> (xvi)

Understanding the role of science in the co-constitution of sex, gender, race and sexuality has been undertheorized (Collins 1999, Subramaniam 2009). By locating the history of evolutionary biology within the logics of race and sex, historians have shown that these categories were co-constituted, where 'the manly European man and the feminine European woman' came to represent not a universal or species-wide sexual dimorphism but rather an advanced evolutionary stage (Markowitz 2001: 391). Race and sex are intertwined in the biological claims of the 'white heterosexual couple' as the pinnacle of human evolution. Anxieties around the non-European were central to the pathologizing of some sexual bodies and sexualities.

But if practices such as phrenology and craniometry have been long discredited and as the numbers of underrepresented groups grow, has not science transformed into a more democratic institution? Here scholars of FSTS respond with a resounding 'no'. Histories of oppression, they argue, have shaped not only the rights and opportunities of various groups but the very categories of science, its cultures and knowledges. History reminds us that bringing diverse bodies into science, while laudable and important for questions of gender and racial equity, is not sufficient to dismantle the deep and systematic structural legacies of domination. Women and racial minorities do not by the virtue of their identity recognize the racism, sexism or other logics of difference that consistently undergird science. Rather, what we need is a thorough understanding and re-conceptions of the epistemologies, methodologies and methods of science.

4. Interrogating science: analysing science-in-the-making

Analysing the structural forces that continually produce a 'logic of difference', Evelyn Fox Keller and Helen Longino argue, 'Gender opened up an entirely new window on the nature of scientific inquiry' (1996: 2). Feminists have shown how poor sample sizes, faulty logic, reductive methodologies, poor methods, unfounded variables or unwarranted conclusions continue to plague science. Complex human behaviours are reduced to simplistic variables and categories (Fausto-Sterling 1985). How do you, for example, measure 'sexual orientation'? Even scientists agree that it is a complex trait and includes a range of traits such as sexual desires, affectionate feelings and behaviours, as well as one's self-conception and self-identity. Rebecca Jordan-Young's (2011) analysis is revelatory. She shows how different studies operationalized sexual orientation in different ways – as sexual attraction, the desires one feels, pattern of falling in love, pair bonding, physical sex of sexual partners, gender of sexual partners or simply whether one identifies as straight, gay, lesbian or bisexual (Jordan-Young 2011). Complex categories are often oversimplified for headline news about the new science of sexuality. Similarly in operationalizing sexuality in animals (often a cornerstone for claims about humans), Jordan-Young points out the utter inconsistencies across studies (Jordan-Young 2011) – in the case of sheep, a ram is considered gay if it mounts another ram. In contrast, a male rat is gay if another male rat mounts it. These are not just different criteria but totally contradictory (Jordan-Young 2011). Yet claims of sexuality as biologically determined persist, along with emerging claims of 'gay genes', even while animal behaviourists widely recognize that animals of both sexes mount and are mounted since mounting behaviour can be about things other than sex, such as play or dominance (Jordan-Young 2011).

Like Jordan Young's more recent analysis, feminists have painstakingly taken apart scientific studies to highlight the political and social assumptions that undergird them (Fausto-Sterling 1985, 2012, Schiebinger 1989, 1993, Hubbard 1990, Rose 1994, Haraway 1997, Birke 1999, Harding 2006). One of the most frustrating aspects of this history is the hydra-like nature of biological determinism. No sooner is one theory discredited than another quickly emerges. This has meant a constant vigilance to refute new studies as they continually appear. The careful attention to method, and the systematic analysis of scientific experiments (in the language of science), has been a great contribution of FSTS. These analyses on the method are shaped by the methodological commitment to the nexus of power and knowledge. It is not accidental that whenever sex differences emerge, the male sex always has the more valued traits! Indeed, with a quick perusal of this history, one is forced to ask – why are we so obsessed with the production of difference?

A focus on language and rhetoric has also proven to be a key contribution of FSTS methodologies. Evelyn Fox Keller documents how the metaphor of the computer 'code' as a model for describing the language of DNA, that is the genetic code, has powerfully shaped the field of genetics. The metaphor of code has shaped frameworks in genetics by generating vocabularies such as 'master' molecule and hierarchical control. As Keller argues, 'We risk imposing on nature the very stories we like to hear' (Keller 1985: 187). Similarly, scholars have shown how the language of human courtship and romance finds itself into the language of reproduction of plants and animals (Haraway 1989, Schiebinger 1989, 1993, Martin 1992, Gowaty 1997, Hustak and Myers 2012). Even single-celled organisms are imagined as heterosexual and imbued with complementary genders where donor and recipient cells are labelled as male and female. Our conceptions of race travel between natures and cultures as the racial politics of human immigration transfers the languages of undesirable aliens and desirable natives onto the qualities of individual plants and animal species (Subramaniam 2001).

Finally, it is important to pay attention to gender and its historical, economic, political and cultural contexts in science. For example, Elizabeth Potter (2001) in her examination of the development of Boyle's law shows how the articulation of gender and class politics in 17th-century England shaped something as foundational as Boyle's law. Indeed, much of modern scientific and technological innovations are best understood as developments mobilized by the increasing pharmaceuticalization of medicine; the increasing geneticization of life; and the increasing commodification of agriculture, health and medicine (Clarke *et al.* 2003, Sunder Rajan 2006, Pollock 2014). A particularly well-developed subfield of analysis in FSTS is the immense growth in reproductive tourism – of assistive reproductive technologies (ARTs) and surrogacy. Feminists remind us that these are not simply innovations that fill human need but that science has been central to creating the desires and needs in the first place. To be sure, medical technologies are important for enabling the harvesting of sperm and eggs, in vitro fertilization, testing and selecting particular embryos and subsequent implantation of the embryo in a uterus. However, the scale of ARTs is possible only because of rising neonatalism and desire for motherhood, the postponement of pregnancy among more wealthy women, the passing of laws that allow the commodification of women's bodies and the transnational inequality of wealth that render some women's bodies as exploitable (Thompson 2005, Cooper and Waldby 2014, Rudrappa 2015). Thus, the circulation of global capital has profoundly shaped scientific priorities and research in contemporary times (Thompson 2002, Sunder Rajan 2006). The old political model where science in the West reigned supreme is being challenged by national initiatives in emerging economies, especially in Asia. These projects, backed by the state, are creating a strong biotechnology industry in Asia and a rising 'bionationalism' that is reshaping global development of genomics as Asian and other developing countries (e.g. India, Mexico and Brazil) are asserting their 'genomic sovereignty' (Benjamin 2009). FSTS reminds us never to isolate scientific innovations but to always examine the political and economic contexts in which any innovation emerges and develops.

5. Moving beyond binaries: studying naturecultures

If feminist studies demonstrate that science is 'constructed', then surely it can also be 'reconstructed' (Subramaniam 2014). If science as an institution has worked in the interests of power, what might a science informed by feminist politics and methodologies look like? What if we had laboratories of our own (Subramaniam 2005)? Who would practise in them and how might this science look like? Helen Longino reminds us that we should 'focus on science as practice rather than content, as process rather than product; hence, not on feminist science, but on doing science as a feminist' (Longino 1989: 47). Doing science as a feminist requires not only new methodologies but also the institutional conditions for such work. Indeed, if sexism, racism and casteism in the academy have functioned to keep structures of scientific labour and pedagogies of domination in place, feminist practices in such institutional settings prove difficult (Connell 2014). Much of the work that has been done in the aid of underrepresented groups in the sciences has done little to change the structures of work. What then are the conditions of doing science as a 'feminist'? I briefly consider the answer at three different levels: practitioners of science, cultures of science and scientific knowledge production.

Work on the underrepresentation of women, racial and caste minorities in the sciences, has shown their continued marginalization in the sciences across the globe, especially the more prestigious sciences and at more senior levels (Rosser 2004, Subramanian 2007, Sur 2011). Studies have repeatedly shown that women are deeply interested in science and indeed perform well academically (Rosser 2004). Women have persisted in their love of science, often under arduous conditions (Rossiter 1982, Alic 1986). Studies suggest this is because of continued inequities within science, and persistent barriers and systematic discrimination (Bystydzienski and Bird 2006, Sur 2011). Yet much of the work on addressing the underrepresentation of groups has focused on mentoring, networking, stopping the tenure clock for pregnancy and rewarding highly successful women scientists as 'models' – what is striking is that the focus remains on 'women' as deserving special attention and rewards and not changing the system or its androcentric culture (Subramaniam 2014). Despite decades of women in the sciences, we continue to hear about cases of repeated and unchecked sexual harassment of women, the most recent being Tim Hunt and Geoff Marcy. These cases remind us that the 'old boy's network' is alive and well. Thus, cultures of science that routinely characterize bad behaviour as idiosyncratic or isolated, and ignore them ultimately, sanction such violence.

At the heart of scientific practice and its culture are its claims to value neutrality and objectivity. The claims that scientists bring no histories or experiences that shape their practice or research agendas rest on an ideology that science has no culture and remains value neutral. What FSTS fundamentally reminds us is that any feminist method when practised within such a disembodied epistemology that inherently ignores social context and history is likely to reproduce the same problems. What needs to change are not only institutions but also scientific methodology and epistemology. However, some work in the sciences gives us a road map for what practising science as a feminist can look like (Subramaniam 2014). Consider, for example, the work of biologists who take on feminist methodology, albeit within a positivist framework of evolutionary biology. Feminists have challenged earlier sexist frameworks where 'coy females' and 'promiscuous males' and male dominance and female subservience characterized the sexes (Zuk 2002). These feminist biologists have used feminist theory to reimagine animal life and have then reimagined and rewritten Darwinian theory to create new frameworks of how the world and especially the two sexes work, one not characterized by universal male dominance (Hrdy 1981, 1999, 2009, Haraway 1989, Gowaty 1997, Strum and Fedigan 2002). Yet other feminists while applauding the rewriting of Victorian sexual mores in Darwinian evolution with more female agency argue that such sociobiology, while feminist, remains grounded in a binary sex system; that is both of these contrasting stories – sociobiology and feminist sociobiology – are variants of the same narrative, where each sex is locked in an oppositional relationship and attempts to outwit the other for reproductive success (Oikkonen 2013). Instead, the critics present more radical visions questioning the very premise of 'sex' and sexual selection as the key mode of evolution. For example, Joan Roughgarden replaces sexual selection theory with social selection theory. Life, she argues, in a very feminist vein, is more than sex and sexual relationship – all forms of sociality occupy us for complex reasons. Roughgarden opens up animal life beyond sexual life and its obsessive and narrow focus on particular modes of reproductive success. Roughgarden challenges the age-old stereotypes of macho males and sexy females that have been so long enduring, and thus adds texture and play to life on earth (Roughgarden 2004, 2009). Lynn Margulis and Dorian Sagan (2003), in a different vein, question the singular focus on sexual reproduction and 'vertical inheritance' down the generations that grounds evolutionary biology. Instead, she highlights the work of bacteria and viruses, and their ability to transfer genetic material across species and individuals, thus producing 'lateral transfer' and inheritance. Again, in Margulis's vision of evolution, the key to variation and diversity is not a battle between the sexes but rather a world teeming with exchange and symbiosis.

Understanding the world as naturecultures offers us an interdisciplinary methodology to study a co-constituted world. Nature and culture cannot be studied on different parts of our campus, and by differently trained and un-communicating researchers. Studying naturecultures requires interdisciplinary explorations that require feminist scholarship and work beyond the silos of disciplinary logic. We need to imagine interdisciplinary spaces – institutional and intellectual – which will allow us to move from the old biopolitics of science to a new feminist politics of biopossibilities (Willey 2016) – possibilities of reimagining our naturecultural world through the liberatory possibilities of feminism.

Note

1 This chapter was published in the *Economic and Political Weekly*, Review of Women's Studies, vol. 51, no. 18, 30 April 2016, pp. 57–63. We are grateful to the editor, *EPW*, for permission to republish this chapter in this volume.

References

Alic, Margaret. 1986. *Hypatia's Heritage: A History of Women in Science from Antiquity through the Nineteenth Century.* Boston: Beacon Press.
Arnold, David. 1993. *Colonizing the Body: State Medicine and Epidemic Disease in Nineteenth-Century India.* Berkeley: University of California Press.
Barad, Karen. 2007. *Meeting the Universe Halfway: Quantum Physics and the Entanglement of Matter and Meaning.* Durham, NC: Duke University Press.
Benjamin, Ruha. 2009. "A Lab of Their Own: Genomic Sovereignty as Postcolonial Science Policy," *Policy and Society*, Vol. 28, pp. 341–355.
Birke, Linda. 1999. *Feminism and the Biological Body.* Edinburgh: Edinburgh University Press.
Bleier, Ruth. 1984. *Science and Gender: A Critique of and Its Theories on Women.* New York: Pergamon.
Bystydzienski, Jill and Sharon R. Bird (eds). 2006. *Removing Barriers: Women in Academic Science, Technology, Engineering, and Mathematics.* Bloomington, IN: Indiana University Press.
Campbell, Nancy. 2009. "Reconstructing Science and Technology Studies: Views from Feminist Standpoint Theory," *Frontiers*, Vol. 30, No. 1, pp. 1–29.
Clarke, Adele, Janet Sim, Laura Mamo, Jennifer Ruth Fosket and Jennifer Fishman. 2003. "Biomedicalization: Technoscientific Transformations of Health, Illness, and U. S. Biomedicine," *American Sociological Review*, Vol. 68, No. 2, pp. 161–194.
Collins, Patricia Hill. 1999. "Moving beyond Gender: Intersectionality and Scientific Knowledge." In Myra M. Ferree, Judith Lorber and Beth B. Hess (eds). *Revisioning Gender.* Thousand Oaks, CA: Sage, pp. 261–284.
Connell, Raewyn. 2014. "The Sociology of Gender in Southern Perspective," *Current Sociology*, Vol. 62, No. 4, pp. 550–567.
Cooper, Melinda and Catherine Waldby. 2014. *Clinical Labor: Tissue Donors and Research Subjects in the Global Bioeconomy.* Durham, NC: Duke University Press.
Didion, Joan. 1979. *The White Album.* New York: Simon & Schuster.
Fausto-Sterling, Anne. 1985. *Myths of Gender: Biological Theories about Men and Women.* New York: Basic Books.
———. 1987. "Society Writes Biology/Biology Constructs Gender," *Daedalus*, Vol. 116, No. 4, pp. 61–76.
———. 2012. *Biology in a Social World.* New York: Routledge.
Fisher, Jill. 2011. *Gender and the Science of Difference: Cultural Politics of Contemporary Science and Medicine.* New Brunswick, NJ: Rutgers University Press.
Foucault, Michel. 1977. In Colin Gordon (ed.). *Power/Knowledge: Selected Interviews and Other Writings 1972–1977.* New York: Pantheon Books.
Fujimura, Joan H. 2000. "Transnational Genomics: Transgressing the Boundary Between the 'Modern/West' and the 'Premodern/East.'" In Roddy Reid and Sharon Traweek (eds). *Doing Science + Culture.* New York: Routledge, pp. 71–92.
Goonatilake, Susantha. 1984. *Aborted Discovery: Science and Creativity in the Third World.* London: Zed Books.

Gould, Stephen Jay. 1981. *The Mismeasure of Man*. New York: Norton.
Gowaty, Patricia. 1997. *Feminism and Evolutionary Biology: Boundaries, Intersection and Frontiers*. The United States: Springer.
Grove, Richard. 1995. *Green Imperialism: Colonial Expansion, Tropical Island Edens and the Origins of Environmentalism, 1600–1860*. Cambridge, UK: Cambridge University Press.
Hammonds, Evelynn. 1999. "The Logic of Difference: A History of Race in Science and Medicine in the United States." Presentation at the Women's Studies Program, UCLA.
Hammonds, Evelynn and Rebecca M. Herzig. 2009. *The Nature of Difference: Sciences of Race in the United States from Jefferson to Genomics*. Cambridge, MA: MIT Press.
Haraway, Donna. 1988. "Situated Knowledges: The Science Question in Feminism and the Privilege of Partial Perspective," *Feminist Studies*, Vol. 14, No. 3 (Autumn), pp. 575–599.
———. 1989. *Primate Visions: Gender, Race, and Nature in the World of Modern Science*. New York: Routledge.
———. 1997. *Modest_Witness@Second_Millennium: FemaleMan__Meets_Onco Mouse*. New York: Routledge.
———. 1999. *How Like a Leaf: An Interview with Thyrza Nichols Goodeve*. New York: Routledge.
Harding, Sandra. 1987. "Is There a Feminist Method?" In Sandra Harding (ed.). *Feminism and Methodology*. Bloomington, IN: Indiana University Press, pp. 1–14.
———. 1991. *Whose Science? Whose Knowledge?* Milton Keynes: Open University Press.
———. 2003. "A World of Sciences." In Robert Figueroa and Sandra Harding (eds). *Science and Other Cultures Issues in the Philosophies of Science and Technology*. New York: Routledge, pp. 49–69.
———. 2006. *Science and Social Inequality: Feminist and Postcolonial Issues*. Urbana: University of Illinois Press.
———. 2012. *The Postcolonial Science and Technology Studies Reader*. Durham, NC: Duke University Press.
Hesse-Biber, Sharlene and Michelle L. Yaiser. 2004. *Feminist Perspectives on Social Research*. Oxford: Oxford University Press.
Hrdy, Sarah. 1981. *The Woman That Never Evolved*. Cambridge, MA: Harvard University Press.
———. 1999. *Mother Nature: A History of Mothers, Infants and Natural Selection*. New York: Pantheon.
———. 2009. *Mothers and Others: The Evolutionary Origins of Mutual Understanding*. Cambridge, MA: Harvard University Press.
Hubbard, Ruth. 1990. *The Politics of Women's Biology*. New Brunswick, NJ: Rutgers University Press.
Hustak, Carla and Natasha Myers. 2012. "Involutionary Momentum Affective Ecologies and the Sciences of Plant/Insect Encounters," *differences*, Vol. 23, No. 3, pp. 74–118.

Jordan-Young, Rebecca. 2011. *Brain Storm: The Flaws in the Science of Sex Differences*. Cambridge, MA: Harvard University Press.
Keller, Evelyn Fox. 1982. "Feminism and Science," *Signs: Journal of Women in Culture and Society*, Vol. 7, No. 3, pp. 589–602.
———. 1985. *Reflections on Gender and Science*. New Haven, CT: Yale University Press.
Keller, Evelyn Fox and Helen Longino. 1996. "Introduction." In Evelyn Fox Keller and Helen Longino (eds). *Feminism and Science*. Oxford: Oxford University Press, pp. 1–14.
Knorr Cetina, Karin. 1999. *Epistemic Cultures: How the Sciences Make Knowledge*. Cambridge, MA: Harvard University Press.
Longino, Helen. 1989. "Can There Be a Feminist Science?" In Nancy Tuana (ed.). *Feminism and Science*. Bloomington, IN: Indiana University Press.
———. 1990. *Science as Social Knowledge: Values and Objectivity in Scientific Inquiry*. Princeton, NJ: Princeton University Press.
Margulis, Lynn and Dorian Sagan. 2003. *Acquiring Genomes: A Theory on the Origin of Species*. New York: Basic Books.
Markowitz, Sally. 2001. "Pelvic Politics: Sexual Dimorphism and Racial Difference," *Signs*, Vol. 26, No. 2, pp. 389–414.
Martin, Emily. 1992. *The Woman in the Body*. Boston: Beacon Press.
Mbembe, Achille. 2003. "Necropolitics," *Public Culture*, Vol. 15, No. 1, pp. 11–40.
McClintock, Anne. 1995. *Imperial Leather: Race, Gender, and Sexuality in the Colonial Contest*. New York: Routledge.
Nagel, Thomas. 1986. *The View from Nowhere*. Oxford: Oxford University Press.
Noble, David. 1992. *A World without Women: The Christian Clerical Culture of Western Science*. Oxford: Oxford University Press.
Oikkonen, Venla. 2013. *Gender, Sexuality and Reproduction in Evolutionary Narrative*. New York: Routledge.
Philip, Kavita. 2004. *Civilizing Natures: Race, Resources, and Modernity in Colonial South India*. New Brunswick, NJ: Rutgers University Press.
Pollock, Anne. 2014. "Places of Pharmaceutical Knowledge-Making: Global Health, Postcolonial Science, and Hope in South Africa Drug Discovery," *Social Studies of Science*, Vol. 44, No. 6, pp. 848–873.
Potter, Elizabeth. 2001. *Gender and Boyle's Law of Gases*. Bloomington, IN: Indiana University Press.
Prakash, Gyan. 1999. *Another Reason: Science and the Imagination of Modern India*. Princeton, NJ: Princeton University Press.
Prasad, Amit. 2014. *Imperial Technoscience: Transnational Histories of MRI in the United States, Britain, and India*. Cambridge, MA: MIT Press.
Raina, Dhruv. 2003. *Images and Contexts: The Historiography of Science and Modernity in India*. New Delhi: Oxford University Press.
Raj, Kapil. 2013. "Beyond Postcolonialism and Postpositivism: Circulation and the Global History of Science," *Isis*, Vol. 1–4, pp. 337–347.
Reardon, Jenny. 2005. *Race to the Finish: Identity and Governance in an Age of Genomics*. Princeton, NJ: Princeton University Press.

Rose, Hilary. 1994. *Love, Power and Knowledge: Towards a Feminist Transformation of the Sciences.* Cambridge: Polity Press.

Rose, Nikolas. 2006. *The Politics of Life Itself: Biomedicine, Power, and Subjectivity in the Twenty-First Century.* Princeton, NJ: Princeton University Press.

Rosser, Sue. 2004. *The Science Glass Ceiling: Academic Women Scientists and the Struggle to Succeed.* New York: Routledge.

——— (ed.). 2008. *Women, Science, and Myth: Gender Beliefs from Antiquity to the Present.* Santa Barbara, CA: ABC-CLIO.

Rossiter, Margaret. 1982. *Women Scientists in America: Struggles and Strategies to 1940.* Baltimore, MD: Johns Hopkins University Press.

Roughgarden, Joan. 2004. *Evolution's Rainbow: Diversity, Gender and Sexuality in Nature and People.* Paperback ed. Los Angeles: University of California Press.

———. 2009. *The Genial Gene: Deconstructing Darwinian Selfishness.* Berkeley: University of California Press.

Rudrappa, Sharmila. 2015. *Discounted Life: The Price of Global Surrogacy in India.* New York: New York University Press.

Schiebinger, Londa. 1989. *The Mind Has No Sex? Women in the Origins of Modern Science.* Cambridge, MA: Harvard University Press.

———. 1993. *Nature's Body: Gender in the Making of Modern Science.* Boston: Beacon Press.

———. 2007. *Plants and Empire: Colonial Bioprospecting in the Atlantic World.* Cambridge, MA: Harvard University Press.

Seth, Suman. 2009. "Putting Knowledge in Its Place: Science, Colonialism, and the Postcolonial," *Postcolonial Studies*, Vol. 12, No. 4, pp. 373–388.

Shiva, Vandana. 1988. *Staying Alive: Women, Ecology, and Survival in India.* New Delhi: Zed Press.

Stengers, Isabelle. 2011. *Thinking with Whitehead: A Free and Wild Creation of Concepts.* Cambridge, MA: Harvard University Press.

Stepan, Nancy. 1982. *The Idea of Race in Science: Great Britain, 1800–1960.* Hamden, CT: Anchor.

Stoler, Ann Laura. 1999. "Colonial Studies and the History of Sexuality." In *Race and the Education of Desire: Foucault's History of Sexuality and the Colonial Order of Things.* Durham, NC: Duke University Press, pp. 1–18.

Strum, Shirley and Linda Fedigan. 2002. *Primate Encounters: Models of Science, Gender, and Society.* Chicago: University of Chicago Press.

Subramaniam, Banu. 2001. "The Aliens Have Landed! Reflections on the Rhetoric of Biological Invasions," *Meridians: Feminism, Race, Transnationalism*, Vol. 2, No. 1, pp. 26–40.

———. 2005. "Laboratories of Our Own: New Productions of Gender and Science." In Elizabeth L. Kennedy and Agatha Beins (eds). *The Future of Women's Studies: Foundations, Interrogations, Politics.* New Brunswick, NJ: Rutgers University Press, pp. 229–241.

———. 2009. "Moored Metamorphoses: A Retrospective Essay on Feminist Science Studies," *Signs*, Vol. 34, No. 4, pp. 951–980.

———. 2014. *Ghost Stories for Darwin: The Science of Variation and the Politics of Diversity.* Urbana: University of Illinois Press.

Subramanian, Jayasree. 2007. "Perceiving and Producing Merit: Gender and Doing Science in India," *Indian Journal of Gender Studies*, Vol. 14, No. 2, pp. 259–284.

Sunder Rajan, Kaushik. 2006. *Biocapital: The Constitution of Post-Genomic Life*. Durham, NC: Duke University Press.

Sur, Abha. 2011. *Dispersed Radiance: Caste, Gender, and Modern Science in India*. New Delhi: Navayana.

Terry, Jennifer. 1999. *An American Obsession: Science, Medicine, and Homosexuality in Modern Society*. Chicago: University of Chicago Press.

Thompson, Charis. 2002. "Strategic Naturalizing: Kinship in an Infertility Clinic." In Sarah Franklin and Susan McKinnon (eds). *Relative Values: Reconfiguring Kinship Studies*. Durham, NC: Duke University Press, 175–202.

———. 2005. *Making Parents: The Ontological Choreography of Reproductive Technologies*. Cambridge, MA: MIT Press.

Traweek, Sharon. 1992. *Beamtimes and Lifetimes: The World of High Energy Physicists*. Cambridge, MA: Harvard University Press.

Willey, Angela. 2016. *Undoing Monogamy: The Politics of Science and the Possibilities of Biology*. Durham, NC: Duke University Press.

Zuk, Marlene. 2002. *Sexual Selections: What We Can and Can't Learn about Sex from Animals*. Berkeley: University of California Press.

6 Researching online worlds through a feminist lens
Text, context and assemblages

Usha Raman and Sai Amulya Komarraju

1. Introduction

Communication in the digital age is a multilayered, multi-directional, multi-mediated phenomenon, its apparent ease and convenience masking a complex system that is both structured and structuring. How do we pin down the ever-shifting, ever-morphing layers of interaction, representation, social-cultural-political formation and circulation in a way that can be studied and understood? Interactions on this space are fleeting and disembodied, individuals represented by what Mark Poster called 'flickers on a screen' (Poster 1997: 217), their words serving as both affect and intent, their affiliations to groups and communities turning into identity markers and their photographs becoming dubious coordinates in a space without longitude or latitude. Built in an invisible, ever-adjusting way, these programmed and algorithmically defined spaces of the Net simultaneously free and constrain us, allowing us opportunities to discard labels and shape identities, form collectivities and experiment with communities, engage in conversation or burrow into solitude cushioned by a rich matrix of information.

Lister *et al.* (2009: 2) remark that studying the Internet, and digitally enabled/structured spaces, is like photographing a breaking wave, which, even with the fastest of cameras, can offer only an instant in motion, its molecules already shifting even as they are captured. But as many others in this volume and in the huge body of work that is social theory and practice have shown, understanding is possible, even if fixing is not. For the purposes of this chapter, we define digital media as all forms of computer-based media, networked and non-networked, that allow for communication, representation, documentation and circulation of ideas and expression. This would include (but is not restricted to) the Internet and its components (search engines, social media, websites, wikis, etc.), video games (online and offline), imaging and publishing software and mobile phones and their applications.

The pervasiveness and ease of use of the 'new' medium make it an important, inescapable space of social research. In fact, digital media are so integrated into the ecology of modern life that it is impossible to separate them from our daily practice (Tacchi 2004, Couldry 2012).

The Internet – and all forms of digitally enabled media – has been the object and subject of social researchers from across disciplines (anthropology, sociology, political science, communications, linguistics, psychology, economics, education), from different perspectives (behaviourist, political economy, humanistic, Marxist, critical, post-structural, postmodernist). It has offered social movements of varying hues, everywhere in the world, an additional space to define, mobilize and carry forward their agendas (Castells 2010).

In this chapter, we explore the possibilities and problematics offered by a feminist approach to the study of the Internet and related technologies. Given the nature of this space (or spaces), what are the specific gendered politics that arise or can be harnessed for study? What questions does it raise for a gendered understanding of the self, community and identity? What approaches may we devise – or co-opt – to further this understanding?

We use current research to attempt to map the questions and suggest some approaches for a contextually situated feminist new media research agenda. In this exploration, we consider some of the main strands of global (cyber) feminist research with a view to reconstructing a space that might take in the subjectivities that characterize a South Asian or even Indian approach to the field. Pulling together the necessarily diverse scholarship in the area, we attempt to understand the contribution of mainstream (offline) feminist thought, research and practice to the online experience, expression and exploration around gender, particularly in the Indian context. What does extant feminist scholarship offer to the study of online gender politics in terms of both concepts and methods?

What, for instance, is the role of standpoint theory in a context where standpoint could be invisible, assumed, fictional or location-blind? How does disembodiment complicate our understanding of gender categories or even gender itself? How does simulation, such as in gaming, confound notions of sexuality in ways that could manifest offline and thereby relate to feminist politics and problematics on the ground? What is the specific nature of the feminist sensibility that one can bring to bear upon an examination of power relations as well as expressive forms in cyberspace? It would be of interest to examine how recent turns in feminist thought and praxis stemming from specific strands of (embodied) identity politics such as Dalit or Ambedkarite feminism, Islamic feminism and other minority feminisms play out in or draw from digital spaces. What sort of issues and what sort of actors tend to become the focus of attention when politics is played out online – in other words, what directions of feminist action or resolution are encouraged or constrained when the conversation is taken primarily to online spaces? These are large interdisciplinary questions, the answers to which can only be partial and continually unfolding and are tackled only in a limited manner within this chapter. But the process of researching them, the tools and epistemological ground from which these examinations proceed, is important to consider.

We begin by revisiting Donna Haraway's formulation of the cyborg and go on to trace the (incipient) boundaries of online feminist research in India and its relationship with online feminist activism. Then, we offer three different ways of approaching feminist digital media studies: raising questions in relation to digital content (text), in relation to the characteristics of the medium (form/space) and a more holistic framework that applies the ideas of actor-network-theory; considering digital media spaces as complexes of human and non-human assemblages (Latour 2005, Law 2009); and combining it with ideas of media as part of everyday practice (Couldry 2004). We then proceed to suggest some methodologies that might help us pursue these questions.

2. The origin myth: reconsidering the cyborg and other cyberfeminist questions

Close to 30 years after it was published, Donna Haraway's *Cyborg Manifesto* (1991) continues to be an important position paper in cyberfeminist studies. It argued for a new language of liberation within the emerging context of a techno-landscape and the possibility of a radical politics that could afford a new un-definition of gender. This set off a debate across feminist Internet scholars from different disciplines about what it meant to be a woman online, whether a postfeminist being was possible in (what was then thought to be) this disembodied, anonymous medium, whether technology ended up enslaving women once again, what sort of sexual politics played out online and so on. A quarter of a century into the Internet age, those debates remain pertinent, and many new ones have arisen, in relation to gender and cyberspace, the transgender movement, the political economy of the Internet and its relationship with the offline world.

The range of theories, debates and practices about the relationship between gender and digital culture is collectively referred to as 'cyberfeminism' (Daniels 2009) or, more recently, 'digital feminisms' (Spiers 2015). *Old* cyberfeminism envisions a utopian and hopeful postcorporeal cyborg that can subvert the patriarchal system. The human–machine cyborg of Haraway's formulation has the potential to shift gender and racial regimes. The *new* cyberfeminists, however, are info-heavy cyber-babes, who confront the 'top-down from the bottom up' by building a secure foundation within the clever information society to create financial opportunities, get funds and perhaps also 'make our own corporations' (Fernandez and Wilding, 2002).

While the cyborg does offer an escape from the limits of embodiment, research on women's use of breast cancer and illness forums (Hardey, 2002, McNamara 2007) questions the notion of 'disembodiment', suggesting instead that the body is never entirely absent even in cyberspace. In fact, as many scholars have shown, online discourse produces the body in specific and marked ways. While the issue of embodiment or its absence constitutes an important part of the cyberfeminist discourse, many Internet researchers believe that we need to go beyond the mind–body binary and attempt to understand digitally created spaces in terms of both possibility and proscription – for bodies, for minds, for relationships, for engagement and for ownership and mobilization. As we shall see later in this chapter, it is more productive to move beyond simple binary oppositions which, while useful as a device for generating questions, mask the nuanced and often necessarily contradictory nature of phenomena.

> Forgetting the body is an old Cartesian trick, one that has unpleasant consequences for those bodies whose speech is silenced by the act of our forgetting; that is to say, those upon whose labour the act of forgetting the body is founded.
>
> (Stone 2000: 525)

Thus, the position we take – and one that we suggest is a more holistic way of thinking about questions of gender in online spaces – is that the body is never completely absent on the Net, and even as we 'escape' it, we recreate it in discourse in much the same way as we might perform it in the material world. Jamie Banks's 'network model of the self' draws on Zizi Papacharissi's 'networked self' (Papacharissi 2010) and the socially mediated 'distributed self' (Baym and Boyd 2012) to (re)imagine the self as a multimodal, multiplexed, multispatial phenomenon that operates/is realized in a context where the human and non-human are 'structured in relation to one another' (Banks 2015: 2), in a way recalling Haraway's cyborg. Brophy speaks of the 'liminality' of the online experience which forces recognition of the body even while being present without it, as the space occupied by the self online is 'an interior (mind) made exterior (visible and/or present to others)' (Brophy 2010: 940).

While cyberfeminist scholars have addressed the gendering of the online self and gendered manipulations of algorithmically constructed forums, others have looked at the mobilizing, expressive and dialogic possibilities that have opened up for women and sexual minorities in social media and other digital spaces. An interesting move away from content to circulation is marked by feminist rhetoric scholars such as Mary Queen, who point to how women's self-presentations online are 'transformed through their circulation within global fields of rhetorical action in ways that "fix" these women within neoliberal frameworks' (Queen 2008: 471). She asserts that this erases the 'multiple ways in which women across the globe use Internet technology to create and claim identities, agency and political activism' (ibid.) and thus urges more work that looks at how digital feminist discourses are appropriated through differential modes of circulation. Queen thus recalls Haraway's caution that extant knowledge–power relations tend to inscribe the socio-technical environment of the Internet (Haraway 1997: 7) that is then 'shot through with material and structural relations of force' (Queen 2008: 472). In order to realize the liberatory potential of Haraway's cyborg, then, one needs to first uncover the ways in which the discourses that could produce her are subject to control and appropriation. However, it is possible to consider online spaces of dialogue as offering a liberatory potential for another reason – that they allow us to engage in a *reflective* conversation that is not constrained by the need for immediate response demanded by embodied interactions. The online/represented (cyber) self in this case is, of course, continuous with the offline/enacted (embodied) self, as posited by Hayles (2008). As Scarry (quoted in Hayles 2008: 195) notes, physical practices have physical realities that can never be fully assimilated in discourse; therefore, it is important to understand how embodiment works 'in conjunction with inscription, technology, and ideology'. For feminist action, this implies that the online world may offer spaces of 'gathering agency' through a more reasoned dialogue and by connecting with supportive networks, and for feminist scholarship, this poses a variety of interesting questions around the limits and possibilities of such liberation and activism.

Yet another strand of scholarship focuses on the gendered nature of the online/offline dialectic, including cyber-labour, ranging from women in call centres to those who do anonymous digital job work (Mirchandani 2004, Kingsley, Gray and Suri 2014). More recently, issues such as hashtag feminism (using social media to raise and make visible feminist concerns) and Gamergate (protesting sexually based violence in video games – Huntemann 2015, McClintock 2015) have pointed to the polarized nature of discussions around gender and cyberspace. Some of the work in this area has urged a move from simplistic 'what is a feminist hashtag' to questions that probe 'who is hashtagging on Twitter in the first place – or who is not?' (Latina and Docherty 2014: 1104), thus giving greater attention to the class and literacy dimensions of action on social media. Hashtag feminism has been credited with unleashing 'a multiplicity of voices that demand recognition of differences across intersections of gender, sexuality, race, and class, so that more effective coalition building might occur' (Clark 2014: 1109). These debates are of particular relevance to Indian feminist research in online spaces, which are even more likely to be dominated by those with technical and other forms of literacy but which, paradoxically, also can be used to form coalitions across geography and, possibly, culture.

Those interested in feminist new media studies could also gain from standpoint theory, which states that knowledge is situated in the material lives of social actors and that the experiences of marginalization are a means to knowledge production. Mohanty's critique of feminist research that considers women as a homogeneous, monolithic category irrespective of caste, class or ethnicity argues that this produces an almost essential 'third-world woman'. The tendency of Western academicians to speak for all women has resulted in the re-colonization (what she refers to as military – prison – cyber – corporate complex) of the already-marginalized subjects. Transnational feminists' contribution in recognizing and reaffirming 'difference' has been very valuable in opening out this discussion.

Though standpoint theory has been critiqued for tending towards essentialism, several scholars have argued that intersections of race, class and economic position give rise to multiple standpoints that are not opposed to difference – so it is not that standpoint theory is not valid; it allows the possibility of nuance based on the specificity of experience (Hesse-Biber 2013: 7). For instance, Collins's (2006: 221) concept of 'shared standpoint' and 'shared intersectionality' puts forward a framework that denies the equivalence of oppressions, stating that the effects of intersecting systems of power vary across groups, something that one would need to keep in mind when studying voices on the Net.

In the context of India, Rege's (1998) work on the Dalit feminist standpoint, pointing out the absence of Dalit women voices from both the women's movement (savarnization of womanhood) and Dalit movement (masculinization of Dalithood), could be of importance to digital media research, in terms of (a) asking questions about the kind of hierarchies that exist in cyberspace and (b) considering it is an entry point to critically engage with questions of how caste intersects with gender, urban/rural and digital divide and issues of access.

Despite the state-sponsored efforts to connect everyone digitally, Omvedt (2001) writes that Indian cyberspace is largely occupied by the Indian elite (upper caste). Ganguly (2005) and Nayar (2014) point out that only a small percentage of Dalits, that is educated Dalits enrolled in universities or those who live in cities, have access to the Internet and have made web-based Dalit activism possible – and one might expect there to be an even smaller number of women or LGBTQ members from Dalit groups online. Other forms of marginalization such as rurality, disability and minority religions would no doubt suffer from the relatively poor presence in online spaces, although we are beginning to see such groups use online forums to build networks and aggregate voices. There is little work on other aspects of digitality in marginalized communities – for instance, the ways in which the very presence and use of devices might introduce elements of agency, or subversive use of such devices.

Jo Tacchi's (2012, 2014) work on the use of mobile phones by 'low-caste marginalized women farmers' takes into account the complex interplay between caste and gender, and develops what she calls 'contextualized affordances', leading to 'meaningful mobility'. As mentioned elsewhere in this chapter (Tacchi 2014: 28), the question of *why* women interact with technologies is as important as *how* they come into such interaction. Tacchi *et al.* (2012) write that in order to understand women's interaction with technology (specifically mobile phones), researchers must also take into consideration the context/setting within which such interaction happens. She cautions that while mobile phones can be agents of change and empowerment, gender, caste, class and status (social, economic, education) act as constraints on such mobility.

There is a need to go beyond understanding women's use of technology in the limited terms of economic and social empowerment. There is also a need to distinguish between digital world(s) and the world with or alongside digital devices. What is it that women feel when they hold digital devices in their hands (Tacchi describes it an as attachment arising out of intimacy with their devices)? What spaces of expression do they open up and why do they use that particular kind of technology?

A meaningful effort to address the problem of digital divide lies not just in providing infrastructure and making it affordable but also in considering the contexts in which they are to be introduced. Cultural and religious stigma around the use of digital devices by women also have to be addressed (Whyte 2014). It is for this reason that Mansell (as quoted in Taachi 2014) suggests that there is a need to focus on people and not on technology to understand the causes and consequences of the digital divide.

Notwithstanding the very real issue of the digital divide, for those who do participate, cyberspace seems to be exactly what Haraway promised us it would be. A space with porous boundaries, no doubt, but whether such boundary confusion is only pleasurable is up for debate and further research. Recent cyberfeminist writing on digital Cartesianism, new materialities (in the context of bringing biology and body back into feminist analysis – Frost 2011: 70) and rejection of the thesis of disembodiment (especially in response to cybercrime and cyberstalking) (Williams 2009) indicates that even though the Internet offers us the possibility of realizing multiple and fragmented identities, or could be a tool of empowerment and resistance, it also carries with it the threat of suppression and reinforcement of offline hierarchies (body shaming and slut shaming: Poole 2013) on social media. Historian Mary Beard, active on Twitter, has often been the object of trolling and vicious verbal attacks on her persona as much as for her opinions (Mead 2014), while in India, feminist and Left-wing activist Kavita Krishnan constantly faces verbal violence on Facebook and other social media (Akram 2015, Roy 2015).

Others, such as transgender feminist philosopher Raewyn Connell, have made use of available online spaces to spark off or respond to a variety of issues concerning gender (*order*) (2012). Connell emphasizes the need to move beyond the totalizing and essentializing binaries of 'men' and 'women'. As Lorber (2005) too notes, there are multiple masculinities and femininities, and what prevails as the only masculinity or femininity has been conceptualized as *hegemonic masculinity* and *emphasized femininity* by Connell (1987). Of her most valuable contributions, 'social embodiment', 'ontoformativity' (Connell 2011: 1372) and gender underline the ways in which 'social realities can be created through historical time' (ibid.: 886). She defines social embodiment as a 'collective, reflexive process that embroils bodies in social dynamics, and social dynamics in bodies'. When understood this way, since cyberspace allows for people to write their realities through blogging, community building, networking and so on, they also set in motion new practices (sharing, tagging, showing: Couldry 2012), and thus, arguably, give rise to new realities.

While acknowledging Connell's point that there are a variety of feminisms, with noticeable tensions between them, we would like to recall Menon's observation that 'feminism is heterogeneous and internally differentiated across contexts. This recognition makes it impossible to articulate a simple "feminist" position on any issue, and alerts us to what Walter Mignolo has termed "diversality" – the recognition of diversity as a universal condition' (Menon 2015: 44).

Apart from the possibility of difference or its erasure in cyberspace, we may consider the categories used by Scott, Semmens and Willoughby (2001) to describe and critique the three different accounts of the 'women and the Internet' narrative by cyberfeminists, namely webbed utopia, flamed out and locked into locality. 'Webbed utopia' (genre: science fantasy) refers to the potential of these electronic feminist networks to create/open up women-friendly spaces and new social and political possibilities; 'flamed out' (genre: horror) refers to the online violence, harassment, cyber-rapists and other kinds of 'male violence'. Cyberfeminists' accounts of underrepresentation of women in online spaces and accounts of women 'still shut away at home' are categorized under the 'locked into locality' narrative.

While the cyborg – its constitution, nature and resultant politics – is one aspect of the digital feminist question, the network within which the cyborg exists – its reach, its texture, its nodes and peripheries – is another. Both aspects are of crucial relevance to global and local feminist research, as struggles for identity, community and communicative power traverse online and offline spaces constantly.

3. Feminisms in Indian cyberspace

The incorporation of the Internet and digital media into feminist activism and scholarship in India has taken the same seamless journey that it has elsewhere. Civil society groups that focused on women's rights, gender-based activism, sexual politics and so on have added these media to their existing toolkit, for social mobilization, fundraising, information dissemination and networking. Activist-academics like Nivedita Menon, Kavita Krishnan and Paromita Vohra[1] have successfully used social media platforms to create and sustain a conversation around issues of gender and gendered identities. While there is relatively less scholarship on cyberfeminism or digital feminism in the Indian context, a number of articles on various news portals talk about cyberfeminism in India. For instance, Badrinath (2011), in his interviews with cyber activists, writes about both the advantages (anonymity and ease of documentation) and pitfalls (inclusion in terms of access). Swarna Rajagopalan (member of Prajnya, a public charitable trust, and one of Badrinath's interviewees), says that Prajnya uses a variety of digital media forms to reach a large number of people at very little cost. A number of articles (Win 2010, Bose 2014, Deshpande 2015) reviewing the research provided by PUKAR (Partners for Urban Knowledge Action & Research) have highlighted the presence of a digital caste system; such accounts can inform the growing feminist scholarship on cyberfeminism in India.

Although it is difficult to state when digital feminist activism exactly took off in India, the Blank Noise project launched in 2003 by Jasmeen Patheja is perhaps one of the earliest projects to have used the Internet to counter street sexual harassment. The success of this project led to a series of activities that made use of their blog, Facebook page and Twitter handle to address 'eve teasing' and victim blaming. On last check, this volunteer-led project had four blogs, two Facebook groups, a YouTube channel and a Twitter account in an effort to create space for 'dialogue between survivors, perpetrators, and bystanders of sexual harassment'. Their work includes both online and offline discussions, testimonials, workshops and internships (Editorial, Indiaspace 2010).

Similarly, offline attacks on pub goers in Karnataka, by Hindu right-wing elements, were countered with the creation of an online Facebook group,

'The Consortium of Pub-Going, Loose and Forward Women' (and men). They planned a mass mailing of pink panties to the Shiv Ram Sene (the group behind the attacks) on Valentine's Day and vowed to flood pubs in Mangalore. Known as the 'Pink Chaddi' campaign (started by Nisha Susan in 2009), it is hailed as one of the most successful instances of digital activism. It garnered widespread attention for ushering in a new mode of non-violent *online* protest in India.

Online campaigns and groups have been labelled elitist, because of issues of access as mentioned earlier, as well as their relatively narrower range of concerns which have to do more with social liberation than the more basic issues of economic and legal empowerment. However, Kamayani, a digital activist, sees the online–offline dichotomy dissolving, with 'kractivist' approaches – 'activism which bridges the gap between online and offline activism'. Her experience as a kractivist shows that online and offline activism complement each other. Social media helped her get support on issues that 'lacked mass appeal' (Das and Chawla 2012).

Facebook groups such as Hyderabad for Feminism, Feminism in India, Indian Feminists, Indian Feministic Society, India Feminist Hub and Feminists India have created spaces for people across genders to engage with ideas of feminism. A recent article by Madabhushi, Wahalang and Joshua (2015) of Hyderabad for Feminism (a Facebook group of around 4,000 members that started as an informal group to organize a midnight march following the Nirbhaya case) in the *Economic and Political Weekly*, in fact, cautions us about the danger of leaving the Internet (social media) spaces to those who want to maintain the status quo. Based on their analysis of the activities (posts shared, liked, commented upon), conversations around issues like sexual violence, rape, marriage, marital rape, feminism, Islamophobia and alternative sexualities emerge as points that see most participation. The circulation of ideas from the Why Loiter? project online has led to it becoming something of a movement, with women across cities claiming their right to public spaces.[2]

The Slutwalk campaign or even the One Billion Rising: 2016 that called for focus on 'most marginalized women and girls' in order 'to bring about deep structural change' (http://www.onebillionrising.org/35963/one-billion-rising-2016-revolution-escalates/) and other feminist campaigns in India have used the dynamic of offline action and online mobilization to further their causes (Raman and Mukhpalkar 2014, Subramaniam 2014). More recently, the continued discourse on nationalism fuelled by student protests in Hyderabad and New Delhi has extended its audiences and participative power through social media. But the potential power and implications of new media are not only tied to radical or dissenting movements; there are also questions of political economy (commercialization, appropriation, cost, access), identity formation, community building, science and technology control (who participates in constructing the medium) and the types of social engineering and re-engineering that emerge within this space.

Any consideration of Indian feminism online cannot ignore issues of access and technological literacy; hence, researchers need to pay attention to how ideas circulate and gain credence; what role social, cultural and economic capital play in this process; and how one might use this understanding to further a more widespread feminist activism. For instance, it is arguable that the protests around the gang rape of a young woman in December 2012 that came to be known as the Nirbhaya incident gained momentum because it fanned out through the Internet from the power centre of Delhi, and was taken up by networks that already had a level of agency. On the other hand, equally horrific incidents such as the death of two young girls from a vulnerable community in Badaun, in rural Uttar Pradesh, while present on social media, led to conversations around issues of representation and circulation rather than any forceful action offline.

4. The problematics and possibilities of new media spaces: investigating socio-technical realities

One of the confounding issues in digital media studies, regardless of perspective, is the definition of this space of the Internet. Rena Bivens, in an attempt to conceptualize social media within the broader research agenda, asks:

> Are social media – like Facebook, Twitter, Tumblr, Instagram, among many others – social spaces, platforms, or networks? Are they content providers, news sources, or advertising meccas? Are they companies, technologies, websites, or mobile apps? Are they software programs, or are they sets of graphical user interfaces, huge databases, and invisible algorithms? At their roots, are social media really just source code? It appears that social media are all of these things and more – but are they all of them simultaneously?
>
> (Bivens 2015: 714)

This question must frame all other questions that a feminist researcher might ask, not only of social media but many other digital media platforms, each of which has its own set of 'affordances', that is the 'material, mediated and emotional aspects of human-technology interaction' (Nagy and Neff 2015). Maintaining that media and communication scholars have found affordances useful only because they continue to see it through a residual screen of technological determinism (Lievrouw, quoted in Nagy and Neff 2015: 2), they suggest instead using the term 'imagined affordances' that emerge between *user*'s perceptions, attitudes, expectations, *designer*'s intentions and perceptions, and physical and digital materiality and functionality of *technology*. 'Imagined' here refers to the 'expectations that users and designers have for technology that are not *fully realized* in conscious, rational knowledge but materialize in the socio-technical systems' (Nagy and Neff 2015: 1, emphasis added).

Judy Wajcman emphasizes the 'material realities' (social relations) of technology production and labours hidden in the appearance of such an object, that is the technological object. Similarly, Bivens and other scholars suggest that we abandon this notion of a technologically inclined definition in favour of a more material approach, which focuses on 'entanglements' (Bivens 2015), or the human relations that are rendered in this space. However, this would necessitate that feminist scholars look at the human – and material – factors that are implicated at various levels: those that go into the making of the space and its maintenance, as well as the relational and community dynamics that occur within it, in other words, entanglements at every locus of the technology-society-individual spectrum that is new media. She further argues, 'We ought to analyze the human and non-human, and the material and discursive together, seeking out their entanglements with one another, their co-existence, interdependence, and multiple causalities' (Bivens 2015: 715). Her own agenda is to go beyond the dominant focus on 'people, content, cultures' to looking at software as a non-human actor, in the manner that actor-network-theory might look at assemblages of human and non-human. Such an approach, she argues, would render visible the 'structural violence embedded within the programmable spaces of our lives' (Bivens 2015: 715). In the Indian context, this might be particularly productive, given the growing IT and IT-enabled services workforce that continues to be largely male. This also takes forward the groundwork laid by these feminist science and technology studies scholars, who emphasize that objects and artefacts are 'part of the fabric that holds society together; they are never merely social or technical' (Wajcman 2010: 149).

Saskia Sassen too emphasizes that 'digital space is embedded in the larger societal, cultural, subjective, economic, imaginary structurations of lived experience and the systems within which we exist and operate' (Sassen 2002: 368–369). Or as Queen puts it:

> Although advocates of Internet technology imagine an unbounded, infinite space in which to enact postmodern concepts of fragmented, multiple, liberated identities through disconnection and disembodiment,

the material reality of the (re)production – both process and product – of cyberspace is neither disconnected nor disembodied.
(Queen 2008: 472)

However, this is not to say that content and medium are irrelevant – they continue to be important focus areas for feminist research in/on digital media – but any analysis of these must be understood against the backdrop of a larger machinery that is at play in the production and circulation of that content or in the structuring of that medium.

The other important framework that we find productive in illuminating the social questions thrown up by digital media is that of Media as Practice, as elucidated by Nick Couldry (2012), and which also aligns well with Jo Tacchi's Communicative Ecologies approach (Tacchi 2006). Couldry holds that media of all kinds (digital and otherwise) have become an intrinsic part of the way modern societies live and commune, and rather than study what media do to people, we need to look at what people do to and with media. Digital media, in particular, have generated a range of practices that are symptomatic of the extent to which our lives are mediated and moderated by their affordances. 'Showing' and 'presencing' through posts and shares and likes on social media, for instance, become important social practices that mark and make our identities and communities (Couldry 2004). Tacchi, in a similar but more anthropological way, and within the framework of action research, describes the value of mapping both qualitatively and quantitatively the media forms and contexts in which the user/individual/group is situated, so as to understand people's relationships with media of various kinds (Tacchi 2006). These two approaches taken together would offer the possibility of drawing a detailed and nuanced map that combines form, content and patterns of circulation within a social space. Overlaying this approach with a feminist perspective could yield rich insights into what people say/do in digital spaces, how this links to their offline life and other parts of their lives and the networks of meaning and belonging that are created/sustained by them either through action or reaction.

5. Digital media spaces/fields and questions for feminist researchers

While the preceding discussion makes it clear that the problematics of digitality and digital media for feminism and for research in general are fluid and multifaceted, it may be useful for us to look at the broad range of questions that are suggested in this field, whether one looks at it as a flow of content, a space of being, an integrated everyday practice or a socio-technical assemblage. Of course, such a separation is only a matter of convenience, as most questions will flow across and from all these ways of understanding the Internet and other non-networked digital media.

5.1 Text/content

Digital media offer a rich variety of content for feminist research, from women's narratives on the blogosphere to hashtag feminism to discussion forums on social media. Some of these, of course, are extensions of what might be analysed offline, but digital media have spawned forms of content that raise different questions in relation to the politics of production and consumption, while also renewing questions around representation. For instance, a close reading of personal blogs of women from the Indian diaspora revealed a complex interweaving of themes that speak to identity performance, the uneasy nexus of personal and political preferences and the sense of homemaking in this online space that is simultaneously both private and public (Raman and Kasturi 2014). The blogosphere also has a significant representation of Indian feminist bloggers, offering a rich space of analysis as both text and networks. A recent study of 'domestic blogs' (women writing from domestic spaces) offers insights into the range of gender politics that express themselves through descriptions of these women's everyday lives.[3]

Others have looked at specific ways in which women speak online, as a form of either self-definition or protest. Liz Lane, for instance, looked at Twitter hashtags to understand how feminist grassroots organizations build an online feminist rhetoric (Lane 2014), while Mary Queen (2008) uses rhetorical genealogy to explore both content and context of online feminist media. Gaming research has received attention particularly in relation to violence and stereotyping of gender roles and representations of women. The way in which gender is constructed within the narrative of the game as well as its 'look and feel' and visual aesthetic are subjects of inquiry, and Indian cyberfeminist research could also raise questions related to ethnicity, class and other forms of intersectionality. The sheer volume of content produced for digital spaces – blogs, wikis, tweets, Facebook statuses and conversations, comments – warrants attention from a feminist viewpoint.

The Indian feminist conversation has expanded considerably in online spaces, as mentioned in the earlier section, offering an increasing amount of material for analysis. Not only has the ease of information generation and distribution allowed more women to become content creators, but it has also allowed more forms of content to be interconnected in interesting ways through practices of sharing, tagging, hyperlinking and embedding. These modes of interconnection allow content to be analysed perhaps in a more situated manner, revealing the dynamics of writing/reading, authoring/consuming, creating/re-creating and inscribing/erasing in the webbed relationships of a text online. The online text is both similar and different from the offline or printed text. Apart from its convergent nature (combines words, images, sound and hyperlinks, possibly also allowing interaction), it is also fluid (editable) and reachable in a variety of unconnected ways (depending on the way it is searched). For the researcher, this means that an online text can never be studied without reference to all these aspects that simultaneously locate it and render it unfixable.

5.2 Context/medium

Medium theory focuses on the nature of the spaces through/within/across which we communicate and interact and, in line with the notion of affordances, considers the ways in which media of communication structure and constrain these communications (Meyrowitz 1985). In relation to digital media, particularly the Internet, scholars such as Holmes (1997) and Papacharissi (2002) have referred to it as 'an environment' within which we communicate rather than a tool that we use to communicate. As mentioned earlier in this chapter, feminist research in digital media spaces could look at the Internet/digital environment both as a space and as a tool and, in addition, consider the ways in which the mechanisms of circulation enable and/or disable certain discourses, ways of being and forms of interaction. Couldry (2015) critiques what he calls the 'myth' of us, charging that we have taken for granted that connectivity leads to a collectivity. How might feminist networks be read, then, or interrogated, as they create, potentially, from the connective tissue of online spaces to the collectivities that are desired?

Taking the ideas of Neff and Nagy forward, can we pose questions that reveal the gendered and gendering nature of digital spaces, both networked and non-networked? In what ways does the *affording* of multispatial, multimodal and multiplexed (Banks 2015) privilege or disprivilege aspects of gender and other identity markers? Radha Hegde (2011) looks at the ways in which global flows of capital and culture affect feminist politics, and one might take similar questions to the online space, which is essentially a space of such flows (Castells 2010). This has particular resonance with transnational feminisms and the building of coalitions but carries with it the attendant risks of co-optation and appropriation. Digital phenomena such as memes and their virality, while opening avenues for the rapid mobilization of audiences for a pithily expressed idea, also carry the risk of trivialization or flattening of ideas precisely because of their rapid movement and resulting transience. What implications does this have for feminist causes that require rapid mobilization *and* sustained consideration or dialogue? A variety of questions may be raised in relation to digital literacies, social-technical-cultural capital that limits or defines access and its extent and the ways in which these literacies and forms of capital afford participation in/with digital media. Considering digital media as form and space also invites us to think about ways of engagement as audience and participant, consumer and producer, and how gendered positions structure experience along these axes.

5.3 Assemblages/socio-technical environments

We sit in front of our screens, large-, small- and mid-sized, and click or scroll or type ourselves into existence on any number of digital platforms, from simple Word processors to instant messengers to blogging communities to wikis or web pages/sites. Where we sit, who we are, the state of mind we occupy as we write, the time of day, the noise around us, our motivations and the motivations and judgements of those who surround us physically and mentally *are all factors that lurk behind our* fingertip actions. These actions translate through a series of coded mechanical and electronic processes into words, images and responses on screen. If we are logged into a network, they travel across cables and through the cloud to find a home on a computer server many miles distant, before being despatched with the next available consignment of signals to make meaning for oneself and others, to be read or acted upon or responded to. Their passage through virtuality and their rendering in other screens are structured and modified in soft and hard ways, both predictably and randomly, by electronica and human intervention, temporality, language and a host of other human and technical factors. At the heart of Latour's actor-network-theory and other approaches that recognize the intimately interconnected nature of all intention, action and reaction is the idea that every element in our conscious, material, un/subconscious and human/non-material (socio-technical) environment has a role to play – not necessarily in predetermined or instrumental ways, but in terms of creating a specific set of possibilities to work with/in.

Pulling back from the specifics of content and medium, to take the long view, allows us to see the various sets of binaries (online/offline, centre/periphery, mind/body, producer/consumer, individual/community, private/public) in relief, as it were, and understand the dynamics and the politics of the digital network in a different way. In an interchange on the website Culture Digitally, Tim Jordan, in conversation with Gina Neff and Joshua McVeigh-Schulz, discusses Latour's idea of the 'factish', which allows us to look at the complexities of networks, 'refusing the opposition between being the thing that "really acts" or is "just part of the construction"'.[4] In their view, the factish, along with the idea of affordances, can give us a way to analyse socio-technical environments without over-privileging either human or technical agency. Banks holds that from such a perspective, 'we can account simultaneously for human objects' *situation* in a network and a human's *subjective experience* of that network – a human may perceive the Self and at the same time relate to other objects in its production' (Banks 2015: 7).

Some feminist scholars, while not overtly referring to the socio-technical paradigm (if one wishes to call it that), do look at the dynamics of the online/offline, which is precisely this way, combining cyberethnography with network analysis and political economy. Anita Chan's work on network peripheries, for instance, argues that digital cultures flourish away from and in ways different from that imagined by the centre (Chan 2014). Rybas and Gajjala, articulating an 'interactive methodology based on epistemologies of doing' argue for a consideration of the specificities of offline location and online presencing in the production of digital and other selves (Rybas and Gajjala 2007). They argue that

> the action of producing oneself in such an environment is enacted through typing; however, the particular participant's agency is produced both through the act of typing and the programming that results through his/her embodied negotiations of socio-cultural literacies, memories, histories, patterns and negotiations. . . . We argue that the ethnographic praxis in technology mediated environments includes both production and consumption of technological artifacts.
> (Rybas and Gajjala 2007)

It is such an ethnographic practice that is mindful of the specificities of location in the offline, yet discerns the possibility of their erasure online, that can yield a fuller understanding of how gendered subjects participate in the digital space. The multiplicity of class–caste markers in Indian linguistic and social communities will be visible in online articulations, readable by those familiar with such markers; and an ethnographer, therefore, can draw out such identities even from behind the supposedly anonymous space of the screen.

The media ecology approach advocated by Tacchi and others (Tacchi, Kitner and Crawford 2012) takes this in a different direction, using a variety of ethnographic tools including mapping and in-depth interviews to understand the intersections of gender, development and technology with reference to digital devices and their use in an everyday context. In the context of feminist media research in India, we would do well to approach questions from such integrative frameworks, which allow for the complexities of caste, class, race and sexual orientation to be considered even as we look at content, flows, political economy and technology. For instance, what questions might arise in relation to technology use if we are interested in migrant women who have access to their husband's low-cost Chinese smartphones for a brief period in the evening and use it to view YouTube videos about maternal health? Or a gay teenager in a private boarding school who has both the social and technological literacy to intervene in online networks?

Approaching feminist questions in digital spaces from the framework of assemblages affords a rich variety of questions and possibilities of analysis and understanding, from meanings arising from content analysis to the politics of production and consumption, issues of representation and oppositional readings, to the flows of information, capital and labour that either reinforce or resist contemporary hegemonies. This echoes Mohanty's exhortation to adopt 'an analytic framework that is attentive to the micropolitics of everyday life as well as to the macro-politics of global economic and political processes' (Mohanty 2003: 509).

6. A question of method

Digital spaces, because of their fluid and hypertextual nature, present a challenge to social researchers. However, the past three decades have seen a rich evolution of anthropological, social and semiotic approaches to analysing digital texts, spaces, culture and social formation. Most of these are derived or adapted from the tools we know well – content and discourse analysis, participant and non-participant observation, ethnography – keeping in mind the character of digital spaces. Also evolving are new ideas about notions of ethical research online. What constitutes the private or the public? Is lurking an acceptable mode of non-participant observation? What are the problems associated with informed consent in a group that might have adolescents and children posing as adults? These questions must be carefully considered as we engage in online research. A more detailed discussion of the ethics of online feminist research is beyond the scope of this chapter, but we would like to flag its importance.

Table 6.1 summarizes some of the methods available to feminist digital media scholars, along with some of the questions that might be pursued in this area.

Table 6.1 An overview of approaches to feminist new media research

Nature of questions	Methodological approaches	Key readings
Identity and performance of self Production of subjectivities Issues of embodiment and disembodiment in cyberspace Anonymity and surveillance Body shaming and slut shaming	*Cyberethnography* *Interactive methodology based on epistemologies of doing* 'This methodology suggests that subjects/objects produce selves – through typing, writing, image manipulation, creation of avatars, digital video and audio – and engage in practices of everyday life at these interfaces' (Rybas and Gajjala 2007)	Rybas, N, and Gajjala, R. 2007, September. "Developing Cyberethnographic Research Methods for Understanding Digitally Mediated Identities," *Forum Qualitative Sozialforschung/Forum: Qualitative Social Research*, Vol. 8, No. 3, Art. 35, pp. 1–15. http://www.qualitative-research.net/index.php/fqs/article/view/282/619 (Accessed December 19, 2016).
Community formations and questions of 'presencing' Online mobilization and activism Empowerment and resistance	Rhetorical genealogy: 'a process of examining digital texts not as artefacts of rhetorical productions, but, rather, as continually evolving rhetorical actions that are materially bound, actions whose transformations can be traced through the links embedded within multiple fields of circulation' (475)	Gajjala, R. 2002. "An Interrupted Post-Colonial/Feminist Cyberethnography: Complicity and Resistance in the 'Cyberfield.'" *Feminist Media Studies*, Vol. 2, No. 2, pp. 177–193. Allahyari, R.A. 2013. "Becoming Feminist Cyber Ethnographers." In Nancy A. Napes and Karen Bojar (eds). *Teaching Feminist Activism: Strategies from the Field*. New York: Routledge, p. 236.

(*Continued*)

Table 6.1 (Continued)

Nature of questions	Methodological approaches	Key readings
Cybercrime – cyberstalking and sexually based violence	WebCA – Web Content Analysis – taking inputs from both discourse analysis and social network theory analysis, the WebCA is a methodologically plural paradigm that includes image, theme, feature, link, exchange, language analyses	Queen, M. 2008. "Transnational Feminist Rhetorics in a Digital World," *College English*, Vol. 70, No. 5, pp. 471–489
Suppression and reinforcement of hierarchies		Herring, S. C. 2010. "Web Content Analysis: Expanding the Paradigm." In *International Handbook of Internet Research*. The Netherlands: Springer, pp. 233–249
Who produces/creates specific technologies for what specific purposes?	Actor network theory – focuses on the connections between human and non-human entities and the creation of new entities from those interactions thereof. ANT researchers ask what it is that brings human and non-human together (paraphrasing Latour)	Latour, B. 1996. "On Actor-Network Theory: A Few Clarifications," *Soziale Welt*, Vol. 4, pp. 369–381
Why and how do women interact with technologies?		Law, J. 1992. "Notes on the Theory of the Actor-Network: Ordering, Strategy, and Heterogeneity," *Systems Practice*, Vol. 5, No. 4, pp. 379–393

Source: Compiled by the authors.

7. Conclusion

Twenty-five years into the Internet, we are still not sure whether what it yields is dystopia or utopia, particularly for those on the wrong side of any power equation. What we do know is that it is fast becoming the most pervasive of media, finding its way into our lives in many ways, and even where physical access remains unavailable, digitality of some sort (bank accounts, universal identification numbers, social welfare schemes that depend on being registered in the digital state) still frames much of existence as a citizen even if not as a private individual. In the early days of the Net, feminist scholars hailed it as a feminist utopia, allowing us to discard the burden of the gendered body and subvert gender in ways that we wished (Paterson 1998, van Zoonen 2002). However, today there is by and large recognition that we cannot really dismiss the body, even when we are completely immersed online. As Brophy points out, specifically about what she calls 'torsion' felt in relation to the materiality of the keyboard (for instance) and the immateriality of words on the screen: 'Users consistently cross between the online world and offline world, and in this liminal state participate in many interactions which involve a complex interplay of self-technology and self-other' (Brophy 2010: 941). While (dis)embodiment is only one aspect in a continuing dialogue around the interplay of gender, power and digital technologies, we need to begin by acknowledging that these are exceedingly complex concepts and their complexity is compounded by the fluid and changing nature of the technology and its pervasiveness. Who codes the structure of the Net and other digital spaces? Who directs such coding? What are the circumstances of access, use and production of information online? What sorts of networks are encouraged and how do they form (or not form)? These are all questions of power, and gender politics must be introduced into what might otherwise remain purely technical questions.

To recall Lee (2006), feminist scholarship in this area tends to focus on 'how women interact with technologies'. Equally important questions as 'why these technologies come into existence' and 'why women come into interaction with technology' need to be engaged with since evolution of information and communication technologies is not natural and that actors are actively involved in designing, creating and producing specific technologies for specific purposes. Also, there is a need for research on 'intersectional' cyberfeminism that asks pertinent questions about technologies of difference. How do categories of class, caste, race and gender intersect and what kinds of technocorporealities get created? What sort of collective subjectivities emerge from global/transnational movements such as the Slutwalk campaign and One Billion Rising? Such an effort would then bring together researchers from various disciplines, and this could then lead to the development of what Pryse (2000) refers to as 'the trans/feminist' methodology.

For digital media or cyberfeminist scholars with a specific interest in how this interplay is expressed and how it may be documented and studied in the Indian/South Asian context, we suggest that the notion of assemblages is a productive one. It is still important to examine new media content, text of various kinds, in terms of meaning, transaction, interaction and representation. It is also important to analyse the flows of content, and the affordances of digital media in terms of alignments, networks and movements. But the shadow spaces of production and consumption, the machinery of the Net, its software and hardware and the materiality of offline contexts must be acknowledged even as we focus on text and medium. A richer, more situated and ultimately more useful analysis could be drawn from such an approach.

Notes

1 Agents of Ishq, a Mumbai-based project focusing on sex and sexuality education, have a vibrant Facebook page, where posters, movies and memes are shared, generating a lively discussion around a variety of topics ranging from desire and pleasure to consent and aggression.
2 The book by Phadke *et al.* has generated a social media presence, and several city-based groups have grown around the idea, each holding its own loitering events (Phadke, Khan and Ranade 2011).
3 Kasturi (2016).
4 'Affordances, Technical Agency, and the Politics of Technologies of Cultural Production'. A Culture Digitally Dialogue between Gina Neff, Tim Jordan and Joshua McVeigh-Schulz, 23 January 2012. http://culturedigitally.org/2012/01/affordances-technical-agency-and-the-politics-of-technologies-of-cultural-production-2/. Accessed 25 January 2016.

References

Akram, M. 2015. "#Selfiewithdaughter Twitter Troll: Activist to file FIR," *The Hindu*, 2 July. http://www.thehindu.com/news/cities/Delhi/selfiewith-daughter-twitter-troll-activist-to-file-fir/article7376806.ece.

Allahyari, R. A. 2013. Becoming Feminist Cyber Ethnographers. *Teaching Feminist. Activism: Strategies from the Field*, 236.

Badrinath, T. 2011, 28 January. Using Technology for Women's Empowerment. http://www.deccanherald.com/content/132672/using-technology-womens-empowerment.html (accessed 18 December 2016).

Banks, J. 2015. "Multimodal, Multiplex, Multispatial: A Networked Model of the Self," *New Media and Society*, pp. 1–20. doi:10.1177/1461444815606616 (accessed 17 January 2016).

Baym, N. K. and D. Boyd. 2012. "Socially Mediated Publicness: An Introduction," *Journal of Broadcasting and Electronic Media*, Vol. 56, No. 3, pp. 320–329.

Bivens, R. 2015. "Under the Hood: The Software in Your Feminist Approach," *Feminist Media Studies*, Vol. 15, No. 4, pp. 714–717. doi:10.1080/14680777.2015.1053717 (accessed 7 January 2016).

Bose, N. 2014, 18 June. How Social Media Is Impacting the Indian Caste System. *IDG Connect*. http://www.idgconnect.com/abstract/8415/how-social-mediasimpacting-indian-caste-system (accessed 18 December 2016).

Brophy, J. E. 2010. "Developing a Corporeal Cyberfeminism: Beyond Cyberutopia," *New Media and Society*, Vol. 12, No. 6, pp. 929–945.

Castells, M. 2010. *The Rise of the Network Society: The Information Age: Economy, Society, and Culture* (Vol. 1). New Jersey: John Wiley & Sons.

Chan, A. S. 2014. *Networking Peripheries: Technological Futures and the Myth of Digital Universalism*. Boston: MIT Press.

Clark, R. 2014. "#NotBuyingIt: Hashtag Feminists Expand the Commercial Media Conversation," *Feminist Media Studies*, Vol. 14, No. 6, pp. 1108–1110. doi:10.1080/14680777.2014.975473.

Collins, P. H. 2006. "Some Group Matters: Intersectionality, Situated Standpoints, and Black Feminist thought." In T. L. Lott and J. P. Pittman (eds). *A Companion to African-American Philosophy*. Malden: Blackwell.

Connell, R. W. 1987. *Gender and Power*. Sydney: Allen and Unwin.

———. 2011. "Southern Bodies and Disability: Re-Thinking Concepts," *Third World Quarterly*, Vol. 32, No. 8, pp. 1369–1381. doi:10.1080/01436597.2011.614799.

———. 2012. "Transsexual Women and Feminist Thought: Toward New Understanding and New Politics," *Signs*, Vol. 37, No. 4, pp. 857–881.

Couldry, N. 2004. "Theorising Media as Practice," *Social Semiotics*, Vol. 14, No. 2, pp. 115–132.

———. 2012. *Media, Society, World: Social Theory and Digital Media Practice*. Cambridge: Polity Press.

———. 2015. "The Myth of 'Us': Digital Networks, Political Change and the Production of Collectivity," *Information, Communication and Society*, Vol. 18, No. 6, pp. 608–626.

Daniels, J. 2009. "Rethinking Cyberfeminism(s): Race, Gender, and Embodiment," *WSQ: Women's Studies Quarterly*, Vol. 37, No. 1, pp. 101–124.

Das, M. and H. Chawla. 2012. "It's a Women's World: Dedicated Activists Who Are Raising Awareness of Social Issues," *Mail Online India*, 8 March. http://www.dailymail.co.uk/indiahome/indianews/article-2111845/Meet-activists-posting-tweets-writing-blogs-raising-awareness-different-social-issues-instead-waving-flags.html (accessed on 18 December 2016).

Deshpande, M. 2015. "Boosting Digital Footprint in Rural Areas," *The Hindu*, 7 August. http://www.thehindu.com/news/cities/mumbai/boosting-digital-footprint-in-rural-areas/article7508689.ece (accessed 19 December 2016).

Editorial. 2010. "Caste Study: Blank Noise," *India Social: Social Media Open*, 27 September. http://www.indiasocial.in/case-study-blank-noise/ (accessed 21 December 2016).

Fernandez, M. and F. Wilding. 2002. "Situating Cyberfeminisms." In Maria Fernandez, Faith Wilding and Michelle M. Wright (eds). *Domain Errors: Cyberfeminist Practices*. New York: Autonomedia, pp. 17–28.

Frost, S. 2011 *The Implications of the New Materialisms for Feminist Epistemology*. The Netherlands: Springer, pp. 69–83.
Gajjala, R. 2002. "An Interrupted Postcolonial/Feminist Cyberethnography: Complicity and Resistance in the 'Cyberfield.' " *Feminist Media Studies*, Vol. 2, No. 2, pp. 177–193.
Ganguly, D. 2005. *Caste: Colonialism and Counter-Modernity, Notes on a Postcolonial Hermeneutics of Caste*. New York and London: Routledge.
Haraway, D. J. 1985. *A Manifesto for Cyborgs: Science, Technology, and Socialist Feminism in the 1980s*. Center for Social Research and Education, pp. 173–204.
———. 1991. *Simians, Cyborgs and Women: The Reinvention of Nature*. New York: Routledge.
———. 1997. *Modest – Witness@ Second – Millennium. FemaleMan – Meets – OncoMouse: Feminism and Technoscience*. Psychology Press.
Hardey, M. 2002. "'The Story of My Illness': Personal Accounts of Illness on the Internet," *Health*, Vol. 6, No. 1, pp. 31–46.
Hayles, N. K. 2008. *How We Became Posthuman: Virtual Bodies in Cybernetics, Literature, and Informatics*. Chicago: University of Chicago Press.
Hegde, R. S. 2011. *Circuits of Visibility: Gender and Transnational Media Cultures*. New York: New York University Press.
Herring, S. C. 2010. "Web Content Analysis: Expanding the Paradigm." In J. Hunsinger, L. Klastrup, and M. Allen (eds). *International Handbook of Internet Research*. Dordrecht, The Netherlands: Springer, pp. 233–249.
Hesse-Biber, S. N. (ed.). 2013. *Feminist Research Practice: A Primer*. Thousand Oaks, CA: Sage.
Holmes, David L. (ed.). 1997. *Virtual Politics: Identity and Community in Cyberspace*. Thousand Oaks, CA: Sage.
Huntemann, N. 2015. "No More Excuses: Using Twitter to Challenge the Symbolic Annihilation of Women in Games," *Feminist Media Studies*, Vol. 15, No. 1, pp. 164–167.
Kasturi, S. 2016. Writing the Everyday: A Study of Blogs by Indian Women. Unpublished dissertation, Department of Communication, University of Hyderabad.
Kingsley, S. C., A. M. L. Gray and S. Suri. 2014. Monopsony and the Crowd: Labor for Lemons. *IPP2014: Crowdsourcing for Politics and Policy-Oxford Internet Institute*, University of Oxford, Oxford, UK.
Lane, L. 2014. Feminist Rhetoric in the Digital Sphere. No. 8. Adanewmedia. org (accessed 17 January 2016).
Latina, D. and S. Docherty. 2014. "Trending Participation, Trending Exclusion?" *Feminist Media Studies*, Vol. 14, No. 6, pp. 1103–1105. doi:10.1080 /14680777.2014.975449.
Latour, B. 1996. "On Actor-Network Theory: A Few Clarifications," *Soziale Welt*, Vol. 47, No. 4, pp. 369–381.
———. 2005. *Reassembling the Social. An Introduction to Actor-Network-Theory*, by Bruno Latour, p. 316. Foreword by Bruno Latour. Oxford: Oxford University Press, September. ISBN-10: 0199256047. ISBN-13: 9780199256044, 1.

Law, J. 1992. "Notes on the Theory of the Actor-Network: Ordering, Strategy, and Heterogeneity," *Systems Practice*, Vol. 5, No. 4, pp. 379–393.

———. 2009. "Actor Network Theory and Material Semiotics," *The New Blackwell Companion to Social Theory*, Vol. 3, pp. 141–158.

Lee, M. 2006. "What's Missing in Feminist Research in New Information and Communication Technologies?" *Feminist Media Studies*, Vol. 6, No. 2, pp. 191–210.

Lister, M. 2009. *New Media: A Critical Introduction*. London: Taylor & Francis.

Lorber, J. 2005. *Breaking the Bowls: Degendering and Feminist Change*. New York: Norton.

Madabhushi, T., M. G. T. Wahalang and G. Joshua. 2015. "Locating 'Hyderabad for Feminism' in the Present Struggle against Violence," *Economic and Political Weekly*, Vol. 50, No. 44, pp. 38–46.

McClintock, L. 2015. November. Serious Games and GamerGate: The Myth of an Online Egalitarian Utopia. In Theresa Petray and Anne Stephens (eds). Proceedings of the Australian Sociological Association Conference, James Cook University, Cairns, Australia. https://www.tasa.org.au/wp-content/uploads/2015/05/McClintock-2015.pdf (accessed 21 December 2016).

McNamara, K. 2007. *Blogging Breast Cancer: Language and Subjectivity in Women's Online Illness Narratives*. Washington, DC: Georgetown University.

Mead, R. 2014. "The Troll Slayer," *New Yorker*, 1 September. http://www.newyorker.com/magazine/2014/09/01/troll-slayer (accessed 21 December 2016).

Menon, N. 2015. "Is Feminism about 'Women'?" *Economic and Political Weekly*, Vol. 50, No. 17, pp. 37–44.

Meyrowitz, J. 1985. *No Sense of Place: The Impact of Electronic Media on Social Behavior*. New York: Oxford University Press.

Mirchandani, K. 2004. "Practices of Global Capital: Gaps, Cracks and Ironies in Transnational Call Centres in India," *Global Networks*, Vol. 4, No. 4, pp. 355–373.

Mohanty, C. T. 2003. "'Under Western Eyes' Revisited: Feminist Solidarity through Anticapitalist Struggles," *Signs*, Vol. 28, No. 2, pp. 499–535.

Nagy, P. and G. Neff. 2015. "Imagined Affordance: Reconstructing a Keyword for Communication Theory," *Social Media+ Society*, Vol. 1, No. 2, pp. 1–9. 2056305115603385.

Nayar, P. K. 2014. "The Digital Dalit: Subalternity and Cyberspace." *Sri Lanka Journal of Humanities*, Vol. 37, Nos. 1 and 2, pp. 69–74. doi:http://doi.org/10.4038/sljh.v37i1-2.7204 (accessed 19 December 2016).

Omvedt, G. 2001. Untouchables in the World of IT. *Panos London Online*. http://www.itu.int/net/wsis/docs/background/themes/development/untouchables-omvedt.pdf (accessed 19 December 2016).

Papacharissi, Z. 2002. "The Virtual Sphere: The Internet as a Public Sphere," *New Media and Society*, Vol. 4, No. 1, pp. 9–27.

——— (ed.). 2010. *A Networked Self: Identity, Community, and Culture on Social Network Sites*. New York: Routledge.

Paterson, N. 1998 "Cyberfeminism." http://www.vacuumwoman.Com/Cyber Feminism/cf.txt (consulted November 2009).

Phadke, S., S. Khan and S. Ranade. 2011. *Why Loiter?: Women and Risk on Mumbai Streets*. New Delhi: Penguin Books.
Poole, E. 2013. "Hey Girls, Did You Know: Slut-Shaming on the Internet Needs to Stop," *USFL Review*, Vol. 48, p. 221.
Poster, M. 1997. "Cyberdemocracy: Internet and the Public Sphere." In D. Porter (ed.). *Internet Culture*. London: Routledge, pp. 201, 218.
Pryse, M. 2000. "Trans/Feminist Methodology: Bridges to Interdisciplinary Thinking," *NWSA Journal*, Vol. 12, No. 2, pp. 105–118.
Queen, M. 2008. "Transnational Feminist Rhetorics in a Digital World," *College English*, Vol. 70, No. 5, pp. 471–489.
Raman, U. and S. Kasturi. 2014. "Performing Transnational Identity Online: Women Blogging from Domestic Spaces." In A. Sahoo and J. G. de Kruijf (eds). *Indian Transnationalism Online: New Perspectives on Diaspora*. London: Ashgate, p. 21.
Raman, U. and D. Mukhpalkar. 2014. "From Social Media to Social Action." In N. Rajan and M. Jayaram (eds). *Covering and Explaining Conflict in Civil Society*. Hyderabad: Orient Blackswan, pp. 151–171.
Rege, S. 1998. "Dalit Women Talk Differently: A Critique of 'Difference' and towards a Dalit Feminist Standpoint Position," *Economic and Political Weekly*, Vol. 33, No. 44, pp. WS39–WS46.
Roy, S. 2015. "Trolling Dissent: Abusing Kavita Krishnan, Shruti Seth Destroys the Point of #SelfieWithDaughter," *F. India*, 1 July. http://www.firstpost.com/living/trolling-dissent-abusing-kavita-krishnan-shruti-seth-destroys-the-point-of-selfiewithdaughter-2319160.html (accessed 21 December 2016).
Rybas, N. and R. Gajjala. 2007. "Developing Cyberethnographic Research Methods for Understanding Digitally Mediated Identities," *Forum Qualitative Sozialforschung/Forum: Qualitative Social Research*, Vol. 8, No. 3 (September), pp. 1–15.
Sassen, S. 2002. "Towards a Sociology of Information of Technology," *Current Sociology*, Vol. 50, No. 3, pp. 365–388.
Scott, A., L. Semmens and L. Willoughby. 2001. "Women and the Internet: The Natural History of a Research Project." In E. Green and A. Adam (eds). *Virtual Gender: Technology, Consumption and Identity*. London: Routledge, pp. 3–27.
Spiers, E. 2015. "Performing the 'Quing of Berlin': Transnational Digital Interfaces in Queer Feminist Protest Culture," *Feminist Media Studies*, pp. 1–2. doi:10.1080/14680777.2015.1093145 (accessed 30 November 2015).
Stone, A. R. 2000. "Will the Real Body Please Stand Up?" In B. David and M. K. Barbara (eds). *The Cybercultures Reader*. London: Routledge, pp. 504–528.
Subramaniam, S. 2014. From the Streets to the Web: Feminist Activism on Social Media. http://cscs.res.in/dataarchive/textfiles/from-the-streets-to-the-web-feminist-activism-on-social-media-sujatha-subramanian-tata-institute-of-social-sciences (accessed 15 March 2016).
Tacchi, J. A. 2004. "Researching Creative Applications of New Information and Communication Technologies," *International Journal of Cultural Studies*, Vol. 7, No. 1, pp. 91–103.

———. 2006. Studying Communicative Ecologies: An Ethnographic Approach to Information and Communication Technologies (ICTs). http://eprints.qut.edu.au/archive/00004400 (accessed 7 February 2016).

———. 2014. "Being Meaningfully Mobile: Mobile Phones and Development." In J. Sarvaes (ed.). *Technological Determinism and Social Change: Communication in a Tech-Mad World*. Lanham, MD: Lexington Books, pp. 105–124.

Tacchi, J. A., K. R. Kitner and K. Crawford. 2012. "Meaningful Mobility: Gender, Development and Mobile Phones," *Feminist Media Studies*, Vol. 12, No. 4, pp. 528–537.

Van Zoonen, L. 2002. "Gendering the Internet Claims, Controversies and Cultures," *European Journal of Communication*, Vol. 17, No. 1, pp. 5–23.

Wajcman, J. 2010. "Feminist Theories of Technology," *Cambridge Journal of Economics*, Vol. 34, pp. 143–152.

Whyte, T. 2014. *Access Denied: Dismantling the Digital Caste System in the New Online Economy*. USA: Global Wire Books (Digital Publishing imprint).

Williams, R. E. M. 2009. Gender, Bodies and Cyberstalking: Embodying Theory, Developing Methodology, Doctoral thesis, Victoria University of Wellington, Wellington, New Zealand.

Win, H. I. 2010. "Social Media and the Caste System in India," *TruthOut*, 22 January. http://truth-out.org/archive/component/k2/item/87760:social-media-and-the-caste-system-in-india (accessed 21 December 2016).

7 The erotics of risk
Feminism and the humanities in *flagrante delicto*[1]

Brinda Bose

1. Introduction

To assure respect for such a female body (and indeed also such a male), the short-term work is law. The long-term work is of imagining the borderlessness that attends to borders. To be borderless is also a pleasure for the female. We cannot deny this pleasure as we are working towards a feminist world, and I do not know what to say to this audience when I am also thinking of the queer (Spivak 2015).

> . . . let the daylight break
> through capitals and monoliths,
> through the shapes that pride can make,
> find a way to trace a grand design
> with living tissue, raise a structure
> never meant to last,
> of paper smoothed and stroked
> and thinned to be transparent,
> turned into your skin.
> 'Tissue' – Imtiaz Dharker

There is a necessity for a more complex, irrational, wanton terrain – 'the borderlessness that attends to borders' – in contemporary Indian feminism, to resist structures of moral policing and panics that have grown endemic to our everyday lives in an increasingly censorious climate. Such a resistant, liminal, shadowy terrain, I suggest, may be created by a methodological shift, by deploying the humanities as a method in gender studies, via sexualities. Sexualities may offer off-roading alternatives to developmental formations of gendered modernity that confine themselves to the tested, the programmatic and the ethical; the humanities as method will give rein to the 'transgressive', a term used not lightly by Foucault in his lectures on literature, language, madness and desire[2] (2015, English translation) – though post-Foucauldian exhortations have pushed the humanities to think about greater risks, as Mackenzie Wark exhorts in his fascinating study of the Situationist International, an avant-garde literary movement:

> There are turning points where the monuments of the critical theory canon intersect with more interesting back alleys: take the streets named Lefebvre, not Lacan; Jorn, rather than Althusser; Debord, not Foucault. Or: praxis, not therapy; form, not structure; situation, not power.
>
> (2015: 159)

Such a humanities method, using sexualities as its tool, could propel Indian feminism from the logics of rights, power and punishment via an engagement with praxis, form and situation into sharp materialist-hedonist possibilities of language, pleasure, profanation, the precarious and the tragic.

The humanities, I submit, both signifies and is signified by risk – a non-sentimental, sometimes dire, sometimes glorious, impermanent, erotic risk that lets go of instincts for safety and responsibility to contend with the ephemeral, the electric, the temporal, the unhappy, the protean. All literature, cinema and art that cut us deepest remind us that nothing ultimately can be learnt or taught because nothing remains, neither the exultations nor the heart-wrenching: at best we may *carpe diem, carpe noctem* – labour, love, hate, toil and strive till death snatches us into oblivion. The humanities, thus, teaches us to shake ourselves out of grand designs to save ourselves or the world – an instinct that could stand potentially at odds with the overarching doxa of women's studies, which is, understandably enough, to rid the universe of its gendered wrongs. Humanities plots against such wrongs, retrieves the memory of minute and momentary victories against it, weeps and laughs and hides and kills in wrestling with it, and tears it threadbare looking for its meanings and signs. So what, then, may be the humanities 'method' deployed in gender studies via sexualities? It may be the dissenting method, the one that risks resistance and that stands in infinitesimal opposition to the vanguardist, the righteous, the responsible, the sacrificing and the caring because its political task is to stand apart, to probe, to think, to weigh, to crawl low into crannies and corners, to charge at windmills and even, perhaps, to fail. The humanities does not look for progress, development and victory but lives in the highs and lows of the moment, simultaneously watching and experiencing life as a kaleidoscope in its quick-shifting patterns.

There is something discomfiting in discussions about the humanities ever since we have declared it to be 'in crisis': our pronouncements are always laudatory and defensive at the same time. Helen Small's ostensible weighing in on *The Value of the Humanities* (2013) raises the same spectre. But her method of appraising the humanities is in itself a lesson in what the humanities can do. Small devotes a chapter to the 'distinction' between the humanities and other disciplines, which is particularly useful in thinking about what the humanities, in turn, can bring to other disciplines (like the social sciences, to which gender studies broadly belongs). She raises the question of 'the force of the etymological connection between "human", "humane", "humanities"' (2013: 24), which most feel is erroneous or at best partial in describing the work (or value) of the humanities, given the centrality of 'critical reflection' or 'critique' in the humanities method. Pointing out that 'the humanistic' which 'operates polemically' (2013: 29) is the most favoured characteristic that other disciplines appear to imbibe from the humanities, enjoying a 'marginal prestige', Small then makes an important intervention:

> It is in such circumstances (offensive and defensive) that the qualities by which the humanities claim distinctive purpose become most sharply apparent: their tendency to value qualitative above quantitative reasoning; their distrust of proceduralism; their greater faith in interpretative than in positivistic thinking; their orientation as much toward historical analysis as toward synchronic structural analysis; and their attention to the role of the perceiver in ascertaining even the most philosophically secure of knowledge claims; (relatedly) their interest in the specificity of the individual response (its content and style) over and above the generalized or collective response, and their concern with what can be known or understood even though it is incapable of empirical verification. On these occasions the humanities project their most forceful self-image outside the discipline, albeit at the price of temporarily losing sight of the other kinds of activity that they also foster.
>
> (2013: 29–30)

Small in this passage footnotes Gayatri C. Spivak's (2009) essay, 'Speaking for the Humanities', where Spivak makes a few similar arguments about forming 'a collective in terms of difference' (2009: 9), inserting gender in the equation:

> A humanities-style education at all levels can let us think of a more just future than rational choice. The issue is not a better definition of the human being, but an undoing of the mechanisms of the production of reason, which shows us reproductive heteronormativity is the matrix

institution. The power to synecdochtize oneself when the situation calls for it in the field of one law for all translates anyone to everyone. Judge this, please.

(2009: 10)

The humanities method, premised not upon the humane, instead 'values' the qualitative, the interpretative, the un-procedural, the historical-philosophical, the subjective, the critical as well as the instinctive even if unverifiable – and thus pushes towards unreason, the non-normative matrix. And this is where, I suggest, sexuality can do the work of the humanities in gender studies.

Sexualities, working 'transgressively' in the interstices of other fretful contemporaneities in India like caste, class, labour, family, education, economy, art, culture and ethics, need to move beyond the question of legal (sexual) rights (within marriage, against violations), which remain mostly within the arena of stable, capitalist modernities. Only a recognition of the many possibilities of sex, not all of them salubrious – as desire, risk, pain, trouble, violence and pleasure – may destabilize the nation-state's onerous march towards a conservative globalism propelled by daily censorings.

2. Perilous method of theory and praxis

At the core of this chapter lies the erotics of risk, parsed as a transgressive, perilous method of theory and praxis, signified by a bold sexuality as much as by a daring humanities. Sex as unlawful, as defiant, as irrational, as courting danger and disaster and death is a gender politics that most Indian feminisms have been inclined to skirt. As Small and Spivak have agreed, the humanities are not to be interpreted as the study of and for humanism, the humane and the humanizing as they often are.[3] In India, the excessive and progressive did come together culturally at certain historical moments, when the arts aspired to become a part of its political canvas – until it was systematically removed by the moral claims of progressive politics. The humanities, as a method, can through sexualities push for interventions in gender studies that hang on a 'borderlessness' – un-procedural, interpretative, historical-philosophical, qualitative, aesthetic, subjective and critical even when unverifiable. One of the first allowances that the humanities opens up for play, then, is a refusal to be restricted by borders imposed by social science disciplines that may be predicated upon ethnographic, located data – 'Indian' contexts to talk about the discipline of gender studies in India, let us say.

I will draw upon resources of critical thinking and praxis without such restraint, attempting to 'do' a humanities/borderlessness turn upon the logics of social science research, talking about India but straying outside its geopolitical boundaries and talking about the contemporary but time-travelling across centuries to find languages and images that we can converse and argue with. What I would like to think about is what might happen when we do this turn on any area or issue in gender studies via sexualities, probing questions of marginality, labour, caste, marriage, rape, desire, family, state, law, entertainment, censorship, education, work, the market and the globe. The humanities turn demands that we allow ourselves a freedom for unfettered-ness, to think about form and structure, about words, images, signs and their multiple shifting meanings and to follow the aesthetic imagination as it soars to fantasy and dives to despair and murder and death. I will traverse four roughly charted territories of the humanities – language, madness and negation; pleasure, ethics and politics; profanation, labour and flânerie; pleasure, precarity, tragedy and revolution – via thinkers and artists, theory and praxis, form and situation, identifying signals by which sexualities can arouse and provoke a dormant gender studies into a politics of the erotic. The humanities studies and interrogates structure and form and content while resisting structure and form and content; its politics lies in the aesthetics of non-conformism and the non-conformism of aesthetics at once.

3. 'Isn't it the most liquid book ever written?' – the languages of reckless voyaging

John Berger, essayist par excellence of the visual and the literary, writes of his first encounter with what is arguably the foremost novel of the 20th century:

> I first sailed into James Joyce's *Ulysses* when I was fourteen years old. I use the words *sailed into* instead of *read* because, as its title reminds us, the book is like an ocean; you do not read it, you navigate it.
>
> . . . The book had been given to me by a friend who was a subversive schoolmaster. . . . When he gave the book to me, I believed it was illegal in Britain to own a copy. In fact this was no longer the case (it had been) and I was mistaken. Yet the 'illegality' of the book was for me, the fourteen-year-old, a telling literary quality. And there, perhaps, I was not mistaken. I was convinced that legality was an arbitrary pretence. Necessary for the social contract, indispensable for society's survival, but turning its back on most lived experience. I knew this by instinct and when I read the book for the first time, I came to appreciate with mounting excitement that its supposed illegality as an object was more than matched by the illegitimacy of the lives and souls in this epic.

> ... This book had that immensity. It did not pretend to it; it was impregnated by it, it flowed through it. To compare the book with an ocean again makes sense, for isn't it the most *liquid* book ever written?
> (2003: 467–468)

Berger, recalling an adolescent reading encounter with all the languid, *liquid* sexuality of a feline stretching in late afternoon sunshine, embodies here the sort of physical and mental immersion in the very materiality, the felt language of literature that enacts the kind of transgression Foucault had talked of. The connection between the potent charge of language and the language of sex is intrinsic to this experience; it is what creates immediacy of effect and affect, both. As we know from *Ulysses*, however, and all other works of art that are so characterized, the sexual is rarely either purely romantic or logical. Foucault in *Language, Madness, Desire* characterizes the 'nature of literature' by figures of transgression, repetition, the forbidden, death and the simulacrum through his readings of Proust, Sade, Chateaubriand, Cervantes, Racine, Diderot and others, finally coming to rest at (what else but) Joyce's *Ulysses*, echoing Berger in many ways (Foucault 2015: 52–65); 'All are figures,' Foucault pronounces, 'I wouldn't say negative, but without any positive aspect at all, in which the being of literature seems to me to be fundamentally torn apart' (2015: 58). Those of us who respond to literature and other arts in this way, looking to be 'fundamentally torn apart', cannot subscribe to an idea of the humanities as benign, healing and restful. It is this torn-apartness that I would wish sexualities to bring to gender studies, drawing upon the madness of desiring that the humanities captures and releases in endless cycles.

There is a tearing apart that is born into language through images. Kumkum Sangari, in her recent study of the socio-economies of sex selection and commercial surrogacy in India, employs a thread of imagery indicated by her title, *Solid: Liquid, a (Trans)national Reproduction Formation* (2015), that allows the reader to find a visceral simulacrum in her otherwise dispassionate, complex findings:[4]

> The fixity of the social body may be gelatinous at its core, while the postsocial body may harden into a fixed position of flexibility. The apparent solidity of the social body and the liquidities of the postsocial body may constitute a dialectic: a dialectic that seizes the duality of capital which compulsively contains or destroys the potential it creates.
> (2015: 155)

Reading Sangari's deployment of this particular set of images (solid:liquid) with a humanities eye bestows upon this leftist-feminist appraisal of the labouring body both the poetic and the erotic; a quickening pulse accompanies our mind picture of a liquefying postsocial body in a dialectic embrace with the solidly social body, and our imagination does a minute's jig in sheer pleasure.

There is no doubt that many philosophers and literary critics perceive the humanities differently, even when thinking in terms of negation. Alain Badiou, in *The Age of the Poets*, his recent book-length discussion of poetry and prose, makes a complicated reading of a fragment of a long poem by Pier Paolo Pasolini, first providing a background for the revolutionary Marxist poet-filmmaker in which he chronicles how his homosexual desire for young poor workers in suburban Rome determined his art and his politics.[5] He analyses a part of Pasolini's poem 'Victory', about young men at war and the impossibility of political hope at a time when they can no longer accept the leadership of the Communist Party and 'become by necessity barbarian and nihilistic people, exactly like the young unemployed of the suburbs' (2014: 89), drawing connections between Pasolini's bitter rejection of war, his memories of his young brother Guido being killed in battle as a resistant fighter and his troubled homoerotic relationships with the poor workers and the unemployed young men in Rome.

> little by little in the barbaric breasts of the sons,
> hate becomes love of hate,
> burning only in them, the few, the chosen.
> Ah, Desperation that knows no Laws!
> Ah, Anarchy, free love
> Of Holiness, with your valiant songs!
> (Badiou 2014: 89)

'The poem', says Badiou, 'is a manifesto for true negation' (2014: 90). However, since Badiou believes that negation 'reconciles destruction and subtraction' and that 'great poetry is always an anticipation, a vision, of the collective future' (2014: 91), he reads Pasolini's grave lament as one from which we can learn that 'to defend the new kingdom of emancipatory politics, we cannot radically exclude all forms of violence', we have to learn 'something of nihilistic subjectivity. The world is not made of law and order, but law and desire' (2014: 92).

But then law and desire are foes, and from Pasolini's excruciatingly painful life and death, lit brightly but only intermittently by firefly-flashes of passion and tenderness, it is difficult to extract such a vision of redemption, what Badiou calls 'subtraction'.

Suniti Namjoshi, Indian-Canadian lesbian-feminist-fabulist, roams the beastly world for uncanny revelations about (in)human meetings, partings, wishes:

> In the forest
> both fawn and I
> lose ourselves.
> . . . I want to go back to that lost forest
> where metaphors mix,
> rub shoulders with each other,
> and everything turns to everything else.
> (Namjoshi 2012: 184)

Both Pasolini and Namjoshi, of times, minds and lands apart, speak of and with a desolation that perhaps only poetry can bring to imperilled life and love. They speak about language that then tells us about living and dying, at that still point 'where metaphors mix'. There are rarely any 'subtractions'/affirmations that survive, and yet the poem holds. Such is the treacherous edge that the humanities teaches us to walk on.

4. Diving into politics: a materialist-hedonist humanities and an ethical feminism

In this inference of the work of the humanities, I would like to establish a dialogue in difference with two recent articles in the *EPW* by Lata Mani. What I wish to deploy here is a methodological tool of the humanities which Helen Small flagged as 'attention to the role of the perceiver in ascertaining even the most philosophically secure of knowledge claims; (relatedly) their interest in the specificity of the individual response (its content and style) over and above the generalized or collective response' (Small 2013). In 'Writing the Present', on 'the specific and productive contribution' that the arts and humanities can make to current social science writing (in which she considers knowledge to be 'instrumentalized' and language 'transactional'), Mani makes an impassioned plea for revitalizing political discourse in contemporary India by drawing upon the differently constituted process of critical thinking in the arts and humanities (Mani 2015: 24–27). If the object of our speculations appears the same, we come to this point via different trajectories. The reason for this difference lies in what I see as the materialist-hedonist charge of the humanities, while Mani desexualizes the humanities to etherize it to a higher, ethical, non-material and integrated plane. There is a holism here, not refraction, and therefore a fear of uncertainty and the sensual which for me is the life blood of the humanities, distinguishing it from the social sciences. This distinction will become clearer when put in conjunction with another essay by Mani on sexualities and Indian feminism.

There is no doubt that Mani's phenomenological intervention in this discourse on humanities and social science critical praxes is important and instructive. Criticizing all writing about 'the present' as demonstrating 'positivist, instrumental, technical – managerial and teleological thinking', Mani regrets how it has

> anaesthetize[d] us to the violence of neo-liberalism, making it seem rational and historically inevitable. The challenges to power have primarily cast their critique within the dialectic of subjugation and resistance, with the affective dimension being comprised of a potent mix of rage, nostalgia, fear and a modicum of hope.
>
> (2015: 24)

She then exhorts that an injection of arts/humanities critical thinking will enable us 'to represent the density, particularity and rich complexity of lived experience' that is abstracted out of current writing about the present, and presents in detail two 'experiments' with multiple art forms that capture this richness of the everyday in the way she would advocate the present to be represented – a video-poem on nocturnal sounds in the city and a multi-genre collection of responses to life on a city street as a development project destroys its regular rhythms. I have no argument with Mani's felt need to record those aspects of urban night and street life destroyed by the manic pursuit of a neoliberal agenda – 'urban life is teeming, not merely endangered', she avows[6] – but this is followed by an abstracting out of all that appears to her to be unseemly in urban life, making it a spiritual life experience.

The 'arts and the humanities could serve to aerate our language', Mani says, and I would agree if that aeration would include the thick sludgy waters of our city rivers, but it appears not: 'The language of social science and that of political discourse has lost the capacity to move us. We can knowledgeably debate poverty without our bodies and hearts physically sensing the true meaning of hunger' (2015: 27). There is a claim here for the pure uplifting power of the arts in opposition to the alleged philistinism of the social sciences, which appears discomfiting on two counts: first, that it seems to deliberately eschew anything of the city that is distasteful by dismissing it as part of a disabling modernity; second, that in claiming this function for the humanities, it de-politicizes the arts and humanities into a romantic Wordsworthian haven of poetic space that even the social sciences are not privy to, let alone the sciences. This seems to me to swing close to the University Grants Commission diktat to have students of science/technology institutes take humanities courses in order to 'de-radicalize' them: it tends towards a dangerous voiding of politics in the humanities, what I would also call, in shorthand, a de-sexing.

In an earlier article in the *EPW*, 'Sex and the Signal-Free Corridor: Towards a New Feminist Imaginary', Mani had also taken issue with modernity and the neoliberal city and ridiculed its unethical nexus with sexual freedom:

> Neo-liberal ideology aggressively constructs the subjecthood of the modern individual as one in which sex, desire and consumption are thoroughly fused.... When we argue against vigilantism solely on the basis of a rights discourse we naturalise sexual desire.... We fail to confront neo-liberalism's valorisation of sex and sexual desire and the implications of this for the relationship of women and men to their bodies, sexuality and sexual health.
>
> (2014: 28)

My argument against vigilantism would be framed not on the basis of a rights discourse but as a politics, a politics claimed for both sexual desire/ freedom and the humanities. Mani writes, 'Politics is the struggle for a form of life that is ethical, fulfilling and sustainable.' I would rather go with Jacques Rancière's oppositional definition of the political as *dissensus*, in which politics is an interruption, a destabilizing and a resistance to the kind of 'ethical, fulfilling' *distribution of the sensible* that Mani seems to be advocating.

Rancière says in his chapter on 'The Ethical Turn in Aesthetics and Politics' in *Dissensus*, 'This tendency of differences in politics and right to disappear in the indistinctness of ethics is also defining of a certain present of the arts and of aesthetic reflection' (2010: 193). It is this disappearance into ethics – for politics, for feminism and for the humanities – that makes me sceptical; I neither believe that politics operates solely for deepening an engagement with ethical and existential concerns, nor do I see such an easy conflation of the 'sexuality-freedom-pleasure-danger nexus' with neoliberalism. Neoliberalism allows no space for the danger and violence of sexuality, its irrational and irresponsible desiring and its suffering and poverty, which are, I think, at the crux of demanding space for its complexities. Mani recognizes that the neoliberal consumptive argument elides the non-moneyed classes but refuses to bring the non-moneyed communities and their sexualities into the equation still: how would the 'ethical and the existential frames' work for those who do not have capital but do have sexual desires? How about sex workers? How about the transgendered who use their visible 'other' sexual markers to beg at street corners? How does the sexual economy work outside the neoliberal urban-educated upper-middle-class framework that appears to be the only lens by which feminist sexual politics is viewed here?

Ethics and spirituality may be eschewed by some because of a transgressive politics, or by others simply because it is a luxury that is irrelevant to their everyday lives. An ethical feminism or an ethical humanities, for that matter, which does not address crucial questions of sexuality and labour, sexuality and class/caste/location cannot claim to be a feminist imaginary that is politically conscious, though it may be politically correct. It is interesting to place Gayatri Spivak's argument for an 'ethico-political' humanities practice here:

> I base social theory on gender. I say that ethical theory, a theory of unconditional ethics, can be practically taught through the literary-philosophical. I base political intervention on a performative contradiction that must presuppose what it wants to achieve. Supplementing work is persistent, I say, and define activism as imaginative training for epistemological performance; in labor movement work, ecological work, among the poor. The thing dearest to my heart is teaching the intuitions of democracy through an understanding of the meaning of the right to intellectual labor, on top as well as below.
>
> (Spivak 2015)

Spivak is concerned with the ethics of a political commitment to a gendered social justice on the ground. One wonders, however, what ethics would stand up to questions of labour and pleasure around the sex worker, for example, for either Mani or Spivak. It is at sex work, pornography and queer sex that Indian feminism will finally have to come to roost for a decisive face-off. The practice of non-normative sexualities is not in itself a radical act, yes, but it has potential for a radical politics when it makes assertions linked with class, caste and labour. It is that transformed sexual-political being that the humanities method creates space for in gender studies, because it does not balk at the liminal and the libidinal.

5. 'The profanation of the unprofanable is the political task of the current generation'

At the end of *Profanations*, Giorgio Agamben's poetic, bristling set of short commentaries on literary and visual texts, he recounts a tale of Don Quixote who lunges forward onto a movie screen to slash it to pieces at the sight of a woman (Dulcinea?)[7] in danger, in the presence of an astonished, enraged audience. Agamben then asks rhetorically,

> What are we to do with our imaginations? Love them and believe in them to the point of having to destroy and falsify them. . . . But when in the end, they reveal themselves to be empty and unfulfilled, when they show the nullity of which they are made, only then can we pay the price for their truth and understand that Dulcinea – whom we have saved – cannot love us.
>
> (2007: 93–94)

Most of the work on sexualities in Indian feminism has not been marked in the least by significations of imagination, risk and pleasure – despite repeated revelations that the subject (woman/Dulcinea) whom it has tried to save often needs an understanding beyond rescue and rehabilitation. In their introduction to *Intimate Others*, an anthology of essays on 'marriage and sexualities in India', Sen, Biswas and Dhawan write grimly of the patterns they have studied through decades of economic and socio-political change: 'The age of open economies and global markets has been marked by the transition of sex as (re)production to sex as consumption' (2011: 1). Indeed, the market economy affects all intimate relationships, from the licit to the illicit, and also ties them to questions of money and labour. But not everything sexual and imaginative is consumptive. Jacques Rancière's *Nights of Labor/Proletarian Nights* provides us with a gripping narrative of the 19th-century factory worker who dreams.

The main subject of this book is those nights wrested from the normal sequence of work and sleep. They were imperceptible . . . where already the impossible was being prepared, dreamt and seen. . . . They were nights of study and intoxication.

> What do their lines of poetry or even the prose in their 'workers' papers' amount to compared with the multitude of day-to-day practices, of acts of oppression and resistance, or of complaints and struggles at the workplace and on the streets? This is a question of method, which tries to link cunning with 'straightforwardness'.
>
> (1982: 248)

It is indeed a question of method. What does the factory worker and the sex worker dream of? What is the poetry they produce in the interstices of their daily/nightly 'work', whether they choose to do it or find themselves in it? In *Seeing Like a Feminist*, Nivedita Menon dismisses the theory that sex workers are deprived of choice, as much as choice operates within a limited set of conditions at a particular time and place. 'Quite simply, sex work is an economically attractive option. . . . The "choice" to do sex work is no more or less constrained than the choice of any other work is under capitalism' (Menon 2012: 183–184). Sex workers Shikha Pal and Mala Das of Sonagachi, Calcutta's red-light district, in Shohini Ghosh's documentary *Tales of the Night Fairies* (2002) insist amid shared raucous laughter and blushes that a sex worker can indeed enjoy what she does, in as much as some of us enjoy the work we get paid for. This would earn her the epithet of *besharam* ('without shame'), to use Pratiksha Baxi's term, like any other woman getting pleasure from sex or flaunting her sexiness:

> It is really very simple. In India, for women to reclaim their rights whatever their class, caste or community, amounts to attracting the allegation of being without shame. Surely we have all been *besharam* for a good part of our lifetimes, and one would hope that we will continue to be – as long as being autonomous amounts to being *besharam* in our culture?
>
> (Baxi 2011)

6. The risky imaginative leap

The connections across class, caste or community, as Baxi formulates it, are emergent – and have percolated to youth movements and campaigns across our cities: *Slut Walk*, *Take Back the Night*, *Why Loiter?* and *Pinjra Tod (Break the Cage!)* are taking on the mantle of fighting battles within and without women's studies in India today.[8] What conjoins these movements is risk-taking and the pleasure embedded in that experience: if all women, whether at university or at jobs, are 'workers', participating in the movements for freedom all around them, then their dreams, their poetry and their graffiti are equivalent to the dreams that Rancière's factory workers dream and the poetry they scribble, however far removed they may be from the working-class ethos in their middle-class comforts and insecurities. Humanities invites us to take that risky imaginative leap.

Walter Benjamin, best-known interpreter of the flâneur, that laconic stroller of streets, draws upon the poetry of Baudelaire to portray this saunterer as one who understood the intricacies of modern city life with ease and depth at once. But Charles Baudelaire, the original flâneur, chronicled in detail the people of the streets who held him in thrall, from the dandy to the prostitute; he sketched the latter glitteringly in an essay in *The Painter of Modern Life*:

> In that vast picture gallery which is life in London or Paris, we shall meet with all the various types of fallen womanhood – of women in

revolt against society – at all levels. First we see the courtesan in her prime, striving after patrician airs. . . . Descending the scale, we come down to the poor slaves of those filthy stews . . . hapless wretches, subject to the most extortionate restraint, possessing nothing of their own, not even the eccentric finery which serves as spice and setting to their beauty. . .

Nothing but pure art, by which I mean the special beauty of evil, the beautiful amid the horrible. . . . It is their moral fecundity which gives these drawings their special beauty. They are heavy with suggestion, but cruel, harsh suggestion.

(Baudelaire 1964: 37–38)

And then there is aura, as Benjamin puts into words what makes aura poetic:

Eyes staring at one's back/Meeting of glances/Glance up, answering a glance

What is aura? . . . To experience the aura of an appearance or a being means becoming aware of its ability [to pitch] to respond to a glance. This ability is full of poetry.

. . . As much aura in the world as there is still dream in it.

(2015)

The case of the ban on Mumbai bar dancers in 2005 is moot for a feminist grappling with questions of sexuality, labour, aura, glance and dream. Flavia Agnes, feminist lawyer and activist who has both challenged and negotiated legal limitations on women's pleasure and sexual assertiveness, is known for her strong interventions throughout this case, which has witnessed a chequered history.[9] Agnes has insisted upon guarantees of safety, both in labour laws and in guarding against physical exploitation; when the ban was first lifted by the Bombay High Court in 2007, Agnes wrote:

A glaring discrepancy in the arguments advanced by the state was in the realm of the agency of the sexual woman. At one level, the state and the pro-ban lobby advanced an argument that the dancers are evil women who come to the bars to earn 'easy money' and corrupt the morals of the society by luring and enticing young and gullible men. This argument granted an agency to women dancers. But after the ban, the government tried to justify the ban on the ground of trafficking and argued that these women lack an agency and need state intervention to free them from this world of sexual depravity in which they are trapped. Rather ironically, the anti-ban lobby also framed its arguments within this accepted 'victim' mould: single mothers, traditional dancers with no other options.

It was important for the anti-ban lobby to make a clear distinction between the dancer/entertainer and the streetwalker, and base its arguments squarely upon the fundamental right to dancing. The eroticism inherent in dancing had to be carefully crafted and squarely located within 'Indian traditions' and the accepted norm of 'Bollywood gyrations' and not slip beyond into sexual advances. The emphasis had to be for a right to livelihood only through dancing and not beyond. . . . So while we were exposed to one aspect of their lives which had all the problems – of parenting, poverty, pain and police harassment – we must admit that this was only a partial projection, an incomplete picture. We could not enter the other part of their world in which they are constantly negotiating their sexuality, the dizzy heights they scale while they dance draped in gorgeous chiffons studded with sequins. Did the problem lie with us and the picture we wanted to paint for them? Well, perhaps yes.

(2007: 174–175)

As Agnes sharply deduces, the pro-ban and anti-ban lobbies had split along the fault-line of the moral and the social: while the anti-ban lobby spoke of labour and livelihood, the pro-ban group pushed to distinguish the bar dancer from the streetwalker. Georges Bataille tries to work through this allure (inadequately, he believed) in a section on beauty in his tortured treatise on *Eroticism*: 'We know that possession of the object we are afire for is out of the question. . . . Beauty is its meaning, what gives it its value, and indeed the element that makes it desirable' (2012: 142). His elucidation of this beauty (in woman) is contradictory, first asserting that 'any suggestion of the animal in human form is repugnant . . . the more ethereal the shapes and the less clearly they depend on animal reality . . . the better they respond to the fairly widespread image of the desirable woman' (2012: 143) and then suggesting that the obverse is true as well: 'The beauty of the desirable woman suggests her private parts, the hairy ones to be precise, the animal ones. Instinct has made sure that we shall desire these parts' (2012: 143–144). The answer to the bar dancer dilemma that Agnes points to may be embedded in the contradiction that Bataille apprehends in his contemplation on eroticism, that the ethereal and the animal must coexist in the genetics of desire. But Rancière's dreaming factory workers in *Nights of Labor* perhaps speak more eloquently to the question that Agnes is raising here about the bar girls: the dizzying sexual beauty of their dancer-selves, those moments of immersive pleasure in chiffons and sequins that are sheer poetry irreducible to monetary benefit, choice, carnal pleasure, victimhood, right and all other vanguardist arguments – this is what the saviour-activists had mostly failed to grasp. This was the moment that transgresses reason and sound moral wisdom, and enters, however hesitantly, guiltily, the arena of contradictory affect, imagination and materiality that the humanities grasps and struggles with daily.

7. 'Not happiness, but hideous grief': the politics of pleasure, precarity, tragedy and revolution

There is at least one understanding of the humanities that shares with fraught sexualities an antinomian spirit, rejecting socially established morality and courting danger for pleasure and death. It is that segment and such a nexus that I invoke for the humanities method in contemporary gender studies in India, in a climate that is ever darkening under the threat of bigoted censorships and incarcerations. The struggle to find a space for difference is continuous. In February 2016, Hansal Mehta's film *Aligarh*, based on the real-life story of Professor Shrinivas Ramchandra Siras of Aligarh Muslim University who was hounded out of the campus for his (homo)sexual preference and died soon after under mysterious circumstances, released to public acclaim. It is significant in the historical context that Siras was so cruelly tortured at a time (2010) when Section 377 of the Indian Penal Code which criminalizes homosexuality had found a brief respite. According to Shohini Ghosh (2016), the film is 'a cautionary tale about the dangers of assenting to live by the dictates of public morality, reiterating instead the importance of constitutional morality'. It is just as significant, then, that Section 377 was reinstated by the Supreme Court in 2013, throwing possible faith in constitutional morality in jeopardy again.

Even before *Aligarh* (2016) released nation-wide, its official trailer was given an A certificate, and upon the film's release its screening was 'unofficially' banned in Aligarh, after a fringe group complained that it reflected badly on the city. While the district authorities denied that they had declared a ban, almost no movie theatre in Aligarh was screening the eponymous film three days past its release, and at least one theatre that it had opened in pulled it after a day. The inferences and implications of a potent public morality aided often by a dank constitutional morality are obvious.

Aligarh raises an obvious comparison with Deepa Mehta's *Fire* (1997), coming two decades after the film that was held responsible for triggering a public consciousness of, and support for, the then-fledgling lesbian-gay-bisexual-transgender movement in the country – a film that showcased lesbian sex in richly textured scenes of lovemaking between its two female protagonists. Its trailer had tracked the flames of desire that brought two women together in a conservative middle-class joint family in the capital city. *Fire*'s explicit love scenes had escaped the censor's scissors but was tripped up by what was perhaps one of the first public Hindutva protests against the 'denigration of Indian culture' to register on a national scale. In 20 years, public morality has joined hands with state/constitutional morality to mount an increasingly impenetrable barrier to freedoms of intimacy. While a tense, tangible sorrow permeates *Aligarh*, there is a strange sense of inevitability about its inglorious end that appears to deny any possibility of rage or revolution.

In this inevitability, perhaps, lies the richest and most difficult traction that the humanities may bring to gender studies through a wrestle with sexualities in which pleasure, risk, danger and desire bring both ecstasy and death. Even as we talk about law and rights and health and ethics, of public and constitutional rights and wrongs, we know it, just as Rahel and Estha knew it in Arundhati Roy's *The God of Small Things*:

> But what was there to say?
> Only that there were tears. Only that Quietness and Emptiness fitted together like stacked spoons. Only that there was a snuffling in the hollows at the base of a lovely throat. Only that a hard honey-colored shoulder had a semicircle of teethmarks on it. Only that they held each other close, long after it was over. Only that what they shared that night was not happiness, but hideous grief.
> Only that once again they broke the Love Laws. That lay down who should be loved. And how. And how much.
> (Roy 1997: 152)

Roy's is the realm of the immediate and the political, in which sex meets caste and class and incest in loops of desire, pleasure, pain and death. We saw it staring women's studies in the face in India at the end of 2015, in the resignation of a group of active members of the Democratic Students Union (DSU), a constituent of the Revolutionary Democratic Front, at Jawaharlal Nehru University, Delhi, alleging that there was within the movement a sustained attempt to suppress any engagement with troubling questions pertaining to gender and patriarchy. Eleven members of the DSU distributed a detailed statement outlining the ways in which intimate relationships are dismissed within the organization as 'sexual anarchy' credited to an imperialist foreign culture.[10] The long statement, in the manner, almost, of the avant-garde manifesto (also published subsequently as 'Revolutionary Sexism – A Critique of Indian Maoism'), addressed their belief that 'with such a patriarchal, feudal-moralist, male-protectionist and patronizing understanding on the crucial question of gender and patrarichy [*sic*], there can no democratization or revolutionary social transformation' (DSU Members' Statement 2015). In a charged rhetorical raging lament, the group of 11 challenged the possibility of a true Marxist-Leninist 'revolution' if the organization remained marooned in an arcane and debilitating sexism.

What is instructive here is that the statement makes a strong and serious allegation that leftist revolutionary thinking largely refuses to acknowledge gender/sexuality as a political category. It is also a corrective reminder to those who assume that reactionary gender politics in the everyday is an exclusive marker of the right. As the earlier contingency unveils, there is really a miniscule divide between those claiming that sexuality is a neoliberal preoccupation of consumptive self-indulgence and those condemning gender relations as the vulgar outcome of an imperialist culture that promotes sexual anarchy through instruments of globalization. The air is clouded by fear and anxiety, a terror of the uncontrollable, of the anarchic, the marvellous and the deviant, which feminism ought rather to embrace in a more robust engagement. Over and over, we see the erotic – desire, pleasure – in a precarious struggle with tragedy, pain and death. This is art, no less – and in this age of sedition, it calls urgently for the recognition of feminist sexuality politics as a revolutionary aesthetics. For

> This is no age for slow desires,
> Desired on lengths of idle beds
> Beside indifferent faces,
> For no smile, however fond, can
> Settle time like a paper weight.
> Kamala Das (2014)

Notes

1 This chapter was published in the *Economic and Political Weekly*, Review of Women's Studies, vol. 51, no. 18, 30 April 2016, pp. 64–71. We are grateful to the editor, *EPW*, for permission to republish this chapter in this volume.
2 Foucault talks about literature as a language of transgression, which is also a simulacrum of the book, directing aggression against the 'feminine essence of the book' – 'Literature is transgression, literature is virility of the language compared to the femininity of the book. . . . What can literature be, precisely, other than the frail, posthumous existence of language?' – in lectures on 'Literature and Language' at Brussels in December 1964 (Foucault 2015: 64–65).
3 The University Grants Commission in January 2013 instructed Indian science and technology institutes to offer humanities courses to its students in order to 'stop radicalization of youth' of the country, defusing any subversive power of the humanities by relegating it to a moral 'soul'-training exercise (reported extensively in *Firstpost*, dated 1 March 2013, and other newspapers and websites). While acknowledging that in contemporary political speech, 'radicalization' has come to mean only the nurturing of potential terrorists rather than the uncompromising pursuit of social and

economic reforms, one can yet deconstruct this myth of morality around the humanities, challenging the propositions that they are either containable by regulation or useful for containing the boldness of youth.

4 Kumkum Sangari in her study of the relation between sex selection and commercial surrogacy in India uses solid and liquid as signifiers:

> It can also sketch the volatile relations between the family, market and state, and describe the cords that bind migrant with embedded labour, the national with the transnational, the social with the postsocial body. The solid may not always be old, the old may be becoming liquid – patriarchal family forms can be liquescent, while the state and market can act as either solvents or hardeners of patriarchal practices.
>
> (2015: 3)

5 Pasolini is also well known for the relationship between his private life and public convictions. Not only was he gay, but this was a part of his political vision . . . he knew perfectly well that desire – and in his own case his desire for young poor workers of the suburbs of Rome – is not independent of our ideological choices. Once more, the task is to inscribe sexual desire in the political negativity not as a purely subversive and destructive feature, but as a creative displacement of the line that separates the individual subjectivity from the collective one.

(2014: 86)

6 The everyday sounds of the night: the symphony of crickets, frogs, the hoot of the owl, the rustling of leaves, the footfalls of humans, snippets of conversation trailing in the wind. . . . Yet the imagined soundscape of the city, or of nightlife as we tend to think of it, hardly ever summons these facts.

(Mani 2015: 25)

7 'Dulcinea del Toboso' (real name Aldonza Lorenzo) is a fictional character who is unseen in Miguel de Cervantes's novel *Don Quixote*. Seeking the traditions of the knights-errant of old, Don Quixote finds a true love whom he calls Dulcinea. She is a simple peasant in his hometown, but Quixote imagines her to be the most beautiful of all women. At times, Quixote goes into detail about her appearance, though he freely admits that he has seen her only fleetingly and has never spoken with her. Two contrasting descriptions of Dulcinea in are testament to the necessary havoc that infatuated love wreaks.

8 Phadke, Khan and Ranade write of the Why Loiter? campaign in Mumbai:

> Loitering is perceived to be risky . . . when women demand the freedom to take risks instead of the guarantee of safety, we are implicitly rejecting this conditional protection in favour of the unconditional right to public space . . . we suggest that they deal very firmly with the aggressors of that violence and not tie up the victims of violence in endless blame games, inane dress codes, and relentless moral policing.
>
> (2011: 181)

9 The ban on bar dancers in Maharashtra has witnessed many decisions both in favour of the ban and against it at the state high court and the Supreme Court since 2005. A newspaper reported on 16 October 2015:

Acknowledging the right of women bar dancers to follow their profession, the Supreme Court suspended Thursday a legal provision banning dance performances in Maharashtra and directed the state government to grant licenses to the bar owners without insisting on the prohibitory legislation. Critical of the 2014 amendment in the Maharashtra Police Act that had imposed a total ban on dance bars and dance performances, a bench of Justices Dipak Misra and P C Pant noted that the state government re-enacted a similar piece of legislation after the top court struck down a prohibitory provision in 2013. . . . However, it added a caveat that 'no performance of dance shall remotely be expressive of any kind of obscenity in any manner' and that 'the licensing authority can take steps so that the individual dignity of a woman is not affected and there remains no room for any kind of obscenity'. The bench said police and other government bodies have sufficient power to 'safeguard any violation of the dignity of women through obscene dances' and they will make sure such performances do not adversely affect public order. See http://indianexpress.com/article/india/india-news-india/dance-bars-to-reopen-in-maharashtra-as-supreme-court-puts-ban-on-hold/#sthash.pXPmpDBW.dpuf.

10 Lacking historical sense and looking at gender relations from the moral prism of common sense, the movement ends up identifying the root of patriarchal oppression in the 'vulgar imperialist culture' promoted by TV, cinemas, internet, novels and even feminism. Far from giving primacy to feudal relations in Indian context, on this issue, the movement ends up looking at sexual violence as a product of this imperialist culture. In all other aspects the movement rightly emphasizes upon the nexus between feudalism and imperialism to unravel the peculiarity of the semi-feudal, semi-colonial context in India. But on the issue of gender relations, we not only see a separation of the two, but also a gross over-emphasis on what it calls 'vulgar' and 'poisonous imperialist culture' promoting 'sexual anarchy'. Here also, the analysis of imperialism is reduced only to the cultural realm. It fails to locate patriarchal oppression within the overall unequal power relations built on the bulwark of brahmanical feudalism which the intrusion of big capital has only bolstered. Simply replace 'imperialist' with 'western', and one cannot miss the uncanny similarity with an extremely reactionary understanding.

(Statement of resignation, DSU members [DSU 2015])

References

Agamben, Giorgio. 2007. *Profanations*. Cambridge, MA: Zone Books.
Agnes, Flavia. 2007. "State Control and Sexual Morality: The Case of the Bar Dancers of Mumbai." In Matthew John and S. Kakarala (eds). *Enculturing Law: New Agendas for Legal Pedagogy*. New Delhi: Tulika, pp. 158–175.
Badiou, Alain. 2014. *The Age of the Poets: And Other Writings on Twentieth Century Poetry and Prose*. Translated by Bruno Bosteels. London: Verso.
Bataille, Georges. 2012. *Eroticism*. London: Penguin Classics.
Baudelaire, Charles. 1964. *The Painter of Modern Life and Other Essays*. Translated and edited by Jonathan Mayne. London: Phaidon.
Baxi, Pratiksha. 2011. In Defence of the Besharmi Morcha. http://www.boloji.com/index.cfm?md=Content&sd=Articles&ArticleID=11301 (accessed 13 January 2016).
Benjamin, Walter. 2015. *Walter Benjamin's Archive: Images, Texts, Signs*. London; New York: Verso.

Berger, John. 2003. "The First and Last Recipe: Ulysses." In Geoff Dyer (ed.). *Selected Essays*. New York: Vintage International (Penguin Random House), pp. 467–473.

Das, Kamala. 2014. "The Fear of the Year." In Devindra Kohli (ed.). *Selected Poems*. New Delhi: Penguin India, p. 2.

Dharker, Imtiaz. "Tissue," *Poems*. http://www.imtiazdharker.com/poems_4-tissue (accessed 29 February 2016).

DSU Members' Statement. 2015. Resignation in Democratic Students Union: What Ails DSU? www.countercurrents.org (accessed 22 November 2015).

Foucault, Michel. 2015. *Language, Madness and Desire: On Literature*. Translated by Robert Bonnono. Minneapolis: University of Minnesota Press.

Ghosh, Shohini. 2002. *Tales of the Night Fairies*. Documentary film, 74 minutes.

———. 2016. A Film That Stuns as Collective Atonement for a Terrible Injustice. https://thewire.in/23051/a-film-that-stuns-as-collective-atonement-and-individual-tribute/ (accessed 28 February 2016).

Mani, Lata. 2014. "Sex and the Signal-free Corridor: Toward a New Feminist Imaginary," *Economic and Political Weekly*, Vol. 49, No. 6, pp. 26–29.

———. 2015. "Writing the Present," *Economic and Political Weekly*, Vol. 50, No. 49, pp. 24–27.

Menon, Nivedita. 2012. *Seeing Like a Feminist*. New Delhi: Zubaan.

Namjoshi, Suniti. 2012. *The Fabulous Feminist: A Reader*. New Delhi: Zubaan.

Pasolini, Pier Paolo. 2014. *The Selected Poetry of Pier Paolo Pasolini* (bilingual edition). Chicago: University of Chicago Press.

Phadke, Shilpa, Sameera Khan and Shilpa Ranade. 2011. *Why Loiter? Women and Risk on Mumbai Streets*. New Delhi: Penguin India.

Rancière, Jacques. 1982. "Preface to Proletarian Nights [1981]." *Proletarian Nights*. Translated by Noel Parker. http://abahlali.org/files/proletarian_nights_excerpt.pdf (accessed 13 January 2016).

———. 2010. *Dissensus: On Politics and Aesthetics*. Translated by Steven Corcoran. London; New York: Bloomsbury.

Roy, Arundhati. 1997. *The God of Small Things*. New Delhi: IndiaInk.

Sangari, Kumkum. 2015. *Solid: Liquid, a (Trans)national Reproductive Formation*. New Delhi: Tulika.

Sen, Samita, Ranjita Biswas and Nandita Dhawan (eds). 2011. *Intimate Others*. Kolkata: Stree.

Small, Helen. 2013. *The Value of the Humanities*. Oxford: Oxford University Press.

Spivak, Gayatri C. 2009. "Speaking for the Humanities," *Occasion: Interdisciplinary Studies in the Humanities*, Vol. 1, No. 1 (15 October 2009). http://occasion.stanford.edu/node/19 (accessed 25 February 2016).

———. 2015. Can There Be a Feminist World? http://www.publicbooks.org/nonfiction/can-there-be-a-feminist-world (accessed 27 February 2016).

Wark, Mackenzie. 2015. *The Beach beneath the Street: The Everyday Life and Glorious Times of the Situationist International*. London: Verso.

8 Impractical topics, practical fields

Notes on researching sexual violence in India[1]

Pratiksha Baxi

1. Introduction

The histories of the women's movements' protests against the manifold injustice towards rape survivors, especially the watershed protests of 1983 and the more recent protests in 2012–13, transformed the discursive and juridical method of constituting rape as an object of reform and research. These histories have pointed to the need to do justice to those who reveal the public secret of rape – 'that which is generally known, but cannot be articulated' (Taussig 1999: 6, also see Nordstrom 1996, P. Baxi 2014). Talking about rape whether in academic or everyday contexts is a 'cultural and political process' (Nordstrom 1996: 156, also see Herman 1992).

In this chapter, I traverse different kinds of registers – protests and law reform, pedagogy and research, testimony and lawyering – to reflect on how publicity, sexual violence and public secrecy constitute a field. I argue that we must pay attention not just to the question of methods in relation to feminist, sociological or anthropological research but also to the question of methods in lawyering and law reform. As Bartlett notes:

> Feminists have developed extensive critiques of law and proposals for legal reform. Feminists have had much less to say, however about what the 'doing' of law should entail and what truth status to give to the legal claims that follow. These methodological issues matter because methods shape one's view of the possibilities for legal practice and reform.
> (1990: 830)

Feminist legal methods include the following:

> (1) identifying and challenging those elements of existing legal doctrine that leave out or disadvantage women and members of other excluded groups (asking the 'woman question'); (2) reasoning from

an ideal in which legal resolutions are pragmatic responses to concrete dilemmas rather than static choices between opposing, often mismatched perspectives (feminist practical reasoning); and (3) seeking insights and enhanced perspectives through collaborative or interactive engagements with others based upon personal experience and narrative (consciousness-raising).

(Bartlett 1990: 831)

Although there has been much debate on this germinal essay, it is not my intention to map the debates on feminist legal methods. Rather, I wish to reflect on my field experience of researching rape trials in a rural and district court in Ahmedabad (1996–98). While a fuller account finds articulation in *Public Secrets of Law: Rape Trials in India* (2014a), in this chapter I ask three interrelated questions. First, is there a relation between social movements and research on sexual violence? Second, what does the conversation around why one researches sexual violence tell us about the way in which sexual violence is framed? Third, how may one think of method in relation to reform and activism? Thereafter, I move to more contemporary moments of reform, to suggest that we need to broaden the question of methods to law reform, lawyering and representational practices. In this sense, the chapter addresses different sites, techniques and representations, to raise questions about how feminist perspectives and sociological methods are adopted, improvised or supplemented.

2. Notes from the trial court (1996–98)

Socio-legal studies of courtroom talk have constituted the rape trial as a privileged site to demonstrate the relationship between law, power and gender (O'Barr 1982, Matoesian 1993, Taslitz 1999). Scheppele (1992) argues that lawyers deploy ordinary storytelling practices to disqualify women's testimonies to rape (also see Ferguson 1996), while Matoesian argues that we need to look at the way the testimony to rape is transformed into statements of 'routine consensual sex through the organization of courtroom linguistic practice' (1993: 1). Philips (1998) argues that spoken law has its own logic, which written law refuses recognition. Analysing courtroom talk in America, Taslitz (1999) argues that during a cross-examination, defence lawyers dominate linguistic space by using repetition as a strategy of breaking down a witness. The survivor has to answer forced-choice answers, demanding a 'yes' or 'no'. Taslitz argues that witnesses resist such linguistic domination by saying, 'I don't remember' or 'I don't know' when they do not wish to 'confirm a detail's accuracy or concede that the point is important enough to remember' (1999: 95). Reform discourses, however, ignore such linguistic and semiotic operations of power in rape cases (Das 1996, Kannabiran 2008, P. Baxi 2014a).[2]

Inspired by this body of literature, my book *Public Secrets of Law* emphasizes everyday processes of the law providing accounts of subjection and resistance to rethink the categories that are normalized by the doctrinal picture of law. It draws attention to how juridical categories inflect feminist discourses eliding the socio-legal processes that underlie the making of testimony. Situating the ethnographic project in a district and sessions court in Ahmedabad, I have argued that the rape trial cannot be addressed by looking at one segment of the trial, as the socio-legal processes that constitute the testimony to rape are configured variably at different institutional sites of the law. To forward an understanding of the different socio-legal routes a case may take and how these possibilities are conserved at different sites of the law, I turned to the case method, which has occupied a dominant place in legal anthropology. The case method has been posited as central to the search of systematic aspects of both procedural and substantive law (Epstein 1978, Nader and Todd 1978). The extended case method has been used to analyse cases over time. As Nader says,

> An extended case may comprise a series of related cases through time, involving some or all of the same actors; or it may comprise one detailed case unsettled over a period of months and years . . . the dispute in question is viewed within the social context in which it develops and is played out, allowing the analyst to trace developments and shifts in the balance of power between the individuals involved.
>
> (1965: 14)

The case method has been favoured within legal anthropology not merely as providing 'opportunities for the elaboration of doctrine'; rather, it has allowed looking at cases as 'imperatives that stem from community life' (Nader 2002: 97). While Llewellyn and Hoebel argued that 'trouble cases' describe the norm or are 'the safest main road into the discovery of law', other scholars argue that 'the case method with its focus on institutionalized dispute settlement or conflict resolution, is unduly restrictive if one is interested in getting a full range of socio-legal occurrences or in grasping differential knowledge of the law' (Nader 2002: 97). Nader argues that in the 'fields of law, where litigation is rare, researchers may get a skewed idea of law if they focus on the trouble-case' (2002: 98). However, the classification between 'trouble' and 'trouble-free' cases presumes that the juridical field is accessible, knowledge of law is uniform or available and it is possible to name the norm from a quantitative predominance of cases, as compared to instances where litigation is rare.

2.1 The locales of fieldwork

The fieldwork by way of participant observation mainly concentrated in two spaces in the trial court – the prosecutor's chambers and the courtroom. I had to learn modes of behaviour and techniques of address while sitting at trial hearings. In a sense, participant observation during the trial proceedings was conducted under the 'judicial stare', which is the 'dogmatic precondition of the narrative structure of the (legal) discourse and is also its normative guarantee of objectivity' (Goodrich 1990: 165). Participant observation in the prosecutor's chambers meant learning codes of behaviour that approximated those imposed on the other women junior lawyers who assisted him with his work. It meant engaging in a network of social relationships with a few lawyers and earning credibility among others over a period of time. This came to mark the very possibility of doing the fieldwork. In a sense, fieldwork was possible only through certain techniques of certification that demonstrated that the research agenda was legitimate.

I first met a High Court judge, a friend of the family's, who put in a word for me with the presiding judge in the District and Sessions Court. I was anxious to secure permission to sit in rape trials that were normally held *in camera*. Other High Court lawyers told me that it was doubtful I would gain permission since at that time the press was animated with reports of the allegation of rape against the inspector general (IG) of prisons by a woman social science researcher. The event was largely constituted in the press and the lawyers I interviewed as 'politically motivated'. The dominant way in which the story was presented in the press was briefly one that concluded that the accused had been framed. There were two versions to this story. One held that the accused was a *respectable* man and could never have raped her; thus, the charge was incredible. The other recognized that a gang, which had sexually abused the victim repeatedly, coerced her into framing him. In both cases, the stories exonerated the accused. However, my presence provided the occasion to voice the caution that granting permission to a woman researcher is fraught with the danger of a false allegation, thus enacting several slippages, such as that the allegation of rape was false, the allegation of rape was made possible because permission was granted to a woman researcher and all women researchers could be potential aggressors of institutional authority. The fieldwork was located in the discursive context whereby the very presence of a woman researcher from a social science background was seen as potentially transgressive to institutional orders. The District judge granted me permission to research *in camera* trials, advising me to maintain that I was a law student and not a sociology student. I could not maintain the fiction of being a law graduate for too long.

Doing ethnographic fieldwork on rape trials begins with challenging the commonplace idea that talking about rape is indecent or immoral. It is in its very conception a project that seeks to transform dominant ways of talking about rape. Most lawyers objected to the choice of my research topic for they felt it was difficult for them to talk about sexual violence, especially with a woman who was unmarried. The motif of shame was accompanied by the idea that the act of witnessing rape trials could damage women. A male defence lawyer, cited earlier, advised me not to document the circulation, witnessing and recitation of narratives of sexual violence. He said, 'You see, your work will affect you. You see varieties of men in the court. You have already seen a lot. It will have a psychological effect on you.' For him, talking about rape did not offer the possibilities of transformation or that 'meanings, in as much as it is established in a chain of signifiers, can always slide, producing new meanings' (Aretxaga 1997: 20). Other lawyers framed the project as 'courageous' and deserving publicity for its audacity. The framing of the research as shameful or courageous, however, is complicit in the public secrecy of rape.

2.2 Cultures of speech, silence and habit

While cultural themes of speech and silence are resources used by lawyers to transform rape into consensual sex during the trial, lawyers do talk about rape in chambers and courtrooms. Medico-legal representations of rape in the court often mediate between legal language of evidence and social categories of shame and stigma. I found that the manipulation of speech and silence is often enabled by medico-legal categories, allowing men and women professionals negotiate the social embarrassment and the potential charge of indecency that such talk ordinarily could engender. Alternatively, the domain of medical jurisprudence is the technique by which language is used to source pleasure.

It was from the Additional Public Prosecutor, whom I call Hirabhai, that I first learnt how medical jurisprudence becomes a vocabulary to talk about the rape law. During the first month of the fieldwork, I made no progress. Just as I had begun to despair, Hirabhai introduced me to a young woman who had come to the court regarding a statutory rape and kidnapping case. He then took me to the courtroom where he requested the bench clerk for the case papers. We sat at a far end of the lawyer's table, and he turned to the medico-legal aspects of the case. As he turned to the accused's medical certificate, he asked me, 'You know what a man's primary sexual organs are, don't you?' A little taken aback, I nodded. Then he turned to the victim's medical certificate. After going over the other details about bodily development and superficial injuries, he asked me, 'Do you know what a hymen is?'

I responded in the affirmative. He drew a vagina to explain the technical terms for injury on the labia minora or labia majora. The discussion carried on in the chamber, where he instructed his junior, whom I call Beenaben, to explain 'it' to me. After he had left, she said, 'Pratiksha, do you know that a man cannot rape a woman by simply touching her, or . . . her.' I nodded even more puzzled and a bit curious now. She carried on 'Well, how do I explain how a man rapes?' I replied, 'Beenaben, do you mean partial or complete penetration?' She nodded in relief.

In performing that which was understood as transgressive in a social sense, Hirabhai transformed that which could not be said by taking recourse to the language provided by the medico-legal textbook. Insisting that medical jurisprudence separates the social from the clinical, Hirabhai maintained that a 'decent' legal practice could coexist with frank discussions on the topic of rape. The route to generating this 'frank' space initiating the research, as he put it, now enabled him to teach his woman juniors how the prosecution could successfully fight rape cases more freely. This linguistic route became his way of teaching me facts of anatomy, sexuality and the rape law.

The space of the court also imposed a specific modality of dress, gait and conduct. Other than adopting saris or *salwar kameez*, I stopped wearing bright colours to court. Once I was instructed to wear my *chunni* properly or not wear a particular *kurta*, for the prosecutor did not think it was modest enough – the only time he found me 'indecent'. I constantly worried about my attire, learning everyday what it meant to look like a modest woman. Nor was it possible always to 'hang around' the court – as one lawyer stopped to say to me, 'Ms. Baxi, if you want to learn law, you must learn to walk faster.' To loiter in a court is to stand out among lawyers who often broke out into a trot between one courtroom to the other.

2.3 Sexual harassment in the field

While I had to learn to tolerate a threshold of everyday sexism in the court, and avoid unsafe chambers, I returned to my university with the question of how universities support women researchers who have experienced sexual harassment in the field, if at all. While this debate has yet to find serious reflection, there are several feminist autoethnographies of sexual violence which interrogate the complicity of anthropological theory and research in the work of public secrecy (P. Baxi 2014b). The silences in sociological and anthropological writings on the experience of rape and sexual harassment in the field have led to a critical interrogation of the very foundations of the discipline. When she returned to Sweden, Moreno recounts,

> My two academic supervisors, on the other hand (both of whom were men), listened to me recount the tale of the attack, but offered little

sympathy and never mentioned the topic of rape again. I later heard that one of them told a female graduate student that I must have acted like a fool in the field. Another senior male anthropologist, upon hearing about the rape, sighed that 'such things happen to women in the field'.

(Moreno 1995: 247)

Such victim blaming discourses rest on the division between the professional and the personal, as if the experience of sexual violence must be dealt only at the personal register. In Moreno's words, it was as if 'anthropologists do not get harassed and raped. Women do' (1995: 246).

Winkler's (2002) autoethnography marks a departure from canonical anthropological representations of the field and the fieldworker by critiquing institutional responses to sexual violence. Loss of tenure is one such wounding response (Winkler 1994, 1995). The disclosure of rape during fieldwork to supervisors or colleagues itself reveals the work of public secrecy. Pandey struggled against the expectation that she write a dissertation without disclosing her experience of sexual assault, even though fieldwork is about 'putting yourself right there' (2009: 114). Ethnographic writing then is not necessarily a form of closure (Pandey 2009).

Reflecting on the need to bear witness to her experience of sexual violence in France, philosopher Susan J. Brison (2008) suggests that one must give the agency to time, for at some point the rape narrative is no longer central to one's biography, although the relationship between memory and time is not a linear. Yet speaking out is about etching solidarity, speaking with others who have been censored. Indeed, one of the few books on male rape narrates such a journey of reframing the experience of sexual violence as a strategy to resist the silencing and stigma of the rape of men by other men (Scarce 1997).

Autoethnographies, then, are not confessional narratives, just as vulnerability is not a sign of weakness. However, Brison points out that when rape is not seen as a form of 'group-based gender-motivated violence against women', rape narratives are often referred to as 'stories' rather specific forms of 'testimony' or 'witnessing' (2008: 192). Hannah Feldman (1993) argues the value of speaking about rape from a personal position does not lie in the confession of the event. Rather, testimony

> works as an act, a reclaiming of history, and does so in a particular manner which asserts the fragility of the silence which counters it. In this way, testimony is a coming to voice, an insistence on speaking and not being silenced or spoken for.
>
> (Feldman 1993: 17)

McChesney (2010) insists not only on the commitments of anthropology as a site of witnessing and testimony but also of producing knowledges that make it possible to bear witness. An 'alternative cultural awareness' found McChesney (2010) during her fieldwork among Hopi women potters giving her 'the means, post-facto, to confront and comprehend' the traumatic sexual violence she had experienced as a child (2010). In relation to adults who have experienced child sexual violence, McChesney suggests that 'the anthropological object lesson of Hopi pottery is that ethnographic knowledge, like temper that strengthens the clay from which these life forms are built, provides a means to amplify a transcultural understanding of traumatic phenomena' (2010: 36). While these writings interrogate feminist epistemologies as acts of solidarity, different sets of challenges meet ethnographic methods and writing, which confront the ethics of researching and representing sexual violence (Mulla 2011). Ethnographies that document perpetrators' narratives of rape raise distinct questions about politics of representation and the limits of rapport during fieldwork (Bourgois 2004).

3. Law reform, 2012–13

Now I address the trance-like global obsession with the mass protests that unfolded in Delhi during the winter of 2012–13, which had created a global desire to 'understand' rape culture in India and how best to transform it (Dutta and Sircar 2013, Sen 2013, Lodhia 2015). As the world consumed spectacularized images of the protests (Roychowdhury 2013, Belair-Gagnon, Mishra and Agur 2014), Western media 'isolated and differentiated India as a crucible for sexual violence, exacerbating global hierarchical power structures' (Durham 2015: 185). These representations remained disconnected with the histories of the anti-rape protests within the feminist and queer movements. While the semantic and performative trajectories of these protests need further nuance, these impulses found reflection in the increasing attention to sexual violence as a field of research and pedagogy, reform and correction and discipline and diagnosis.

The vocabulary of protest was not singular, changing its grounds as more voices debated what needed to change in real and virtual worlds. During the protests, we saw the emergence of many kinds of publics. There were many interventions against the emergence of a retributive public, where the cry for death penalty became a dominant vocabulary of protest. Castration acquired a retributive currency not witnessed in earlier protests against sexual assault. And the male juvenile now acquired a hypercriminality.

Moving away from patriarchal languages of shame and honour, protective frameworks of 'rescue', or carceral politics of retributive justice, we heard the powerful slogan for *azadi* (freedom). The protestors included loud voices of dissent, which named rape as an act of power, not sex. As a form of gendered and sexualized violence, rape and other forms of sexual assault found powerful critique. The victim blaming discourse that women provoke men to rape found visceral challenge – leading to a series of images, art and performances – which sought to create alternate imaginations of what it may feel like to inhabit life without the fear of rape.

This was a protest, which drew attention to the continuum of violence from the everyday forms of sexual harassment to the aggravated forms of sexual assault. Slogans of *azadi* from the patriarchal control of the father, brother, husband, state repression and enforced sexuality resounded during the protests (Prakash 2014). The call for *azadi* was semantically rich able to incorporate within it different forms critique of patriarchal violence, humiliation and censorship. The protestors addressed the humiliation enforced by Section 377 of the IPC, the criminalization and medicalization of LGBTQI sexualities; critiqued marital rape; demanded the repeal of emergency laws such as the Armed Forces (Special Powers) Act 1958; and insisted on respecting the sexual choices made by consenting adults. In other words, the call for *azadi* both memorialized narratives of resistance against sexual violence and offered an alternate imagination of a gender-just world.

If law met love in *Naz Foundation v. Government of India and Anrs* [WP(C) No.7455/2001, Delhi High Court, 2 July 2009], law reform met the cry for freedom (Narrain 2014). The critique of heteronormative feminism, heightened during the intense debate on the question of gender neutrality of the rape law, was folded into the call for freedom from compulsory heterosexuality during the protests (Prakash 2014). The decision to replace the language of retribution that was based on a series of identification and misrecognition by the language of *bekhauf azadi* (fearless freedom) was deliberate. Krishnan (2013) talks about how the politics of producing discomfort interrupted the symbolic and political capital that rested in the retributive public. And the slogan for *azadi* marked a movement away from *suraksha* (protection), from rescue (paternalism), from policing (sexual regulation), from pathologizing (medicalizing sexualities) and, most important, from a juridical notion of retributive justice (also see Krishnan 2014). Not only did it challenge the public–private divide, but it also made visible all kinds of bodies – children, men, women, gay, lesbian, inter-sex, transgender, queer. It made visible the everyday and the extraordinary, the custodial and the public, the structural and the collective. It marked a significant participation of men who did not adopt the protectionist approach by proffering to regulate presence but insisted on women's freedom and autonomy as a condition for equality (see Prakash 2014). The protests spoke directly to law reform in proliferate ways.

3.1 Justice Verma Committee

The Delhi protests led to the constitution of the three-member Justice Verma Committee (JVC), headed by retired justice J.S. Verma with retired

188 *Pratiksha Baxi*

justice Leila Seth and solicitor general Gopal Subramanium on 23 December 2012. The stated objective of the committee was 'to look into possible amendments of the Criminal Law to provide for quicker trial and enhanced punishment for criminals committing sexual assault of extreme nature against women' (JVC Report 2013). A public notice was issued, inviting recommendations on issues relating to 'extreme sexual assault' and questions of stricter punishment by the fifth of January.[3] Gopal Subramanium recounted:

> When we looked at the protesters, we realized that their demonstrations were not just about the gang rape. They were looking for a kind of liberation. It was like one of the first congregations in South Africa for the freedom struggle.[4]

Expanding the terms of reference of the committee, the JVC provided a manifesto to the protesters. The relationship between the JVC and its publics was intimate. Other than the 80,000 submissions received, the JVC organized 'an oral consultation' with 'particularly the women's social action groups and experts in the field' (JVC Report 2013: iii).[5] The temporality of law reform altered dramatically, keeping pace with the spectacle of TV debates, protests and the parliamentary debates (U. Baxi 2012).

3.2 *Methods used by the JVC*

Rather than enumerate the recommendations of the JVC report, I highlight the methods used by the JVC, which may find contrast with law commission reports (Sen 2010). While the JVC did not reflect on the question of feminist legal method in law reform, a reading of the report illustrates how the committee mirrored the work of the women's movement, feminists and queer scholars and activists. First, the JVC recognized that law is not unitary, recognizing thereby the multi-sited nature of law, with different claims to truth (see Smart 1992). While law reform recognized the proliferate sites of law, before which the rape survivor stood in humiliation, the task of codification meant that law's customariness was beyond the limits of reform.[6] Second, the JVC hearings and interviews privileged experiences of women, children and sexual minorities. The JVC, for instance, noting that it felt 'very strongly that an assault on a woman is an assault on the person of the woman', quoted Sohaila Abdulali, 'a rape victim, who recounts her experience that took place 32 years ago in Mumbai:

> Rape is horrible. It is not horrible because you lose your 'virtue'. It is not horrible because your father and your brother are dishonored. . . .

If we take honor out of the equation, rape will still be horrible, but it will be a personal, and not a societal, horror. We will be able to give women who have been assaulted what they truly need: not a load of rubbish about how they should feel guilty or ashamed, but empathy for going through a terrible trauma.

(JVC Report 2013: 94–95)

While the JVC privileged the experiential, it did not reflect on the horror or voyeurism that scripts official accounts of sexual violence (see Jeganathan 1998).

Third, the JVC asked what Bartlett (1990) calls the 'woman question' by enumerating the exclusion of women's experiences from the life of male-dominated institutions. It upheld a person's right to choose whom, when and if to marry. And it recommended the deletion of the marital rape exception in the rape law, holding that the matrimonial relation cannot be cited as a legal defence to rape a wife. However, the JVC did not take Dalit feminism as an epistemology of resistance seriously. The JVC almost entirely ignored the judicial interpretation of rape as atrocity other than in its reference to the violent role of *khap panchayats* in creating bloody scenes that annihilate intercaste marriages.

Fourth, the JVC recognized that 'some features of the law may be not only non-neutral in a general sense, but also "male" in a specific sense' (Bartlett 1990: 837). Citing Indira Jaising, the JVC stated that 'we are further of the opinion that merely facial [*sic*] gender neutral laws and policies cannot deny what has perceptively called "differential access to justice faced by women seeking to engage with the legal system"' (2013: 65). Noting that rape is a male crime, the JVC, thereby, recommended that all survivors irrespective of their gendered identity must be recognized as victims of rape and allowed to prosecute their male assailants. However, unlike the 172nd Law Commission report, the JVC did not recommend the repeal of Section 377 of the IPC. While this critique named rape of queer bodies, displacing the heteronormative feminist concern with the biological female body, it did not offer a manifesto for the future marked by the overturning of *Naz* by the Supreme Court (see Khaitan 2014).

Finally, the JVC called upon sociologists, especially eminent women sociologists, to participate in law reform innovations, especially in relation to its recommendation to constitute employment tribunals that would redress sexual harassment (JVC Report 2013: 132), thereby pointing out that academics need to engage with feminist interventions and research on sexual harassment, as a constitutional duty to actualize the promise of equality. While this may be seen as a cunning gesture of the state to incorporate feminist sociology into what has been called 'governance feminism' (Halley *et al.* 2006), it may also be read as an acknowledgement of a specific picture of the social in law.

3.3 Questions for pedagogy and research

Does the teaching and research of law and society respond to the demand for reform, diagnosis and correction? Commenting on the teaching of rape law, in *Virender v. State of NCT of Delhi*, Justice Gita Mittal, also cited in the JVC report, noted:

> The issue with regard to teaching of offences regarding sexual assault and rape itself has been a source of much discussion. I am informed that there are instances of even legal educators being bashful and embarrassed about teaching such subjects.
> (cited in JVC Report 2013: 302–303)

Justice Mittal rightly noted that most law schools marginalize feminist perspectives on law. Academics teaching social sciences in law schools often struggle with the privileging of 'law' courses over 'non-law' courses. Kalpana Kannabiran (2005), for instance, has interrogated how legal education must look at not only how law is embedded in the social but also how gender is a critical category to the very pedagogy of law.

In the 1950s, Lotika Sarkar was not allowed to teach criminal law at the University of Delhi on the grounds that a woman law teacher could not possibly teach the law on rape to men and women students. Ironically, as a co-author of the *Mathura Open Letter*, Sarkar with Baxi *et al.* (1979) catalysed the first national rape law reform in independent India. The *Open Letter* critiqued the Supreme Court for acquitting two policemen who raped and molested a young tribal girl in a police station in Maharashtra. The decision to write an 'open letter' was what Baxi calls 'an invention out of exhaustion' (also see U. Baxi 1994, 2014). The *Open Letter* adopted a *feminine* form of writing against the masculine cannon of judicial writing. The signatories knew that they ran the risk of contempt since the *form* itself was a political tactic. This was a context when social action litigation was yet to make place in the judiciary and the role of law in social change, especially to interrogate the status of women, was taking shape, acting as a precursor to feminist jurisprudence.

A decade or more later, Ved Kumari described her struggles to teach rape law by bringing it into the classroom in the 1990s (Kumari 1994, Dhanda and Parashar 1999). In recent years, law academics such as Mrinal Satish, Jhuma Sen and Saptarshi Mandal have inaugurated courses on sexual violence in law schools, while contributing significantly to research and reform. Yet it is fair to argue that rape, in law or social science, is underresearched and underrepresented in pedagogy. The public debate on sexual violence then does not necessarily mean the incorporation of feminist critique in research methods syllabi in law or social sciences (Huff 1997). Nor do the many accounts of researchers who have written about the experience of sexual violence in the field find citation in sociological works on method in India.

3.4 Displacing scripts of horror and anger

While the 2013 protests gave rise to a number of satirical performances that mocked the idea of men gaining pleasure or power through rape, simultaneously, there was an important interrogation of whether or how the protests offered survivors epistemologies of solidarity. Did representations of sexual violence in the circuits of publicity only generate horror or anger as the primary response? Or can women also forge solidarity with each other by representing violent experiences to each other through parody, rather than mimic the socially dead? (Goldstein 2003).

I cite the reflections of a law student (SJ), who was interning with a judge during the protests in December 2012:

> Last December was momentous for the feminist movement in the country – almost an entire population seemed to rise up spontaneously against the violence on women, and the injustices of a seemingly apathetic government. In the strange irony of situations that our world is replete with, the protests were the backdrop of my own experience. In Delhi at that time, interning during the winter vacations of my final year in University, I dodged police barricades and fatigue to go to the assistance of a highly reputed, recently retired Supreme Court judge whom I was working under during my penultimate semester. For my supposed diligence, I was rewarded with sexual assault (not physically injurious, but nevertheless violating) from a man old enough to be my grandfather.[7]

The protests made a specific kind of demand on women to speak out in anger and indignation, at a time when institutions and hierarchies remained unchanged, especially in the dark chambers of our courts. SJ further says:

> While the incident affected me deeply, I felt little anger and almost no rancour towards the man; instead I was shocked and hurt that someone I respected so much would do something like this. My strongest reaction really, was overwhelming sadness. . . .

> This emotional response was also completely at odds with the powerful feelings of righteous anger that the protestors in Delhi displayed. I am not trying to say that anger at the violence that women face is not a just or true response, but the polarization of women's rights debates in India along with their intense emotionality, left me feeling that my only options were to either strongly condemn the judge or to betray my feminist principles. . . . If the shared experiences of women cannot be easily understood through a feminist lens, then clearly there is a cognitive vacuum that feminism fails to fill.

This critique of the 'cognitive vacuum' of feminist discourses questions the epistemology of solidarity, identifying the burden on survivors of violence to speak out by complaining to the police or the workplace, irrespective of whether or not they wish to choose to speak out in this way. And is testifying about violence simply about anger? Has feminism placed a burden on women by expecting them to be angry? Was writing itself not an act of feminist resistance?

> The incident is now a while behind me, and they say time heals all wounds. But during the most difficult emotional times, what helped me most was the 'insensitivity' of a close friend whose light-hearted mocking allowed me to laugh at an incident (and a man) that had caused me so much pain. Allowing myself to feel more than just anger at a man who violated me, something that I had never done before, is liberating! So, I want to ask you to think of one thing alone – when dealing with sexual violence, can we allow ourselves to embrace feelings beyond or besides anger, and to accept the complexity of emotions that we face when dealing with any traumatic experience?

While SJ's testimony ultimately travelled to the court to fix accountability, and raised the issue of sexual harassment in law schools, she also raised important questions about how women define feminism. She insisted that laughter and parody as a form of self-reflexive mode of being is as feminist as marching and shouting slogans in anger. The images of feminist protest that script anger as the appropriate response to sexual violence and the criminal complaint as the privileged act of resistance find powerful displacement in this narrative.

During the protests, many women protestors experienced sexual harassment by co-protestors and the police. Those working in the media narrated how their workplace sexualized for salacious and titillating interest in sexual violence stories was also extended to inappropriate comments and gestures to women reporters. And there were other cases where writing, talking and protesting against rape figured as the background for sexual harassment or rape. The nature of forensic reporting of what was done to the victim's body also created a pornographic public – where reporting not only directed male desire to geographies of sexual colonization but also produced pedagogies of sexual violence.

Yet MS,[8] narrating her own experience of sexual harassment by a senior lawyer, notes that the discursive context also communicated solidarities.

> What has changed now – after months and months of debate over sex crimes – is that women don't pity themselves anymore. They feel there is a small group, a small segment of society that will stand by them.
>
> It took me a while to be able to talk about my experience, and to express the conviction that I felt violated because I did not think I fit the idea of someone who is victimized or vulnerable. . . . I did not want to see myself as a victim, I told myself it was not as bad as it could have been and there are others who have it worse, and I was also a little crippled by shame and fear – of not speaking out, and of the potential consequences of doing so.[9]

MS recounts her struggles at her workplace around naming this experience of unwanted sexual advances as discrimination and the productive of a hostile work environment. Feminism provided her a language to name sexual harassment as also represents her experience reflexively in conversation with SJ.

> Feminism did not fail me. It gave me a vocabulary and a discipline to think beyond the binaries and assumptions of litigation and to interrogate the double binds that women operate under in these cases – that silence equals complicity, but speaking out and spoiling the office atmosphere means there was a good reason to fire you and therefore you are just making it up to take revenge. Or that you have to be traumatised to X degree in order for it to be harassment, and if you are traumatised to that degree, you are incapable of providing a lucid testimony.

These testimonies foreground the feminist premise by highlighting materiality and embodied nature of knowledge. They point to the multiplicity of feminist discourses, some more subjugated than the others, indicating the fragilities of feminist epistemologies as acts of solidarity. The Dalit or queer feminist critique, for instance, offers an internal challenge to dominant ways of constructing the woman as a universal subject. Yet what these accounts offer is the possibility of thinking of feminist lawyering as a concrete and embodied modality of inhabiting a male-dominated profession which challenges the binary between abstract body of law and the lived experience of lawyering.

It is here that we see that the ways in which feminist lawyers intervene in their workplaces mark the beginnings of the transformation of the entrenched sexism of legal language. In *Additional District and Sessions v. Judge 'X' Registrar General, High Court of Madhya Pradesh and others*,[10] Jaising argued that the characterization of her opposing counsel of her interjections as 'delightful' amounted to sexism. I cite what transpired from the judgement:

> Learned counsel for the High Court, well-meaning and deferential as he always is, responded by observing, 'The interjections by the learned senior counsel for the petitioner, are always delightful.' Learned senior counsel for the petitioner, had serious objection to the term, 'delightful' used, with reference to 'her'. She questioned, the use of the term, 'delightful' by posing to the learned senior counsel, whether similar interjections by men, were also considered by him as delightful. Why then, she questioned, should 'her' interjection be found 'delightful'. In expressing her view, she went on to describe the response of the learned senior counsel as 'sexually coloured'. Having given our thoughtful consideration to the response, of the learned counsel for the petitioner, we may only say, that she may well be right.
>
> There is a lot to be learnt, from what she innocuously conveyed. Her sensitivity to the issue, one may confess, brought out to us, a wholly different understanding on the subject.
>
> (At para 17)

Jaising's challenge of the use of sexist language in a case where the complaint of a woman judge against a senior male judge is adjudicated finds rare acknowledgement in a judgment. The importance of feminist lawyering as a technique of transforming courtroom talk brings to legal practice a practical feminist method, which transform legal consciousness as a method of lawyering. Feminist lawyering is not just about winning cases about gender equality. Rather, it places a specific demand on a radical transformation of the conduct of legal experts – in the chambers, the courtroom and the law school.

4. Conclusion

Rather than elaborating what it means for feminist lawyers to adopt linguistic strategies to change courtroom culture, I wish to cite one among many scenes in the foyers of the academia which I remember. A senior white academic said to me, 'It is not important to ask why men rape women, rather the more important question is: why I wont rape you?' This is the modality of sexist speech, which personalizes a philosophical question about why someone may or may not break a rule. I use this example not as a reflection on the problems of translation but to highlight how academic interactions can also feel 'uncomfortable' during talk about researching rape. Yet it is not a matter of common sense to include in methods courses discussions on what it means to research sexual violence.

Despite the 2013 protests, feminist jurisprudence or queer perspectives on law do not inform the more *masculine* and core topics such as contract or criminal law. In fact, those who do not directly research gender do not think that feminist legal theory, philosophy or sociology has anything to offer pedagogy. Many colleagues often prefer to think that it is their feminist/women colleagues who should teach feminist jurisprudence, theory or method, if such pedagogy is needed at all.

It is easy to leave prevention and redressal to a few feminists, rather than deploying feminist methods to transform work and life. Further, most feminist academics are expected to serve committees instituted to redress sexual harassment, while such committees are caricatured and represented as a threat to a heterosexist academic community. Feminist academics also are caricatured for introducing norms seen as marking governmentality under the sign of prevention of sexual harassment at the workplace. Yet there is scarce recognition of the myriad forms of violence such as domestic violence, forced marriages, threat of so-called honour crimes, stalking and rape that exists in the lives of those who find life in a university. These cases also become the calling of a few feminist academics, while the rest of the academia remains untouched by the need for professionalizing services for those who survive violence. Further, when talk about equality, freedom and dignity of women and sexual minorities enters the politico-jural realm of censorship, bans and boycott, the academia-publisher-law combine re-inscribes the public secrecy of rape.

Notes

1 This chapter was published in the *Economic and Political Weekly*, Review of Women's Studies, vol. 51, no. 18, 30 April 2016, pp. 80–88. We are grateful to the editor, *EPW*, for permission to republish this chapter in this volume. Many thanks to Kalpana Kannabiran, Padmini Swaminathan, Svati Shah, Rupal Oza, Uma Chakravarti, Shirin Rai, Upendra Baxi, Ghazala Jamil, Arvind Narrain and Mani Shekhar Singh for the productive comments. To the reviewer, much appreciation.
2 Taslitz is cited in the report of the Justice Verma Committee (2013), discussed later in its discussion on education but not in relation to courtroom speech.

3 http://blog.blanknoise.org/2012/12/public-notice-justice-verma-committee.html.
4 http://india.blogs.nytimes.com/2013/02/04/a-conversation-with-former-solicitor-general-gopal-subramanium/?r=0. Accessed on 29 February 2016.
5 See Vrinda Grover at http://www.tehelka.com/2013/04/remembering-justice-verma/. Accessed on 29 February 2016.
6 While the JVC recommended changes in the law pertaining to medical examination of the survivors, it did not address the way medico-legal textbooks are written and used in courts of law.
7 https://jilsblognujs.wordpress.com/2013/11/06/through-my-looking-glass/. Accessed on 29 February 2016.
8 http://www.legallyindia.com/201311184119/Legal-opinions/indias-most-sexist-profession-harassment. Accessed on 29 February 2016.
9 http://blogs.wsj.com/indiarealtime/2013/11/25/women-dont-pity-themselves-anymore/. Accessed on 29 February 2016.
10 *Additional District and Sessions v. Judge 'X' Registrar General, High Court of Madhya Pradesh and others*, Supreme Court of India, Writ Petition (Civil) No. 792 of 2014.

References

Aretxaga, Begoña. 1997. *Shattering Silence: Women, Nationalism and Political Subjectivity in Northern Ireland*. Princeton, NJ: Princeton University Press.

Bartlett, Katherine T. 1990. "Feminist Legal Methods," *Harvard Law Review*, Vol. 103, No. 4, pp. 829–888.

Baxi, Pratiksha. 2014a. *Public Secrets of Law: Rape Trials in India*. New Delhi: Oxford University Press.

———. 2014b. "Sexual Violence and Its Discontents," *Annual Review of Anthropology*, Vol. 43 (October), pp. 139–154.

Baxi, Upendra. 1994. *Inhuman Wrongs and Human Rights: Unconventional Essays*. New Delhi: Har Anand Publications.

———. 2012. "Because Women's Rights Are Human Rights," *Indian Express*, 27 December.

———. 2014. Unlearning the Law with Lotika Sarkar. The First Lotika Sarkar Memorial Lecture, Campus Law Centre, University of Delhi, 22 February. http://clc.du.ac.in/full-Event.aspx?id=13.

Baxi, Upendra, Vasudha Dhagamwar, Raghunath Kelkar and Lotika Sarkar. 1979. "An Open Letter to the Chief Justice of India," *Supreme Court Cases*, Vol. 4, pp. 17–22.

Belair-Gagnon, V., S. Mishra and C. Agur. 2014. "Reconstructing the Indian Public Sphere: Newswork and Social Media in the Delhi Gang Rape Case," *Journalism*, Vol. 15, No. 8, pp. 1059–1075.

Bourgois, P. 2004. "The Everyday Violence of Gang Rape." In N. Scheper-Hughes and P. Bourgois (eds). *Violence in War and Peace: An Anthology*. Oxford: Blackwell, pp. 343–347.

Brison, Susan J. 2008. "Everyday Atrocities and Ordinary Miracles, or Why I (Still) Bear Witness to Sexual Violence (but Not Too Often)," *Women's Studies Quarterly*, Vol. 36, No. 1–2, pp. 188–198.
Das, V. 1996. "Language and Body: Transactions in the Construction of Pain," *Daedalus*, Vol. 125, No. 1, pp. 67–91.
Dhanda, Amita and Archana Parashar (eds). 1999. *Engendering Law: Essays in the Honour of Lotika Sarkar*. Lucknow: Eastern Book Company.
Durham, Meenakshi Gigi. 2015. "Scene of the Crime," *Feminist Media Studies*, Vol. 15, No. 2, pp. 175–191. doi:10.1080/14680777.2014.930061.
Dutta, Debolina and Oishik Sircar. 2013. "India's Winter of Discontent: Some Feminist Dilemmas in the Wake of a Rape," *Feminist Studies*, Vol. 39, No. 1, p. 293.
Epstein, A. L. 1978. "The Case Method in the Field of Law." In A. L. Epstein (ed.). *The Craft of Social Anthropology*. New Delhi: Hindustan Publishing Corporation, pp. 205–230.
Feldman, H. J. L. 1993. *More Than Confessional and the Subject of Rape*. Monograph. New York: Whitney Museum of Art.
Ferguson, Robert A. 1996. "Untold Stories in Law." In Peter Brooks and Paul Gewirtz (eds). *Law's Stories: Narrative and Rhetoric in Law*. New Haven and London: Yale University Press.
Goldstein, D. M. 2003. *Laughter Out of Place: Race, Class, Violence, and Sexuality in a Rio Shantytown*. Berkeley: University of California Press.
Goodrich, Peter. 1990. *Languages of Law: From Logics of Memory to Nomadic Masks*. London: Weidenfeld and Nicolson.
Halley, Janet, Prabha Kotiswaran, Hila Shamir and Chantal Thomas. 2006. "From the International to the Local in Feminist Legal Responses to Rape, Prostitution/Sex and Sex Trafficking: Four Studies in Governance Feminism," *Harvard Journal of Law and Gender*, Vol. 29, pp. 335–423.
Herman, Judith Lewis. 1992. *Trauma and Recovery*. New York: Basic Books.
Huff, Jennifer K. 1997. "The Sexual Harassment of Researchers by Research Subjects: Lessons from the Field." In Martin Schwartz (ed.). *Researching Sexual Violence against Women: Methodological and Personal Perspectives*. Thousand Oaks, CA: Sage, pp. 115–128.
Jeganathan, P. 1998. "'Violence' as an Analytical Problem: Sri Lankanist Anthropology after July, '83'," *Nethra: Journal of International Centre Ethnicity Studies*, Vol. 2, No. 4, pp. 7–47.
Kannabiran, Kalpana. 2005. *Towards an Inclusive Praxis in Law: Questions on Pedagogy, Diversity and Rights*, Paper presented at the National Conference on Women's Studies, Goa, May.
Kannabiran, Kalpana. 2008. "Sexual Assault and the Law." In Kalpana Kannabiran and Ranbir Singh (eds). *Challenging the Rule(s) of Law: Colonialism, Criminology and Human Rights in India*. New Delhi: Sage, pp. 78–118.
Krishnan, Kavita. 2013. India's Anti-Rape Movement – Experiences, Reflection and Strategies for the Future, Public talk delivered at SOAS on 3

October. http://freedomwithoutfearplatformuk.blogspot.in/2013/12/indias-anti-rape-movement-experiences.

———. 2014. "Women's Liberation, Everyone's Liberation," *Green Left Weekly*, 5 July. https://www.greenleft.org.au/node/56790.

Kumari, Ved. 1994. "State's Response to the Problem of Rape and Dowry." In Lotika Sarkar and B. Sivarammaya (eds). *Women and the Law: Contemporary Problems*. New Delhi: Vikas Publishing House, pp. 104–128.

Lodhia, Sharmila. 2015. "From 'Living Corpse' to India's Daughter: Exploring the Social, Political and Legal Landscape of the 2012 Delhi Gang Rape," *Women's Studies International Forum*, Vol. 50, pp. 89–101.

Matoesian, G. M. 1993. *Reproducing Rape: Domination through Talk in the Courtroom*. Cambridge: Polity Press.

McChesney, L. S. 2010. "The Body Breaks: Narrating Child Sexual Abuse through Transcultural Metaphors of Bodily Disease," *Voices*, Vol. 10, No. 1, pp. 31–37.

Moreno, E. 1995. "Rape in the Field: Reflections from a Survivor." In D. Kulick and M. Wilson (eds). *Taboo: Sex, Identity and Erotic Subjectivity in Anthropological Fieldwork*. London and New York: Routledge, pp. 210–250.

Mulla, Sameena. 2011. "Facing Victims: Forensics, Visual Technologies, and Sexual Assault Examination," *Medical Anthropology: Cross-Cultural Studies in Health and Illness*, Vol. 30, No. 3, pp. 271–294.

Nader, Laura. 1965. *The Ethnography of Law*. Menasha, WI: American Anthropological Association.

———. 2002. *The Life of the Law: Anthropological Projects*. Berkeley: University of California Press.

Nader, Laura and Harry Todd (eds). 1978. *The Disputing Process: Law in Ten Societies*. New York: Columbia University Press.

Narrain, Arvind. 2014. What Happens to a Dream Deferred? On Law and Love, 22 January. http://duqueercollective.wordpress.com/2014/01/22/what-happens-to-a-dream-deferred-arvind-narrain-on-law-and-love/.

Nordstrom, C. 1996. "Rape: Politics and Theory in War and Peace." *Australian Feminist Studies*, Vol. 11, No. 23, pp. 147–162.

O'Barr, W. M. 1982. *Linguistic Evidence: Language, Power and Strategy in the Courtroom*. London: Academic Press.

Pandey, A. 2009. "Unwelcomed and Unwelcoming Encounters." In P. Ghassem-Fachandi (ed.). *Violence: Ethnographic Encounters*. New York: Berg Publishers, pp. 135–144.

Philips, Susan. 1998. *Ideology in the Language of Judges: How Judges Practice Law, Politics, and Courtroom Control*. Oxford and New York: Oxford University Press.

Prakash, Anant Narayan. 2014. Politics of Anti-Rape Law Reform: A Socio-Legal Analysis of the Criminal Law Amendment Act, 2013. Unpublished MPhil dissertation, Centre for the Study of Law and Governance, Jawaharlal Nehru University, New Delhi.

Roychowdhury, Poulami. 2013. "'The Delhi Gang Rape': The Making of International Causes," *Feminist Studies*, Vol. 39, No. 1, pp. 282–292.

Scarce, M. 1997. *Male on Male Rape: The Toll of Stigma and Shame*. Cambridge, MA: Perseus Publishing.
Scheppele, K. L. 1992. "Just the Facts, Ma'am: Sexualized Violence, Evidentiary Habits, and the Revision of Truth." *New York Law School Law Review*, Vol. 37, No. 123, pp. 123–172.
Sen, Rukmini. 2010. "Law Commission Reports on Rape, Women's Studies Review," *Economic and Political Weekly*, Vol. XLV, No. 44 (30 October), pp. 81–87.
———. 2013. "The Need for an Everyday Culture of Protest," *Economic and Political Weekly*, Vol. 48, No. 2 (January), p. 12. http://www.epw.in/journal/2013/02/web-exclusives/need-everyday-culture-protest.
Smart, Carol. 1992. "The Woman of Legal Discourse." *Social and Legal Studies*, Vol. 1, pp. 29–41.
Taslitz, A. E. 1999. *Rape and the Culture of the Courtroom*. New York: New York University Press.
Taussig, Michael. 1999. *Defacement: Public Secrecy and the Labor of the Negative*. Stanford: Stanford University Press.
Verma, J. S., Leila Seth and Gopal Subramanium. 2013. Report of the Committee on Amendments to Criminal Law. 23 January. http://www.prsindia.org/uploads/media/Justice%20verma%20committee/js%20verma%20committe%20report.pdf. Accessed 5 March 2016.
Winkler, Cathy. 1994. "Rape Trauma: Contexts of Meaning." In T. Csordas (ed.). *Embodiment and Experience: The Existential Ground of Culture and Self*. Cambridge: Cambridge University Press, pp. 248–268.
———. 2002. *One Night: Realities of Rape*. Oxford: Alta Mira Press.
Winkler, Cathy with Penelope J. Hanke. 1995. "Rape Attack: Ethnography of the Ethnographer." In Carolyn Nordstrom and Antonius C. G. M. Robben (eds). *Fieldwork under Fire: Contemporary Studies of Violence and Survival*. Berkeley: University of California Press, pp. 155–185.

Part II
Exploring themes

Section 3
Development

9 Planning for modernization?
Feminist readings of plans and planned development in India

Padmini Swaminathan

1. Introducing and contextualizing the problematic

Feminists across the globe through their research practices have constantly and consistently attempted to transform the methodologies and epistemologies of their disciplines; in the process, their research has substantively questioned the received wisdom that 'good research methods are supposed to be culture free, value free'. On the contrary, feminists have demonstrated not only that 'value-free research is an unachievable ideal' but that 'it is also an undesirable one' (Harding and Norberg 2005, 2010). A more productive approach adopted by feminists has been to involve oneself in 'socially engaged research' where 'research holds itself ethically and politically accountable for its social consequences' (ibid.: 2010). Such research constantly produces new knowledge that enables interrogation of existing knowledge and phenomena, while asking new questions as the worlds around us are transformed and as our interactions with people change.

Socially engaged research whether undertaken in the countries of the South or North has brought out several common concerns and dilemmas characterizing gender and gendered relationships, whereby gender as a mechanism contributes to the reproduction of social structures. Feminist research in present times corroborates what West and Fenstermaker wrote way back in 1995, namely how womanly and manly natures continue to

> achieve the status of objective properties of social life. They are rendered natural, normal characteristics of individuals and, at the same time, furnish the tacit legitimation of the distinctive and unequal fates of women and men within their social order. . . . This arrangement provides for countless situations in which persons in a particular sex category can 'see' that they are out of place, and if they were not there, their current problems would not exist.
>
> (West and Fenstermaker 1995: 22)

An abiding project of feminists across space and time has been to constantly study how gender 'takes on social import, how it varies in its salience and consequence and how it operates to produce and maintain power and inequality in social life' (ibid.: 22). The Gender Mainstreaming (GM) project that emerged in the 1990s building on the empowerment discourse of the 1980s was defined by the United Nations as the integration of gender into the 'design, implementation, monitoring and evaluation of policies and programmes in all political, economic and societal spheres' (ECOSOC 1997: chapter IV, quoted in Parpart 2014: 384). It was built on the assumption that transforming unequal and unjust power relations is doable and that it 'simply required GM to be everyone's responsibility, everyone's job' (UNDP 2002: 6, quoted in Parpart 2014: 384).

Within a short time, the operationalization of the GM transformative agenda has demonstrated the pervasive nature of resistance to the project and to the instability of the concept itself. Drawing on feminist theory and critical development analysis, Parpart (2014) describes how, notwithstanding the wide acceptance of the notions (and policies based on such notions) of gender equality and women's empowerment, the same is constantly subverted, that gender has become a synonym for women and girls, '*and GM a promise of inclusion, rather than transformation*' (emphasis ours) (ibid.: 389).

Even as the volume of literature that the implementation of GM project has generated demonstrates an overall depressing track record of transformation, what is to be noted here is that it is the deployment of feminist methodological lens that has enabled a nuanced interrogation and reading of this rich haul of information. Mainstream development agencies (World Bank's *World Development Report, 2012*, UNDP's 2003 Report on *Transforming the Mainstream*, to name a few institutions and their publications) have generally sought solutions within established institutional structures and practices. Feminists, on the other hand, have critically examined these 'solutions' for their politics, practicalities, implementing strategies and outcomes, and in terms of their transformative abilities.[1]

A realization that has increasingly got strengthened but that, nevertheless, does not deter feminists from attempting to work towards a step-by-step, incremental transformation of inimical entrenched structures and power relations is the protracted nature of the struggle to challenge assumptions that are deeply embedded in people's consciousness reinforced by powerful institutions and regarded as normal by both men and women. Precisely because GM necessitates transformation that in turn poses a threat to existing power structures and persons who have benefitted and continue to benefit from these structures, feminists are aware that the nature of change they desire cannot be a short-term strategy; neither is it about merely changing men's behaviour and attitudes.

The Indian subcontinent has contributed in no small measure to the earlier literature on gender equality/GM through its examinations of, among other things, the agendas of plans, welfare programmes; government initiatives in setting up of committees and commissions to inquire into the status of women in general and of the nature of 'women's work' in particular; the nature and consequences of interventions in the educational field through the institution of women's studies centres and departments; movements of 'autonomous' and/or political party–affiliated women's organizations on a range of themes; the implications of women's agenda when sought to be furthered either through foreign-funded non-governmental organizations (NGOs) or through state-funded ones; and the repeated attempts to sensitize and urge official data-collecting agencies to ensure collection of gender-sensitive gender-disaggregated data.

This chapter aims to highlight a very small part of the earlier findings; it focuses in particular on the methodologies used by scholars and by government organizations and NGOs to arrive at their prognosis on the status of Indian women, what in their opinion contributes to the persistence of gender inequality despite 68 odd years of planned development and where, in their opinion, if any, lies the resolution to this problem and why. Given the vast terrain covered by literature, it would be foolish to pretend that an exhaustive account of existing knowledge will be presented. Rather, the attempt here is to engage primarily with the theme of planned development using a feminist lens to reveal the gendered nature of planning for economic development of the country.

The choice of the theme stems from the significant role that five-year plans and planning has played in the life of the nation. In fact, as the struggle for independence gained momentum, the leaders of the movement in anticipation of independence began the process of planning long before 1947. Women's role in a planned economy was an important document that came out of this exercise way back in 1939; post-independence, as the voices of scholars (through their writings) and of people from movements (through their actions on the ground) from different corners of the country became more strident, the authorities in power had to be seen to be active as well. The Report of the Committee on the Status of Women in India, 1974, and the Report of the National Commission on Self-Employed Women and Women in the Informal Sector, 1988, need to be seen in this light.

It took a gender-sensitive member of the Planning Commission to take unprecedented measures so that a Committee of Feminist Economists could be constituted to undertake the task of 'Gendering of Plans'. Given the role of the Planning Commission, which, among things, was also the nodal agency for plan grants to the states of the country, it was hoped that not only would the exercise of gendering the plans go at least some way in making the polity sensitive to the nature of exclusion and multiple deprivations/burdens suffered by rural women in particular because of inadequate development or maldevelopment, but it would also result in devolving more funds to schemes identified as addressing such deprivations. This vision of the Planning Commission member and the hope that *change is possible* drove the Committee of Feminist Economists to race against time to examine, from a feminist lens, each draft chapter of the 11th Five-Year Plan, which exercise was repeated during the 12th Five-Year Plan as well.

Given a situation today where the Planning Commission has been officially disbanded, it is important to record this journey of planning and the role that feminist scholars have played in trying to read and rewrite the plans from a feminist perspective, even though this exercise at the end of the day has in no way *transformed* the lives of the poor and marginalized; neither have the feminists succeeded in their agenda of addressing the contentious issue of 'inclusion'; rather, as pointed out by Eapen and Mehta (2012), inclusion is and remains elusive.

This chapter is divided into four sections. In Section 2 that follows the Introduction, we discuss in some detail the pre-independence document mentioned earlier, namely women's role in a planned economy. In Section 3, the discussion turns to a feminist reading of the recommendations of a few of the seminal documents of the post-independence period to reinforce our conviction as feminists whether or not such recommendations serve/do not serve the cause of gender equality. In Section 4, our conclusion, we revisit the theme of transformation versus integration in the light of our discussions in Sections 2 and 3.

2. Revisiting *women's role in a planned economy*

2.1 *Planning for women's role in independent India: an introduction*

Maithreyi Krishnaraj (1995), Nirmala Banerjee (1998) and Leela Kasturi (1995) have made visible[2] in their own ways the contents of a subcommittee report, namely 'Women's Role in Planned Economy' (WRPE), which had been prepared in the late 1930s for the National Planning Committee of the then Congress Party. The significance of this pre-independence document lies, as Banerjee points out, in its recommendations that were way ahead of its times and certainly not warranted by the conventional terms of reference given to it. What does not come as a surprise today (as will become clearer as we proceed) is the wholesale burial of the radical part of the recommendations (discussed later) of the report immediately after independence; but what remains a mystery to this day is, to put it in Banerjee's own words:

> Many of the women who came to occupy various positions of importance in independent India had originally been members of the subcommittee set up for the WRPE . . . even though all of them had not fully agreed with the earlier document, they were aware of it and there is no record that they opposed it. So why was it that they never mentioned it or revived any of its ideas when they became part of the country's power group?
>
> (Banerjee 1998: WS-6)[3]

Banerjee goes further and also notes that

> not even the CSWI (Committee On the Status of Women in India) Report seemed to have any awareness of it although members of the (CSWI) committee had diligently explored most available sources of information about the trajectory of women's status during this century.
>
> (Banerjee 1998: WS-4)

Implicit in these observations are several unanswered questions and conundrums; however, there are lessons as well, the most important flagged by Banerjee herself, wherein she expresses her dismay at the Indian's women's movement in post-independent India, which, according to her,

> is no more sure that it has the strength to frontally challenge household-based patriarchy than were those stalwarts working 60 years ago on the WRPE. We are still looking to the state to curb the patriarchal forces and to give women autonomy over their lives.
>
> (Ibid.: WS-7)

That Banerjee's fear is not unfounded will become clear as we begin with a discussion of the recommendations made by the WRPE in 1939 and later move to a discussion of the recommendations made by a Group of Feminist Economists,[4] constituted by the erstwhile Planning Commission (now National Institute for Transforming India [NITI] Aayog) during the making of the 11th Five-Year Plan and subsequently also during the making of the 12th Five-Year Plan. Discussions on these last two plan documents will immediately make clear, not only that we, as women and as feminists, are still dependent on the state (howsoever patriarchal it may be) to fight patriarchy at the household level, but equally, if not, more than ever, '*how we have moved from a position of working to bring about transformation to one*

210 *Padmini Swaminathan*

of seeking accommodation through inclusion a la Parpart (2014)', quoted earlier (emphasis added).

2.2 The WRPE document, 1939[5]

Introducing the WRPE Report, Kasturi points out that Jawaharlal Nehru, as chairman of the National Planning Committee, appointed several sub-committees (as many as 29) to report on various aspects of 'national life and work' and to make recommendations in accordance with a predetermined plan. One of these dealt with the place of women in the planned economy of a free India. The subcommittee's terms of reference included the consideration of the social, economic and legal status of Indian women; in particular, it was to concern itself with family life and organization and women's employment in the house; marriage and succession, and the laws governing these; the conditions of employment of women in various sectors; social customs and institutions that hindered women's development; and appropriate types and methods of education which would enable women to play their due roles in the household, professions and national services (listed in Kasturi 1995).

A question that immediately arises in the context of the earlier mandate is: on what sort of evidence did the subcommittee prepare its report in 1939? Kasturi says the following about the committee's report:

> The work of the Sub-Committee was hampered by scarcity or unevenness of information. Questionnaires, quite stunningly comprehensive, were issued widely and the replies and reports analysed. These form the basis of the text of the Report. The Sub-Committee could not build a structure of any firmness on the foundations supplied to [it] in the shape of data but laid down the main principles on which a structure could be built. The Report may therefore be regarded as a framework of principles – a sort of work plan.
>
> (Kasturi 1995: 10)

We reproduce some of the observations that Kasturi herself has reproduced from the text of the subcommittee report; these observations at once reveal the far-sighted thinking and vision embedded in them:

> Woman cannot be free until the means and training for economic liberty have been assured to her, and until the functions which nature and society impose on her are organized in such a way that while fulfilling them woman still retains the right to mould her social and economic life in any way she chooses.
>
> (Kasturi 1995: 9)

We do not wish to turn woman into a cheap imitation of man or to render her useless for the great tasks of motherhood and nation-building. But in demanding equal status and equal opportunity, we desire to achieve for woman the possibility of development under favourable circumstances of education and opportunity, and while so doing, urge upon the State its responsibility towards women in this respect.

(Kasturi 1995: 10)

Kasturi emphasizes that the drudgery of the housewife was openly acknowledged and that the demands of the WRPE for health, leisure and recreation for women meant two things: the hard work a woman puts in as mother, wife and homemaker and therefore the right of a woman to recover her energies and to have something left over for herself as an individual. The concept that housewives are also *working women* is a running thread of the report, further that, all women work regardless of class and that, '*in homes where men and women work, they should not only share expenses but domestic responsibilities as well. Men of every class should learn housework and "domestic science"*' (emphasis added).

The WRPE, according to both Kasturi (1995) and Banerjee (1998), not only chose to concentrate heavily on the issue of women's economic rights but went further and emphasized that such rights were contingent on each woman being treated as a separate unit in the economic structure, a radical stand when viewed against the present continuing mainstream stand of generally taking a household as the unit of analysis and subsuming women's position within it. Giving examples, Banerjee demonstrates how many of the recommendations of the WRPE underscore the notion of a woman as an independent entity in her own right.

One, the WRPE stated categorically that a worker woman should have full control over her earnings; two, it condemned the practice of throwing women out of their jobs consequent to marriage; three, with regard to night work and of such work considered as unfit for women, the WRPE was of the strong view that instead of barring women from such work, it is the work organization that needs to be altered so that the environment becomes safe for women to work: 'What is meant to safeguard a worker should not act to her detriment' (quoted in Banerjee 1998: WS-3).

The radical nature of the recommendations becomes starker when one studies the document for why it opposed making the family as a unit of economic activities, namely that family as a unit rendered women as subsidiary or secondary earners and that family as a unit justified payment of lower wages to women. The WRPE carried its radical stance further when it critiqued trade unions of several industries that had sacrificed married women's interest at times of wage negotiation or job rationalization on grounds that the husbands of these women had jobs. Instead, the WRPE recommended that, instead of a family wage, the wage should strictly be fixed on the principle of equal pay for equal work regardless of 'status of worker, whether married or single, whether he or she has to support a family or not' (ibid.: WS-3).

The WRPE also engaged with the theme of women's unpaid labour performed either as part of the family enterprise or the routine work of reproduction. On unpaid family enterprise labour, the WRPE was clear that the economic value of such work needed to be recognized and, that, in lieu of payment, the family enterprise worker must be allowed to claim all benefits given to other workers – medical help, crèche facilities, training and so on – a remarkable foresight indeed. On unpaid household work, the WRPE recommended as compensation women's absolute control over part of the family income and also an inalienable right to a share in the husband's property. There was also a mention that men should learn and practice household skills. Banerjee says it all when she observes: 'It is indeed surprising how many of the WRPE recommendations, especially on issues relating to economic empowerment are still a part of the unfulfilled demands of the Indian women' (ibid.: WS-3).

Kasturi goes further and demonstrates how the report also attempted to place the economic rights in a larger context. Thus, for example, the WRPE stated that women's prospects for economic independence would be improved if they could claim equal rights to property as well. The WRPE was aware that property rights of women varied under different personal laws; however, it averred that such rights are not absolutely denied but are limited.

The subcommittee even considered the rights of children and made several modern pronouncements. The child is an individual who has rights and needs help and protection from the state (Kasturi 1947:43–44). Child labour particularly in the unorganized sector was recognized as an evil. Among its recommendations were compulsory universal education up to the age of 14 and a legal prohibition of such labour (Kasturi 1947: 81–83, 149).

The need for crèches was reiterated throughout the report. Whole-time crèches should be provided where all mothers needing leisure, rest, tension-free convalescence or childcare arrangements during working hours could leave their young children. *This subcommittee realized the needs of mothers other than those working outside the home.* Crèches are normally associated only with the latter. This, according to Kasturi, is an extraordinary acknowledgement of all women's need to be free of childcare for reasons of personal development and the recovery of their health. 'The state must provide for the maintenance of crèches and nursery schools under a system of social insurance', suggested the subcommittee (emphasis added).

The report of the subcommittee, in Kasturi's opinion, may be summed up as the first attempt to assess the status of Indian women and to define the parameters of their development. Although the analysis was not that of a group of professional sociologists or economists, as committed intelligent women they based their conclusions on their knowledge of society and the data they received. Some aspects of women's lives were emphasized and some were not, but most of the issues were outlined. We see that they were not against tradition or in favour of modernization, but they were certainly in favour of women's development as individuals.

Progressive for its time, this document disappeared in the years after independence, was forgotten, misplaced and overlooked, so concludes Kasturi.

2.3 Discussion

Then as of now, it has become clear to feminist economists engaged in comprehending 'women's status' in India that radical restructuring of the economy and through it of society (which is one important reading of the WRPE) has never been on the agenda of even the most ardent votary of 'modernization', namely Jawaharlal Nehru, whose term as the first prime minister of the country set the basic pattern of economic development that was followed for upwards of three decades. In fact, Banerjee's (1998) work is replete with quotes from observations made by Nehru at several fora where his obsession with growth (but not necessarily growth with employment), his reasons for promoting girls' education 'for making better homes, better family and better society' and whose understanding of women's role did not rise above seeing them as 'chiefly responsible for running the home . . . in an orderly and aesthetic way', in no way justify, from a feminist perspective, the adage of statesmanship that is often used to describe him.

Feminist scholars dealing with the themes of transformation of the state in industrial countries of the West, particularly the Organisation for Economic Co-operation and Development (OECD) countries, have sketched the trajectory that states in these countries have followed to address the issue of gender inequality, the outcomes of which have, in turn, led to change in state structures (e.g. Jenson 2009, O'Connor 2015). This trajectory traces the manner in these societies, which have moved from a male-breadwinner model to adult-worker model family to dual-earnership models – all of which is premised on women being part of the labour force. Feminist examination of these models has revealed the persistence of gender inequalities despite large numbers of women being part of the labour force. One set of mainstream policy makers has explained this persistence in terms of 'incomplete revolution' in women's roles, necessitating therefore more attention in three areas (education, employment and entrepreneurship); another set has emphasized social investment in response to the 'inability of traditional economic and social policy frameworks to address changing demographic trends, including population ageing and declining birth rates in most OECD countries, high unemployment, child poverty and the intergenerational transmission of poverty and disadvantage' (O'Connor 2015: 487).

Despite the significance of the social investment strategy to go some way towards combating the inequalities resulting from the incomplete revolution argument, feminist scholars have critiqued this strategy for its failure to address the 'structural bases of gender inequality in the here and now while making women central to the demographic stability of the population and the prevention of intergenerational poverty transmission' (O'Connor 2015: 488).

The relevance of the aforementioned point to our discussion lies in the remarkable manner in which the contents of the WRPE document (discussed in Section 1.2) combined the incomplete revolution argument, namely centrestaging the need for women to work and be recognized as workers and earners in their own right, and the social investment strategy (urging the necessity of social investment in a range of activities that would enable women to participate in public life). That the WRPE document was aware of the structural bases of gender inequality is discernible, among other things, from its emphasis on the need for legislation to guarantee women right to property, inheritance rights, right of every child to education and so on. The WRPE went even further when it averred that men needed to learn and practise household skills.

3. Post-independence

3.1 *Report of the Committee on the Status of Women in India (CSWI), 1974*

During the 1970s, in response to protests by women's groups across the globe against their unequal status in society, the United Nations (UN) took a decision that urged member states to submit reports on the status of women in their countries. Vina Mazumdar (1985) provides an interesting account of the manner in which the Government of India (forced to respond to repeated reminders from the UN) finally arrived at the answer to the question: *Who in the government is responsible for women?* It was left to the Department of Social Welfare (the only agency that had something to do with women) to constitute a Committee on the Status of Women in India (September 1971) under the leadership of the then union minister for social welfare, Dr. Phulrenu Guha.

The CWSI Report (GOI 1974) is a much-discussed and written-about report, and a seminal document as far as the Indian women's movement is concerned. The emphasis in this paper is limited to comprehending what informed the set of recommendations that the CWSI put out – were these aimed at the transformation of Indian society, or were they more tuned to integrating women in the development process as envisaged by the then ongoing five-year plans of the country?

It is our contention that, unlike the WRPE document, whose adoption and implementation *would* have meant radical restructuring of the household and of the economy, the CWSI Report in its Chapter V, dealing with roles, rights and opportunities for economic participation, centre-staged the theme of 'integrating women into the process of development at all levels'; it spoke of the need for 'acceptance by society of the multiple roles of women as home workers and mothers as socially and economically productive in the same manner as direct participation in the economic process'; it emphasized the fact that marriage and motherhood 'which contributes to the continuation of the nation should not become disabilities in the gainful participation of women in the economic process'; it listed out a set of supportive services and institutionalized aids without which 'these dual roles will continue to impose a tremendous strain on the physical and mental resources of women. It will also affect the welfare and development of the future generation through inadequate care in childhood' (ibid.: 230).

Even as the CSWI Report made the right noises about women being excluded from active participation in the productive process as the economy attempted to transit to a modern one, and of inadequate measures having been instituted to remove 'women's disabilities and handicaps', it saw no contradiction in simultaneously stating that 'the experience of some countries has shown that it is possible by public policy to accelerate women's employment in new areas of work, by finding solutions to their problems of family life and child care' (ibid.: 231). Some of the solutions suggested consisted in extending the scope and coverage of the Maternity Benefits Act, 1961, in provision of crèches, integrated development of training and employment and the like.

The CWSI Report is a far cry when viewed against the emphatic statement made by the WRPE that as soon as a woman is not considered as an independent worker but viewed in conjunction with her role in a family, then, more often than not, she is liable to be considered a secondary earner and hence paid lower wages. This powerful understanding, among several others, finds no echo in the CWSI Report. Methodologically, therefore, the CWSI recommendations emphasized more 'practical gender needs' in the hope that eventually this would address 'strategic gender needs'.

3.2 'Women and development' chapter in Indian five-year plans

Swaminathan (1991) has commented on the perspectives from which the five-year plans of the country have viewed 'development' in general and women's role in such development. She points out that, precisely because much of 'development' is measured in terms of, say, *growth rates* of agriculture, industry and other sectors, and in terms of the *quantum* of different materials produced like steel, fertilizers and cement without a *qualitative assessment* of what development has meant to the lives of the people (in terms of availability of very basic necessities of life), one finds, plan after plan, that the component which really addresses itself to the vast majority of, specially, the rural population (the Minimum Needs Programme) is being relegated to the end chapters of the plan document. This is also the section that gets its share of resources substantially axed whenever there is a resource crunch.

By its very definition, the Minimum Needs Programme covers the barest minimum requirements of the population, namely drinking water, fodder, fuel, rural health and sanitation. The *Draft* Fifth Five-Year Plan (Government of India, Planning Commission, 1974–79) is the only document that spoke of a National Programme of Minimum Needs aimed at establishing throughout the country 'a network of certain essential services on a coordinated and integrated basis, given certain predetermined criteria of uniformity and equality' (p. 87). More important, the *Draft* recognized that

> the emphasis placed under this programme on the integrated planning of various services and facilities with a view to bringing about their physical convergence also necessitates the adoption of new procedures, for physical planning, decision making and the delegation of responsibility.
>
> (p. 91)

Subsequent plan documents (including the Fifth, Sixth and Seventh Five-Year Plans), while dealing with the different components of a minimum need programme under separate headings, have abandoned this integrated approach to the whole issue of survival, especially in the rural areas. Worse, starting from the Sixth Five-Year Plan, a number of such issues that should rightly form the domain of so-called planning for a just society have found their way into the chapter on 'women and development' and from then have continued to been seen and discussed as 'women's issues'.

The manner in which the chapter on women and development was conceived and dealt with in the Sixth Five-Year Plan and thereafter not only foreclosed any limited option there might have been of 'including women' in the main body of the plan; its designation of a number of issues as women's issues reinforced the oppressive effects of an ideology based on what feminists have termed

> the male model of work and the sexual division of labour implicit within it. . . . Implicitly, it (the male model of work) presumes that domestic tasks will be taken care of by someone else at home full time. The male model of work does not 'fit' with children whatever the childcare arrangements.
>
> (Sassoon 1987: 165–166)

In Section 3.4 we will discuss in some detail attempts made by feminist economists to 'gender' the 11th and 12th Five-Year Plans.

3.3 The report of the National Commission on Self-Employed Women (NCSEW) and women in the informal sector, 1988

> Despite the existence of various Constitutional and legal provisions safeguarding women's employment a large number of women workers particularly in the unorganized sector suffer from various disadvantages relating to their working lives as well as in their homes. . . . Government of India feel that it is necessary to conduct a comprehensive examination and study of self-employed women workers as it is in this area that the lack of access to credit, marketing, health and social security are most discernible. It has therefore been decided to constitute a Commission on Self-Employed Women.
>
> (GOI 1987, quoted in NCSEW Report 1988: 332)

Among the several terms of reference listed in Government of India's letter constituting the aforementioned commission, the following is of particular significance for our argument:

> vii) To suggest measures relating to all sectors for removing the constraints *which adversely affect the integration of self-employed women in the national development process* (emphasis added).
>
> (Ibid.: 332)

Once again, as in the case of the CSWI Report, we find that 'integration into existing development processes' takes precedence over 'transformation' of the existing order of society; once again, reading through the voluminous set of recommendations contained in the NCSEW Report, we find, for example, that the understanding that addressing issues pertaining to provision of 'drinking water, energy and environment' constitutes important attempts 'to reduce *women's drudgery* considerably' (emphasis ours) (NCSEW 1988: 274) has come to stay; it is not simply reiterated plan after plan and only in plan documents, but has found its way into documents of officially constituted committees and commissions presided over and consisting of women activists with long years of engagement with the women's movement in India.

The dilemma that such phrasing of the important issue of basic infrastructure poses for feminists is the proverbial Hobson's 'choice' embedded in the phraseology itself: choose between 'practical' gender needs or forgo 'practical needs' and wait for 'strategic' gender needs to materialize. Given the particular manner in which economic development has been taking place in the country since the dawn of independence, where citizens cannot demand basic services as a right, there is no scope as yet for some of the practical gender needs translating, even if gradually, into strategic gender needs. Hence, even the most vocal and radical of feminists find themselves acquiescing, under these circumstances, to go along with the demand for provision of sufficient investment in basic infrastructure even if the latter is seen as addressing women's issues and not that of the household. Given a 'male model of work', the partial-/poor-quality services provided by the state and the almost static traditional role of men have meant very little change in the quality of rural women's lives in particular, with the result that women are forced simply to do more and accept double/triple shifts.

A few quotes from the reports of the NCSEW (1988) will help clarify how and in what manner women's subordination gets continually restructured even as the economy ostensibly attempts to provide new opportunities through its welfare measures for women as citizens and as workers.

> The problem of safe drinking water is very acute. Poor women have to spend a number of hours every day and have to walk long distance to fetch water. This responsibility is exclusively theirs. . . . There should be increased plan allocation for providing drinking water to villages and stepping up the implementation of programmes as water is a basic right of women. Non-availability of it adds to their drudgery, and ill-health, besides denying them a few hours daily which could be profitably used in income-generating activities.
>
> (NCSEW 1988: 258)

Planning for modernization? 219

Since one of the reasons for poor enrolment of a girl child and even poorer retention of their enrolment is their contribution in helping the working mothers in domestic work and looking after younger children, and also contributing to the family economy as child labour, it is necessary that there should be shifts for girls at suitable times so that they can assist their mothers in work and go to school. It would be preferable to have a regular crèche attached to the primary school where the younger children could be taken care of so that the older child can attend the school.

(Ibid.: 284)

This report has brought out in quantitative and qualitative terms the deteriorating position of the rural population and the urban poor and of women in particular. Yet underlying its recommendations are some fundamentally problematic assumptions, most important being *either* the state provides services, or the family (read woman of the family) has to shoulder these responsibilities. The less the state does, the more is done or has to be done by women. This form of feminism automatically looks to the state to provide the servicing work now being done by women in society without questioning the complex interrelationship that exists between the organizations of production, the domestic sphere and the limits of state intervention.

3.3.1 *Implications of NCSEW recommendations for feminist politics*

The NCSEW Report is full of recommendations such as the earlier ones that are hugely problematic from a feminist perspective. We begin with juxtaposing the contents of the earlier two quotes against the recommendations that the WRPE made way back in 1939, emphasizing in no uncertain terms the banning of child labour, making education mandatory for all children as part of child rights and emphatically stating that the state must provide for the maintenance of crèches and nursery schools under a system of social insurance so that women are free to pursue their vocation. The NCSEW recommendation on the other hand, in essentializing the role of girl children, takes the clock right back. The question then arises: why has feminism taken a beating in the post-independent period? Or, were the authors of NCSEW simply being pragmatic?

The Commission recognizes the fact that in the rural areas there are not enough trained women who can be appointed as teachers. Urban based teachers posted in rural areas do not tend to stay in the village to which they are posted resulting in loss of school hours for the children. The Commission, therefore, recommends an innovation in the basic requirements of school teachers. For primary schools, girls who have completed secondary school or have achieved even middle school level, may be given an intensive training for a period of one year or nine months in certain training colleges of the state government. Their training, boarding and lodging should be free. After the training, they should be posted in their home villages or in the vicinity of their villages. Only in this manner will it be possible for the schools to have women teachers who will stay there and not absent themselves from schools.

(Ibid.: 285)

The preceding observation reads almost as if it is the precursor to the institution of para-teachers that has today become the norm as far as teacher appointment is concerned. The wave of decentralization that ensued following the 73rd Constitutional Amendment in the mid-1990s came in handy for some state governments to decentralize partially or wholly their teacher management system. 'Para-teacher' is a generic term applied to characterize teachers appointed on contract. Initially not much attention was paid to such appointments because of the perception that such appointment is a passing phase. However, not only is it continuing, but it is also expanding.

Across the country, to meet the surge in demand for teachers consequent to explosion in enrolment, and at a time when states were and still are facing fiscal deficits, the contractual appointment of teachers was facilitated by the centre to minimize the permanent recurring liability of teacher salaries in state budgets. Studies (e.g. Govinda and Josephine 2004, Kingdon and Sipahimalani-Rao 2010) mention that several states have discontinued hiring regular teachers altogether in government schools; new hires are only para-teachers; such teachers are paid just one-third of the amount paid to regular teachers. Further, what is also at stake is the poor investment that the state makes in training such teachers.

In 1988 the commission would not have anticipated that a recommendation made by it in the interest of furthering girls' enrolment and their retention in school would in the mid-1990s take on a wholly different avatar. To be fair to the commission, the origin of the institution of para teachers in the country is not traced to the commission but to a combination of national and international factors: the growing embarrassment that the country faced in being ranked low in Human Development Index (an important component in the calculation of the latter being the level of literacy of the population), the race to fulfil the millennium development goal (MDG) requirement of universal literacy by 2015, the growing demand internally for education by almost all sections of the population and so on. Despite these compulsions, the governments of the day did not substantially increase the proportion of national income to meet educational expenditure commensurate with demand; instead, economy of expenditure was sought to be achieved through recruitment of para teachers, poor maintenance of existing infrastructure and gradual privatization of the educational sector as a whole.

The feminist concern in all of the aforementioned that we wish to highlight and question is the notion implicit in the commission's recommendation (but today made explicit by officially sanctioning the appointment of para-teachers): simply because urban-based regular teachers posted in rural areas do not tend to stay in the village, is it fair to subject rural children to poorly trained teachers? Increasingly, government schools have become synonymous with the education of children of Dalits and of girl children.

Further, the studies mentioned earlier, namely Govinda and Josephine (2004) and Kingdon and Sipahimalani-Rao (2010), reveal that several of the para-teachers may not have undergone the length of training that regular appointees undergo because governments are in a hurry to meet targets of enrolment. However, in terms of qualifications, most of them are at par or even better qualified than regular teachers. This then raises another question: if in terms of qualifications, there is not much difference between regular and para-teachers, is it fair to monetarily exploit such teachers? The inability of the economy to generate decent employment in the non-farm sector, and therefore the inability of these educated youngsters to get an employment of their choice even after some level of education, has necessitated their acceptance of the job of para-teachers in the hope that the system would regularize their employment at some point in future.

At another level and equally of concern to feminists is the inability or the poor upward mobility of generations of 'rurally educated' children. Field-based studies, not necessarily deploying a feminist lens, demonstrate that significant upward mobility in contemporary India is, by and large, contingent upon being educated in English medium in an urban educational institution and such other characteristics that are simply absent or not available to rural households. Hence, these studies, contrary to feminist recommendations, emphasize that '*promoting social mobility*' may be more practically rewarding than addressing inequality through large-scale redistribution of productive assets, such as land reforms (emphasis ours) (Krishna 2013). These have important messages and implications for feminist struggles aimed at 'gender mainstreaming' and/or 'empowering' women, struggles that have hitherto concentrated more on acquiring land and pattas for and in the name of women.

3.4 Feminist economists' engagement with the 11th and 12th Five-Year Plans

In a foreword to a document (Government of India, Engendering Public Policy 2010) published by the Planning Commission subsequent to the adoption of the 11th Five-Year Plan (2007–12), Dr. Syeda Hameed, member of the then Planning Commission, spoke of history having been created: 'This was the first time that an effort was made to engender the entire five year plan. The formation of the Group of Feminist Economists was the means to achieve this end.'

In a separate joint contribution, Hameed and Jain (2009) not only provide a brief historical account of 'women and the plans' but also bring their feminist lens to critically examine, among other things, how despite the emergence and presence of a strong women's movement, the disjunction between policy makers and the women's movement continued to exist and even widen. The reasons put forth by these authors for such disjuncture are worth reproducing for their continued validity even today.

According to the authors, three main reasons emerge from their reviews of the situation: the first is that they find a resistance to the accommodation of the knowledge that women are providing of the situation on the ground and of women's actual location in the Indian political economy as the main contributors to its economic sectors; the second is the failure of the women's movement to forge a semblance of unity on public issues, which would gain them a space in the political discourse; the third is the very nature of women's construction of knowledge and its use. The authors demonstrate how 'the tendency to question every notion or concept which attempts to arrive at a boundary for identity fixing' negates any bonding and 'impedes the participation of women in policy as a political presence drawn from a collective identity'. This formidable realization and situation notwithstanding, the efforts to bring together a group were not given up, and as the authors put it, 'when there was a call from the Planning Commission for a consultation, the response was immediate and complete'.

In the same contribution, Dr. Hameed recounts her predicament as an official of the Government of India (first as member of the National Commission for Women and then as member of the Planning Commission), in being unable to reconcile the invisibility of women in official agendas in sharp contrast to what she repeatedly witnessed on the ground, namely 'multiple burdens and multiple deprivations of women' made worse by the fact that the 'excellent schemes drawn up at the planning level did not seem to reach the ground level'. Convinced that women's issues should cut across all sectors, Hameed writes: 'I realized that my primary goal would be Gendering the Plans,' the outcome of which was the establishment of a formal committee, namely the Committee of Feminist Economists.

The Group of Feminist Economists, constituted in March 2007, was mandated (a) to review all sectoral reports of working groups and steering committees for the 11th Plan with respect to their gender content and make suggestions regarding gender issues, promoting gender equality and so on, and (b) to examine and make suggestions as to how the 'inclusive growth' approach envisaged for the 11th Plan could be translated into sectoral plans with appropriate institutional arrangements and adequate financial allocations, so as to promote gender equality and growth with equity.

The outcome of the preceding exercise was the report, Engendering Public Policy. This report documents the complex process evolved by the Group of Feminist Economists to engender the 11th Five-Year Plan. Subjecting every draft chapter of the 11th Five-Year Plan to gender audit enabled the committee to bring to the fore with evidence:

1 The economic contribution of women by including a section on unorganized sector and on home-based workers, both of which have heavy female concentration
2 The specific locations of women such as in agriculture, where the establishment has yet to come to terms with women as farmers so essential to access extension, credit and marketing services
3 The significance of highlighting best practices from the field to demonstrate where what has worked, in what context and under what circumstances
4 The need to include in plans, areas and sectors hitherto uncovered, such as urban and rural livelihoods. Within this, the committee had also identified the specific sectors that contributed to both growth and employment and which therefore needed to be supported.

In a nutshell, the 'gendering of plans' exercise by the committee was focused on drawing out women's role as economic agents, whether paid or unpaid. While the exercise did not get into the next step, namely that of calculating or imputing value to such work, it was fairly able to provide an idea of the vast and diverse range of women's economic role, and how such work enabled households to cope with the 'multiple deprivations' mentioned by Hameed earlier.

The Planning Commission reconstituted the Working Group of Feminist Economists for the 12th Five-Year Plan. While the subtitle of the 11th Five-Year Plan emphasized a move towards inclusive growth, the 12th Plan, not to be outdone, spoke of 'faster, sustainable and more inclusive' growth. In a paper titled 'Gendering the 12th Plan: A Feminist Perspective', two members of the reconstituted Group of Feminist Economists, Mridul Eapen and Aasha Kapur Mehta (2012), begin by asking some very pertinent questions: how will inclusion occur? What are the mechanisms for including the excluded and how will this be measured or continuously monitored over the plan period?

More damaging, they question why there is no evidence of growth having been inclusive during the 11th Plan despite the fast rate of growth of the economy.

> There is a shying away from providing a report card on why the Eleventh Plan that promised so much by way of more inclusive growth of excluded/marginalized groups including women failed in these objectives. Inclusiveness through planned development has remained elusive.
>
> (Ibid.: 43)

A little later the authors answer their own question by pointing out the distance between the planners and the Group of Feminist Economists in the understanding of the term 'inclusion':

> In the view of the planners, inclusion is to be achieved through the distribution of the gains through flagship programmes and handouts to the needy. In other words, if gains from growth do not trickle down to all as expected, equity among citizens is to be ensured through special policies that cater to the needs of vulnerable sections. Perhaps this is why the approach paper is not overly concerned about the failure of the economy to generate additional employment during the Eleventh Plan period.
>
> (Ibid.: 44)

In the case of the 11th Plan, the Group of Feminist Economists spent considerable time and effort in demonstrating and establishing what gendering of plans entails and how this exercise enabled to centre-stage the economic contribution of the poor labouring section of the population, women in particular. During the exercise involving the 12th Plan, dismayed at the continuing phenomenon of denial of gains of growth to large sections of the population as well as the poor quality of whatever employment got generated, the main emphasis of the group was on urging the planners to make livelihood and decent employment generation the driving force of growth. Speaking the language of economics to address a Planning Commission that largely understood only this language, the group emphasized how 'shifting to a livelihood-led growth strategy or an employment oriented macroeconomic strategy can have many direct and indirect positive effects through strong multiplier effects, even for other policy measures' (ibid.: 49).

Consequent to a change in government in 2014, not just the 12th Plan but the institution of the Planning Commission has been disbanded and replaced by the NITI Aayog.

4. Conclusion

We begin with Amy Mazur's (2013) pertinent question asked in the context of post-industrial democracies but nevertheless relevant to the theme of our chapter given the long and fairly intensive engagement that scholars, feminists or otherwise have had with plans and planned development in this country, namely, does feminist policy matter? The question assumes relevance since over a long period a highly active and individually successful community of scholars has grappled in several different ways in working towards the goals of mainstreaming gender and of improving women's lives at the margin. To what extent has this been achieved and how do we assess its achievement?

If *outputs* of plans and policies are measured in terms of

1 *government programmes*, then we have innumerable welfare programmes, most of which are indeed women-specific;
2 *structures*, then over a long period governments of the day have created separate departments, cells, women police stations and so on;
3 *instruments*, then we have managed to bring forth several legislations and laws to address gender-specific issues;
4 *funding*, then tools such as gender-budgeting, earmarking of funds for women-specific institutions and programmes such as maternal heath do exist and also function.

In the light of the aforementioned, there is no doubt that over the years successive plans have much to show in terms of *administrative outputs*. It is only when administrative 'outputs' are differentiated from 'practice' on the ground a la Mazur (2013) that we begin seeing the growing disjuncture plan after plan, and between plan rhetoric and ground reality. We couldn't agree more with Mazur:

> Identifying outputs AND practice is particularly important in feminist policy formation where elected officials may be willing to sign-off on a policy that promotes gender equality, establish mechanisms to implement and evaluate, but less supportive of the potential politically costly

process of putting into action those policy instruments. Therefore, promoting 'concrete' activities, rather than 'symbolic' gestures, may take more political will and bottom-up pressure than just setting up administrative machinery.

(Mazur 2013)

Eapen and Mehta's (2012) work mentioned earlier concretely captures some of what Mazur has expressed earlier.

Engaging with the theme of planned economic development has enabled us to unearth several dilemmas that we as feminists need to confront even if we may not all agree on how we read and interpret them. But read them we must, since it has implications for our politics, the strategies that we wish to adopt, for the sequencing of our actions on the ground for achieving the goals that inform our politics in the first place. Right at the beginning we had endorsed Parpart's (2014) observation of how the transformation (of unequal and unjust power relations) agenda had fallen by the wayside and replaced with a promise of inclusion. That we in India have not even managed the agenda of inclusion is a telling commentary on the nature of our struggle and our politics as feminists.

Acknowledgement

I am extremely grateful to Bhavani Arabandi for her critical and close reading of the chapter.

Notes

1 A special issue of the *Journal of International Development*, Vol. 26, No. 3, April 2014 (which includes Jane Parpart's paper referred to in our text), interrogates the theoretical underpinnings of gender mainstreaming and argues for a rethinking of the received notions of agency and transformation.
2 Nirmala Banerjee (1998) credits Maithreyi Krishnaraj for having resurrected the WRPE from archival sources; Leela Kasturi's piece (1995): *Development, Patriarchy and Politics: Indian Women in the Political Process, 1947–1992* (New Delhi: Centres for women Development studies), was accessed on 2 April 2016.
3 Devaki Jain takes issue with Nirmala Banerjee on this point. According to Jain, several of the architects of the WRPE, Durgabai, for instance, preferred to work outside the government system as 'social workers', a term not to be read as synonymous with becoming apolitical. Durgabai was a pioneer in setting up several institutions that became a focal point for women's issues; for retention of autonomy in the functioning of these institutions, Durgabai had to directly confront the state. These institutions, according to Jain, had an important place in the political landscape of the country. Important as these observations are, and even granted that persons like

Durgabai were very much in the public space but politically active in their own way, Jain's observations still do not answer the question that Banerjee raises, namely what accounts for the silence on the part of the authors of WRPE, when say, for example, there is absolutely no mention of the WRPE in the First Five-Year Plan of the country (Jain, D. Women's Contribution to Political Economy. Accessed on 16 April 2016)?

4 Group of Feminist Economists for the 11th Plan (2007–12) constituted by the Planning Commission vide its letter dated 29 March 2007.

5 This section is based on Banerjee (1998) and Kasturi (1995).

References

Banerjee, N. 1998. "Whatever Happened to the Dreams of Modernity? The Nehruvian Era and Women's Position," *Economic and Political Weekly*, Vol. 33, No. 17 (25 April), pp. WS-2–WS-8.

Eapen, Mridul and Aasha Kapur Mehta. 2012. "Gendering the Twelfth Plan: A Feminist Perspective," *Economic and Political Weekly*, Vol. XLVII, No. 17 (April), pp. 42–49.

Government of India. 1974. *Towards Equality: Report of the Committee on the Status of Women in India*. New Delhi: Ministry of Education and Social Welfare, Department of Social Welfare, December.

———. 1988. *Shramshakti: Report of the National Commission on Self-Employed Women and Women in the Informal Sector*. New Delhi: Department of Women and Child Development, Ministry of Human Resource Development.

———. 2010. *Engendering Public Policy: Report on the Work of the Working Group of Feminist Economists during the Preparation of the Eleventh Five Year Plan, 2007–12*. New Delhi: Planning Commission.

Govinda, R. and Y. Josephine. 2004. *Para Teachers in India: A Review*. Paris: International Institute of Educational Planning, UNESCO, October.

Hameed, S. and Devaki Jain. 2009. Feminist Economists Engage with India's Eleventh Five Year Plan. Paper for the IAFFE *Conference on Engendering Economic Policy*, Boston. devakijain.com/pdf/jain_engenderingindias5year-plan.pdf (accessed 2 April 2016).

Harding, S. and K. Norberg. 2005. "New Feminist Approaches to Social Science Methodologies: An Introduction," *Signs*, Vol. 30, No. 4, pp. 2009–2015.

Jenson, Jane. 2009. "Lost in Translation: The Social Investment Perspective and Gender Equality," *Social Politics: International Studies in Gender, State and Society*, Vol. 16, No. 4 (December), pp. 446–483.

Kasturi, L. 1995. "Development, Patriarchy and Politics: Indian Women in the Political Process, 1947–1992," *Occasional Paper No. 25*, New Delhi: Centre for Women's Development Studies.

Kingdon, Geeta G. and V. Sipahimalani-Rao. 2010. "Para-Teachers in India: Status and Impact," *Economic and Political Weekly*, Vol. XLV, No. 12 (20 March), pp. 59–67.

Krishna, A. 2013. "Making It in India: Examining Social Mobility in Three Walks of Life," *Economic and Political Weekly*, Vol. XLVIII, No. 49 (7 December), pp. 38–49.

Krishnaraj, M. 1995. *Remaking Society for Women: Visions – Past and Present.* New Delhi: Indian Association for Women's Studies, December, Published by Systems Vision.

Mazumdar, Vina. 1985. "Role of Research in Women's Development: A Case Study of the ICSSR Programme of Women's Studies." In R. S. Ganapathy, S. R. Ganesh, Rushikesh M. Maru, Samuel Paul and Ram Mohan Rao (eds). *Public Policy and Policy Analysis in India.* New Delhi: Sage, pp. 208–251.

Mazur, Amy G. 2013. Does Feminist Policy Matter in Post Industrial Democracies? A Proposed Analytical Roadmap. www.csbppl.com/wp-content/uploads/2013/09/Does-Feminist-Policy-Matter-in-Post-Industrial-Democracies.pdf (accessed 27 March 2016).

O'Connor, Julia S. 2015. "The State and Gender Equality: From Patriarchal to Women-Friendly State." In Stephan Leibfried, Evelyne Huber, Mathew Lange, Jonah D. Levy, Frank Nullmeier and John Stephens (eds). *The Oxford Handbook of Transformations of the State.* Oxford, UK: Oxford University Press, Chapter 25, pp. 482–498.

Parpart, Jane L. 2014. "Exploring the Transformative Potential of Gender Mainstreaming in International Development Institutions," *Journal of International Development*, Vol. 26, No. 3 (April), pp. 382–395.

Sassoon, Anne Showstack (ed.). 1987. "Introduction." In Anne Showstack Sassoon (ed.). *Women and the State: The Shifting Boundaries of Public and Private.* Berkley, CA: Hutchinson Education, University of California, pp. 15–47.

Swaminathan, P. 1991. "Science and Technology for Women: A Critique of Policy," *Economic and Political Weekly*, Vol. 26, Nos. 1–2 (5 January), pp. 59–63.

UNDP. 2002. *Transforming the Mainstream: Gender in UNDP.* UNDP: New York.

———. 2003. *Transforming the Mainstream: Gender in UNDP.* New York: UNDP.

United Nations Economic and Social Council (ECOSOC). 1997. *Mainstreaming the Gender Perspective into All Policies and Programmes in the United Nations System.* New York: United Nations.

West, C. and S. Fenstermaker. 1995. "Doing Difference," *Gender and Society*, Vol. 9, No. 1 (February), pp. 8–37.

World Bank. 2012. *World Development Report, 2012.* Washington, DC: World Bank.

10 Unpacking 'win–win'
How feminists interrogate microfinance

K. Kalpana

1. Introduction

In recent years, feminist research has systematically, and with growing rigour, explored the interfaces between gender and development, seeking to provide nuanced and complex understandings of the 'gendering' of statist developmental discourses and projects, both in the advanced capitalist countries and in the post-colonies. In many parts of the post-colonial world, including India, a former marginalization of women from the exercise of 'planning for development' has been reversed dramatically in the past two decades of the 20th century and beyond, in tandem with the ascendance of neoliberal capitalism. Consequently, feminist research engagement with the development experience of Third-World countries has sought to make sense of how, why and to what ends 'women in poverty' have emerged as an enormously important constituency, valorized and invoked by development policy makers in different ways and for diverse purposes. Refuting the idea that the sheer numbers of women participating in state-crafted developmental initiatives is ipso facto evidence of gender transformative change, feminist scholarship has interrogated the terms on which women are 'mainstreamed' into developmental initiatives that promote their income-earning strategies in a number of ways.

Feminist enquiries into this phenomenon are particularly salient given that women of land-poor and low-income households have emerged as the primary constituency of microfinance/credit-based development projects, since the last decade and a half of the 20th century. These projects involve forming residence-based peer groups that save and rotate their money (as micro-loans) to group members and seek credit from the formal financial sector, including commercial banks and other financial institutions. The growth of microfinance has taken place even as many parts of the world have experienced a declining governmental commitment to social sector provisioning and employment generation in the face of neoliberalism-inspired macro-economic reforms and social policy transformations. In this context, women microcredit borrowers are expected to use their micro-loans to defray the costs of procuring basic amenities and essential services (e.g. drinking water, health and education) and finance micro-enterprises and other self-employment-based revenue-generating activities, contributing thereby to the survival of their households and communities undergoing economic stress (Rankin 2001, Mayoux 2002).

If neoliberal capitalism has dismantled social protectionist policies, depressed wages for the working classes and reduced job security overall, it has nevertheless managed, Fraser (2009) argues, to elaborate a new romance, a 'feminist romance' of women's advancement and gender justice. This 'romance' appeals to women across the class spectrum, including professional women of the middle classes, Special Economic Zone workers, migrants, microcredit borrowers and domestic workers – women who are seeking material security and liberation from traditional authority and have poured into the labour force in large numbers in some parts of the world. The feminist romance has succeeded, in effect, in harnessing the dream of women's emancipation to the engine of capitalist accumulation (Fraser 2009). In this chapter, I map some of the important ways in which feminist scholarship in the domain of gender and development has problematized the feminist romance that Fraser describes by disentangling the agendas of capitalist accumulation and women's emancipation, where these are intertwined in complex ways. My aim in this chapter is to show how gender, as a category of analysis, has been deployed in ways that have opened up new questions, insights and understandings at the level of both policy conceptualizations and their trajectories in the field.

In order to demonstrate this, I use the case of women-targeted microfinance, which is an exemplary instance of an anti-poverty intervention that derives its rationale from the 'synergy' argument (Jackson 1996) for 'investing' in women. Synergy-based claims are enormously popular in the development establishment and have won microcredit programmes a diverse spectrum of institutional supporters ranging from commercial banks to national governments to international donor agencies. In seeking to unpack the multiple claims made on behalf of these interventions, feminist researchers have honed particular, productive methodological tools – the subject of discussion of this chapter. Besides discussing this, I also show how feminist research has offered us a critical reading of the discursive/representational shifts that constituted women in poverty as deserving and worthy of development assistance, in consonance with the rise of both the 'anti-poverty' and the 'efficiency'-based gender planning paradigms in the past two decades of the 20th century.

2. Why invest in women?

Razavi (1997) observes that the global reassertion of poverty concerns in the 1990s, in response to documented findings of the adverse social impacts of neoliberal economic reforms in many parts of the world, influenced the gender and development discourse in two distinctive ways. The 'feminization of poverty' argument, advanced by development policy institutions and women's organizations worldwide, posited that women were over-represented among the poor, that an increasing number of households had become female-headed and that the poorest households were more likely to be headed by a woman than by a man. Targeting female-headed households with development resources (microcredit or other productive inputs and technologies) was therefore seen as simultaneously reaching the poorest households, rendered vulnerable by male desertion, divorce, out-migration or death. The second position, largely promoted by advocates within the World Bank, emphasized the multiple social gains or 'spin-offs' of investing in women such as child survival, fertility reduction, the increase of family incomes and consumption spending on basic needs of the family, protection of the environment and the enhancement of food security. The 'human capital' argument for investing in women, as it came to be called, deemed women's participation crucial for enhancing the efficacy and delivering optimal outcomes on a range of development programmes and represented women as the 'missing link' in low-cost poverty alleviation strategies (Razavi 1997).

In constituting women as the ideal target group of development programmes, policy makers, planners and programme implementers have assumed that the interests of women necessarily and automatically coincide with all other development goals in an unproblematic manner. Feminist scholars have rigorously questioned this synergy argument (Jackson 1996) and the 'integrationist' strategies (Kabeer 1999) it fuels. Kabeer (1999) notes that gender advocates in development organizations, seeking to engender mainstream policy making, have attempted to integrate women into the poverty agenda as the 'poorest of the poor' or the efficiency agenda as 'under-valued food producers and micro-entrepreneurs'. While these approaches may well deliver short-term payoffs, she cautions that integrationist strategies can remain limited within the parameters set by institutional priorities and their transformative potential stunted. It is also the case that the structural relations of disadvantage that constitute poverty may not always or entirely overlap with those that constitute gender inequality. And hence, the possibility of conflicting interests between the two agendas (of gender justice and poverty reduction) requires that they *not* be conflated with each other, warranting instead the 'rescue' or retrieval of gender as a distinctive analytical and conceptual category from the 'poverty trap' (Jackson 1996).

Feminist scholarship has therefore established that we must ask the hard question of precisely how and through what pathways specific poverty-targeted development interventions improve women's well-being, enhance their autonomy or contribute to other attainments, valued from gender-transformative perspectives. Anti-poverty and other economic development interventions must be interrogated, keeping in mind that the pursuit of multiple programme goals can imply the overriding of one by the other and that synergies and 'win–win' scenarios may not always ensue. In the following sections, I show how these conceptual frameworks and the methodological insights they inspired have paved the way for a meticulous interrogation of dominant microfinance paradigms from a gender perspective. In particular, I show how they have skilfully taken apart the win–win hypothesis (Mayoux 1998, Morduch 2000) that underpins the microfinance edifice.

3. Unpacking win–win: a gendered institutional analysis

The win–win hypothesis rests on the claim that microfinance-centred development interventions alleviate poverty (by financing micro-enterprises of the poor) and empower women (by making available a valued resource to poor households through their female members), even as they offer the prospect of commercial viability and profit margins for lending institutions (by enforcing on-time loan repayment and charging the poor near-market interest rates). Microfinance delivery to poor households through informal, grassroots-based peer groups of women is thus seen to simultaneously meet the needs and interests of multiple stakeholders: the commercial viability imperatives of banks and other lenders, the social empowerment interests of the women in question, the poverty alleviation needs of their households and the growth needs of the economy at large. Researchers have mobilized the analytic power of gender to unsettle win–win scenarios by showing how multiple programme goals compete and conflict with each other, producing outcomes that do not necessarily advance women's interests. In doing this, they have raised several pertinent questions, the foremost being, why target women at all and how did the focus on women savers and borrowers originate?

While microfinance institutions have responded to emergent global concerns regarding 'mainstreaming' women in development, ethnography-based analyses of institutions (e.g. Bangladesh's well-known Grameen

Bank) have revealed that the complex effects of patriarchal ideologies have played a significant part in constituting women as the desired borrowers of microcredit worldwide (Rahman 1999). When compared to men, the relative ease of lending to and recovering loans from women derives from the ability of microfinance projects to mobilize and harness as *resources* traditional gendered social norms and practices such as women's limited physical mobility and their availability in and around their homes, their greater susceptibility to public and peer shaming in case they are unable to repay their loans, men's propensity to respond more vigorously when the honour (*izzat*) of their female kin is at stake and the women borrowers' relative inability to challenge the authority of the loan dispensers – the field staff of microcredit projects. The 'positional vulnerability' (Rahman 1999) of women, figuring prominently in the field narratives of project staff or the 'hidden transcripts' (Scott 1990) of microfinance projects, anchors programme implementation more closely to loan repayment, rather than empowerment-derived concerns and imperatives.

My research on the self-help group (SHG)-bank linkage programme in India has also dwelt on the question of how the idea of banking with *women*'s SHGs gained widespread acceptance and support since its origin in the early 1990s. Ranging between 12 and 20 members, the SHGs are neighbourhood-based peer groups that save and make loans to group members for a six-month period after group formation, subsequent to which they become eligible to apply for loans from commercial banks, India's specialized development banks (the regional rural banks) and state-owned credit cooperatives. The Indian state's encouragement and official support to SHG-banking schemes has coincided with the onset of macro-economic reforms or the Structural Adjustment Programmes adopted since the 1990s. India's financial policy makers, such as the central bank of the country, the Reserve Bank of India (RBI) and the National Bank for Agriculture and Rural Development (NABARD), have constructed the SHG-bank linkage project in ways that appeal to the commercial interests of banks by aligning its operational principles with the banking sector's efficiency concerns of recovery performance, institutional viability and transaction costs reduction (Kalpana 2017). These concerns have, in turn, grown increasingly salient since the inception of banking sector reforms, initiated as part of overall economic reforms (Ramachandran and Swaminathan 2002).

The policy documents of RBI and NABARD acknowledge that SHG-banking has evolved in a macro-economic environment dominated by the concerns of rural banks damaged by the 'twin problems of non-viability and poor recovery performance' (RBI Bulletin 1997: 70). Concomitantly, the women members of SHGs are represented, in the public utterances and speeches of high-ranking bank officials, as valuable assets whose 'trustworthy', 'sincere' and 'committed' natures; 'excellent' repayment record; and willingness to use peer pressure will guarantee the timely repayment of bank loans (Dadhich 2001). It is apparent that the case for women's access to bank credit is advanced not so much from the viewpoint of redressing a former exclusion and the attendant injustice but of mobilizing women's repayment capacities in the interests of promoting the portfolio health of rural banks. In other words, India's financial policy makers have sought to legitimize women's claim to bank credit for the instrumental purpose of attaining other objectives, rather than intrinsic reasons. At one level, we might ask whether and why this should matter. For instance, in a different context, Razavi (1997) takes issue with what she identifies as a scholarly feminist critique of arguments for gender equality (advanced by gender advocates within development organizations) that draw on instrumental rather than intrinsic reasons for investing in women. She points out that this critique fails to take into account the compulsions of policy advocacy that operates in the world of real (not abstract) politics, defined by compromises, aberrations and alliances.

In the case of SHG-banking, the deployment of essentialized assumptions and images of women's 'nature' and the promise of disciplined fiscal behaviour on the part of women have, to an extent, served strategic purposes. They have, in part, contributed to opening the doors of the formal sector to women from hitherto 'unbanked' land-poor and low-income households and communities. Nonetheless, the strategy of invoking women's responsible repayment behaviour, as the prime rationale for lending to women, resonates through the banking sector in ways that have disconcerting implications at the grassroots and marks the interfaces between SHGs and banks in particular ways. If the rhetoric of the upper echelons of the financial sector in India celebrates the instrumental advantages of lending to women, branch-level bankers have sought to appropriate women's much-vaunted diligence in loan repayment, in ways not anticipated or intended by bank policies. Bank branch managers have often pressured the SHGs who seek bank loans to fully repay any individual-targeted loans that the banks may have formerly made as part of older, long-defunct schemes to the male kin (husbands, sons, even in-laws) of the women members of these groups. The failure (by even a few group members whose male kin had unpaid overdues) to do so could mean the denial of bank loans to the SHG as a collective, regardless of the group's eligibility for loans otherwise.

Faced with recalcitrant bank personnel, SHG women have often incurred debt in order to repay loans borrowed by their male kin, usually several years prior to the formation of the SHGs. Not infrequently, banks have also insisted that the women members of SHGs become the unremunerated loan collectors, who expend considerable time, effort and energies to ensure loan repayment by all residents in the village panchayat, including *non*-kin male members in order to 'earn' their access to bank loans sanctioned by policy (Kalpana 2008, 2017). As is apparent from the case discussed here at some length, the use of a gender lens to examine SHG-banking enables us to not only identify but also problematize the instrumentalism that suffuses the whole enterprise. It helps us perceive that the loan collection tactics employed by branch-level managers have primarily worked because the groups consist of women whose responsibilization (vis-à-vis themselves, their peer group members and their households) has been manipulated in ways that do not serve their interests.

In the foregoing discussion, it is important to note that the banks have mobilized in their favour the gendered understanding that cuts across all participating institutions (the banks themselves, the non-governmental organizations [NGOs] that promote the SHGs and rural households) that women must honour commitments made by their male kin. This calls for a careful analysis of the gendered dynamic that shapes the actors and personnel involved in 'integrating' women in development, as part of engaging with the institutional matrices within which all development interventions (including microfinance) are situated. Goetz's (1997) work offers us valuable methodological leads on how this might be done. She proposes that we study the 'gendered archaeology' of organizations by examining eight elements that include institutional/organizational histories, the gendered cognitive context of organizations, organizational cultures, authority structures, incentive and accountability systems, the sexuality of organizations, gendered space and time and gendered participants. She helps us understand why institutions change so little even when introducing new actors (women) and new concerns (gender equity) by reminding us that gender preference systems are embedded in the norms, structures and practices of all institutions, including those generally believed to be gender-neutral territory. Drawing an analogy between the functioning of institutions and the rules of a game, Goetz (1997) asks us to imagine what happens when new actors enter the arena. If pygmies wanted to play football, could they bend the rules of the game?

To return to the case of SHG-banking, a thoroughgoing gendered institutional analysis of its actors and processes in ways similar to those outlined by Goetz illuminates dynamics that remain obscure otherwise. Nationalized commercial banks, subject to multiple and often conflicting priorities and compulsions, are expected to fulfil the mandates of a developmental state by complying with 'priority sector' lending quotas that include loans to women's SHGs, among other components.[1] Simultaneously, the performance orientation of banks in India has intensified in a reform-oriented environment since the onset of banking sector reforms (Kohli

1997). In this institutional context, bank personnel interact with women, new entrants to the formal financial sector, who are disempowered by the intersecting social relations of class, caste and gender. Yet the banks make no allowance for the women's lack of experience when dealing with bank paperwork, procedure and protocol or for their need to have unfamiliar processes explained to them. The rural women members of SHGs often report distressing encounters with irritable branch managers who display little respect for the women's time constraints or their work commitments at home and outside. The marginal status of rural women marks them out for discriminatory treatment by bank personnel who respond to them, not as valued customers representing the aspirations of social groups hitherto excluded by the formal credit sector but as potential defaulters whose small-sized loan accounts are barely worth the trouble and effort of transactions.

By making the organizational histories, gendered cultures, authority structures and practices of the banking sector the object of study, my research shows that SHG-banking does not mean pro-poor or gender-sensitive banking given that it does not transform banks into hospitable environments for women or the poor. Rather, it requires that the women make the necessary adjustments and mould themselves to 'fit' better within reform-oriented banking institutions (Kalpana 2008, 2017). The embedded class and gender biases that animate the banking sector are revealed with stark clarity in the contrasting treatment of 'privileged' defaulters, belonging to the elite classes, whose political clout and social and institutional networks and contacts enable them to evade scrutiny and punitive consequences. Corporate entities, whose unpaid debt to public sector banks often run into millions of rupees, are rarely, if ever, subject to the 'naming and shaming' logic that women of the SHGs bring to bear on each other, especially when the groups' repayment of bank loans is at stake. Take, for instance, the recent case of Vijay Mallya, the liquor baron and owner of a prominent private airline in India. Charged with defrauding the publicly owned IDBI Bank of Rs 900 crore, Mallya was 'permitted' to flee the country despite ongoing investigations against him. Earlier, the Central Bureau of Investigation had requested a consortium of 17 banks, led by the State Bank of India, to declare loans worth Rs 10,000 crore to Mallya as fraud (Asian Human Rights Commission 2016). The case of Vijay Mallya compels us to ask how 'performance-oriented' banks have really been on the question of challenging the impunity of powerful defaulters.

4. Re-configuring the 'gender order'

The discussion thus far has elaborated how the use of gender as a category of critique and analysis allows us to perceive that synergy-based claims (of win–win) do not inevitably lead to positive outcomes for women microfinance borrowers. How then has feminist research charted the ways in which these projects impact women's lives and choices? One of the ways it has done so is to ask how these programmes reshape the gender order that women negotiate on an everyday basis in diverse regional, institutional and socio-cultural settings. Kabeer (1999) makes an important conceptual point when she reminds us that gender relations do not exist in a social vacuum, but are constituted and reconstituted as relations of difference and inequality by the institutional domains of households, communities, markets and states. This conceptualization of the re-making and un-making of gender relations has significant methodological implications insofar as it enables us to formulate precise questions about the ways that microfinance projects re-configure the social relations and dominant ideologies of gender at play within each of these domains. Do they challenge, for instance, the ideologies of familial domesticity that embed women within kin and community-based social spaces and networks? Do the projects that foster women's market engagement address the oppressive structures of disadvantage that confine women petty commodity producers to the lower segments of the informal sector? What mediates women's transition from the status of workers to entrepreneurs in family-owned enterprises and how might a gender perspective enrich our understanding of women's varied and complex engagement with markets?

Rahman's (1999) work on the Grameen Bank and my research on SHG-banking in India suggest that the first question is an important vantage point from which to interrogate microfinance. As already discussed, the two studies showed how women's kin relationships and community-based social ties are instrumentally invoked by lending institutions in ways that re-embed women within these relations, underscoring these identities as primary, 'essential' ones and undercutting their agency as autonomous actors. While the imperatives and strategies of microfinance provider institutions are important to observe and critique from a gender perspective, they do not preclude the question of whether the women borrowers of microcredit use the spaces, resources and opportunities provided by these projects to tilt in their favour the many 'patriarchal bargains' (Kandiyoti 1988) they routinely conduct with household, kin and community structures. Interestingly, debates among feminist scholars on microfinance have been most charged on the theme of its intersection with intra-household gender dynamics. The issue in question relates to differing evaluations of women's ability to control their loans (vis-à-vis their male kin) and make decisions on how they will be used once they enter the household. Kabeer (2001) makes an important methodological point when she notes that indices such as 'managerial control', which some studies have used to measure women's control over the loans they borrow, cannot substitute as proxy variables for programme outcomes such as empowerment. These outcomes, she argues, must be independently examined, keeping in mind that membership in credit programmes is likely to be empowering even for women who hand over loans to their male kin. Kabeer's intervention in this debate is important in terms of cautioning against the perfunctory use of indices of empowerment or well-being, abstracted from the specific local contexts that give them meaning and value.

The critical edge of the second question on women 'micro-entrepreneurs' in the unorganized sectors of the economy draws from feminist scholarship that dates back to the period when a multitude of small-scale, NGO-implemented, donor-sponsored enterprise promotion projects for women were launched between the late 1970s and the early 1980s, gaining momentum in the wake of the Nairobi International Women's Conference of 1985 (Moser 1993: 55–82, Mayoux 1995). On the one hand, these projects sought to expand women's income-earning opportunities within the informal sector assumed to possess the autonomous capacity to generate employment sufficient to absorb the 'working poor'.[2] Feminist research, on the other, provided more complex formulations of the informal sector, of women's work within it and of its relationship to the formal (capitalist) sector. Early studies of home-based production systems showed that the concentration of women in the occupations that bore a structural resemblance to their family/domestic roles made it possible for capital to install productive processes within the heart of the family. Feminist analyses laid bare the mechanisms by which gender relations and ideologies, in articulation with capitalist relations of production, facilitated the extraction of surplus value via the piece rate system of wage payment to women, shut off from access to employment outside their homes and neighbourhood spaces. Where women worked in family-owned enterprises, the non-availability of ideologies of autonomous entrepreneurship for women rendered them a labour force *par excellence* that fed male entrepreneurial success (Mies 1981, Moser and Young 1981).

The early feminist critiques that probed women's self-employment in the lower rungs of the informal sector resonate powerfully in the current era of microfinance. In 1997, when this researcher began to work with SHG federations in the southern districts of Tamil Nadu, I found that women (in Kanyakumari district) frequently borrowed loans from their groups, the financing banks and the NGO-organized federation in order to intensify their involvement in the most widely available income-generating activities in the region, namely coconut and palm leaf thatching. Heavily feminized, these activities were carried out by women in their homes or in small clusters within their neighbourhoods. While the loans financed the women's purchase of raw material from the middlemen and were valued for this reason, it was not uncommon for the women to work till midnight to complete the greater quantum of work they had taken on. The structure of work remained the same, with the middleman's control of raw materials, markets and wages undisturbed. Undoubtedly, these economic activities (and a multitude of others like them in different parts of the country) make available valuable incomes (even if meagre) directly earned by women. However, a gender analysis of these productive activities obliges us to go beyond noting their immediate utility for women and to problematize state developmental initiatives that rely on the strategy of expanding women's work performed under difficult conditions, and at considerable costs to themselves, in order to mitigate household poverty.

A critical gender perspective also warrants that we explore whether there has been a commensurate improvement in the bargaining strength of women informal sector workers (including those managing petty enterprises and other credit-financed self-employment activities) vis-à-vis their male kin, private capital and the state. For instance, we might ask (as feminist researchers have) if household care responsibilities get re-negotiated in a more equitable manner between male and female members and what other (unintended) consequences may ensue when women earn incomes they may not have earlier. Drawing on their study of women's and men's savings groups in Bangladesh, Kelkar, Nathan and Jahan (2003) found that an increase in women's economic activities had increased their working hours and that the women resented men's greater leisure. However, men had begun to share domestic work (however small their contribution), and women's increased involvement in income-earning activities, by increasing the pressure on their time, had led to the abandonment of labour-intensive household chores, such as the manual pounding of rice.

Insofar as women's involvement in family-owned enterprises is concerned, research from a gender perspective has sought to understand if women's labour investment in these enterprises is accompanied by the acquisition of new skills and knowledge on their part. Do microfinance projects merely make available women's loans for male-owned and dominated businesses, reproducing established power hierarchies in the process? Or do women learn to maintain books of accounts, handle cash, cultivate market networks and contacts and confidently interact with (non-kin) male acquaintances? Leach and Sitaram (2002) discuss the challenges involved when women silk-reelers of the scheduled castes in the state of Karnataka attempted, through an NGO-led project, to become entrepreneurs in the face of a dominant gender order that has always used women's labour in silk-reeling and spinning, but promoted men's control of marketing and finance. In the project area, the women were intensively trained and skilled through residential courses aimed at building their motivation and self-confidence as well as escorted visits to the cocoon and the silk markets, in order to facilitate on-site learning and direct observation.

Leach and Sitaram (2002) document the many reasons the project floundered and failed, even though the women reported, in the early stages, a perceived increase in economic and social status, the satisfaction of earning their own income and 'thinking as businesswomen' and of being self-employed rather than the employees of others. Since the NGO insisted that the women (and not their kinsmen) visit the local cocoon market and the Silk Exchange over 170 kilometres away in Bangalore city, they had to rely on their husbands to drop them at the bus stop in the neighbouring village and wait long hours for their wives' return in the late evening or the night. It appeared that the formal exclusion of men from the project, even if they were informally involved, had undermined it from the start. The price fluctuations in the silk market, the volatility that marked the business and the women's inexperience led to their husbands berating them for their 'ignorance' and 'incompetence' and their houses being mortgaged to the NGO to repay the capital invested. This case study raises serious questions about the risks and costs of a programme that exclusively targets women from the poorest households working in an overwhelmingly male-dominated industry and expects them to function autonomously in a fluctuating market they have little control over, exposing them, in the process, to hostility and backlash within their households.

The exclusion of women from market spaces is not a universal characteristic that marks all social and regional contexts. Acknowledging this, research on the gender dynamics of markets has sought to capture the tremendous cultural and regional variation in household structures, women's histories of market engagement and access to public spaces. A case in point is an NGO-organized microcredit programme in Ghana. The researchers found that almost all the women had some business experience before they joined the programme and that women in Ghana were usually involved in trading commodities such as plantains, cassava, tomatoes and oranges. Appropriation of women's loans by men was rare, and there was a near-complete absence of the husbands' interference in decision-making about loan use in the study region. However, in some cases, men reduced their contribution to the household in the face of their wives' growing financial independence, forcing the women to hide their loans and businesses from their respective spouses. Women continued to exercise little control over how much money the men gave them for household expenses or how the latter spent the rest of it (Cheston and Kuhn 2002).

5. Conclusion

Women have emerged as a desired and sought-after constituency of microfinance and micro-enterprise-based development interventions, in consonance with the ascendance of neoliberal capitalism. Theorists such as Nancy Fraser (2009) argue that neoliberal capitalism has advanced an alluring feminist romance that harnesses the dream of women's emancipation to the engine of capital accumulation. In this chapter, I have attempted to show how research on microfinance using the analytical category of gender contributes to disentangling, in concrete ways, the distinct agenda of women's emancipation from the imperatives and strategies of capital accumulation in the microfinance sector. This chapter has discussed both the broader feminist critique of synergy-based approaches to investing (development resources) in women and the specific methodological perspectives that feminist research has drawn upon to unpack the win–win claims that underpin microfinance. While the win–win hypothesis assumes that women's interests always coincide with those of the other actors involved, be it the poverty-related concerns of their households or the financial viability-related goals of microfinance provider institutions, feminist research on microfinance has uncovered the many ways in which these synergistic assumptions may not hold true. The efficiency-related imperatives of microfinance providers may override empowerment-derived concerns or even actively harm rather than promote women's interests. A gendered institutional analysis or a gendered archaeology (Goetz 1997) of the multiple actors, agencies and personnel involved in delivering microfinance, or more broadly, in integrating women in development, has illuminated these contradictory outcomes.

As part of unravelling the ways in which microfinance re-configures the gender order in diverse socio-cultural contexts, feminist research has interrogated the 'female entrepreneurship' that these projects ostensibly generate. It has demonstrated that it is not enough to ask whether (or not) microfinance projects allow women to set up and manage income-generating activities, to a greater degree than before. Research, using the gender lens, has tackled the issue of whether women's (microcredit-financed) income earning modifies in some ways intra-household gender relations and mitigates their domestic responsibilities. It has delineated the conditions in which women's engagement in household enterprises might allow them to acquire subjectivities that expand the social horizons and physical boundaries demarcating their lives. It has shown that the gendered social and economic structures within which microfinance and micro-enterprise projects operate, in particular local settings, mediate the impacts the latter have upon women's lives.

Besides asking if microfinance projects produce visible changes in gender relations in households, markets and community spaces, feminist research has taken a critical lens to the official promotion of women's income-earning strategies in the face of state and macro-policy failure to effectively address structures of economic disadvantage and deprivation. These critiques call into question state-promoted anti-poverty approaches and paradigms, which assume that women's time and labour efforts are infinitely elastic and freely available resources that may be harnessed through low-paid income-generating activities or entirely unpaid volunteerism. In their analysis of *Kudumbashree*, the women-targeted anti-poverty project of the state government of Kerala, Devika and Thampi (2007) argue that the project has inscribed the image of the income-generating woman, who brings in monetary benefit for the well-being of her low-income family, within the female domestic ideal of Malayalee society, without countering or challenging prevailing gender norms regarding appropriate feminine behaviour. Women's groups formed through the scheme are focused on thrift, credit and micro-enterprises and conceived as instruments by which women may eradicate poverty within their families, *not* as collectives that foster consciousness-raising through which women might challenge multiple patriarchies. Devika and Thampi (2007) also point out that the real concern of women's double burden or the lack of leisure hardly figures in discussions of women-focused and state-led poverty alleviation projects.

While it is not microfinance-centred, Molyneux's (2002) account of the expansion of community-based, self-help projects during the 1990s in several Latin American countries is equally pertinent to this discussion. She takes to task international development agencies and national governments alike for mobilizing women as the (unremunerated) organizers and managers of health, education and neighbourhood food and housing programmes, in order to mitigate the disastrous social effects of irresponsible macro-economic policies that have impoverished their households and communities. If dominant development discourses have valorized women's perceived capacity to improve the performance and impacts of multiple development interventions, feminist research has relentlessly examined the new orthodoxies that have moved women, the missing link, from the margins to the centre of the world of development and have raised, in the process, as many concerns as they have attempted to address.

Notes

1 Nationalized banks in India are mandated to direct 40 per cent of net bank credit to 'priority' sectors that include agriculture, micro-enterprises and small enterprises, education, housing and designated 'weaker sections' such

as small and marginal farmers, artisans, village and cottage industries and so on (RBI 2013).
2 By the early 1970s, frustration at the failure of the 'trickle down' of growth had shifted international policy attention to the agenda of employment promotion and the target group of the working poor, who were seen to need most attention. In this development context, the informal sector teeming with the productive activities of the self-employed poor was perceived as the solution (Moser 1978).

References

Asian Human Rights Commission. 2016. "Fleeing Mallya Rakes Up the Deep Rot in Indian Democracy," *Countercurrents.org*, 11 March. http://www.countercurrents.org/ahrc110316.htm (accessed 12 April 2016).

Cheston, S. and L. Kuhn. 2002. "Empowering Women through Microfinance." Paper commissioned by the Micro Credit Summit Campaign + 5, New York, 10–13 November. Published by UNIFEM. http://www.seepnetwork.org/filebin/pdf/gender/71_Empowering_Women_Through_Microfinance.pdf (accessed 20 December 2015).

Dadhich, C. L. 2001. "Micro Finance – A Panacea for Poverty Alleviation: A Case Study of Oriental Grameen Project in India," *Indian Journal of Agricultural Economics*, Vol. 56, No. 3, pp. 419–426.

Devika, J. and Binitha V. Thampi. 2007. "Changing Regimes of Empowerment and Inclusion in the Public: Women and the Kudumbashree in Contemporary Kerala." In M. A. Oommen (ed.). *A Decade of Decentralization in Kerala: Experience and Lessons*. New Delhi: Institute of Social Sciences and Har-Anand Publications Pvt Ltd, pp. 175–208.

Fraser, Nancy. 2009. "Feminism, Capitalism and the Cunning of History," *New Left Review*, Vol. 56 (March–April), pp. 97–117.

Goetz, A. M. 1997. "Introduction." In Anne Marie Goetz (ed.). *Getting Institutions Right for Women in Development*. London and New York: Zed Books, pp. 1–28.

Jackson, Cecile. 1996. "Rescuing Gender from the Poverty Trap," *World Development*, Vol. 24, No. 3, pp. 489–504.

Kabeer, Naila. 1999. "From Feminist Insights to an Analytical Framework: An Institutional Perspective on Gender Inequality." In Naila Kabeer and Ramya Subrahmanian (eds). *Institutions, Relations and Outcomes: A Framework and Case Studies for Gender-Aware Planning*. New Delhi: Kali for Women, pp. 3–48.

———. 2001. "Conflicts over Credit: Re-Evaluating the Empowerment Potential of Loans to Women in Rural Bangladesh," *World Development*, Vol. 29, No. 1, pp. 63–84.

Kalpana, K. 2008. "The Vulnerability of 'Self-Help': Women and Microfinance in South India," *IDS Working Paper 303*. Brighton, UK: Institute of Development Studies. http://www2.ids.ac.uk/futurestate/pdfs/Wp303.pdf (accessed 19 December 2016).

———. 2017. *Women, Microfinance and the State in Neo-Liberal India*. New York: Routledge.

Kandiyoti, D. 1988. "Bargaining with Patriarchy," *Gender and Society*, Vol. 2, No. 3, pp. 274–290.

Kelkar, Govind, Dev Nathan and Rounaq Jahan. 2003. "We Were in Fire, Now We Are in Water: Micro-Credit and Gender Relations in Rural Bangladesh," *Working Paper Series No. 19*, New Delhi: Institute for Human Development.

Kohli, Renu. 1997. "Directed Credit and Financial Reform," *Economic and Political Weekly*, Vol. 32, No. 42, pp. 2667–2676.

Leach, Fiona and Shashikala Sitaram. 2002. "Microfinance and Women's Empowerment: A Lesson from India," *Development in Practice*, Vol. 12, No. 5, pp. 575–588.

Mayoux, Linda. 1995. "From Vicious to Virtuous Circles? Gender and Micro-Enterprise Development," *Occasional Paper 3*, Geneva: United Nations Research Institute for Social Development.

———. 1998. "Microfinance Programmes and Women's Empowerment: Approaches, Issues and Ways Forward," *DPP Working Paper No. 41*, Milton Keynes: The Open University.

———. 2002. "Women's Empowerment or Feminisation of Debt? Towards a New Agenda in African Microfinance," *Report Based on a One World Action Conference*. London, March 2002. https://static1.squarespace.com/static/536c4ee8e4b0b60bc6ca7c74/t/543810e2e4b06169c234b37d/1412960482860/49.Womens+Empowerment+or+Feminisation+of+Debt.pdf (accessed 20 December 2015).

Mies, Maria. 1981. "Dynamics of Sexual Division of Labour and Capital Accumulation: Women Lace Workers of Narsapur," *Economic and Political Weekly*, Vol. 16, No. 10/12 (March), pp. 487–500.

Molyneux, M. 2002. "Gender and the Silences of Social Capital: Lessons from Latin America," *Development and Change*, Vol. 33, No. 2, pp. 167–188.

Morduch, Jonathan. 2000. "The Microfinance Schism," *World Development*, Vol. 28, No. 4, pp. 617–629.

Moser, C. O. N. 1978. "Informal Sector or Petty Commodity Production: Dualism or Dependence in Urban Development?" *World Development*, Vol. 6, No. 9/10, pp. 1041–1064.

———. 1993. *Gender Planning and Development: Theory, Practice and Training*. London and New York: Routledge.

Moser, C. O. N. and Kate Young. 1981. "Women of the Working Poor," *IDS Bulletin*, Vol. 12, No. 3, pp. 1–9.

Rahman, Aminur. 1999. "Micro-Credit Initiatives for Equitable and Sustainable Development: Who Pays?" *World Development*, Vol. 27, No. 1, pp. 67–82.

Ramachandran, V. K. and Madhura Swaminathan. 2002. "Rural Banking and Landless Labour Households: Institutional Reform and Rural Credit Markets in India," *Journal of Agrarian Change*, Vol. 2, No. 4, pp. 502–544.

Rankin, K. N. 2001. "Governing Development: Neoliberalism, Microcredit and Rational Economic Woman," *Economy and Society*, Vol. 30, No. 1, pp. 18–37.

Razavi, Shahra. 1997. "Fitting Gender into Development Institutions," *World Development*, Vol. 25, No. 7, pp. 1111–1125.

Reserve Bank of India (RBI) Bulletin. 1997. "Role of Non-Governmental Organisations in Rural Credit Delivery System," Inaugural address by Dr. C. Rangarajan, Governor RBI at the 35th Excom Meeting of APRACA at Bangalore on 28 October 1996 reported in the *RBI Bulletin*, January, Mumbai: Reserve Bank of India.

———. 2013. "Master Circular – Priority Sector Lending – Targets and Classification," RBI/2013-14/107, 1 July. http://rbidocs.rbi.org.in/rdocs/notification/PDFs/107010713PSLFL.pdf (accessed 20 December 2015).

Scott, James. 1990. *Domination and the Arts of Resistance: Hidden Transcripts*. New Haven, CT: Yale University Press.

11 Globalizations, mobility and agency
Understanding women's lives through women's voices[1]

Bhavani Arabandi

1. Introduction

In 'The Messy Relationship between Feminisms and Globalizations', Manisha Desai (2007) contends,

> The interrelations [between gender and globalizations] are fraught and in some instances have furthered inequalities among women. But this does not preclude other possibilities . . . [. . .] feminists have used globalizations to further women's agency and their political, economic, and cultural empowerment. To see these other stories, one needs to define globalizations in the plural and to understand feminists as both constitutive of, and important actors in, globalizations.
> (Desai 2007: 797–798)

In order to understand how gender and globalizations interact, we need to understand, first, the variety of globalizations and, second, what feminist research entails for those different contexts.

Women's lives around the world have been transformed by globalization through the flexibilization of workers, occupational segregation and informalization of the economy. Feminist scholars have observed that the growing labour markets of the global economy are increasingly feminized (Salzinger 1997, Freeman 2000, Swaminathan 2004). These studies have tended to focus on the particular demographic dynamics of those niches of the global economy dominated by female labour where work is commonly concentrated at the lower rungs of manufacturing and services sector such as call centres, and the care economy. This body of work is important and useful for understanding women's tenuous work experiences, because women are typically funnelled into low-skilled, low-paying occupations lacking job security. While this is an area where the majority of women in the Global South are employed, it would be short-sighted to think that this is the only story from the South. Millions of educated women employed in 'creative economies' like the technology sector in countries such as India, for example, have tended to receive less scholarly attention, with notable exceptions such as Fernandes (2000), Radhakrishnan (2011) and Upadhya and Vasavi (2008). Educated, high-achieving women exemplify both a successful investment in human capital and labour market mobility. They are forerunners, who set standards for other women to emulate in their educational, work and family arrangements (Stone 2007). This group's entry into the high status and predominantly male professions signifies that it is at the front line in the battle for gender equality, effects cultural transformation and contributes to the diversification of knowledge production. Transnational feminists have critiqued Western scholars who treat the experience and claims of non-Western scholars as additional data points fitting within the dominant framework of globalization, rather than seeing them as alternative loci to Western knowledge production (see e.g. Bhambra, Shilliam and Orrells 2014).

Feminist researchers use a diversity of methods from various disciplines ranging from natural to social sciences. A shared goal among these different perspectives is to prioritize women and their knowledge, and, most important, recognize that women are not a homogeneous group (Mohanty 1988). Some common elements in feminist research are posing new questions, selecting critical methods, locating women at the centre of the research process, using an intersectional lens, focusing on women's lived experience and being aware of power dynamics in the research process (Hesse-Biber and Leckenby 2004). This reshaping of the epistemological position of the research agenda enables feminist researchers to view women and their subjectivities with a critical socio-historical, economic and political lens. Thus, instead of using broad strokes to paint women in the Global South as marginalized, exploited and without agency, feminist researchers attempt to identify the interstitial spaces and complex ways in which women exercise agency, even as they are operating within normative and patriarchal structures (Kandiyoti 1988). Sociology, in particular, has been critiqued by feminists (see e.g. Reinharz 1985, Millman and Kanter 1987, Hesse-Biber and Carter 2000, Sprague 2005) as being overly Western, positivist and androcentric in its research undertaking, especially in dichotomizing the area of work and family, where men were studied solely in their role in the public work sphere, while women were observed only within the seclusion of the private home sphere (Hesse-Biber, Leavy and Yaiser 2004). Mainstream economics, too, has been criticized for assuming gender, race and class neutrality, and overlooking the fact that people's relations to production depend on their structural position in society (Barker and Feiner 2004).

Thus, instead of theorizing women's work and lives as a dichotomy of empowerment or exploitation, this article is written from the emic perspective of what women think about their own work, family and gendered lives. I use their voices and stories to link dynamic macrostructural processes to the micropolitics of everyday lived experiences (Kingsolver 2001). Engaging with Mohanty's (1997) argument, this research uses feminist analysis to situate women's work in 'the ideological construction of jobs and tasks in terms of notions of normative femininity, domesticity, (hetero)sexuality, and racial and cultural stereotypes' (1997: 6), and considers how women use agency to construct their own lives. Taking a page out of feminist economist analysis, this chapter recognizes not only the centrality and profound impact of gender, race/caste, class and nationality on work and workers but also their relationship to work that is considered valued and devalued (Barker and Feiner 2004).

2. Context and methods

While economic liberalization policies have exacerbated inequalities in the informal sector in India, they have also created opportunities for young English-educated and skilled professionals. Urban women's lives especially have been critically transformed by educational investments by their families and the state, and the expansion of employment opportunities in the private sector. This generation of women is different from that of their mothers who were predominantly homemakers, and yet their identities are complicated by the politics of nationhood and respectability (Radhakrishnan 2011).

The data for this chapter comes from an ethnographic study conducted in 2005 and 2006 at three different sites in Hyderabad, India. While the data is a decade old, the work and family experiences of these professionally employed women are still relevant, if not more relevant, given that India is facing a crisis in decreasing female labour force participation (see the report from the International Labor Organization 2012). The first two sites – TechSolutions and Global IT – are pseudonyms for large global corporations with headquarters in the United States and a growing presence in India. The third site – First Bank, also a pseudonym – is a private Indian bank that has a strong foothold in India, with growing global aspirations. Although TechSolutions, Global IT and First Bank provide different products and services, all of them belong to the privatized services sector and have a global presence (albeit not all to the same degree). I use this contrast between transnational corporations and a domestic company to make a larger point that even as global corporations localize, Indian businesses actively adopt global business standards in order to compete effectively in local and global markets. This also serves to locate overlapping social structures and normative cultural practices that are seen as dissimilar because they are situated across different sites and yet are experienced and articulated by workers in similar ways (Upadhya 2008). Utilizing a feminist perspective allows me to ask how men and women make sense of the ongoing economic and cultural transformation in India, and disabuse assumptions that these changes impact them in exactly the same ways. And finally, comparing the perspectives of workers occupying diverse class, caste, gender and religious backgrounds and different positions (from trainees to mid-level workers to managers) in these organizations enables me to go beyond, what standpoint theorists argue as, situated and partial knowledge (Collins 1997).

The location of the study, Hyderabad, is the capital city of the south Indian state of Telangana. It is a perfect site for analysing the socio-economic transition taking place in India. It is the fourth largest city in India, with a population of 6.8 million people, and is considered a major urban centre undergoing rapid change. Economic liberalization at the national level, and the successful solicitation by the then[2] Andhra Pradesh government of transnational corporations seeking investment prospects to set up offices in Cyberabad (a hi-tech city on the outskirts of Hyderabad), provided an unparalleled opportunity in a strategic location to investigate changing work culture and gender relations in the Indian middle class.

I gathered data using semi-structured interviews, participant observations and focus group discussions from 58 employees – 31 men and 27 women – at all three sites (24 employees at TechSolutions, 20 employees at Global IT, and 14 employees at First Bank) via snowball sampling. Informants ranged in ages from 21 to 45 years. A majority of informants (53 individuals) have graduate degrees (engineering, MA, MBA, MS Computer Science or CA – an advanced degree in accounting). Most of my informants originated from lower-middle to middle-class backgrounds, and a majority had mothers who were homemakers (N = 45). Interestingly, all the interviews were conducted in English at the insistence of the informants even though I mentioned that I was a native speaker of Telugu (the local language) and Hindi. This use of language represents the vernacular terrain in which my informants described themselves in empowered ways. In most cases, fieldwork establishes a hierarchical relationship between the researcher as the 'expert' and the researched as the 'subject', and has power differences built-in (Purkayastha *et al.* 2003). Further, the researcher has control over both the research process and the interpretation of the findings (Sprague 2005).

However, employees I interviewed were not only well educated but were also aware of their role and contribution to the global workforce and their membership in a transnational class. Marcus (cited in Upadhya 2008) argues that in such cases, the researcher needs to understand that knowledge is more intensely co-produced than in the usual fieldwork process. Upadhya (2008), however, sees it as an advantage because the researcher can use this relationship to discuss findings and check theories, which could, in turn, open new avenues for research. During my research, my interlocutors did not hesitate to correct me if I had misinterpreted something they said. For instance, in discussing the constraints on the physical mobility of women, I asked how their families perceived night-time work given the discussion in the media about the sexual exploits in call centres during graveyard shifts. My female interlocutors were quick to distance themselves from women workers in call centres and resisted any suggestion on my part to lump them in the same category. They not only reminded me that they had higher education and that their work was more value added than the work in call centres but also used notions of respectability to construct their femininity in contrast to the questionable moral characterization and lower-class location of the women employed in call centres. It should be noted that it was women's reputation under discussion in the media and not the men's. Thus, I learned the ways in which women deliberately construct their identity as modern global workers and 'good' Indian women simultaneously, because women had much to gain by repudiating the circulating discourse.

In terms of my own social location, I was both an insider and outsider to the research context and process. Even though I often shared a similar gender, class, caste, national and religious background with my informants, I was considered an outsider, as I had not lived in India for almost a decade at that point, having left for the United States to pursue graduate study. There were far more differences than similarities that I began to identify as my research progressed. Some of these differences were immediately apparent in terms of gender, age and marital status (being a single woman in my thirties and not having children) and work status (being a doctoral candidate while many of them were on their second job), while other differences were more obscure, such as my aspiration to be an academic with, what my informants considered, a very low pay in a foreign country while India was booming. These differences served to make the familiar unfamiliar and enabled me to pay attention to nuances that I might have otherwise missed. More important, for a feminist epistemology, the difference in social location reduced most power distinctions between my role as the researcher and their roles as informants.

The next sections draw on my ethnographic work to illustrate how women work as agents in constructing their new work identities, resisting and contesting gender roles within the household and redefining their previously marginalized identities in novel ways. Relying on a tradition used successfully by feminist ethnographers, I integrate interpretive and materialist (culture, political economy and structural) approaches (Harrison 2007) to produce a critical analysis of women's lives at the intersection of work and family.

3. Women as drivers of change

Indian middle-class women are poised at a moment in history that is undergoing rapid transformation. They are poised between an old India ravaged with bureaucratic redundancies and a 'new' India with its high growth rate and a place in the global economy; between an old middle class, which is steeped in upper-caste membership and Sanskritization of the lower castes, and a new middle class, which has heterogeneous caste origins and is seen at the helm of a new India; and between mothers who did not work outside the home and daughters who will grow up with career-oriented mothers. These educated middle-class women are the first generation of women to have the potential to make a significant contribution to the 'knowledge society' in the global economy.[3] While I started the research with an aim of examining work culture, my female informants often turned the discourse to the transformation of the middle class and changing gender norms. They actively set themselves apart from the previous generations and saw themselves as pioneers of a new India. Thus, while I cannot claim that my sample is proportionally representative (a common limitation of qualitative research), it allows me to explore interrelationships and linkages that go forward and backward, and connect and at once distance the 'old' from new middle classes.

3.1 'Middle-class girls ... want to be someone'

Madhavi, 36 years, is a financial analyst and had been with First Bank for six years. Making an observation about how the middle class has changed over the years, she offers:

> Ten years back if you [were to] see a middle class girl, the parents *and* the girl also were of the view *ki* [that] educate [her] to a certain extent and then get her married and be a housewife. They never had any career plans or [the idea that] she has to become someone! Build a house, save some money, and give it to the daughter so that she has a good future in her in-laws' place. *That's it!* [with emphasis] *That* was the middle class mentality. For boys, parents were insisting on good education, good job, good promotion prospects. . . . Lot

of expectations! But now things have changed. Now in the middle class, girls have started feeling that, yes, they also should do something on their own. *Be someone*! And parents are supporting this by educating them. My own parents took loans to make sure that my sisters and I got an education. I am a CA [Chartered Accountant] because of them. My father tells people about me [whether] they ask or not (laughs)! I see the happiness and pride in their [parents] faces.

Madhavi's outburst about the shifting priorities of the middle class reflects a changing reality observed by work–family scholars in India. Rajadhyaksha and Smita (2004) examining the status of work and family research find that while there is very little research on working women (a minority in themselves) in India, in the mid-1970s to the mid-1980s research on urban women in dual-earner families focused on women's role conflict in balancing work and family and determined that women prioritized family over work. They conclude that women's working status did not translate to more egalitarian positions within the family despite holding class constant. By contrast, studies (still far and few in between) in the mid-1990s shifted to focus on career-oriented women in high-status jobs. Here, they noted the changing attitudes of men in support of their wives' productive roles. However, further probing revealed that this support did not extend far. Although men supported their spouses working outside the home, they were no more inclined to help with housework than their fathers, leaving women with a dual burden.

Studies also showed that though working women had a say in decision-making at home, husbands controlled important financial decisions. While it appears that little has changed in terms of women's status in three decades and, in fact, working women experience high work–family conflict, what the authors overlook is the historicity of change in gender norms (Pearse and Connell 2016). Though women in the 1970s, 1980s and 1990s mostly pursued work for economic reasons and struggled with family responsibilities, they paved a path for subsequent generations of women to have careers and develop their own human capital potential to, as Madhavi states earlier, 'Be someone!' It is worth noting that in contrast, when my male informants discussed the new middle class, it was in terms of a shift from public to private sector orientations, increasing opportunities and competition for jobs, lack of work–family balance and growing consumerism.

Pearse and Connell (2016) note that gender norms do not exist in a vacuum but are embedded in every aspect of cultural life and institutions, and need to be understood as a set of interrelationships between individuals and groups that have the power to both reproduce them and exercise agency to change them. Later in the interview, Madhavi revealed that her mother was the driving force for her and her sisters to attain higher education at a time when higher education for girls was not a popular idea. Madhavi's mother was not very educated, having been married off right after high school, but insisted that her daughters become independent women and not a housewife like her. Pearse and Connell (2016) note that assuming the sway of gender socialization, or smooth passing on of gender norms from generation to generation, without recognizing change runs the risk of undervaluing the agency of social actors, one that can be corrected only by tracking change overtime. Further, they argue that normative change can occur in a number of ways.

> It is common to think of change in gender as resulting from forces external to gender relations themselves: economic requirements, technology, modernization, democratisation, and so on. There is truth in this, but it is very important to recognize that gender also has internal dynamics of change.
> (Pearse and Connell 2016: 43)

Accordingly, though economic liberalization policies set the stage for women's increasing presence in the public sphere, it would be mistaken to claim that liberalization alone brought about changes in gender norms. If anything, economic liberalization served as a catalyst to thrust women into the limelight in India, work that has been a long way in the making by women in the previous generations breaking ranks in the workplace and changing attitudes within the family. Recognizing the arrival of women in the workplace, current research too is shifting from examining psychological aspects of working women to organizational factors that hinder and support women in the workplace (see e.g. Bhattacharyya and Ghosh 2012 regarding women in the Indian IT sector and Hewlett *et al.* 2013 on women facing challenges when they return to work after career interruptions).

3.2 'I don't want to be a tortoise!'

The growth of employment opportunities in the private sector provided a jump-start for the socio-economic and cultural transformations in India. Here, while capitalist patriarchal structures use gender scripts to construct the ideal worker as an unencumbered man who can work long hours and where Indian culture uses normative femininity to construct women as mothers first and workers next, middle-class professional women are slowly working to dislodge these ideas. At 27 years, Arti was one of the youngest branch managers at First Bank, a mother, and invested in her career growth. She moved from a nationalized bank to the private sector recently, and when asked if she would return to the public sector, Arti replied:

> No, no, no. I don't want to go back to public sector because there you will be like a tortoise. I don't want to be a tortoise (laughs)! I want to grow fast. This is a challenging job and I can never rest. I'm given challenges day-in and day-out. That's what I enjoy. I got changed to it [sic]. I got used to this atmosphere now, and I want some fast growth in my career. And here, for the upper management positions, they will not take someone from outside [the bank] generally. They'll promote [from] inside. That is one good thing about First Bank. When they think of promotions, they'll think of people inside the organisation first. If they don't find anyone, then only they take someone from outside. I want to be in a position where I am noticed.

Q: Do you think men and women have equal opportunities to be promoted?
ARTI: Definitely! They [First Bank] do not care whether you are a man or a woman. As long as you perform and you have talent, you will be promoted. [Reflectively] I know that I'll be losing something in my personal life but I thought that this is a good trade-off.
Q: What do you mean when you say, 'losing something in personal life'?
ARTI: Because [First Bank] is a little bit hectic when compared to any other bank. I put in long hours at work but people working with public sector banks hardly [work] 8 hours. So, compared to them, I miss out on family time, spending time with my son. My role model is Chanda Kochhar, who [in 2006] is the first woman and youngest Deputy Managing Director at ICICI [one of India's largest private domestic banks]. I really appreciate how [she] handles such a big position being a woman and having personal responsibilities. So I take her as my inspiration. Being a woman I feel many times that I should leave the job, and be with my kid, especially when he is not feeling well. I really feel, 'Why am I working?' But then I consider that *I* [with emphasis] also should become something. I should not waste my life. I want my son to be proud of me.

Several scholars have posited that the demands of the workplace are antagonistic to the strains of home, and women experience greater conflict in balancing work and family than men (Rothbard 2001, Wharton and Blair-Loy 2006). In addition, notions of 'intensive mothering' (Hays 1996), where women are expected to be nurturing with their children but competitive at work, deepen the tension in women's work–life balance.

In India too, although the dominant framework of normative femininity stresses that married middle-class women should be 'maternal goddesses' (Donner 2008) devoting their time to the household, children and their education, some women resist these norms by their continued and intense participation in the workplace. Despite being married with children, neither Madhavi nor Arti shows any signs of slowing down their pace at work and, in fact, invest in their careers and actively seek upward mobility. Recognizing that career success in the privatized workplace is defined by how much one contributes to the company, Arti said that she did not mind the long hours. She uses the time to go beyond the tasks assigned to her, making her successful at her job. For instance, Arti found ways to cut short the time taken for some banking transactions and improved the productivity of the branch as branch operations manager. She also took it upon herself to train new employees in efficient ways of doing things. Recognizing her talent, First Bank promoted her to branch manager in just one-and-half years. 'But there is no time to rest,' she says, because she knows one can be demoted for not delivering, and she does not want to be in that situation, 'Chanda [Kochhar] did not get to the top position by sitting on her hands,' Arti reminds me.

As Arti demonstrates, 'good jobs' that are creative and have growth prospects for the cultivation of satisfying careers and other exchangeable forms of social capital allow for a change in the status of women. However, the path to success is not straightforward. Women continue to face discrimination and sexism at work, and their commitment to their jobs is often seen as suspect. At the home front too, women are bogged down by cultural expectations of being primary caregivers. These issues need to be addressed along with men's attitudes towards providing care and the state's support for families, if there is to be real change. Sweet *et al.* (2016), doing a cross-national study of employees in 11 countries working in seven multinational companies, find that there is very little difference in career centrality between men and women when job quality is taken into consideration, that is if women have the same opportunities as men to enter higher-quality jobs, they will invest in their careers in a comparable manner.

4. Agency and empowerment: negotiating and challenging gender norms in marriage

Agency is understood as control over resources, freedom to pursue opportunities and making strategic life choices where women act as agents of their own well-being (Sen 1985). The path from individual empowerment to large-scale social transformation is not direct, but agency has the potential to lead to empowerment when women practise it to challenge gender norms, institutions and injustices that subordinate them and other women (Kabeer 2008). Mason (2005) examining what empowerment means for women within the domestic sphere in five Asian countries emphasizes its relational nature. By this, she means the consensual nature of interrelationships that exist in any particular context where some members of the group (mostly men) have the right over resources and access to greater power. However, when women are empowered, they not only gain individual capabilities but also create a shift in collective consensus about their right to resources and opportunities. Mason also points to the uneven multidimensionality of empowerment. Women might have power in the private sphere but not in the public sphere. Thus, empowerment is not a zero sum game – that either one has it or one does not. A more nuanced analysis reveals that women use power and agency in one dimension to navigate other dimensions. This section illustrates how women use their position as successful professionals in the public sphere to negotiate their status with their parents and future families after marriage.

4.1 'He should understand my work timings'

Arranged marriage is one of the last strongholds of the caste system, with the largest proportion of marriages in India being organized in this manner. In my sample, the majority of informants who are married (N = 30) have had arranged marriages (N = 21). But merely considering these numbers does not reveal the strategies and negotiations that women employ in changing the 'rules of the game' (Kandiyoti 1988) of this long-standing institution. Lalitha, 27 years, a finance manager with Global IT, discusses her plans for marriage:

Q: Have you given any thought to marriage? Do you have anything specific in mind?
LALITHA: (Laughs) Everyone points out that I'm 27 and unmarried. But I want to proceed carefully because this is for a lifetime. Education-wise he must be a postgraduate. Must be an engineering or MBA graduate. But more importantly, [he should be] a nice person who can understand me because you know with guys and girls working in MNCs [Multinational Corporations] there are no set timings. You should have proper understanding because the work atmosphere is like that. You can come and go anytime. It is not standard timing that you go in the morning, and are home in the evening; nothing like that. [I want to be with] a person who can understand the demands at the office and wants to be with me . . . and, of course, a loving person [laughs].
Q: Why is this important to you?

LALITHA: [Matter-of-factly] Because I want to keep working after I get married. Earlier they never used to let a girl work in the night. Now it is fine because, everybody is working at one or the other MNC. And everyone understands that there is no particular time when the person is coming or going. It has become common.

Q: Everyone . . . like your parents, you mean?

LALITHA: Yes, but again there are some people in society that are still not aware of it. Take me as an example. When a couple of proposals came my way, my parents told them my work timings . . . like, she is going to work late at times and asked them if their family was going to be okay with it. They were like, 'Oh my God! She is going to come home around 10 o'clock? No, that is not good.' We rejected those matches outright. I cannot be in family like that. So you see, your parents might understand but when you go to another family after you get married, they might not take it. There is another example. One of my friends has got recently engaged [*sic*] and had a great job. It is a love marriage. But her mother-in-law said strictly, 'If you are going to work in the night shift, you better quit your job. If you find a job in the day, you can continue. I cannot afford to send you in the night.'

Q: So what did your friend do?

LALITHA: (Laughs) After marriage she persuaded her husband to move to Hyderabad [from Bangalore] away from her in-laws, to work at our branch. She requested a dayshift and continues to work.

Unlike in a romantic relationship where one gets to know the other person over time, in an arranged marriage there is pressure to make a decision quickly. Women such as Lalitha, who are employed in the new privatized services sector and participating in the global economy, represent the new Indian women who not only negotiate with their parents about when and who they marry, but are also comfortable asking tough questions of prospective bridegrooms and in-laws. To them, their jobs meet more than an economic need. They invest in their careers and expect an equal partnership in marriage. Thus, while their parents and relatives might vet the prospective grooms, women are not only voicing their opinions but also have a final say in who they get to marry. In anticipating their married lives, women want to make sure that their family life is not in conflict with their work life.

Several scholars have noted that work and family act as oppositions where women are concerned because the positions they occupy within and outside the home are governed by gender ideologies that in turn shape women's decisions to stay or leave the labour force (Crompton 2000, Stone 2007). Accordingly, young marriageable women reason that they can mitigate work–family conflict to some extent by carefully selecting future partners and in-laws.

258 *Bhavani Arabandi*

Other scholars (e.g. Radhakrishnan 2011) similarly find that professional women in India play a major role in planning their futures. This new trend of arranged marriages where women are consulted by their families indicates the fluidity of women's changing position at the intersection of work and family. At the same time, the embodied nature of social control on women is evident in the case of Lalitha's friend who had to give up a lucrative job that involved a night shift. Even so, we should not disregard that she and her husband moved to Hyderabad, ostensibly to be away from the surveillance of the in-laws, and she continues to work and might even end up taking on night shifts. Thus, even as they go along with arranged marriage, women are not just submitting to cultural expectations but bending and asserting social relations to achieve what they want from a marriage.

4.2 'Why should I pay him a dowry?'

Before economic liberalization polices were introduced in 1991, the practice of dowry advantaged families with boys who were employed in the public services sector because these jobs were coveted, had status and assured a secure future for the family. Families of such eligible young men had a wide choice of brides and could demand any amount of dowry.[4] Some unscrupulous in-laws, however, demanded more after marriage, and when the parents of the bride are unable to provide, the in-laws would be violent towards the bride, sometimes resulting in a dowry death. Far from receding, dowry in neoliberal India is exacerbated such that status is represented by conspicuous consumption – lavish and lengthy weddings funded almost entirely by the bride's family, and exchange of luxury commodities such as flats, cars and vacations abroad (Uberoi 2009). However, not everyone is comfortable with this trend. Most of my informants – both male and female – claimed to be against dowry, and some women took steps to stop the practice in their own marriages. Savita, 25 years, an employee at TechSolutions is engaged to a man of her choice. She is quite outspoken about dowry:

> In my case, luckily, my father-in-law did not ask any dowry. That was good. *Really good* [with emphasis]! If he had asked for something, I would have rejected my fiancé and the marriage. That's how strict I am about dowry! Why should the bride's family give money? If both the bride and groom are earning . . . I'm the same like him, am I not? I am earning equally to him. So why should I pay him a dowry?

Savita's passionate resistance against dowry comes from a growing awareness of self-worth and gender equality bolstered by her economic independence. Her determination to hold her principles above her 'heart' is evidence to a growing backlash from educated women who are active in the labour force and against the practice of dowry. Socially conscious movies and some individuals who go against the system are making an impact on young people's minds. One case that made the headlines in 2003 is about Nisha Sharma, a young, college-going woman in Delhi, who had the bridegroom and his father arrested at the venue of the wedding when they asked for a dowry. Nisha became famous both nationally and internationally, with women's groups praising her actions and prospective grooms coming forward to marry her without a dowry. Several of my informants brought up Nisha as evidence of changing times and to show that they too were against dowry.

The catalyst for this change is the entrance of middle-class women into IT jobs and their high-earning potential. Working women and their families are aware that once married, women's financial contributions stay in the husband's household; therefore, they question the need to provide a dowry in addition. Despite these trends, one cannot generalize the protest against the practice of dowry to the entire generation because women are still negotiating within the confines of a patriarchal system.

Savita is a well-educated, professionally employed, independent woman who has selected a spouse on her own. Such women are a minority in India, and deep-rooted structural inequalities need to be addressed before the practice of dowry completely disappears. We should also be reminded that individual human capital achievements in education and paid employment do not automatically determine women's empowerment (Kabeer 1998); rather, the impact of individual capabilities is interceded by cultural norms and gender ideologies (Mason 2005). However, Kandiyoti persuasively argues, 'Patriarchal bargains are not timeless or immutable entities, but are susceptible to historical transformations that open up new areas of struggle and renegotiation of the relations between genders' (1988: 275). Middle-class women in India are situated at such a historic moment of transformation that has the potential to improve women's worth and impact the practice of dowry.

5. Shifting identities within the home

Feminist economists such as Bina Agarwal (1997) and Notburga Ott (1995) posit that gender relations within a household are based on a cooperation and conflict model, and involve negotiation between family members. The distribution of resources and responsibilities are outcomes of this negotiation. Therefore, by having a good job (in terms of money, status and prestige), women can bring much to the bargaining table and escape the drudgery of unpaid household labour that is both devalued and has opportunity costs. These are small steps in using social capital to improve one's position within the household.

5.1 'I am not a good girl'

Prema, a single woman of 26 years, has an MBA and had been with Global IT for over five years.

Q: How do you spend your time over the weekends?
PREMA: I don't know how to cook and I don't go into the kitchen or help out with anything at home. I even work late! No . . . (laughs) *I am not a good girl* [emphasis added]. Over the weekends, I sleep in and make plans to go to the movies or dinner with my friends.
Q: Has it always been like this or since you started working?
PREMA: I am the youngest in the household, so to some extent I did not have much responsibility at home but since I started working, there is even more of a difference. Now I am not *allowed* to do much. My parents take so much care [*sic*] of me. They see it as: 'She is going in the morning and working hard till late night, so let her rest.' The caring is more.

Prema's autonomy and capacity to dictate her own schedule are the envy of many working Indian women. At the same time, she feels compelled to frame this aspirational arrangement, even if jokingly, as a moral failing, an abdication of her inherent responsibilities as a woman. This shows us how deeply entrenched the household division of labour is. Recent reports have indicated that Indian men do a fraction of the housework compared to Indian women; for instance, the Global Gender Gap Report 2014 by the World Economic Forum, shows that India is ranked at the bottom in terms of household division of labour. These statistics at the country level, however, do not discuss why men take on such little work or the structural inequalities that reinforce this unequal division of labour. More important, from a feminist perspective, these data also do not reveal the differences between women in various groups. For example, urban middle- and upper-class (and caste) families can afford to hire domestic help to do menial tasks from which lower-class and lower-caste women have no escape (as workers and within their own households).

Analysing data from my study show that unmarried middle-class women like Prema, pursuing higher education and/or working in lucrative jobs, can negotiate decreased (if not escape) household chores in order to focus on their work outside the home; and parents often go along with such arrangements. Married women, however, cannot do it to the same extent. Here, there is a further difference. Married women in patrilocal arrangements have greater housework, child and elder care responsibilities than married women living in neolocal arrangements. But even in this context, employment status matters. Married women in patrilocal arrangements working in high-status jobs and bringing home a significant salary can negotiate a decreased workload at home and even tap in-laws for childcare arrangements. Thus, merely surmising that Indian women do the majority of housework misses the nuances involved. Compared to women, unmarried men in the study did not bring up housework in their interviews. Married men, on the other hand, expressed some guilt and remorse at not doing enough to help their wives (whether they were employed or homemakers) within the household, but specifically with regard to children and not in terms of general housework.

Returning to Prema's reflection earlier, being 'bad' is connected to discursive ideas of normative femininity that many women appear to accept, but resistance to these norms problematizes the idea that norms are passed down smoothly (Pearse and Connell 2016). Knowing how to cook, keeping a nice home and taking care of the elderly are considered quintessential qualities of good girls. In a context where middle-class women are defined by their relationship to their family, in terms of being daughters, wives and mothers, and where women's physical and temporal mobility is strictly governed by family members and society, being good is an important quality to strive for. But far from being penalized for flouting this norm and conventional cultural standards, Prema is being treated, in essence, as a young man who is absolved of any household responsibilities and has no restrictions on mobility outside the home. Prema attributes this treatment to her educational attainment and employment in the new global economy.

However, one must be careful not to exaggerate this newfound freedom of young women. While it is becoming acceptable for women to work into the night at IT companies, hanging out with friends at a pub or dating is still unacceptable behaviour for good girls. Even as Prema revels in her freedom of movement, she carefully constructs her identity within 'good girl' standards and stresses, 'My parents know where I am at *all* times.' She distances herself from women who work in call centres and those associated with 'loose' characteristics. In a larger sense, though the presence of educated, upwardly mobile women traversing public spaces after dark and resisting responsibility within the home unsettles traditional notions of women's place both inside and outside the home, its actual impact on women and their families is complex. Against the background of increasing violence against women, such 'freedom' can be taken away anytime and women are cautious about not 'misusing' or overusing it.

5.2 'My in-laws respect me more'

Madhavi, mentioned previously, a financial analyst with First Bank, discusses the differential treatment given to her by her in-laws:

> I'll tell you, I've seen the difference in my in-law's house itself. I am educated *and* working. My other two sisters-in-law [husband's brothers'

wives] are not much educated and they're housewives. So the treatment my in-laws give me is different from what they give my sisters-in-law. They give me more respect. If I say something, they listen. If they [sisters-in-law] say something, my in-laws don't listen; they discount their viewpoint. But they will like to take my viewpoint because they feel, she's interacted with people, she's seen much larger society, much larger world, she's educated, so let us listen to her. So, *that* recognition will come when you're educated, and working.

Madhavi garners respect from her family and finds it fulfilling. As a financial analyst for a private bank, she not only uses skills she learned at work to invest her own money but also advises her in-laws about their investments. Her in-laws in turn treat her better than their other daughters-in-law and also help with childcare for Madhavi and her husband. Both Prema and Madhavi work in male-dominated professions and bring home a big pay cheque. In Prema's situation, she earns more than her father did when he retired. And in Madhavi's case, her salary is much bigger than her husband's, making her the primary breadwinner. But more than that, they bring home an exposure to the outside world that was not part of the world view of middle-class women from previous generations. These women are among the first to be well educated and working in prestigious occupations in their families.

Many of the women I interviewed focused their energies into building careers and, over time, got their families to recognize them as working professionals. This is not to say, however, that Indian middle-class women are suddenly being treated like men and there is gender equality. Married women still struggle with the burden of housework and childcare. While Madhavi's husband is proud of her position in the bank and leaves the financial decision-making to her, she still has to feed the family when she gets home from work. 'He does not even start the rice cooker,' she complains. 'I have to do everything because he will not enter the kitchen. He sees it as my domain.' India is poised at a moment where its patriarchal traditions are at odds with the global image that it wants to cultivate as a modern nation-state. Women from diverse class and caste backgrounds are making strides in education and slowly gaining a foothold in the workplace. If India is to truly make use of its human capital, it will have to undergo deliberate and significant transformation in the area of gender equality. The scope of what these middle-class women can do has opened up new futures for succeeding generations of women in India.

6. Conclusion

While it may take a long time for institutional and social and cultural barriers to be removed, changing attitudes towards gender equality, education and employment are making significant changes in the lives of middle-class women. Informants in my study self-identified as serious economic actors and did not look at work merely as a job or pastime. They actively invested in their careers and made plans for the future. In a context where women's work is both undercounted and undervalued, middle-class women are slowly entering male-dominated occupations without causing many ripples but making sure they are not invisible within the workplace or the household. In the current charged milieu with a focus on violence against women in India, it is easy to miss the more-nuanced changes taking place within the private and public spheres. Feminist perspectives, thus, are integral to highlighting the novel findings about labour, household and social dynamics. Future work in this area would benefit from research using feminist methodologies that raise new questions about whether the conditions for women have changed at the intersection of work and family. Analysing the interaction between transformational macrostructural processes and everyday dynamics exposes interstitial spaces where gender relations are being modified. Such modifications might not be groundbreaking, but they should not to be dismissed either.

Notes

1 This chapter was published in the *Economic and Political Weekly*, Review of Women's Studies, vol. 51, no. 18, 30 April 2016, pp. 89–97. We are grateful to the editor, *EPW*, for permission to republish this chapter in this volume. I am thankful to the editors, Padmini Swaminathan and Kalpana Kannabiran, and the blind peer reviewers in guiding this work and helping me sharpen my analysis, and to Jeff Mantz for reading several drafts and always inspiring me to do my best.
2 The state of Andhra Pradesh was reorganized into the states of Telangana and Andhra Pradesh in 2014. Hyderabad, the capital of Telangana, is also the temporary capital of the state of Andhra Pradesh till the new capital is built in Amaravati.
3 The World Bank's recent focus on the knowledge society theme argues that access to science and technology is key to closing the gap between the South and the North (World Bank 2002). This reasoning comes from the realization that the global economy is transforming in a way that makes higher education a basic condition for economic competitiveness and, thus, for economic development (Naidoo 2003).
4 Of course, those employed in the private service sector also commanded a high dowry, but those employed in the public sector far outnumbered those in the private sector prior to 1991.

References

Agarwal, Bina. 1997. "'Bargaining' and Gender Relations: Within and beyond the Household," *Feminist Economics*, Vol. 3, No. 1, pp. 1–51.

Barker, Drucilla and Susan Feiner. 2004. *Liberating Economics: Feminist Perspectives on Families, Work, and Globalization*. Ann Arbor: University of Michigan Press.

Bhambra, Gurminder, Robbie Shilliam and Daniel Orrells. 2014. "Contesting Imperial Epistemologies: Introduction," *Journal of Historical Sociology*, Vol. 27, No. 3, pp. 293–301.

Bhattacharyya, Asmita and Bhola Nath Ghosh. 2012. "Women in Indian Information Technology (IT) Sector: A Sociological Analysis," *Journal of Humanities and Social Science*, Vol. 3, No. 6, pp. 45–52.

Collins, Patricia Hill. 1997. "Comment on Hekman's 'Truth and Method: Feminist Standpoint Theory Revisited': Where's the Power?" *Signs*, Vol. 22, No. 2, pp. 375–381.

Crompton, Rosemary. 2000. *Restructuring Gender Relations and Employment: The Decline of the Male Breadwinner*. Oxford: Oxford University Press.

Desai, Manisha. 2007. "From the SWS President: The Messy Relationship between Feminisms and Globalizations," *Gender and Society*, Vol. 21, No. 6, pp. 797–803.

Donner, Henrike. 2008. *Domestic Goddesses: Maternity, Globalization and Middle-Class Identity in Contemporary India*. Aldershot: Ashgate.

Fernandes, Leela. 2000. "Rethinking Globalization: Gender, Nation and the Middle Class in Liberalizing India." In Marianne deKoven (ed.). *Feminist Locations: Global and Local, Theory and Practice*. New Brunswick: Rutgers University Press, pp. 147–167.

Freeman, Carla. 2000. *High Tech and High Heels in the Global Economy*. Durham, NC: Duke University Press.

Harrison, Faye. 2007. "Feminist Methodologies as a Tool for Ethnographic Inquiry on Globalization." In Nandini Gunewardena and Ann Kingsolver (eds). *The Gender of Globalization: Women Navigating Cultural and Economic Marginalities*. Santa Fe, NM: School for Advanced Research Press, pp. 23–31.

Hays, Sharon. 1996. *The Cultural Contradictions of Motherhood*. Princeton, NJ: Yale University Press.

Hesse-Biber, Sharlene and Gregg Carter. 2000. *Working Women in America*. New York: Oxford University Press.

Hesse-Biber, Sharlene, Patricia Leavy and Michelle Yaiser. 2004. "Feminist Approaches to Research as a Process: Reconceptualizing Epistemology, Methodology, and Method." In Sharlene Hesse-Biber and Michelle Yaiser (eds). *Feminist Perspectives on Social Research*. New York: Oxford University Press, pp. 3–38.

Hesse-Biber, Sharlene and Denise Leckenby. 2004. "How Feminists Practice Social Research." In Sharlene Hesse-Biber and Michelle Yaiser (eds). *Feminist Perspectives on Social Research*. New York: Oxford University Press, pp. 209–226.

Hewlett, Sylvia Ann, Laura Sherbin, Tara Gonsalves and Catherine Fredman. 2013. *On-Ramps and Up-Ramps India*. New York: Center for Talent Innovation.

ILO. 2012. *Global Employment Trends for Women*. Geneva: International Labour Organization.
Kabeer, Naila. 1998. "'Money Can't Buy Me Love'? Re-Evaluating Gender, Credit and Empowerment in Rural Bangladesh," *Discussion Paper 363*. Brighton, UK: Institute of Development Studies, University of Sussex.
———. 2008. "Paid Work, Women's Empowerment and Gender Justice: Critical Pathways of Social Change," *Pathways Working Paper 3*. Brighton, UK: Institute of Development Studies, University of Sussex.
Kandiyoti, Deniz. 1988. "Bargaining with Patriarchy," *Gender and Society*, Vol. 2, No. 3, pp. 274–290.
Kingsolver, Ann. 2001. *Nafta Stories: Fears and Hopes in Mexico and the United States*. Boulder, CO: Lynne Rienner Publishers.
Mason, Karen Oppenheim. 2005. "Measuring Women's Empowerment: Learning from Cross-National Research." In Deepa Narayan (ed.). *Measuring Empowerment: Cross Disciplinary Perspectives*. Washington, DC: The World Bank, pp. 89–121.
Millman, Marcia and Rosabeth Kanter. 1987. "Introduction to Another Voice: Feminist Perspectives on Social Life and Social Science." In Sandra Harding (ed.). *Feminism and Methodology*. Bloomington, IN: Indiana University Press, pp. 29–36.
Mohanty, Chandra. 1988. "Under Western Eyes: Feminist Scholarship and Colonial Discourses," *Feminist Review*, No. 30, pp. 61–88.
———. 1997. "Women Workers and Capitalist Scripts." In M. Jacqui Alexander and Chandra Talpade Mohanty (eds). *Feminist Geneologies, Colonial Legacies Democratic Futures*. New York: Routledge, pp. 3–29.
Naidoo, Rajini. 2003. "Repositioning Higher Education as a Global Commodity: Opportunities and Challenges for the Future Sociology of Education Work," *British Journal of Sociology of Education*, Vol. 24, No. 2, pp. 249–259.
Ott, Notburga. 1995. "Fertility and Division of Work in the Family: A Game Theoretic Model of Household Decisions." In Edith Kuiper and Jolande Sap (eds). *Out of the Margin: Feminist Perspectives on Economics*. New York: Routledge, pp. 80–99.
Pearse, Rebecca and Raewyn Connell. 2016. "Gender Norms and the Economy: Insights from Social Research," *Feminist Economics*, Vol. 22, No. 1, pp. 30–53.
Purkayastha, Bandana, Mangala Subramaniam, Manisha Desai and Sunita Bose. 2003. "The Study of Gender in India: A Partial Review," *Gender and Society*, Vol. 17, No. 4, pp. 503–524.
Radhakrishnan, Smitha. 2011. *Appropriately Indian: Gender and Culture in a New Transnational Class*. Durham, NC: Duke University Press.
Rajadhyaksha, Ujvala and Swati Smita. 2004. "Tracing a Timeline for Work and Family Research in India," *Economic and Political Weekly*, Vol. 39, No. 17, pp. 1674–1680.
Reinharz, Shulamit. 1985. "Feminist Distrust: Problems of Context and Content in Sociological Work." In David Berg and Ken Smith (eds). *The Self in Sociological Inquiry*. Beverly Hills: Sage, pp. 153–172.

Rothbard, Nancy. 2001. "Enriching or Depleting? The Dynamics of Engagement in Work and Family Roles," *Administrative Science Quarterly*, Vol. 46, pp. 655–684.
Salzinger, Leslie. 1997. "From High Heels to Swathed Bodies: Gendered Meanings under Production in Mexico's Export Processing Industry," *Feminist Studies*, Vol. 23, No. 3, pp. 549–574.
Sen, Amartya. 1985. "Well-Being, Agency and Freedom: The Dewey Lectures 1984," *Journal of Philosophy*, Vol. 82, No. 4, pp. 169–221.
Sprague, Joey. 2005. *Feminist Methodologies for Critical Researchers: Bridging Differences*. Walnut Creek, CA: Alta Mira Press.
Stone, Pamela. 2007. *Opting Out? Why Women Really Quit Careers and Head Home*. Berkeley: University of California Press.
Swaminathan, Padmini. 2004. "When Women Take on Wage Work: A Report from Tamil Nadu's Export Processing Zone," *Manushi*, Vol. 144, pp. 31–38.
Sweet, Stephen, Natalia Sarkisian, Christina Matz-Costa and Marcie Pitt-Catsouphes. 2016. "Are Women Less Career Centric Than Men? Structure, Culture and Career Investments," *Community, Work and Family*, Vol. 19, No. 4, pp. 481–500.
Uberoi, Patricia. 2009. *Freedom and Destiny: Gender, Family, and Popular Culture in India*. New Delhi: Oxford University Press.
Upadhya, Carol. 2008. "Ethnographies of the Global Information Economy: Research Strategies and Methods," *Economic and Political Weekly*, Vol. 43, No. 17, pp. 64–72.
Upadhya, Carol and A. R. Vasavi. 2008. *In an Outpost of the Global Economy: Work and Workers in India's Information Technology Industry*. New Delhi: Routledge.
Wharton, Amy and Mary Blair-Loy. 2006. "Long Work Hours and Family Life: A Cross-National Study of Employees' Concerns," *Journal of Family Issues*, Vol. 27, No. 3, pp. 415–436.
World Bank. 2002. *Constructing Knowledge Societies: New Challenges for Tertiary Education*. Washington, DC: The World Bank.
World Economic Forum. 2014. *The Global Gender Gap Report*. Geneva: World Economic Forum.

12 'Ladkiyaan phir aage?'
Towards understanding the formal school system

Kumkum Roy

1. Introduction: fools rush in . . .

Virtually every year the print media celebrates what seems to be a welcome relief from the routine grim and gory headlines that have become our daily fare. These reports, often accompanied by visuals of cheerful young girls jumping, hugging, thrusting sweets into one another's mouths and so on, proclaim that girls have performed better than boys in the two major examinations that define the school regime across the nation – those at the end of classes X and XII. That girls perform better in these tests evidently reassures us that we are on the right track, that we are making progress and that all is well with the world.

At one level, this perception is evidently and eminently justified – there have been visible improvements in enrolment and retention rates of girls in schools, and access to school education has expanded considerably over the past two decades. If, in addition, girls perform better than boys within the system, in spite of a skewed sex ratio, surely this calls for celebration? Without attempting to detract from the achievements of these young women, who succeed in a gruelling and incredibly demanding competitive world that is very different from the one in which I grew up about 40 or 50 years ago, I will attempt to unpack what this success means.

Let me state at the outset that this is by no means a unique endeavour. As Pappu and Goswami (2015: 160) remind us:

> The need for any further analysis or understanding of what can be done or should be done in relation to girls' education is in danger of being neglected due to a misplaced sense of having bridged the 'gap' without really achieving the goals of gender equity.
>
> In fact, there is a continued need, perhaps urgency as well, for the examination of a large and complex gamut of issues under the rubric of gender and education in India. In undertaking explorations of these kinds the location of the educational institution, the class, caste and

religion of the management, teachers and students would necessarily have to be taken into account, because gender (as has been demonstrated through the rich tradition of feminist scholarship that has developed over the past two decades in India) is not only about girls and boys or about women and men but is inextricably intertwined with other critical markers including region, religion, class, caste, sexual orientation and disability.

Pappu and Goswami also draw attention to the relatively low visibility of feminist perspectives and analyses of education within the vast body of feminist scholarship that has emerged (ibid.: 161), suggesting that the everyday violence that the system generates 'is not easily recognized'. Further, they identify a painful paradox. On the one hand, the Right to Education Act (2009) has notionally expanded access to education. At the same time, we are in the throes of major structural changes – of privatization of education at all levels and the consequent urge to package education as a private good (ibid.: 163). Besides, discussions on the New Education Policy that is currently on the anvil indicate that we are likely to be faced with a situation in which students are visualized as consumers, with teachers as service providers.

The critical discourse on education, if not always explicitly feminist, has been incredibly rich and troubling. I will not attempt to engage with it at length here but will simply highlight some concerns in terms of themes and methodologies. My perspective, at once inevitable and perhaps unenviable, emerges from the margins. While I am a teacher (of history), and have been concerned with pedagogy for decades, I am not a specialist in education. And yet, that location may be of some value; after all, feminisms have, fortunately or otherwise, resisted mainstreaming and have more often than not been resisted by the mainstream.

A recent conference organized by the Comparative Education Society of India (CESI) in December 2015, on the theme *Education: Domination, Emancipation and Dignity* (abstracts available as an e-book), provides a snapshot of the concerns within the field. 'Gender, Patriarchy, and Education' figures as one of the 30 subthemes.

Some issues are worth flagging, with the caveat that abstracts obviously cannot capture the nuances of a full paper and a lively discussion. First is the overwhelming tendency to focus on school education (over 70 papers, Appendix 12.1a). While this is both necessary and enriching, it also means that there is a distance between the researcher, almost invariably located in the higher echelons of a highly stratified educational system, and the subjects of research, whether learners, teachers or administrators. As an extension of this, the social identities of the subjects of research are often systematically and empathetically foregrounded, even as those of the researcher remain in the background. What this means is that questions about ethnographic methods also, therefore, tend to be assumed as resolved, rather than opened for scrutiny in most instances. As a corollary of the aforementioned point, there is a relative paucity of papers pertaining to higher education (20 papers, Appendix 12.1b), and of studies of educational administrators, who remain virtually invisible in this domain. Twenty-three papers deal with other themes.

Can we implicate ourselves within the ethnographic process even as we 'use' it? My entry into this set of issues began through exploring ways and means of intervening creatively and constructively in a postgraduate classroom that has, for the past decade or so, combined diversity with homogeneity in terms of the composition of the students, even as the social profiles of teachers (and possibly educational administrators) changed far more slowly. Many of us could no longer take our positions as upper/middle class/caste apparently gendered, relatively privileged persons for granted.

Moreover, these are not our only locations. We negotiate several hierarchies within the domain of higher education, which is rapidly differentiating. In a scenario of increasing privatization, the social sciences are becoming relatively marginalized, as the focus shifts to what are perceived as commercially viable courses. Again, within the social sciences, history is considered to be relatively 'traditional' with an element of condescension (whether this perception is justified is another matter). Therefore, history teachers and learners tend to compete with relatively 'unconventional' options such as women's studies, media studies and discrimination and exclusion studies, as well as with other traditional social sciences such as economics, sociology and political science. To add another layer to the hierarchy, within history, modern history occupies pride of place, often viewed by students as the most exciting and 'relevant' part of the discipline. Needless to say, students (and sometimes teachers) of ancient history tend to view themselves as relatively marginalized. Further, these disciplinary hierarchies are reinforced by structural hierarchies inbuilt into the educational system – between administrators and teachers, teachers and learners and among teachers.

Within these structures, the classroom where I teach in is only a superficially homogeneous social space. To some extent, *ladkiyaan phir agey* would describe it as well. Most students are women, upper/middle class/caste, from relatively privileged urban backgrounds, with a reasonable fluency in English. The men, almost invariably in a minority, come from relatively less privileged backgrounds in terms of class and caste, and often from what are perceived as non-metropolitan urban, if not rural areas. Also, almost invariably, they are far more fluent in Hindi. Sexual orientations may be varied but are not explicitly demonstrated in public spaces, even as same-sex friendships/alliances are apparent.

Again I cannot escape assigning these identities a fixity that is by no means self-evident or even accurate. In effect, these are more often than not in the process of being made and remade, through constant negotiations, contestations and conflict. Some of the issues involved are brought out, for instance by Lori Horvitz (2011: 3), where she remarks that because of not being marked as African American or differently abled in North America, 'I have the privilege of "passing" into the dominant sexuality, of hiding who I am.' She also acknowledges 'how coming out is a process, and how I'm still processing' (ibid.).

Thus, as feminist practitioners within educational institutions, our locations are complicated. On the one hand, we may be expected to engage in 'simple social reproduction' (Spiegel 2011: 26), reiterating and reinforcing the status quo. Yet, as Horvitz (2011: 4) notes, learning and teaching demands that we move into areas that have the potential to cause discomfort. In order to do so with responsibility means that we engage relentlessly in interrogating ourselves as well as those who entrust themselves to us. This is by no means easy and painless. And yet, it is, I would argue, both possible and necessary.

Given that I teach a course on social history, where issues of caste, class, gender and sexual orientation are integral to our discussions, one of the issues I try to grapple with is how learners who entered the classroom experience these and other issues (including disability and regional/ethnic/religious identities). One of the entry points was through conversations about their experience of formal schooling.

I prepared a set of questions regarding the ways in which schooling was experienced. The questions were wide-ranging: on the medium of instruction; modes of transport; experiences of gender, caste, class, community, regional and ability-related diversities in terms of learners and teachers; subjects that were thought to be interesting; and infrastructure. There were also questions on family backgrounds, including siblings and their educational aspirations/opportunities. All the questions were circulated through e-mail, prior to the scheduled discussions, although I discovered that most students had simply glanced through them before coming, partly because of the pressures of the academic calendar.

We generally met in groups of three to six over several hours. Three students, who did not attend classes but invariably appeared for the examinations and cleared them, did not participate. I realized that I was unable to persuade them that I was interested in learning from them rather than upbraiding them, an acute reminder of the ways in which power relations between teacher and taught are perceived. In the course of the conversations, some questions were extended into sub-questions.

The conversations reinforced what I had already learnt through secondary readings and participation in teacher training workshops: social sciences were insignificant within the school curriculum. If an understanding of society was communicated through the formal system, English was one possible site to examine. This led me to explore the examination system. Once again, I discovered that the rich discourse on education has relatively little to offer on this, as well as the guidebooks that enable students to negotiate these, and override the textbooks and other pedagogical practices. And yet, the learners and teachers who bridge the gap between school and higher education in everyday lives traverse through these grey zones to 'arrive'.

What follows then are perspectives on formal schooling from two different vantage points. One is oral histories, recalling memories of school, especially in terms of issues of homogeneity and diversity. These pertain to the hidden curriculum rather than their experience of examinations, my second focal point. The latter, as most practitioners know, fade from memory rather rapidly as learners tend to negotiate them following a last-in-first-out strategy, even as for most students, cracking the examinations is regarded as a marker of success. This perception is shared and indeed derived from a wider social context, including parents and kin networks, generating and reinforcing aspirations that are regarded as legitimate. The school (including administrators and teachers) is often perceived as the location for ensuring that the goal is achieved, and anything else, in terms of less instrumental pedagogical interventions, is dismissed or marginalized as irrelevant or distracting.

To what extent do these two, that is the everyday experiences of the formal school and the definition of 'success' in the examinations, converge or diverge? I will attempt to address this through juxtaposing the insights from this situated ethnography with a discussion of an examination paper in English Communicative, a common course for the Central Board of Secondary Examination (CBSE), class X. The CBSE schools have an all-India reach, even if they are spread somewhat thinly across different states. About half the students who reached my classroom had cleared the CBSE; of the rest, one-third had come through the 'rival' Indian School Certificate Examination and two-thirds, most men and some less privileged women, had come through state boards. What is important is that the CBSE forms a point of reference even for boards that do not conform to it.

Clearly, other entry points are possible and even fruitful. However, in using these, I hope to draw attention to the chasm that exists between research on schooling and higher education and the urgent need to bridge this, especially, but not only from a feminist perspective that values and engages with the challenges of democratization.

Let me add a few more qualifiers. First, to state the obvious, the school system in our country is highly differentiated at present and is becoming increasingly more differentiated. Thus, at one end, there are private schools that offer the International Baccalaureate and are tied into a global educational market. These cater to the privileged, upper class, both boys and girls, and are beyond the reach of most of the growing, and diverse, middle class. At the other end are the government schools, in varying degrees of array and disarray, offering the bare minimum in terms of infrastructure and pedagogical inputs, and sometimes not even that, to the underprivileged, who cannot afford anything else. In a situation where resources are scarce, poor families tend to send girls to government schools, while their siblings are sent to more expensive private schools, in the hope of providing access to routes towards upward mobility. Also, in terms of caste, government schools often cater to those at the lowest rungs of the hierarchy, who cannot afford alternatives.

In a sense, the classroom in the public university represents these diversities in a microcosm – the most underprivileged women do not find space in these relatively rarefied reaches of higher education; at the same time, the most privileged men are expected, generally, to pursue more profitable professions, and rarely make it to the ancient Indian history classroom, even as they may retain an amateur interest in the past. Also, most students who made their way into the classroom had not studied history in high school and sometimes not even in college. Why this was so is another story. But to summarize, parental, peer and institutional pressure very often determined 'choices' of subjects, and science and commerce were almost invariably privileged over the social sciences.

2. 'Classifying' students

The CBSE has a set of three books for class X for a course designated as English (Communicative): the *Main Course Book* (2011), the *Workbook* (2012) and the *Literature Reader* (2014). We will refer to them by these titles, as these are authored by teams and are regarded as collective productions.

The preliminary pages outline the focus of the books. For instance, the *Literature Reader* (2014: viii) states:

> Like the Main Coursebook [*sic*], this Literature Reader also carries pieces which have been identified and selected with a bearing on social issues and universal values. In other words, the literary pieces remind us all of the importance of values such as telling the truth, good health, respect for older people, and the role of law and order.

If we are looking for pieces that would encourage the learner to work for social transformation, or even critically evaluate the social order in which she or he is located, we are clearly in the wrong place.

At another, and more subterranean, level, chapters and exercises in language books are almost invariably built around named protagonists. Some of these are well-known figures; others are purportedly names for ordinary people. It is the latter that open up possibilities for engaging with similarities and differences on an everyday basis, as opposed to spectacular but often empty gestures towards inclusivity or integration. They offer spaces for challenging stereotypes and for introducing issues of diversity in ways that are plausible rather than platitudinous. How is this potential space used?

Consider the names used in the *English Course (Communicative) Workbook* for class X (2012). Here, I work with the commonsensical assumption that names derived from Sanskrit and related languages are generally read as Hindu, those of Arabic or Persian derivation are understood as Muslim and English-/European-sounding names are often regarded as Christian. There are around 170 names derived from Sanskrit. Only 15 names are derived from Persian/Arabic/Urdu and an equal number from English/European languages (see Appendix 12.2).

Names, as we know, reveal caste and region as well. Many language books work with the assumption that caste can be erased by not mentioning it. Therefore, most protagonists are distinguished only by their first name; in the rare instances where surnames are mentioned, these tend to be implicitly or explicitly upper caste. Again, names that seem distinctively south Indian are few and far between. And for what has come to be designated as the Northeast, there is a single girl named Mary – unless we are expected to understand that all the English-sounding names, which are not too many, signify people from this region. A name such as that of Nido Tainam, for instance, the young man who lost his life when he was attacked in a marketplace in Delhi in January 2014, would remain unfamiliar to students passing through the system. Interestingly and ironically, there is an attempt to achieve gender parity, so the numbers of names of women and men are more or less equal.

These names are built into routine exercises of grammar and syntax, the staple of a language curriculum. As such, they offer immense potential for introducing a variety of names derived from different naming practices and traditions. That this opportunity is left virtually untapped may not be deliberate – nonetheless, it is troubling as it indicates the almost subconscious choices made by the authors/compilers of these exercises, which renders the very existence of diverse populations virtually invisible.

Compare this with experiences of schooling. For most of those who had worked their way through the government schooling system, almost all their schoolmates shared a common background. Virtually all students, with a few exceptions, came from the majority religious community. Students from schools in Uttar Pradesh, for instance, with the exception of one from Azamgarh, recollected having only a handful of Muslim classmates. Jains, Buddhists, Christians, Sikhs? In most instances, even from students of elite private schools, the answer was in the negative. After some reflection, one young woman who had opted for humanities said: 'Of course, there would have been Jains in the science and commerce class.' Thus, opportunities for interacting routinely with students from other communities were almost absent. Students from other regions, likewise, were virtually absent; the exceptions were in a handful of schools in metropolitan areas, and some government schools targeting parents with transferable jobs.

The profile of teachers is also significant. While some teachers in government schools were drawn from neighbouring provinces, most tend to be from the same state. Also, virtually all were recognized as belonging to the majority community. Most schools did not have teachers with disabilities. By and large, this pattern seems to be replicated in private schools outside the major metropolitan cities as well, including cities such as Jodhpur, Jaipur, Lucknow and Allahabad. In other words, certain homogeneities tend to be reinforced by both text and context. If feminisms encourage engaging with diversities meaningfully, the formal school then provides a challenge rather than an opportunity.

At another level, a middle-class, if not upper-class, world is taken for granted with remarkable ease in the course material, evident in standard exercises about students going on holidays or for further education. In the *Workbook* (2012), these places include Canada, Cornell, the United States, Switzerland, America and London (2012: 48, 88, 95, 242, 122, 129, 160). One of the few Indian universities mentioned is Patna University (*Workbook* 2012: 48). In a rare instance does a young girl suggest a trip to Shillong (ibid.: 204).

As part of this scenario, cars are taken for granted (*Workbook* 2012: 15), as are expensive clothes (ibid.: 173). Further, issues of health that are highlighted include sleep deprivation, associated with typically middle-class jobs (*Main Course Book* 2011: 3–6) and obesity (ibid.: 22–24), while stress-busters include recommendations of laughter yoga (ibid.: 18–20). Not surprisingly, less exalted occupations are almost invisible.

Even when they occur, representations of poverty are problematic, to say the least. For instance, the learner encounters generic statements such as the following (*Workbook* 2012: 49):

> It is impossible to ignore the beggars on the roads.
>
> (Ibid.: 51)

The same perspective is reinforced in the examination. Consider the following (CBSE 2012, Gupta n.d.: A.36):

> The park in front of your house has been illegally occupied by some people. They have set up temporary dwelling units and are a security threat to the colony residents. Write a letter to the President of the Residents Welfare Association drawing attention to this threat.

As is evident, the learner is not even expected to enquire into why 'some people' may have set up these 'temporary dwelling units'. In other words, troubling issues of class differences, privilege and the lack of entitlement to basic amenities are simplified and converted into 'a security threat'. All that is expected of the learner is to address this neatly circumscribed issue rather than exploring more disturbing realities that may lie beyond what is perceived to be an encroachment. Can we even begin to visualize what answering such a question might mean to a first-generation learner from an underprivileged background, who may be part of those who are represented as a security threat?

Another question, apparently appropriate in a country periodically reeling under heat wave conditions, again typically envisages a middle-class student as the learner (CBSE, Gupta, n.d.: B28–B29):

> Look at the following visual which brings out how the heat wave can be dealt with if we follow some simple precautions in our lifestyle. Using these inputs and ideas of your own, write a letter to your friend on how you are taking care of yourself despite the month-long temperatures being about 43 degree C.

The accompanying visual shows a young girl with the options of showering/bathing/swimming; using a solar hat/cap; reading; watching TV; playing indoor games; wearing loose, light, cotton clothes; carrying an umbrella; drinking *nimbu paani* and *aam panna* (lemon juice and raw mango juice); eating fruit salad; and using slippers and sandals instead of shoes. That many of these luxuries, including regular access to water, would be beyond the reach of many first-generation learners is obviously invisible and/or irrelevant to the examiners.

Interestingly, while the textbook and the examination paper work with the understanding of a more or less homogeneous middle class, learners have vivid memories of the ways in which class differences were manifested in school. Those who had been through navy schools, for instance, remembered the sharp difference between the children of sailors and those of officers. Areas of residence, in quarters, were different. Besides, as teachers were often 'officers' wives', they were perceived to be treating the children differently. 'They [i.e. sailors' children] were treated harshly,' an officer's child observed. What about the children? She remembered the children of sailors as being 'more reserved', not readily responding to her gestures of friendship. At the same time, in the course of the conversation, she recollected how, when the sailors' children won the school elections, the teachers reacted by claiming that the elections had been rigged. Obviously, bridging the gulf requires much more than goodwill.

There were other markers of wealth that students readily identified, in spite of the standardization imposed by the school uniform – access to the Internet, cable TV and what one watched, cell phones, water bottles, tiffin boxes, shorter skirts for the uniform, tattoos, casual wear when permitted, the use of 'fancy stationery', colour printouts for projects, modes of transport; many of these were perceived by the less privileged as 'flaunting one's status'. For the less privileged, even acquiring the mandatory school uniform was a major event. One young man recalled getting his first pair of shoes, and pant and shirt, in class X.

Inevitably, caste and class were inextricably linked. Students from less-privileged-caste backgrounds experienced discrimination routinely, in subtle and not-so-subtle ways. In one government school, the seating arrangement in the classroom privileged the upper castes. One particularly energetic young man remembered how teachers almost invariably asked upper-caste students to fetch drinking water for them. Thus, this routine chore was etched in his memory as a marker of discrimination. This was extended to what was seen as participation in prestigious activities such as cultural events or sports. He was good in sports but was denied opportunities because his clothes and shoes were considered inadequate. *Narial se basket ball kheltaa thaa* (I would play basket ball using a coconut). His energies were drawn on when required – for digging the soil when saplings had to be planted, yet his contributions, he felt, were rarely acknowledged. Even when his academic performance was among the best, he was not recognized, because the teacher did not know his name. His recollections of Independence Day celebrations are particularly poignant – while he was in a junior class, one of the 'ma'am's' recognized his potential and encouraged him to participate in *naara-baazi* (raising slogans). Later, in senior classes, he was ignored, in spite of his punctuality and other qualities: *tab main man me naaraa lagaataa thaa* (then I would simply repeat the slogans in my mind). The same young man was routinely expected to help in cleaning the school premises – *jhaaroo pochhaa lagaanaa* (sweeping and mopping the floor). Remarkably, he did not resent this but was hurt that he was never asked to participate in the recitation of the Monday prayers, obviously regarded as a prestigious activity, reserved for the more privileged. Nor was he encouraged to read out aloud from the newspapers, again, evidently an important activity in the school schedule. In the course of our conversation, he stated, with obvious pride in his ability to work hard, his indefatigable energy and perseverance: *Mujhe dayaa nahin chahiye* (I do not want pity).

3. 'Eradicating' caste

Given the intersections between caste and class, it is interesting that while the latter is treated as an unmarked category within the examination system, the former is effectively eliminated in both textbooks and examinations. For instance, when figures like the noted Tamil Dalit woman writer Bama are introduced, their caste identities are glossed over. These are replaced by relatively innocuous statements such as the following (*Main Course Book* 2011: 68):

- Multi-faceted personality-woman with extraordinary courage, conviction, resistance to any form of oppression
- Keen eye for beauty in nature, profound insight into issues pertaining to caste, religion, women
- Clear thoughts and expression
- Dedicated to the uplift of the downtrodden: passion-Teaching: Mission-Building a casteless society.

Contrast this silencing with the omnipresence of caste in the matrimonial advertisements in the newspapers. The listings for a single day mention more than a dozen caste-related affiliations, sometimes (as in the *Times of India*), arranged alphabetically, in other cases (as in the *Dainik Jagaran*), in terms of the dominant caste order. If the school curriculum and examination could encourage an understanding of how such identities are constructed, maintained and occasionally challenged, this opportunity to recognize, contextualize and problematize caste is lost, if not deliberately ignored.

And yet, as we have seen, caste sharply etched in students' minds as part of the hidden curriculum. When I asked a young woman whether caste was in an issue in her school, an expensive private institution, she replied:

> No, it was not an issue, but I remember one incident. This was during the National Talent Search. That's a very tough test – one girl cleared it and the rest wondered, how did she? Then we found out that she belonged to the SC. And some girls felt, 'she belonged to the SC, she is my friend, she never told me'.

The tensions and pressures evident in concealing and revealing identities are palpable.

The caste identities of teachers, often masked under the category 'general', were experienced in a variety of ways. One student from a less privileged background remembered how the physical education teacher, also in charge of the hostel, was a Brahmin, good-looking, strict and prone to use abusive language. Those from privileged caste backgrounds were more hesitant to discuss the caste of their teachers. In one instance, when a student reflected back on her experience, she said, thoughtfully, 'I suppose most of them were from the same castes, brahmins or Rajputs.'

One of the quotidian practices that students from less privileged castes identified as reinforcing caste identities in the classroom was the method of recording attendance. While some schools used first names, others included surnames. A young man remarked: 'The way they (the teachers) mention your title tells you what they think.' He enacted the different modes, which obviously cannot be captured in a bald narrative. In other instances, roll numbers were called out. This was more impersonal and was simultaneously less discriminatory and more easy to subvert – *bacche bhaag jaate they* 'students would run away,' observed one young woman.

Yet it was not only students who ran away – some of the less privileged, whose options were limited to government schools, recounted how teachers were often absent, busy with private tuitions, while formal classes remained unaddressed.

4. Gender and sexuality: visibly invisible

How is gender addressed in the course material and examination? There is a combination of two strategies. On the one hand, gender is abstracted from caste, class, and regional contexts, and figures as a neat, delimited category. Not surprisingly, there are accounts of achievers – women astronauts, for instance, figure in vivid detail in the *Main Course Book* (2011: 102–108). Such narratives may have inspirational value – however, one wonders why virtually all the heroes of rags to riches stories are men. Narratives about less privileged women succeeding in life are conspicuous by their absence.

In the *Literature Reader*, only 2 of the 12 selected authors are women (*Literature Reader* 2014: 35–46, 97–98). Thus, readers may get the impression that women authors are exceptional. Further, while short biographies are provided for most authors, Vikram Seth, whose poem 'The Frog and the Nightingale' (ibid.: 86–91) is anthologized, is denied any further acknowledgement. Is it because of the discomfort in mentioning his sexual orientation and his support for decriminalizing homosexuality?

Women characters are virtually absent from 6 of the 12 pieces and only marginally present in 2 of the others. Moreover, the women characters represented are not particularly exciting or complex. Consider 'Two Gentlemen of Verona' (ibid.: 3–7), a story of two young boys who do everything possible to earn money for the treatment of their elder sister, a young woman struck with tuberculosis. She appears affectionate, vulnerable, weak and dependent. The three other pieces where women are present include a woman who insists on organizing séances (ibid.: 35–46), a set of scheming society women who try to outsmart one another through ostentatious displays and even blackmail (ibid.: 13–16), and two sisters who quarrel about the things they hope to inherit from their father (ibid.: 137–154). The most challenging, at once talented and tragic female character in the entire text is provided by Seth's animal fable, in the figure of the nightingale (ibid.: 86–91), who ultimately dies, pushed and prodded relentlessly by the manipulative frog.

Compare this with the range of boys and men presented in the text. These include the two young boys mentioned earlier, who demonstrate enterprise, perseverance and affection in looking after their sister, as well as two others who are caught within a web of virtual reality but make their way out of it (ibid.: 72–78). There is excitement and tension in the narrative.

Also, men are part of more complex narratives, where they are seen, and see themselves, from different perspectives. This is evident in the poignant story titled 'The Letter' (ibid.: 23–29), where a poor old man waits patiently for a letter from his daughter. The irate post office employees who initially ridicule him ultimately empathize with his experience, even though it is apparently too late. Also thought-provoking is the sketch of 'Patol Babu, Film Star' (ibid.: 55–66), which traces the way in which the principal protagonist responds to the offer and challenge of playing a minor role in a film. D.H. Lawrence's short poem on his encounter with a snake (ibid.: 125–127) also takes the reader through a range of conflicting emotions.

Apart from this, there are the staple excerpts from classics, including the works of Shakespeare (ibid.: 103–104 and 158–178), Shelley (ibid.: 107) and Coleridge (ibid.: 112–114). While these are intended to evoke grand, heroic and tragic emotions, the contexts of texts such as the *Ancient Mariner* may be quite remote for learners in the 21st century.

If the *Literature Reader* suggests that women are few, silly and manipulative, consider the implications of answering the following examination questions. We learn (CBSE 2012, Gupta n.d.: A-62):

> The implementation of Right to Education Act has ensured education for all children 4–14 years of age. The government has also started new schemes to especially educate the girl child, for it is rightly said, if the woman is educated the family is educated. Inspite of efforts made by the government to educate girls, we still come across incidents of

disparity maintained between boys and girls' education. Using hints from the Unit on Education of your MCB [*Main Course Book*] and your own ideas write an article in about 100–120 words on the importance of educating the girl child.

Two issues stand out in the way in which the question is framed. First, it is not addressed to the girl child – others are expected to answer it on her behalf. Second, the response is squarely located within a framework of domesticity; the girl child who may attempt to look beyond the family has little or no justification for claiming a right to education. How would young girls and boys respond to such a question? In order to succeed in the examination, there is no scope for questioning the framework – rather what is inculcated is acceptance of the premises and fitting a response within this circumscribed space.

An identical perspective underlies yet another question (CBSE 2012, Gupta n.d.: B 55):

You are Anish/Ashna of Class X, the head of the School Social Science Club. You have witnessed that crime against women has increased in the country whether it is female infanticide, rape, murders, physical and emotional assault. As a concerned citizen of this country, write an article in about 100–120 words, on 'How to Make our Women Secure'?
Hints:

- Crime against women have increased
- Unsafe for women to move out at any point of time
- Stricter laws
- Vigilant police force, etc.

Once again, the exercise provides little or no space for potential young women to express their opinions directly, nor does it allow for the recognition of possibilities of domestic violence, or of violence perpetrated by the police. In other words, the discussion is confined within 'safe' limits.

What about the hidden curriculum? For learners passing through coeducational schools, the proportions of girls and boys vary substantially according to streams. Therefore, students passing through science or commerce streams found more boys than girls in their class, whereas students in the humanities found the opposite situation. Boys opting for the humanities often felt particularly stigmatized as they were perceived as letting down those who had greater expectations of them.

There are other, more insidious ways in which gender plays out. Many young women remembered the trauma of the mandatory white skirt or the white salwar or churidar as part of the school uniform, and the anxiety of menstrual stains showing up. One young woman described a stark contrast: 'From class VIII we had to wear white churidars, while the boys wore black pants.' Another young man recalled the change as well: 'Till class IX boys wore navy blue pants while girls wore navy blue skirts, and then from class X the girls had to switch to a white salwar, white dupatta, and navy blue kurta.' Incidentally, the young men from government schools in Uttar Pradesh and Bihar had somewhat different memories of the school uniform – it was regarded as a sign of showing off, and many students came to school, as and when they did, in casual clothes.

Also, in some co-educational schools, both boys and girls recollected that a standard form of punishment for troublesome boys was to make them sit in the rows meant for girls. This was obviously meant to be humiliating for the boys. What it meant for the girls to be routinely regarded as degraded and less than equal was evidently immaterial.

Issues of adolescent sexuality remain as troubling memories. One young woman remembered:

> Also there was a girl who studied till the 10th, she was tomboyish – there were days when we could wear coloured dresses – she wore jeans and tee shirts – so the eco teacher told her, I'm going to cut your hair. The others were more sensitive – they felt she had a mental problem, a hormonal problem. Some of the teachers understood.

This terse, tense narrative encapsulates the experience of a young girl who did not quite conform and the way this was understood and handled. Creating space for a diversity of sexual experiences/orientations is obviously not regarded as an option within the structured space of the school.

In yet another instance from a co-educational school, young girls from the class were singled out for a not-particularly-enlightening discussion on menstruation. To add to their embarrassment, the boys, who knew what was clearly an open secret, kept asking, 'Where have you been?' In addition, teachers kept a close surveillance on cross-sex relationships, which were discussed in parent–teacher meetings.

More generally, those who had been through the government school system interacted primarily with male teachers, especially in the science and commerce streams. As one student succinctly summarized the situation:

> Junior section mein ladies theen, senior mein men. (There were ladies [women teachers] in the junior section, while the senior section had men).

In other words, gender hierarchies were perceived as part of the routine structure of the school system. In private schools, the gender profile of teachers was remembered differently, with a majority of women teachers and a handful of male teachers who handled technical and non-academic subjects. In many instances, students categorically identified the background of teachers: as one remarked: 'Most teachers were army wives.'

5. Of success and survival

It is obvious that we have simply touched on the tips of several icebergs. We have considered only one examination board, the CBSE. How different/similar would the picture be if other examination boards were considered? Also, we have chosen one language/subject – would the picture become more complex if we were able to consider others? And the students who have shared their experiences are exceptional – they have not made their way into engineering/management/commerce/medicine. Would other students share their perceptions? Would access to the perceptions of teachers and administrators have provided different insights? Babu, Singai and Mahajan (2015) draw attention to these possibilities. Clearly, and perhaps fortunately, there are no easy answers. As Roy (2015: 190) reminds us, even apparently marginalized girl students succeed, within limits, in redefining the experience of schools for themselves and others.

At the same time, there are deafening silences that demand urgent attention. Students and teachers with disabilities were rare, if not non-existent, in most schools. One student recollected the poignant experience of a classmate with hearing problems, who sat quietly in class. She realized that this young girl had a disability only after befriending her. In other words, the student was apparently left to fend for herself in a 'normal' classroom, without any formal acknowledgement of her special needs or any provision for support. The possibility of transgender categories existing within the classroom was equally, if not more, unimaginable.

For many students, the experience of relative homogeneity in terms of class, caste, community, region and sexual orientation, within a simplistically construed and reiterated gender binary, was re-created/reinforced in college, unless they moved to institutions in the metropolitan cities. Even where diversities were far more visible, responses often varied from formal acknowledgement to active negotiation, with the possibility of stereotypes being reinforced as one of the easiest options. Rathod *et al.* (2015) draw attention to the significance of this domain. Higher education in public universities provides one of the few precious spaces available for engaging with diversities and differences meaningfully and constructively – through pedagogic practices, content of courses, dialogue and debate, even as we must acknowledge that access to these spaces remains effectively restricted to the middle class, fortunately in itself differentiated. The learners who reach us, moreover, come through the hurdles of several examinations, of which the school examination remains by far the most important.

What does succeeding or excelling in the school examination mean? Does it mean that the learners internalize the not particularly exciting or demanding understanding of society that runs through the textbooks and workbooks and is further circumscribed by the questions posed and the answers expected in the examination? Or is the penetration of the examination process skin deep, something that is negotiated and then conveniently forgotten, overrun by the pressures, pleasures and challenges of coping with and surviving in a far more complex real world? And, of course, there is a range of possibilities between these two poles. How do we, as feminists in the broadest sense of the term, engage with pedagogical precepts and practices to both recognize and challenge differences, diversities and hierarchies of privilege that are at once palpable and naturalized? Sreenivas (2015) provides thoughtful reflections on some of these issues. She reminds us about the need to acknowledge the importance of our shared experiences.

But, beyond that, there are other questions. How do we intervene effectively in the formulation of educational policies, their implementation and practices in an increasingly differentiated scenario? How can we continue to dream, meaningfully, about the transformative potential of education? Hopefully, interventions, praxis and theorization will continue to evolve in many directions as we engage with these challenges.

Acknowledgment

I would like to thank all the students who generously shared their experiences of formal education with me. All these conversations took place through March and April 2015 as part of a project on the teaching and learning of history that has been possible because of a fellowship awarded by the Nehru Memorial Museum and Library, New Delhi. I am also grateful to Kalpana Kannabiran and Padmini Swaminathan for their patience, and to the anonymous referee who compelled me to rethink and rewrite much of what I took for granted. Errors and lacunae, conceptual and otherwise, that remain are mine.

References

Babu, Savitha, Chetan Singai and Anupama Mahajan. 2015. "Teaching in College: Exploring Experiences, Examining Identities." In *Education: Domination, Emancipation and Dignity*. Bengaluru: Comparative Education Society of India (e-book), pp. 276–279.

English Course (Communicative), Literature Reader. 2014. New Delhi: Central Board of Secondary Education (reprint, revised edition 2010, first edition not mentioned).

English Course (Communicative), Main Course Book, a Textbook for English (Communicative). 2011. New Delhi: Central Board of Secondary Education (revised edition 2011, first edition 1994).

English Course (Communicative) Workbook, a Textbook for English Communicative. 2012. New Delhi: Central Board of Secondary Education, 2012 (reprint, revised edition 1998, first edition not mentioned).

Gupta, R. K. n.d. *Golden English Communicative (with Sample Papers)*, Class X, Term I and II, New Delhi: New Age International (P) Limited Publishers (containing questions from CBSE examinations up to 2014).

Horvitz, Lori. 2011. "Introduction." In Lori Horvitz (ed.). *Queer Girls in Class: Lesbian Teachers and Students Tell Their Classroom Stories.* New York: Peter Lang, pp. 1–4.

Pappu, Rekha and Nirmali Goswami. 2015. "Introduction," *Indian Journal of Gender Studies*, special issue, Current Issues in Gender and Education, Vol. 22, No. 2, pp. 159–169.

Rathod, Sadaf, Bharat Rathod, Kalpana Dixit, Anagha Tambe, Vinayak Lashkar, Swati Dyahadroy, Snehal Sharma and Sangeeta Kamat. 2015. "Democratizing Higher Education: Collaborative Research for Equity and Social Justice in U.S. and India." In *Education: Domination, Emancipation and Dignity.* Bengaluru: Comparative Education Society of India (e-book), pp. 261–262.

Roy, Sangeeta. 2015. "Why Should Holidays Come in the Way of School? Situating Girls' Experiences of Schooling," *Indian Journal of Gender Studies*, Vol. 22, No. 2, pp. 170–193.

Spiegel, Michelle. 2011. "The Personal as Productive?: Sexual Embodiment and Identity in the Women's Studies Classroom." In Lori Horvitz (ed.). *Queer Girls in Class: Lesbian Teachers and Students Tell Their Classroom Stories.* New York: Peter Lang, pp. 21–26.

Sreenivas, Deepa. 2015. "Between Politics and Discipline: Gender Studies in an Institutional Setting," *Indian Journal of Gender Studies*, Vol. 22, No. 2, pp. 265–281.

Appendix 12.1a

CESI 2015 papers related to school education ('SD' in parentheses indicates explicit mention of social diversities, including gender; 'E' indicates use of ethnographic methods, '*' indicates mention of both school and higher education)

1. A.R. Sitalakshmi, 'Faclitiating [*sic*] Knowledge Construction through Constructivist Pedgagoy [*sic*] in Senior Secondary Science Classroom in India', p. 1 (E).
2. Aditi Kundra, Nishitha Sony and Shafali Sharma, 'Vision for an Inclusive Society: A Micro Socio-Economic Survey of Educational Aspirations of Urban Poor', pp. 2–5 (SD; E).
3. Alfeno Marie Shivakumar and Indira Vijaysimha, 'Educational Achievement of Children from Urban Slums of Bangalore', pp. 6–8 (SD; E).
4. Alka Malvankar, 'Domination, Emancipation and Dignity in Lives and Schooling of Students', pp. 9–11 (SD; E).
5. Amar Singh and Ravi Verma, 'Discrimination and Isolation of LGBTs in Schools', pp. 12–14 (SD; E).
6. Amar Singh, 'Dichotomy of Government and Private Schools and Socio-Economic Inequality in Ikbalpur Village', Rajasthan, pp. 15–17 (SD; E).
7. Ankit Saraf, 'Teacher Leadership: Towards a New Professionalism?', pp. 18–20.
8. Ashwini Kp, Pradnya Sanghajit Garud and Areesh Kumar Karamala, 'Intersection of Caste and Gender: Experiences and Challenge of Dalit Children in Schools', p. 32 (SD; E).
9. Ata Mallick, 'The OL Script and Santal Education in West Bengal', pp. 70–72 (SD).
10. Atima Singh, 'Investigating the Perceptions of Elementary School Teachers about Assessment and Learning', pp. 33–37.
11. Avinash Kumar Singh, 'Right Based Approach to Education and Development: Policies and Practices', p. 38 (SD).
12. Barnali Biswas, 'Education and Social Inequality: Exploring the Dynamics of Street Vendor's Children in Delhi', pp. 39–41 (SD; E).

13 Binay Pattanayak and Giridhari Gaunjhu, 'Domination Related to Children's Language, Emancipation and Dignity in Multilingual Jharkhand . . . An Ongoing Experiment', pp. 47–48.
14 Bishnu Mishra, 'The Ethnography of an Alternative School in Rajasthan', pp. 49–51 (E).
15 Deepshikha Singh, 'Inclusion of Children with Disabilities in Early Childhood Education: Challenges in Teachers' Practices', pp. 61–64 (SD; E).
16 G.C. Pal, 'Pre-School Education, Access to Knowledge and Social Exclusion: Insights from the Integrated Child Development Services', pp. 88–91.
17 Gayatri Panda, 'Perennial Private Interventions for School Success: An Exploratory Study of the Seeding of Unequal Educational Chances', pp. 96–98 (SD).
18 Ghazal Gulati and Praveen Khanghta, 'A Pragmatic Framework for Private School Regulations', pp. 99–100.
19 Gurumurthy Kasinathan, 'Domination and Emancipation: A Framework for Assessing ICT and Education Programs', pp. 101–104.
20 Indrajeet Dutta and Rashmi Soni, 'Transition from "Agents of Change" to "Victims of Change": Changing Contour of Teacher Identity', pp. 112–114 (E).
21 Jaya Singh and Shekhar Singh, 'Understanding Assessment: Need for Reform', pp. 115–118.
22 Jyoti Bawane and Damayanti Rajpal Raut, 'Survival of Elementary Education as a Public Good in This Era of Privatization', pp. 129–131 (E).
23 Kalyani Akalamkam, Deepika Papneja, Kanika Ahuja and Megha Dhillon, 'Mapping Conflict in Schools: A Step towards Creating Peace and Equity', pp. 132–134 (E).
24 Kanika Saraff, 'Identity and Power in an Early Childhood Classroom: Reflections from the Ground', pp. 135–137 (SD; E).
25 Khushbu Singh, 'Equality of Educational Opportunity and Social Justice: Is 25 per cent Reservation under the RTE Act, 2009 a Way Out?', p. 139 (SD; E).
26 Leena, 'Corporal Punishments in Educational Institutions and Its Implications in Indian Context', pp. 152–155 (SD; E).
27 Marie Mc Andrew, 'Inequalities in the Educational Pathways of Ethnic Minority Youth: The Role of Systemic Factors', pp. 154–157 (SD).
28 Mary Vayaliparampil, 'Participatory Action Research in Education: Photovoice', pp. 158–161 (SD; E).
29 Maxine Berntsen, 'Pragat Shikshan Sanstha: Three Decades of Engagement with Social Justice', pp. 172–176 (SD; E).
30 Meera Gopi Chandran, 'Teachers' Work Lives and Search for Identity', pp. 177–180 (E).
31 Megha Dadhwal, 'Curriculum of Teacher Education in Colonial India', pp. 181–183.

32 Monica Gupta, Sailaja Modugu and Aparna Joshi, 'Emancipation through Ecological Living: A Journey from Philosophy to Praxis', pp. 184–188 (E).
33 Nadim Khan, 'RTE Act and Inclusive and Discrimination Free Schools', pp. 193–195 (SD).
34 Nandhini Nanjappan, 'Understanding Exclusion in Education: A Study of Female Dropout in Dharmapuri District of Tamil Nadu', pp. 196–198 (SD; E).
35 Naseem Akhtar and Shivani Taneja, 'Aims of Education – Manifestation in Schools', pp. 199–201 (SD; E).
36 Navprit Kaur and Lallan Baghel, 'Growing Up Dalit: Caste and Experience of Getting Educated in a Modern City', pp. 202–204 (SD; E).
37 Nidhi Gaur, 'Educational Experiences of Rural Girls', pp. 209–211 (SD; E).
38 Nirmali Goswami, 'Costs, Security, Discipline: Engendering the Debate on School Choice in India', pp. 216–217 (SD; E).
39 Nishi, 'Assessment in Policies and in Schools', pp. 218–221.
40 Noopur, 'Examining Low Fee Private Schools in India under the Frame of Right to Education Act, 2009', pp. 222–223 (SD; E).
41 P.S. Raju Vetukuri, 'School Education among Dalits in India', pp. 224–228 (SD).
42 Pallavi Chhabra, 'Technology in Classrooms: For What Purpose?' pp. 229–231.
43 Pamela Dasgupta, 'Girls' Education and Empowerment in Rural Areas: A Study in Uttar Dinajpur District of West Bengal', pp. 232–234 (SD; E).
44 Parimala Rao, 'Official Discourse on Native Morality: Some Explorations on Female Teachers and Students in the Nineteenth Century India', pp. 235–236 (SD).
45 Parul Malik, 'Denying Them and in Denial of Young People's Sexuality: Narratives of Desires and Conflicts at School', pp. 237–238 (E).
46 Prakash C. Bhattarai, 'Challenges for Ethics of the Educational Administrators: A Case of Nepal', pp. 244–245 (E).
47 Priyanka Padhy, '"I Am What I Learn": Industry and Inferiority in School Children Enrolled through Quota for Weaker Sections and Disadvantaged Groups', pp. 246–249 (SD; E).
48 Reshmi Chakraborty, 'Middle Class Narratives in Education: The Dynamics of Power and Change in the Capital City of Assam', pp. 251–252 (SD; E).
49 Ritesh Khunyakari and Shikha Takker, 'Contemplating Issues Related to Teacher Professional Identity: Towards a Conceptual Framework', pp. 253–256 (SD; E).
50 Rupamanjari Hegde, 'Constructions of Unequal Citizenship: A Sociological Study of a School in Delhi', pp. 257–260 (SD; E).

51 Sadananda Kadel, 'English as a Medium of Instruction: Challenges for Community Schools in Nepal', pp. 263–265.
52 Sangita Dey, 'Policy Analysis of Mid Day Meal Programme: From Governance Perspectives', pp. 269–271.
53 Sanket Karkare, 'Gender and Media Literacy amongst Teenagers in India', p. 272.
54 Satya Prakash Pattanaik, 'Benefits of Studying at KGBV: A Micro Study in Rajasthan', pp. 273–275 (SD; E).
55 Sehar Saeed, Saba Saeed and Farrah Saeed, 'Disparities in Education along Socio Economic Lines in Pakistan', pp. 280–281 (SD).
56 Sehar Saeed, Saeed Piracha and Ahmad Dawood, 'Children's Literature Festival – Beyond Texts and Test for Promoting a Culture of Multiple Narratives and Critical Thinking', pp. 282–283 (SD; E).
57 Shashi Bhusan Mishra and Arijita Dutta, 'Efficiency of Primary Schools in West Bengal: Measurement and Determinants', pp. 284–286 (SD).
58 Shrikant Kalokhe, 'Dialects and Domination of Dalits in the Discourse of Marathi Language', p. 295.
59 Shruti Chopra, 'Teachers as Inquirers: A Reflective, Inquiry-Based Approach to Understanding of Nature of Science among Pre-Service Teachers', pp. 296–298 (E).
60 Sonia Sawhney, 'Understanding the Play of Tacit Social Modelling in Classroom Interactions', pp. 303–305 (SD; E).
61 Soumali Banerjee, 'Education: Domination, Emancipation and Dignity: The Condition of the Indigenous and Tribal Students in India', pp. 306–308 (SD; E).
62 Suhail Mir. 'A Gini Approach to Inequality of Educational Opportunity in India: Evidence from NSS', pp. 316–320 (SD).
63 Sujatha Rao, 'Who Am I and Why Am I Here? The Role Conflict and Ambiguity of Being a Head Teacher in Government Schools in India', pp. 321–323 (SD; E).
64 Sumedha Jain and Manisha Wadhwa, 'Engaging with Pluralism in Primary Classroom', pp. 324–326 (SD; E).
65 Sunaina K, 'Texts, Contexts and Voices in Social Writing: A Study of Development of Critical Consciousness among School Students in Kerala', p. 327 (SD; E).
66 Suvasini Iyer, 'To Understand How Middle Class Subjectivities Are Shaped through Private Schooling', p. 331 (SD; E).
67 Syeda Farwa Fatima, 'Learning for Access: Case of Out of School Children of Pakistan', p. 332 (SD; E).
68 Tamal Krishna Kayal, 'Efficacy of Input-Based Policies in Primary Education: An Empirical Investigation in India', pp. 333–335 (SD).

69 Tasha Agarwal, 'A Study of Education Voucher Program Design in Delhi', pp. 336–338 (SD).
70 Tripti Bassi, 'Gendered Socialization Experiences of Rural Sikh Girls in Ferozepur, Punjab', pp. 339–341 (SD; E).
71 Tushar Savarkar, 'Factors Affecting Educational Attainment of Youth in India', pp. 342–344 (SD).
72 Usashi Kundu De, 'Effect of Gender on Secondary Students' Performance in Mathematics', pp. 345–347 (SD).
73 Vachaspati Shukla, 'Expansion of Educational Opportunities, Inequality in Education, and Its Impact on Income Inequality: Cross-Section Evidence from India', pp. 348–349 (SD*).
74 Vidya Mahambare and Sowmya Dhanaraj, 'Closing the School Achievement Gap: What Factors Matter', pp. 350–351 (SD; E).
75 Vijitha Rajan, 'Educational Exclusion of Children of Distress Seasonal Migrants in India', pp. 352–355 (SD).
76 Yamini Agarwal, 'Minority Educational Institutions, Issues of Identity and Culture: The Case of Sikh Community in Delhi', p. 359 (SD; E).
77 Yashpal Jogdand and Steve Reicher, 'Humiliation in Classrotom [*sic*] Interactions: Identification, Experience and Interventions', p. 360 (SD).

Appendix 12.1b
CESI papers related to higher education

1. Aruna Bajantri, 'History of Bombay University of the Nineteenth Century: A Study of Adaptation of Western Education in India', pp. 28–31.
2. Bharat Rout, 'Three Worlds of Education Welfare States in South Asia: Investigating to the Processes of De-Commodification and Stratification', pp. 42–43.
3. Binay Kumar Pathak, 'Information Processing, Choice and Governance in Higher Education: A Study of Select Institutions', pp. 44–46.
4. Chandra Lekha Singh, 'Central Hindu College: The Progenitor of Banaras Hindu University', pp. 52–54.
5. Firdous Ahmad Sofal, 'Occupational Efficacy and Administrative Behaviour: An Empirical Assessment of Educational Administrators Working in Indian Universities', pp. 73–78 (SD).
6. Emon Nandi, 'Selectivity and Hierarchy in Higher Education Market: Evidences from Select Engineering Colleges in West Bengal', pp. 79–83.
7. Gauri Khanduja and Mathangi Subramanian, 'Inclusion of Sexual Minorities in Higher Education Institutions of India', pp. 92–95 (SD; E).
8. Jharna Kewalramani, 'Critical Pedagogy and the Family', pp. 119–121 (E).
9. Jinusha Panigrahi, 'The Funding Patterns of Public Higher Education Institutions: The Concerns and Strategies', pp. 122–123.
10. Jyothsna Belliappa, 'Pedagogy for Equity and Emancipation: Reflections on a Course in Gender Studies for Future Educators', pp. 127–128.
11. Khalid Khan, 'Privatization, Dominance and Higher Education in India: An Empirical Analysis', p. 138.
12. Mathew Anthony, 'Higher Education in Indian States: Policy Evolution on Critical Aspects', pp. 162–164.
13. Matthew Witenstein, 'Thinking beyond Quality: Defining Educational Value in the Indian Higher Education Context', pp. 165–168 (E).

14 Neha Aggarwal, 'Critical Pedagogy and Classroom Discourse: A Study of Dialectical Teaching Method in Undergraduate Programme', pp. 205–208 (SD; E).
15 Pradeep Kumar Choudhury, 'Determinants of the Student's Choice for Institutions and Courses of Study in Engineering Education: Evidences from Delhi, India', pp. 239–243.
16 Sadaf Rathod, Bharat Rathod, Kalpana Dixit, Anagha Tambe, Vinayak Lashkar, Swati Dyahadroy, Snehal Sharma and Sangeeta Kamat, 'Democratizing Higher Education: Collaborative Research for Equity and Social Justice in U.S. and India', pp. 261–262 (SD).
17 Savitha Babu, Chetan Singai and Anupama Mahajan, 'Teaching in College: Exploring Experiences, Examining Identities', pp. 276–279 (SD; E).
18 Solomon Arulraj David, 'Re-Stratification of the Hierarchy of Academic Disciplines: The Complex Intersection of Academic, Economic, Social Values in Economic, Social Values in India', p. 302.
19 Srivastava Ritika, 'Bilingualism in B.Ed Course of University of Lucknow Opening or Blocking Gateways of Knowledge for Student Teachers', pp. 309–311 (SD; E).
20 G.V. Subitha, 'Improving Professional Development of Teachers in the Age of Reforms Role of Policy Processes and Systems', pp. 312–315.

Appendix 12.2

Derivation of proper names used in the *English Course (Communicative) Workbook*, 2014. Figures in brackets indicate instances where more than one name is found on a particular page.

Names derived from Sanskrit

p. 7 (3)
p. 13
p. 14 (2)
p. 18
p. 21
p. 26
p. 27 (3)
p. 36
p. 47
p. 49 (3)
p. 51 (3)
p. 53
p. 54 (2)
p. 56
p. 59
p. 60 (2)
p. 65 (3)
p. 67
p. 68 (2)
p. 72 (4)
p. 73 (2)
p. 77 (2)
p. 80 (2)
p. 82 (2)
p. 83 (2)
p. 86
p. 87
p. 88 (2)
p. 89 (2)

p. 94 (3)
p. 95
p. 97
p. 98
p. 100 (3)
p. 102
p. 103 (2)
p. 105
p. 107
p. 110
p. 111 (3)
p. 120 (4)
p. 125
p. 133 (5)
p. 144
p. 155
p. 157
p. 160 (2)
p. 161
p. 164
p. 165 (2)
p. 168
p. 169
p. 170 (3)
p. 171 (2)
p. 172
p. 173 (2)
p. 174
p. 178

Towards understanding the formal school system

p. 179 (3)	p. 240
p. 181	p. 242 (2)
p. 191 (3)	p. 245 (2)
p. 198 (2)	p. 246
p. 199	p. 250 (4)
p. 201 (2)	p. 252 (2)
p. 204	p. 253
p. 206 (2)	p. 254 (3)
p. 207	p. 255
p. 208 (2)	p. 257
p. 210 (3)	p. 262
p. 213	p. 263 (7)
p. 214	p. 264 (3)
p. 228	p. 269
p. 232	p. 278
p. 233	p. 280 (4)
p. 235	

Names derived from Arabic or Persian

p. 16	p. 170
p. 26	p. 174
p. 66	p. 198
p. 72	p. 199
p. 132	p. 201
p. 154	p. 213
p. 155	p. 237
p. 165	

English-/European-sounding names

p. 13	p. 45
p. 18 (3)	p. 154
p. 20	p. 168
p. 21	p. 169
p. 25	p. 181
p. 26 (2)	

Section 4
Health

13 Researching assisted conception from a feminist lens

Sarojini Nadimpally and Anindita Majumdar

1. Introduction

The rise and significance of assisted reproductive technologies (ARTs), a group of technologies that assist in conception or in the carrying of pregnancy to term, such as in-vitro fertilization (IVF), has also been accompanied by the associated conversation on the construction and discourse surrounding the use of these technologies. ARTs occupy a significant politico-economic space today, which has to be seen in relation to the reproductive tourism industry, the social and medical status of infertility in India and the kinds of laws that govern the use of the technology.

In this chapter we analyse how the need to study and critically engage with ARTs and their significant offshoot commercial gestational surrogacy has marked our decade-long engagement as a women's health group. Sama, a Delhi-based resource group[1] working on women's and health issues, has been engaging with ARTs, raising concerns around gender and health rights emerging from the unchecked proliferation of ARTs, including surrogacy. Research initiatives by Sama on this issue have contributed to uncovering the social, medical, ethical and economic implications of ARTs, including commercial surrogacy on the lives of women accessing them, as well as the various issues regarding access to these commercialized technologies as part of the ART industry. The findings and conclusions have enabled the location of discussions and debates on ARTs within the framework of women's health, women's rights and social justice, and have contributed to the consolidation of existing knowledge and analysis of ARTs and of the reproductive tourism industry.

We draw from two of our studies on ARTs and on commercial surrogacy in India. The study on ARTs (Sama 2010) was meant to map the ways in which infertility treatment in India constructed the idea of assisted conception. In the process of looking at infertility clinics in different parts of India, the study unearthed the way in which treatment was meted out and the rhetoric surrounding ARTs. The study on commercial surrogacy (Sama 2012) was aimed to establish a philosophical and conceptual understanding, located firmly within a feminist and public health framework, that aimed to move beyond the liberal imaginary of victim versus agent, which had led to a polarized understanding of reproductive labour, to develop an understanding of the locations, motivations and concerns of surrogate women, and of how they are relating to the surrogacy arrangements. This meant that women's experiences and standpoint must be grounded in the larger social and political context of culture.

In the process, we also seek to engage with our research methods and position them firmly within a feminist paradigm. Feminism emerged out of the women's movement, which posed challenges to existing thinking and knowledge. Due to the inadequacy of existing research methods to fully conceptualize women's lives and social realities, feminists evolved a kind of research methodology that re-conceptualized methods of knowing, representing and understanding feminist issues. Feminist perspectives carry messages of empowerment that challenge the knowledge claims by those who occupy privileged positions. It is not the method that makes feminist research but the feminist framework, perspective, principles and the way it is conducted. Feminist research is not simply having women engaged as researchers, nor is it about studying gender as a category or including women as a variable in research. Feminist research is about taking women's location and standpoint in the world as the basis for research drawing from women's perspectives and needs.

This chapter traces the kind of methodological issues that came to mark our concerns and engagements with ARTs in India. As a women's group, the focus was always on reproductive rights and the contextualization of reproductive labour in relation to the surrogate. Thus, the reflections on our ethnographic practices unearth not only our methodological challenges but also the kind of activism and policy advocacy that the same fuelled.

It is also important to note that while embedded in an Indian setting, our research was certainly not only reflective of local concerns. Due to the transnational character of commercial surrogacy in India (attracting not only foreign couples but also a transnational trade in oocytes and technology), we began to reflect on our research from a more global perspective. Fuelled by emerging studies on surrogacy, our research also began to reflect on the conversations around transnational feminisms. In many ways our ethnographies began to reflect the challenges that transnational feminisms had begun to bring forth in the study of ARTs and commercial surrogacy.

In seeking to bring together the conversations around and on transnational feminisms, the rhetoric on reproductive technologies has also become a flashpoint (John 2011). Thus, Michelle Murphy (2012) faults American feminists for having paved the way for the proliferation of 'travelling technologies' of preventing conception to the Third World, which is then effectively usurped by foreign-funding bodies such as the World Bank and the Ford Foundation. In a similar vein, the academic conversations around reproductive technologies have also been at loggerheads about creating viable connections for a form of feminism that can speak to each other and not against (Gupta 2006, Loblay 2010, John 2011).

Thus, it began with sex selective technologies (Menon 1995, John 2011) and then moved to ARTs (Gupta 2006, Loblay 2010) and finally to commercial surrogacy (Pande 2011, Majumdar 2014). The desire to create or trace transnationalism in feminist thought and methodology is attributable to the transnational nature of reproductive technologies, meaning that there can never be a unified analysis of their impact (Inhorn and Birenbaum-Carmeli 2008). This is more than evident in the case of commercial surrogacy wherein the Indian surrogate is also necessarily linked to infertile women from the West who hire them to have children (Pande 2011). The paradox of 'stratified reproduction' began to adversely impact the quest for transnational feminism in methods that found themselves crippled with how to represent both sides of the picture. Methodologically, narratives of surrogates have dominated the anthropological study and representation of surrogacy (Roberts 1998, Berend 2010, Teman 2010), giving insight into how reproductive technologies, kinship and bodies intermingle in a complicated social and economic exchange. But this has meant a form of engagement that is restricted to the narrativization of cultural particularities and peculiarities, whether American or Israeli.

It is in resurrecting these discussions and debates and looking at the issues that arose from both of our studies that we wish to bring the methodological challenges to the fore. This chapter thus first discusses some of the challenges we faced in our ethnographic work, followed by highlighting findings from our research on ARTs in the next section. We reflect on our feminist moorings and their impact on methodology by looking at our critique of the draft bill on the Regulation of Assisted Reproductive Technologies in India, which has provoked future research and questions regarding the role of research and policy advocacy. It has also led us to reflect on how we position ourselves within a feminist discourse while looking at the larger ethical debates on commercial surrogacy in India. Thus, the section on commercial surrogacy primarily deals with our conversations with the law in an endeavour to reflect the ways in which our ethnography always goes back to the law and its feminist engagements.

2. Methodological challenges

The studies on ARTs and commercial surrogacy in India were carried out in 2008–9 and 2010–11, respectively. While we carried out ethnographic research on ARTs in the states of Orissa, Madhya Pradesh and Tamil Nadu, the research on surrogacy was carried out in Punjab and Delhi. We identified the providers in the selected sites through Internet searches, through the Indian Society for Assisted Reproduction directory and through lists drawn up for previous research studies on ARTs, noting the number of institutions offering surrogacy arrangements in each instance. Clinics offering both IVF and surrogacy services were fewer in number in Punjab than those offering IVF services alone. Since there is no single source of information or official database of all clinics – and since not all the clinics featured in the Internet search – some of the clinics offering these services were identified during the course of the fieldwork. Within these sites, variables such as temporality (when clinics were established) and selection of clinics on the basis of the profiles of surrogates or commissioning parents were considered while conceptualizing the research goals. However, due to severely restricted access, and, more commonly, the unwillingness or reluctance of the various actors involved to share their experiences, such variables did not prove to be conclusive as selection criteria. In order to capture the heterogeneity and plurality of the industry, a few third-party agencies were also identified, such as medical tourism agencies, surrogacy agencies and individual agents offering services of contacting and arranging for surrogates and ensuring their surveillance.

Research tools such as the interview guide, the consent form and the permission letter were prepared in consultation with the members of the advisory committee. A formal letter describing the objectives of the study was also prepared for providers towards seeking interviews with them, surrogates, agents and any other players. The informed consent form was developed in the local languages of the respondents to provide participants with information about the purpose and intent of the study, and to assure them that the data being collected would remain confidential. The form was signed by both the respondent and the researcher, and a copy of the form was given to the respondent. This procedure and its importance were also explained to the respondent verbally. Interview guides were developed for each of the varied players – surrogates, providers and agents. It included open-ended questions and checklists for pursuing a desired line of enquiry covering particular themes. It was a flexible tool, meant to be adapted by the researchers according to the time duration and the nature of the interaction that was possible with the respondents. The guide was also modified for conducting repeat interviews according to the quality of the data collected previously. A field diary, which included the notes and observations of the researchers during the fieldwork, was maintained.

2.1 Access to data

In the absence of a credible, centralized and government-run or government-certified database/registry of functional ART clinics, there is no adequate and accurate way of knowing the exact number of operational ART centres in a particular area; the research team had to rely on a network of informal sources for information.

Secondary literature, particularly on the Indian context, was found to be insufficient. It was difficult for Sama, as a non-governmental organization in general and a policy monitoring and advocacy group in particular, to garner access to actors such as ART clinics, sperm banks, surrogacy agents and hostels, surrogates and ART users. In comparison, it is perhaps easier for students and researchers, both Indian and foreign, to gain legitimacy and entry due to their institutional affiliation to established and recognized universities.

While we did not allow Sama's politics or positions to reflect in the interviews conducted, in some instances, clinics had heard of Sama in relation to our previous advocacy efforts demanding regulation, which may have created some biases and preconceived notions in the providers about our project. Since the providers are the point of entry/access for the researchers, it is a challenge when providers are unresponsive and disinterested, or when they refer the researchers only to women users who are 'success stories'.

2.2 Nature of interactions

The nature of the interviews conducted was contingent on several factors. The doctors often insisted that the interviews be conducted within the hospital premises. Similarly, the agents insisted that the interviews be conducted under their supervision or at their office or home. In all cases except two, we were able to talk to the women at such venues in a separate room without actual physical supervision. A medical tourism agency arranged the first meeting with two surrogates at its office premises and the second meeting at the surrogate home run by it. In each case, the interviews had to be conducted in the presence of an agent. In these instances, we were not able to talk to the surrogates for a long duration, and such settings had an inhibiting influence on the surrogates. It was also difficult to explore in depth questions about the surrogates' relationships with other actors such as doctors, agents and commissioning parents in this setting, or to probe further into their narratives. It was not always possible to interact with surrogates repeatedly. It was possible to hold in-depth repeat interviews with four surrogates. There was a considerable difference in the quality of interviews where the first-time interaction took place in doctors' clinics or at agents' homes.

When interviews were conducted at the surrogates' own residences, they were far more comfortable and candid. During the interviews, we were able to explore and discuss some themes with each surrogate, taking up a particular line of inquiry in more detail depending on both the time we were able to have with the surrogate and her willingness to engage. During the interviews with the surrogates, which were very intensive, we tried to keep emotions at low key. And very often switching roles from activist to a researcher dealing with an emotionally loaded issue was very challenging.

Gender norms make it difficult to interview women in certain spaces (e.g. the waiting rooms of hospitals, which are usually crowded) or ask certain questions openly, particularly when more intimate details may be sought in the company of husbands or mothers-in-law. Further, it may be upsetting for women to narrate their experiences of childlessness and the associated stigma and despair, as a lot of these are traumatic to recount and relive.

It is difficult to conduct certain interviews because of logistical problems. For instance, some providers conduct IVF in batches/camps, which are held only on certain days of certain months, and allow a small window to access a large number of women users.

2.3 Generalizability issues

By tracking the rising use of ARTs and the demographics of those who seek out these procedures, potential barriers to access come clearly into view. These include wealth/income, costs, marital status, sexual orientation, religion and caste. While there was no conscious attempt to include predominantly Hindu respondents, they formed the majority of users in this purposive sample. This is also related to their demographically higher proportion in the population.

Though our sample has users from across the caste spectrum, this should not indicate that the market is blind to caste, thus bearing the potential to liberate us from ascriptive identities. In India, given that caste is classed, access to ARTs must be understood as mediated most significantly by class, and *therefore* by caste, because of this overlap.

Several providers did not want to share the costs of their services with us. Of the ones who did give information on costs, the figures quoted were vague and offhand, and providers did not detail what they did or did not include, such as hospital stay and cost of drugs. Again, in the absence of a registry or database, we could not verify/cross-check these figures, except by also asking users (who could be equally unclear about the exact among spent and its break-up, given the long-drawn nature of treatment).

In conducting ethnographic research, we aimed to bring together elements of our community-level advocacy among grassroots organizations and the disciplinary requirements of conducting ethnography – making our findings so much richer and nuanced. In many ways we were participating in the field as beyond observers, as we grappled with our role as feminist activists *and the resulting difficulties that our political stance brought*. This was most in evidence in relation to medical practitioners who were aware of our work and critique of the draft bill, and were vary to engage with us initially. In the sections that follow, we reflect on our findings and the kind of policy deliberations that the findings led to.

3. Reviewing infertility technologies

Sama's work in assessing the impact and realities of ARTs in India has led to deliberations on how a largely flawed technology is played out in public discourse and understanding. Through a mixture of ideas that position the technology as alleviating women's suffering and fulfilling idealized aspirations of motherhood to creating a mirage of the ARTs that render them affordable and part of a growing social demand, we discuss the ways in which reproductive technology is sold. Also part of our deliberations is a critique of the draft bill on the Regulation of Assisted Reproductive Technologies in India, which has been under construction since 2008 under the aegis of the Indian Council of Medical Research.

3.1 *Assisting reproduction, resisting adoption*

In Sama's study on ARTs (2010), research pointed towards a culture that essentially positioned ARTs as a gendered technology aiming to 'alleviate' suffering and stigma that infertile women endure in India. This is part of an elaborate marketing strategy that also aims to position itself as catering to the needs of women suffering from infertility. Thus,

> the images, language, and slogans used to promote ARTs serve to reinforce the 'tragedy' of childlessness and the sentimentality of childbearing, particularly mother-hood, while deliberately ignoring, omitting, or playing down the concerns and complications that come with medical intervention, such as side-effects, efficacy, and costs. While ARTs may 'deliver' women from the social pressure to be mothers, they do not question or challenge this pressure.
>
> (Nadimpally, Marwah and Shenoi 2011: 4)

Within such an understanding, ARTs become 'pro-women' and 'emancipatory' (Arora 1996).

Similarly, the culture of 'tall claims' that ARTs espouse positions them as affordable and successful technologies that nonetheless hide many inherent costs and sacrifices that men and women undertake to have children. Such rhetoric is pandered through aggressive advertising and displays that sell the expertise of the clinician based on the number of babies born in the clinic.

> Many clinic waiting rooms display photographs of the provider carrying newborn babies, with captions proclaiming 'firsts', and other breakthroughs and landmarks. Like any other commercial venture, the ART industry operates in a competitive market environment, which fuels claims of providers to milestones and successes apparently achieved by clinics. These serve to establish the credibility and competitiveness of the clinics, towards attracting users. . . . Inflating success rates to attract consumers is also common in the ART industry. In order to promote their services and expand their clientele, ART providers quote success rates that are often exaggerated or unclear and misleading. Success rate can be reported in various ways by clinics. Many report the embryo implantation or pregnancy rate as the success rate; these are higher than the live birth rate because a pregnancy may end in miscarriage, or induced abortion, or stillbirth. Clinics rarely quoted the take-home-baby or live birth rate as the success rate, and users are generally unaware of the difference. Moreover, the success rates quoted by clinics are nearly never substantiated on the basis of the number of users or the time period with regard to which they were calculated. This makes it difficult to discern the extent of the 'success' denoted by stand-alone figures and percentages. Further, success rates vary with the type of procedure used, whether IUI, IVF, or ICSI. Clinics, however, often quote one success rate, without any qualification indicating the specific procedure to which the rate refers.
>
> (Nadimpally, Marwah and Shenoi 2011: 6)

Thus, one of the clinic display boards proudly exhibited:

> Our pregnancy rates at 65–70% are among the highest in the world Today we have a success rate of 40–50% per treatment cycle. The success rate of ICSI & Test Tube Baby is 50% to 60% comparison to best Laboratory in the World.
>
> (Ibid.: 6)

But the authenticity of such success rates is questionable as they do not adhere to any form of standardization or global markers.

The overt biologization that follows the accompanying conversations on ARTs means that adoption fast becomes positioned as a 'non-option' for many infertile couples and their families (Bharadwaj 2003). This includes creating an idea of motherhood that is essentially biological and linked to the 'birth' of a child, such as this long tagline from the advertising material of a clinic:

> When nature lets you down, our IVF experts step in and resume the process to bring you the gift of motherhood. They say women make the world go round. How true! It is because they are mothers: The creators and sustainers of every generation. . . . The moment a child is born, the mother is also born. She never existed before. The woman existed, but the mother, never. A mother is something absolutely new.
> (Nadimpally, Marwah and Shenoi 2011: 5)

Within such a context ARTs have fuelled a new understanding of parenthood, gender and reproduction in formats that remove all forms of intimacy and connectedness, replacing it with neoliberal considerations, the interventions of a women's health group became essential. This led us to our ongoing debate and discussion with the law on ARTs in India – signalling the most important aspect of our engagement methodologically with our area of research, policy advocacy.

3.2 Critique of the bill

Since 2008, the draft bill has been part of public conversations primarily because it is the only form of recognizable quasi-legal regulation governing the use of ARTs and commercial surrogacy. The bill has had a 2010 avatar, which was circulated for public debates and discussions.

The draft bill is designed to protect the interests of the infertility medicine industry, which seeks to minimize legal conflicts in its operation and management. Many of the provisions in the bill are problematic, especially the conversations on eligibility for parenthood, the setting up of ART banks and, most important, the rights of the surrogates. The *draft bill* seeks to define and prohibit practices and relationships that do not conform to an idealized social norm. Here, the norm comes to be overwhelmingly defined by heterosexual marriage, thereby impacting notions and ideas regarding parenthood, in particular motherhood. The bill (2013 draft) defines 'couple' as 'a relationship between a male person and female person who live together in a shared household through a relationship in the nature of marriage' (ICMR 2010: 3).[2] As per this definition, it seems that the bill also includes people living together without getting married (live together in a shared household through a relationship in the nature of marriage). Even if it is to some extent self-explanatory, there needs to be more clarity as far as the definition is concerned, for a better understanding. It is clear that the definition excludes gay couple(s) from accessing ARTs in India, which has now been implemented through a Ministry of Home Affairs directive in 2013 restricting access to surrogacy to married heterosexual couples whether Indian or foreign. In 2015, the government introduced a new surrogacy bill that aims to completely ban commercial surrogacy and allow altruistic surrogacy. Thus, single men and women, divorced men and women, unmarried couples living together and the LGBTQ (Lesbian, Gay, Bisexual, Trans and Queer) community are deemed redundant by a few lines of definitions. They are also simultaneously excluded from the right to have a family and to procreate.

Society gives value to the relationship of procreation through the ties of marriage – the two give each other validity. Thus, the possibility of procreation that ARTs and surrogacy promise to those 'excluded' from marriage and reproduction becomes a real threat to the norm of the heteronormative family (Butler 2002). It is important to note here that the family as imagined in legal norms of eligibility is always heterosexual and within the boundaries of marriage, which is why gay couples are automatically exempt (Butler 2002). Unfortunately, the positioning of the gay family as 'choice' and not 'biology' (or linked through the ties of procreation and marriage [Weston 1991]) is used to exclude the LGBTQ community from accessing reproductive technologies to create and form their own families just like the 'heteronorm'.

Thus, eligibility becomes a form of mapping of bodies, identities and selves. The medical criteria of primary/secondary infertility may or not may not be used to identify suitability – but it is important to note that ARTs and surrogacy especially are seen to pose grave 'threats' to the conceptualization and persistence of the norm.

The draft (in continuation with its 2010 version) also defines 'ART banks' as 'an organization that is set up to supply . . . surrogate mothers to the assisted reproductive technology clinics or their patients'. Caution, therefore, needs to be taken before allowing ART banks to recruit and 'supply' surrogate mothers, as we know most of them come from marginalized communities and classes in India. Further debate needs to be organized around the pros and cons of commercial surrogacy vis-à-vis altruistic surrogacy, before a law is made commercializing surrogacy to an extent of buying wombs from a bank by allowing ART banks to supply surrogate mothers. The bill should take this into consideration as we know that in poverty-ridden conditions, the easy 'availability' of surrogates will override considerations regarding their safety and any rules or standards that need to be followed.

Agents or intermediaries have become important components of the fertility industry. However, the intermediaries or brokers are also many a times potential sources of exploitation for the donors and surrogates. One of the clauses states:

> The use of individual brokers or paid intermediaries to obtain gamete donors or surrogates shall be an offence under this Act, punishable with imprisonment for a term which may extend to three years or fine which may extend to rupees five lakh or with both.
>
> (Clause 68)

Such a step will prohibit ART clinics and banks from engaging with intermediaries or brokers to obtain surrogates. However, at the same time, couples and individuals should be made aware of such a provision, and also discouraged from entering the arrangement through any intermediary. The role and responsibility of the ART bank needs to be streamlined and better regulated.

As our policy interventions began to provoke conversations regarding the exploitative nature of the infertility industry, we began our interventions into the emerging transnational market in commercial gestational surrogacy. It is important to note that commercialization began to mark our conversations on surrogacy, leading us to engage with conversations on reproductive labour.

4. Seeking to legitimize commercial surrogacy: the dilemma of policy advocacy

In 2015, when Sama participated in and co-organized a policy-level deliberation on commercial surrogacy and the draft bill with the National Commission for Women, Government of India, the problems regarding our involvement in research and advocacy led us to reflect on our methodological challenges.

These challenges were beyond those of access, consent, confidentiality and research protocols but had more to do with the ways in which policy-level interventions, feminism and real-life ethnography could be blended together in a more effective way. To that extent, Sama authored an information brief for the general public to understand and comprehend the complications involved in participating in a commercial surrogacy arrangement, especially on the part of the surrogate. But our most important work began in constructing a legitimate critique of the draft bill and its take on surrogacy that would not lead to its ban and at the same time protect the rights of the surrogate. The critique is what we focus on next to showcase the ways in which research can reflect on advocacy and activism in ways in which neither has to compromise on the ethics of the other.

A large part of building an alternate discourse on commercial surrogacy in India meant that as a women's group in post-colonial India, we had to seek the support of fellow feminists – many of whom are against surrogacy (what) in any form. The process of building consensus on legitimizing surrogacy began with our critique of the bill but was ably supported by our fieldwork. Some of our primary criticisms and suggestions are mentioned to bring forth a more nuanced discussion regarding the ways in which feminist ethnography can and must provoke conversations regarding laws and socio-medical practices.

4.1 Legalizing genetic surrogacy

The draft bill makes genetic surrogacy illegal, that is a surrogacy arrangement that involves the woman bearing a child using her egg (oocyte) and the commissioning man's/donor's sperm. The prohibition of genetic surrogacy is part of the process of creating complete biological ownership in the commissioning parent, thereby deliberately separating the surrogate mother from the child she is carrying. However, the fact that a human body nurtures the pregnancy has nothing to do with biology. But to create a sense of lack of genetic–biological connection, the compulsory use of IVF is advocated in surrogacy, which is medically a more invasive process than intrauterine insemination (IUI) – involving the direct introduction of the sperm into the uterus. We advocate that both genetic and gestational surrogacy should be allowed.

4.2 Insurance for the surrogate

The present bill also states that

> the commissioning parent(s) shall ensure that the surrogate mother and the child she delivers are appropriately insured until the time the child(ren) is handed over to the commissioning parent(s) . . . till the surrogate is free of all health complications arising out of surrogacy.
>
> (2013, Clause 60(22))

However, the bill does not elaborate on the nature and kind of insurance to be extended. There is also no mention of post-delivery and follow-up care of the surrogate mother. The bill should, thus, explicitly state the kind of care and compensation to be extended to the surrogate, including reimbursement of all her expenses made during the pregnancy, such as travel to the doctors and medical check-ups, and provision of free legal aid in case any conflicts arise during the surrogacy arrangement. These aspects will be essential in maintaining greater transparency, accountability and well-being of the child(ren). Therefore, the proposed bill needs to specify such details for better implementation of its clauses.

4.3 Breach of contract

The bill does not deliberate on the course of action to be taken in case of breach of contract. For example, if the parents of the child do not pay the entire contractual amount to the surrogate, will the surrogate get to keep the child? It is suggested that even in cases of breach of contract, the custody of the child should be given to the parents of the child, but a complaint may be filed with the commission (if set up under the act) or with the appropriate civil/criminal court for the breach. Additional provisions should include prosecution of non-resident Indian or foreign couples who do not fulfil their obligations in the contract, including giving powers to the police to act upon a complaint filed by the surrogate mother by preventing the parents from leaving the country.

4.4 Administration and monitoring of the surrogacy contract

The present draft bill is also silent on issues of the administration of the contract between the surrogate and the couple. Therefore, questions such as the following remain unanswered: Who makes the contract and monitors that it is not breached? How would the money transaction actually take place? And in cases where the surrogate is directly hired by the couple, how would the ART bank come into the picture and what would be the significance of the surrogate's contract with the ART bank? Since the bill allows known persons, friends and relatives to act as surrogates, it should also clearly list mechanisms for the proper administration and monitoring of the contract drawn between the surrogate and the commissioning parent(s) in such cases.

4.5 Status of the child

The present draft bill has a provision of including only the names of the commissioning/genetic parents in the birth certificate of the child(ren). The draft bill should, however, also consider granting a parental status to the surrogate mother. When a woman gives birth to a child, the birth must be officially documented and that women must *be the natural parent of the child born to her*. This aimed to give recognition to the role and act of gestation, which is mired in secrecy and denial throughout the arrangement. Recognition also meant that the surrogate would be able to demand health rights and benefits that are denied to her primarily due to her overt 'invisibilization' within the arrangement. This can be followed by a transfer of parenthood, to the intended parents, either through adoption or another system devised specifically for the arrangement.

The aforementioned clauses form some of the core issues within the draft bill that need immediate attention and deliberation. Having said that, we believe that no law should be passed without engaging in entirety with the present clauses. For this, there is an immediate need to make all policy deliberations open for public debate and discussions.

As commercial surrogacy comes to mark Indian and overseas public opinion in interesting ways, it also provokes the most livid debates on questions of choice and ethics. Here, in this section, and in this chapter, we have tried to reflect upon how a feminist methodology can come to orient deliberations regarding gendered policy and state interventions.

5. Conclusion

Nancy Scheper-Hughes in her now iconic ethnography *Death without Weeping* notes how the positioning of reproductive nurturing among women comes to be canonized in academic research on women, but 'these theories [are] inadequate insofar as they posit a very specific cultural "norm" as general or universal and thereby alienate the experiences of many poor, working class, and Third World women, who become a feminist version of the non-Western other' (1993: 401).

It is this point of view that seeks to reflect upon the feminist in methodology by invoking it and at the same time critically engaging with it that comes to mark our study of ARTs and commercial surrogates in India. Here we integrated the core issues in various feminist epistemologies and the feminist perspectives on various research methods to reflect upon the ways in which this can inform our work as activists. Our most important questions through our ethnographical engagements continued to inform our advocacy and community outreach and vice versa. In that sense, the dynamism of our research will always remain relevant.

Notes

1 Sama – Resource Group for Women and Health is a Delhi-based organization working on the issue of ARTs since the past ten years through research

and advocacy. Sama looks at issues of women and health through a caste, gender, class and rights perspective.
2 The draft bill has seen many avatars, with the latest being discussed in October 2015. Many of the versions have been made public, while those from 2014 were not similarly available. Most of the provisions of the bill have remained constant except for those involving eligibility to commission or contract the arrangement. Thus, from 2013 a parallel process involving the Ministry of External Affairs, Government of India, has made it illegal for foreign gay couples and later foreign couples to access commercial surrogacy in India.

References

Arora, Dolly. 1996. "The Victimising Discourse: Sex-Determination Technologies and Policy," *Economic and Political Weekly*, Vol. 35, No. 37 (9 September), pp. 420–424.

Berend, Z. 2010. "Surrogate Losses," *Medical Anthropology Quarterly*, Vol. 24, No. 2, pp. 240–262.

Bharadwaj, A. 2003. "Why Adoption Is Not an Option in India: The Visibility of Infertility, the Secrecy of Donor Insemination, and Other Cultural Complexities," *Social Science & Medicine*, Vol. 56, No. 9, pp. 1867–1880.

Butler, Judith. 2002. "Is Kinship Always Already Heterosexual?" *Differences: A Journal of Feminist Cultural Studies*, Vol. 13, No. 1, pp. 14–44.

Gupta, J. A. 2006. "Towards Transnational Feminisms: Some Reflections and Concerns in Relation to the Globalization of Reproductive Technologies," *European Journal of Women's Studies*, Vol. 13, No. 1, pp. 23–38.

Indian Council of Medical Research. 2010. *Draft ART Regulation Bill*. New Delhi: Ministry of Health and Family Welfare.

Inhorn, M. C. and D. Birenbaum-Carmeli. 2008. "Assisted Reproductive Technologies and Culture Change," *Annual Review of Anthropology*, Vol. 37, No. 1, pp. 177–196.

John, M. E. 2011. "Sexing the Fetus: Feminist Politics and Method across Cultures," *Positions*, Vol. 19, No. 1, pp. 7–29.

Loblay, Victoria. 2010. "Experiments in Methodology on Reproductive Technology: Feminisms, Ethnographic Trajectories and Unchartered Discourse," *Economic and Political Weekly*, Vol. 45, Nos. 44–45 (30 October), pp. 56–62.

Majumdar, A. 2014. "The Rhetoric of Choice: The Feminist Debates on Reproductive Choice in the Commercial Surrogacy Arrangement in India," *Gender, Technology and Development*, Vol. 18, No. 2, pp. 275–301.

Menon, N. 1995. "The Impossibility of Justice: Female Foeticide and Feminist Discourse on Abortion," *Contributions to Indian Sociology*, Vol. 29, Nos. 1–2, pp. 369–392.

Murphy, M. 2012. *Seizing the Means of Reproduction: Entanglements of Feminism, Health, and Technoscience*. Durham, NC: Duke University Press.

Nadimpally Sarojini, V. Marwah and A. Shenoi. 2011. "Globalisation of Birth Markets: A Case Study of Assisted Reproductive Technologies in India," *Globalization and Health*, Vol. 7, No. 1, pp. 1–7.

Pande, Amrita. 2011. "Transnational Commercial Surrogacy in India: Gifts for Global Sisters?" *Reproductive Biomedicine Online*, Vol. 23, No. 5, pp. 618–625.

Roberts, E. F. 1998. "'Native' Narratives of Connectedness: Surrogate Motherhood and Technology." In Robbie Davis-Floyd and Joseph Dumit (eds). *Cyborg Babies: From Techno-Sex to Techno-Tots*. New York: Routledge, pp. 193–211.

Sama. 2010. *Constructing Conceptions: The Mapping of ARTs in India*. New Delhi: Sama Resource Group for Women and Health.

———. 2012. *Birthing a Market: A Study of Commercial Surrogacy in India*. New Delhi: Sama Resource Group for Women and Health.

Scheper-Hughes, Nancy. 1993. *Death without Weeping: The Violence of Everyday Life in Brazil*. Berkeley: University of California Press.

Teman, E. 2010. *Birthing a Mother: The Surrogate Body and the Pregnant Self*. Berkeley: University of California Press.

Weston, Kath. 1991. *Families We Choose: Lesbians, Gays, Kinship*. New York: Columbia University Press.

14 RUWSEC Clinic
Challenges faced by a grassroots feminist clinic

Subha Sri B. and T.K. Sundari Ravindran

1. Introduction and background

Sexual and reproductive health and rights were incorporated into international policy frameworks after the 1994 International Conference on Population and Development in Cairo and the Beijing Declaration of 1995. However, the feminist movement had identified and started working on women's sexual and reproductive rights and health long before then.

Globally, the publication of *Our Bodies, Ourselves* in the early 1970s with its emphasis on women taking charge and control of their bodies shaped the way the feminist movement looked at women's bodies (Boston Women's Health Collective 1973). Around the same time, there were several initiatives from feminist groups from many developed countries – the United States, Canada and Australia and countries of Europe – to demystify medical knowledge, challenge medical control over women's reproduction, start women's health clinics and advocate for women's health policies. Inspired by this, several initiatives started in different parts of the world to increase women's knowledge and awareness of their own bodies and improve their access to health and health care (Gray Jamieson 2012).

In India, the 1970s was a time of radical change. A regressive political context at the national level led to a strong students' movement across the country. This was also a time when the feminist movement strengthened in the country and Left-inspired women's groups came up in different parts of the country. The movement's focus initially was on sexual and state violence against women and laws pertaining to these. Some groups also focused on oppressive population control policies and hazardous contraceptive methods. The prevalent political environment of radical politics also provided a backdrop that promoted reflection by some feminist groups on women's bodies and how it shaped women's lives and health in the Indian context (Saheli 2000).

It is in such a context that Rural Women's Social Education Centre (RUWSEC) came into being. In this chapter, we give a brief background on RUWSEC's work on sexual and reproductive health and rights among rural Dalit women before describing and reflecting on one particular effort where RUWSEC attempted to provide reproductive health services to marginalized rural women through a clinic built on feminist rights-based perspective.

2. Rural Women's Social Education Centre

In the late 1970s, the National Adult Education Programme (NAEP) was active in the villages around Chengalpattu, a small town in present-day Kancheepuram district, about 70 kilometres outside the state capital of Madras (now Chennai). Volunteers inspired by the Left students' movement in Madras facilitated the learning in this programme and introduced Freirean methods[1] that used the learners' personal experiences as a tool for literacy, while simultaneously prompting political analysis of the learners' lives. This programme resulted in the emergence of village-level leadership of both men and women with clear political ideas. When the NAEP was withdrawn, these village-level leaders decided to work on development in their communities by formalizing themselves into an organization, the Rural Development Society (RDS).

Discussions with women's groups during the adult education programme had led to the realization that if women were to become agents of social change, they had to overcome the oppression that arose from the lack of control they had over their own bodies and the powerlessness caused by this. The women leaders who were part of RDS expressed the need to better understand their bodies, which led to collective readings of Our Bodies Ourselves facilitated by one of the authors of this chapter. This soon expanded into small group discussions led by the women leaders with women in their respective villages. This eventually strengthened the idea that strengthening women's understanding about their bodies and their control over childbearing and sexuality was a much-needed area of work in the village community. The women leaders decided that they needed a separate space to focus on this. Thus, 12 Dalit women leaders from the area who were a part of RDS formally founded RUWSEC in 1981, along with one of the authors of this chapter.

From the beginning, the founders were committed to working with low-income, Dalit women in the area on issues of social justice. They also believed women's health was a product of interaction between biological factors and various social determinants. Thus, they organized women to collectively realize their entitlements to various determinants of health and demand for them.

Over the next decade and a half, RUWSEC's work spanned four interconnected areas (Ravindran and Balasubramanian 2007).

- *Changing women's 'being'* by mobilizing them and creating a culture of collective demand to resources that affected their health and well-being, including access to water, roads, transport, better wages and living conditions.
- *Changing women's 'consciousness'* by helping them reflect and analyse the different factors including caste, class and gender that led to their oppression at multiple levels.
- *Changing women's health-seeking behaviour* by making them feel entitled to care, helping them access simple cures including self-care at home, helping them identify when they needed medical care and promoting judicious use of the health care services while simultaneously improving their means to access these services.
- *Influencing the health system's commitment and ability to meet women's health needs* by representations to health authorities, systematic attempts to work with local public health facilities and developing women's leadership to engage with and demand better services from these facilities.

2.1 The choice to provide services

After about 15 years of RUWSEC's work in the local community, women had better access to resources, felt somewhat entitled to seek care and also had become judicious seekers of health care through access to information on when to seek health care. All of this resulted in a situation where women started demanding reproductive health care services.

Meanwhile, the public health system in Tamil Nadu was also making efforts to improve its services. It had appointed and built capacities of a whole cadre of auxiliary nurse midwives, called village health nurses, who were expected to provide services to the community in their own villages (Muraleedharan, Dash and Gilson 2011). While this move greatly strengthened public health services, these services were restricted to those for pregnancy and childbirth and for immunization. Services for other reproductive health needs were not provided either in the primary health centres or at higher levels of facilities in the public health system. Even when provided, women were satisfied with neither the technical quality of the services nor the behaviour of the service providers. This forced women to often seek services in the private sector – however, this sector also did not offer good-quality services, and the costs were often prohibitively expensive for women; often, unnecessary tests and investigations were ordered, and treatment was limited to ineffective drugs and palliative care.

In such a context, with increasing realization for the need for better reproductive health services, women started demanding that they have a health facility of their own where they could get the services that they felt they badly needed.

While this demand from women persisted over a course of time, RUWSEC's women leaders were initially very hesitant and reluctant to start service provision as part of their programme in the community. Since RUWSEC was an organization completely run by grassroots women, it was felt that they lacked the capacities to run something as 'technically demanding and intense' as a health care facility.

However, the demands from the community persisted. Meanwhile, ongoing studies and engagement with the public health system revealed repeatedly the clear absence of reproductive health services and, even when present, their poor quality (Komala and Ravindran 1991). There was thus a lot of frustration that was built up over the lack of a viable alternative for health services.

Simultaneously, other events took place that had an impact on RUWSEC's decision to start a clinic. Globally, in the Western world, women's health clinics inspired by the feminist movement had been set up in the 1970s – these were led by women themselves and were aimed at women taking charge and control over their own bodies (Gray Jamieson 2012). At another level, the International Conference on Population and Development (ICPD) had happened in Cairo in 1994, and this led to a wider discourse of comprehensive reproductive health services being provided from a human rights perspective. This also led to a situation where international agencies were willing to provide funds for service provision for reproductive health services. All of this created a climate in which RUWSEC was able to act on the community's demands and therefore led to the starting of the clinic.

2.2 *An alternative clinic*

RUWSEC clinic was envisioned by the grassroots women in the organization as a clinic that was meant to be an alternative in every sense. The original project proposal for the setting up of the clinic states:

> We envisage the RUWSEC Women's Health Clinic to be an alternative health facility in all respects: in the quality of health care it provides; its approach to women's health as intimately related to their low status;

its focus on enabling women to take charge of their health instead of being passive recipients of health care; in its treatment of women as intelligent and capable persons who will work towards improving their health if given the means to do so.

Thus, the principles of the clinic from its conceptualization are as follows:

- Women-centred, gender-sensitive care
- Technically good-quality care
- Leadership by local rural women

It has now been 20 years since the RUWSEC Reproductive Health Clinic came into existence. In the following sections, we reflect on the clinic's achievements; the challenges the clinic faced in the past two decades to ensure it adhered to its original vision and principles; and the clinic's successes, failures and learnings.

2.3 Service provision in the clinic: scope and quality

RUWSEC had since the beginning worked with grassroots rural women to enable them to understand their own bodies and take control over it. One of the key strategies towards this had been to make them aware of means of self-care and traditional home-based remedies. The clinic was meant to fulfil a need for services when the need for health care could not be met just through traditional home-based remedies. Thus, by its very design, the clinic was meant to provide mainstream medical services.

The scope of services to be provided in the clinic was decided in consultation with women at various points in the clinic's history. Initially, the clinic was meant to provide outpatient services for reproductive health problems while facilitating referrals of women who needed surgeries, including those for family planning and abortions to other centres in Madras. Since reliable laboratory tests were unavailable in the neighbourhood, the clinic also housed a clinical laboratory that offered basic investigations. A pharmacy that allowed women to buy drugs at affordable and subsidized costs was also introduced. All of these services were started in 1995 in a two-storey rented building in the town close to the villages RUWSEC worked in, Chengalpattu, so that women would have good geographic connectivity and access to the clinic.

However, within a few months, based on demands from the women, the scope of services was expanded to include abortion services, family planning services and delivery services. This range of services was provided for a few years before being again restricted to outpatient services, delivery services and minor procedures – the backdrop to this is discussed later on in further sections.

While providing allopathic care, RUWSEC was also aware of and engaged in the feminist critique of the biomedical focus of modern medical systems. Thus, efforts were made to ensure medical pluralism, and services in alternative forms of medicine, for example in *Siddha* and homeopathy, were also offered.

Simultaneous to defining the scope of services of the clinic, several measures were also put in to ensure that the services adhered to good technical quality. Some of them are described below:

- Since the clinic was run by grassroots women with very little technical medical knowledge, RUWSEC set up an advisory committee of experts, the Medical Advisory Committee (MAC), to help them understand and address technical issues. The committee consisted of experts with knowledge and skills in different areas, including different systems of medicine, different aspects of the clinical services, for example laboratory services, and also public health programmes; these experts were also sympathetic to and supportive of RUWSEC's vision for the clinic. The MAC met at regular intervals along with grassroots women involved in running the clinic, looked at data regarding patients and services and helped in addressing any technical issues that arose. In addition to these regular meetings, individual MAC members were asked to help with specific systems and engaged in quality control measures.
- One of the other steps taken to ensure quality of care was to put in place standard guidelines and policies that spelt out steps to be taken to ensure quality. These policies, for example, talked about guidelines for prescriptions, those for specific procedures like abortions and sterilization surgeries. In addition to technical quality issues, these guidelines addressed issues of access to treatment, for example, by stating explicitly that no person should be sent home without a full course of antibiotics even if the person is unable to pay for it.
- Another means of ensuring quality of care was to create a drug list for the pharmacy that ensured that only those drugs on the essential drug list of the World Health Organization or Government of India were included for sale in the pharmacy. The drug lists were made through a process of consultation, which included members of the MAC and also grassroots women. The process considered several aspects of the

drugs, including their need in the local context, efficacy, cost, ease of use and length of treatment before finalization of the drug list.
- Quality assurance of services in the laboratory was made through regular standardization of tests done by a member of the MAC with expertise in laboratory methods.
- Monitoring and evaluation was a key step to ensure quality. Regular feedback was collected from clinic users through various means, including exit interviews, feedback from community health workers, introduction of a suggestion box and use of a coloured token system to express satisfaction with the service. In addition, institution of audits of different aspects of service provision, for example, of prescriptions, of referrals, was done with the support of experts in the MAC.

2.4 Women-centred, gender-sensitive care

Gender as a core social determinant of health had been internalized and understood by women in RUWSEC over several years of work in the community. This understanding was reflected in the design of the clinic and its services.

Consultations with local women helped design the clinic's physical structure, both when it was in rented premises in Chengalpattu and later on when the clinic moved to its own building in a village at the heart of its field area. Women expressed through different means like drawings what they wanted the physical structure to look like – this included clean, ventilated spaces, adequate toilets, running water, adequate sheltered waiting areas and space for small children to run around safely.

The women in RUWSEC also attempted to make the clinic women friendly in other ways. Thus, the timings of the clinic were fixed based on when it was most convenient for women to access care. Similarly, ambulance services were provided for picking up women from their homes when they did not have access to other transport facilities, dropping them back and also when they needed to be referred to higher centres.

In addition, the understanding of gender and its interplay with health reflected in the clinic, including in its scope of services for a broad range of reproductive health issues. Thus, abortion services were introduced, a broad range of contraceptive services were offered, sexual and reproductive health services were offered to adolescent girls and boys and women affected by violence were provided health care and support services. Box 14.1 describes the services offered for women affected by violence as an illustrative example of how the clinic attempted to integrate gender as a core social determinant in its service provision.

Box 14.1 The clinic's role in RUWSEC's prevention of domestic violence programme

From the time of its founding, RUWSEC has found domestic violence, especially spousal violence, to be an integral part of women's lives and has provided social, legal and economic support to its own staff and workers as well as other women in the community affected by it. However, after the death of one of its own fieldworkers due to spousal violence, where the community by and large shielded the perpetrating husband from the police, it was realized by the women leadership in RUWSEC that it was necessary to systematically engage with the community to create attitudinal change regarding violence. Thus, RUWSEC created its 'Violence Against Women – Prevention and Support' programme (Balasubramanian and Ravindran 2010).

As part of this programme, pressure groups were formed in villages in RUWSEC's field area to champion the prevention of gender-based violence, especially spousal violence. These groups consisting of specially identified and trained young women and men formed 'Women's Protection Committees' and provided support to women facing violence in their own villages. The support has included challenging male violence against the women within their communities, active intervention to offer shelter within the community to the woman experiencing violence and linking them to staff of RUWSEC's violence prevention programme when access to legal or other services is needed. Presence of such young women and men challenging domestic violence in their own communities has resulted in breaking the myth that husbands beating wives is acceptable, and has slowly resulted in attitudinal change in the younger generation in these villages.

RUWSECs clinic has also been an integral part of the violence prevention programme. All staff in the clinic, including nurses and technical staff, have undergone training on the issue and perceive violence against women as a gender and rights issue. They are also trained in identifying clinical markers that may point to domestic violence and thus are able to suspect and identify the presence of violence in women seeking services for various reasons, including physical injuries, mental health issues, repeated reproductive infections or unwanted pregnancies.

In addition, RUWSEC clinic's counsellor, a trained person from the local community, screens all women attending the clinic for history of violence; this offers an opportunity for women to open up about their experience of violence in a protected, confidential space. The counsellor then discusses with the woman possible ways to address the issue and supports the woman in whatever way she wants. The counsellor also links the women up with members of the committee in her village who then provide her ongoing support.

The clinic also offers specific services for women facing violence, including treatment of physical injuries, counselling and treatment for mental health issues and safe abortion services for women with an unwanted pregnancy. In addition, clinic staff help women facing sexual violence at the hands of their husbands choose an appropriate form of contraception and provide services for the same. Another area where the clinic coordinates with the violence prevention programme is by clearly documenting in the medical records details of injuries that occur as a result of violence; the woman is informed that such documentation is available if she should at any time need it for legal action against the perpetrator.

2.5 Focus on helping women take charge of their health

One of the key features of RUWSEC's clinic was its attempt to ensure that the clinic treated women as active participants in their health care and helped them take charge of their health. Several measures were put in towards this.

From the beginning, the clinic had a counsellor who saw every woman who came to the clinic. The counsellor was a local grassroots woman who had received training, and her responsibilities included counselling the women accessing services on the nature of their problem and possible choices for treatment, and helping them make a specific choice of treatment modality and the need for follow-up; in addition, the counsellor explored with the woman other determinants that could have led to her medical problem, for example domestic violence, nutrition, mental health issues, and helped her take measures to whatever extent possible to address these problems. The role of the counsellor was seen by both RUWSEC and the users of the clinic as crucial in making women active agents in their own care and also in providing medical care that was socially relevant to the woman's need and context.

One other way in which women were made to have control over the medical process was by employing traditional birth attendants (TBAs) in the clinic to provide women-centred care to women seeking pregnancy and delivery services on an equal footing with nurses and doctors who provided modern medical care. The TBAs and nurses were also trained on ensuring that technically good care was provided to women in labour while simultaneously ensuring their dignity.

Another key measure in supporting women's active participation in their care was the provision of information to women on different aspects of reproductive health and health care. Thus, pamphlets on common reproductive problems, various contraceptive methods and care during pregnancy and childbirth were all produced in the local language and disseminated free of cost – these pamphlets included technical details regarding the health issue and various treatment options available; in addition, they brought in women's perspectives on the health issue and its care based on RUWSEC's fieldwork in the community over the years.

RUWSEC's broad network of community health workers and volunteers in the villages it worked in also ensured that there was constant feedback back and forth between the clinic and the field programme. This ensured that women continued to receive care and follow-up well beyond the confines of the clinic itself.

2.6 Grassroots rural women leading the clinic

RUWSEC's work over several decades has been to empower women to take charge of their health. Even while starting a health facility, the women had seen themselves as leading and providing direction to the facility. In stark difference to other community-based health projects, RUWSEC, when starting its services, did not have an exemplary medical practitioner who had made a choice to work with a rural community or rural organization. The organization initially put in several measures to ensure rural grassroots women's leadership to the health facility, some of which are described here.

- A well-defined record keeping system was put in place, and consolidated reports were generated every month on different aspects, including client flow patterns, appropriateness of treatment provided and adequacy of follow-up. These reports that were in the local language were shared with the RUWSEC women in addition to the members of the MAC.
- A senior woman leader of RUWSEC, one of its founding members who had a clear vision of the aims of the clinic and was also known for her tough skills in negotiating with everyone, was made in charge of 'clinic–field liaison'. She visited the clinic every week and filled in a form based on her observations on cleanliness, the attention paid to clients, waiting time, provider–client interactions and client satisfaction. In addition to her, RUWSEC's fieldworkers who accompanied clients to the clinic were asked to fill out the form based on their

experience of the clinic. All of these were then discussed during weekly clinic review meetings where representatives of all field staff and all clinic staff participated – the feedback from clients was then discussed, and any measures needed to address dissatisfaction were put in place.
- Field-level workers from RUWSEC's villages were also in rotation given duties in the clinic alongside clinic staff – this ensured their constant presence in the clinic and observation of its practices, thus serving to provide feedback to the clinic staff.
- Patient feedback was also constantly encouraged through the presence of a suggestions box, which was periodically checked and collated to identify any emerging issues.
- In addition to above measures, active community participation in the clinic was ensured through the constitution of a review committee that consisted of men and women from the local community who had been associated with RUWSEC and understood its vision – this committee met at regular intervals and reviewed the clinic's functioning and patient feedback. It also served as a monitoring mechanism for the clinic. Later, once community monitoring was instituted under the National Rural Health Mission, these review committee members used the experience of monitoring the RUWSEC clinic to attempt monitoring of public health facilities.

Thus, while RUWSEC as an organization ensured rural women's leadership through its presence in governance bodies like the executive committee of RUWSEC, several efforts were made to institutionalize similar structures for promoting grassroots women's leadership in the clinic.

However, within a short period, this grassroots women's leadership conflated and conflicted with the clinic's engagement with the medical profession – this is detailed in the next section. Over the course of time, we found that the clinic was successful in being led by grassroots women in certain domains where it involved working with the community on reproductive health and rights issues, for example on domestic violence; these were also domains that were outside traditionally of the medical system or those that were seen by the medical professionals as 'not their area'. In others, especially in technical areas related to health care, by the very design of mystified medical knowledge and jargon, women found it extremely challenging to establish their leadership.

2.7 Challenges in engaging with the medical profession

RUWSEC clinic was expected to provide health care services beyond what women themselves could do on their own in terms of self-care or traditional remedies. In a state like Tamil Nadu where modern medical care was a widespread aspiration, RUWSEC set out to provide in its clinic such modern medical care that was technically sound. This meant engaging services from the medical profession.

Even while RUWSEC did not have medical professionals in its core group, it had, as members of its MAC, a set of dedicated professionals who understood its vision and goals. In the beginning, when services were restricted to outpatient services, the clinic services were led by two nurses, with some members of the MAC making visits from Madras on specific days of the week to provide outpatient services. However, the introduction of services for deliveries meant that doctors had to be available on call even during the nights, and this started a period of engaging with the local doctors in Chengalpattu who were hired to provide specific services. Specific doctors came in part-time to provide outpatient, delivery and family planning services, and soon, a full-time obstetrician also was employed.

Within the first two to three years, however, this resulted in a lot of conflict between the rural women who saw themselves as leading the clinic and doctors who believed they were the natural leaders of any health care facility. Medical professionals did not appreciate being asked to account for their timings, performance and behaviour by 'illiterate, ignorant women'. Simultaneously, due to a need for better management of technical details of the clinic, a retired nurse matron from the local medical college had been appointed. While bringing in much-needed efficiency, this move also resulted in consolidation of power by the doctors and nurses on one side versus the grassroots women on the other side.

The quality of services offered by the clinic and the subsidised costs it offered them at also made the clinic attractive to the women from the local middle class in Chengalpattu town. The doctors and nurses from the local town also encouraged their use of the clinic. This gradually resulted in a situation where providers were seen to be indulging in preferential treatment and behaviour with the local urban women, and the rural women from RUWSEC's field area felt discriminated against. RUWSEC's women leaders repeatedly raised these issues in the review committee meetings.

Matters came to a head when a maternal death took place in the clinic and doctors refused to be accountable to the rural women who instituted an enquiry into the death. This resulted in serious reflections within RUWSEC on the direction the clinic was taking, and a decision was made to shift the clinic out of the urban area it was housed in to a village in the heart of RUWSEC's field area – it was felt that this would result in better utilization of the clinic by the women it was originally meant to provide service to. It also led to reflections on what the limits up to which services could be provided by a grassroots women's organization were. The annual report of 1998–99 captures this reflection as follows:

> Setting up and running this clinic has taught us many lessons about the working of the medical system and the power of the medical establishment. We have a better insight into what ails our health care system, and who we can work with and who we cannot. One important error of judgement was our failure to appreciate how near impossible the task of working with medical personnel trained within the present health services was going to be, leave alone getting them to provide client-centred and gender sensitive services. We had believed that developing an institutional structure in which clients wield considerable influence, a clear-cut policy for day-to-day functioning, mechanisms for enforcing accountability and regular monitoring would gradually change the practices and perspectives of medical officers. If we were to start all over again (which we are trying to), we would first look for a service provider with the right perspective and ideology, before we do anything else.

Thus, the clinic was shifted to a village in the field area of RUWSEC, and it started functioning as an outpatient service in 2001 and started providing inpatient services from 2004. However, the first five to six years in the rural area saw the clinic struggling with availability of doctors to provide services. Doctors were not interested in travelling to a relatively remote area to provide services; young doctors joined for short periods of time while waiting for admission to postgraduate courses or while waiting to set up private practice. This saw a huge turnover of doctors and adversely affected rapport building in the local community. This also meant that the clinic struggled just with the question of survival, and issues related to women's leadership and quality of services took a backseat. Professionals from alternative medical systems and nurses continued to provide services but did not necessarily share the vision for women-centred care. Newly recruited women health care providers like nurses also subscribed to the dominant medical paradigm and were not enthused about grassroots women leading the clinic.

It was only after 2006 that two women doctors, one a specialist obstetrician and another a retired government medical officer, joined the clinic and stayed on for the next several years. Another male doctor with a public health education joined a few years later. This period lent stability to the clinic. Since two of these doctors also shared the feminist ideals of the clinic, this period also saw a lot of efforts being made to ensure both technical quality and women-centredness in the clinic while simultaneously making efforts to improve its linkages with the local community women and women leaders.

However, these efforts were dependent on the individual medical doctors and were not based on any change in the medical establishment. Thus, when some of these doctors left, the positive changes in the direction of the original vision for the clinic could not be sustained. This has resulted in a situation in the present day where services of reasonably good technical quality continue to be provided in RUWSEC's clinic, while, however, efforts at women establishing leadership in the clinic and its community engagement processes still face challenges.

3. Discussion

In the previous sections, we have detailed how the RUWSEC clinic was started as a response to a felt need by grassroots women for gender-sensitive and good-quality care and the successes and challenges in achieving these objectives. Here we discuss how we see this journey from the perspective of creating an alternative health facility and what this means for women's health care.

As detailed earlier, the clinic came into being at a point in time where women demanded technical care that needed physician-centred services to deal with their reproductive health issues. Grassroots rural women leaders decided to create a space for such health care and sought to lead and control it. Technical aspects of such care were to be provided through professionals who would be hired and paid for services provided. Gender sensitivity and women-centredness was planned to be made a core focus of the care by providing guidance on such care to the hired professionals through grassroots leadership and institutionalization of structures that promoted such women-centredness, rural women's leadership and accountability structures.

However, in reality, such grassroots leadership was limited in its scope to a few areas, which were not traditionally led by the medical establishment. When they sought to establish their leadership over the clinic, which was seen by physicians as their territory, grassroots women faced severe backlash from the medical establishment that did not see itself being answerable to, let alone be controlled by 'lay' persons, more so, rural women with little formal education. The power hierarchies inherent in the negotiations between a powerful medical lobby and an articulate, rights-aware group of women from marginalized sections were too huge. In retrospect, this power inequity was underestimated at the time of founding the clinic. The fact that the medical lobby was entrenched in an ideology that was polar opposite to what the women expected – it was steeped in power, patriarchy and commercialization – was naively overlooked while designing the clinic.

Feminist scholars have critiqued the formal medical system in the past. It has been seen as mechanistic, reductionist, interventionist and lacking focus on social determinants. This has led to experiments with setting up women's health spaces that are informed by feminist values and promote self-care. Feminists have also advocated for a more egalitarian therapeutic relationship between patient and doctor that respects patient autonomy and the right to informed consent, and an openness to alternative approaches (Ruzek, Clarke and Olesen 1997, Canadian Women's Health Network 2009).

The medical system in India, both public and private, has been dominated by patriarchal values that imbue it with tremendous power. Medical education in India teaches young professionals to essentialize women's bodies. The content of medical education is steeped in misogyny, and gender sensitivity is not a value that is sought to be imparted through such education. Professionals coming out of such education systems then get absorbed into health systems where such misogyny and patriarchal values are perpetuated through various institutional structures (Subha Sri B. 2010). It is a unique medical professional who, even while being part of this education and health system, retains a sense of empathy and sensitivity to patients, including women. Such 'unique doctors' are a rare species and are not easily found.

There are examples from other countries where efforts have been made to integrate gender into undergraduate medical and nursing education. Monash University in Australia has tried to adapt the medical curriculum to produce 'gender-competent doctors' while simultaneously making efforts to restructure the medical profession so more women can be included who will challenge medical science from excluding women's knowledge and experience (World Health Organization 2007). Similarly, efforts have been made in integrating gender into medical curriculum at the Chulalongkorn University in Thailand. One key feature here has been the inclusion of gender as a core area in students' assessments (World Health Organization 2007). Canada had made sustained efforts over many decades to gender mainstream medical education and to promote opportunities for women's leadership in academic medicine. This was possible only because of the major reforms in medical education per se to make it people-centred and mindful of diversity. In these settings, while there is no evidence to show that unique doctors are the norm, they are likely to be more common than in India.

RUWSEC clinic's experience describes what is possible in terms of women-centred medical care and what are its limitations in the absence of such unique doctors. Others who have initiated similar experiments in India to create a space for women-centred care have chosen to limit the space to such technology that can be delivered by the women themselves, and have equipped themselves with skills so that such technology can be provided without the active engagement of professionals from the formal system. For example, women have learnt to perform speculum examinations and screening tests for cervical cancer in such an initiative in rural Maharashtra (Masum 2016).

What does RUWSEC's experience in attempting to move beyond such limits therefore mean for the women's movement or the health movement that aspires to make gender-sensitive, rights-respecting health care widely available to all women (and others) through the public health system?

First, we believe that in spite of all the challenges and failures we have faced over the years, RUWSEC's experience with running a health facility has brought with it several successes. Even when confronted with the medical hierarchy, the rural women leaders of RUWSEC have held their own over certain stretches of time and have internalized a feeling of being entitled to better care, both technically and in terms of its gender sensitivity. This has fostered an alternative imagination of what is possible and has led to sustained demands from the women in the community for better health care both from RUWSEC's clinic and, more important, from the public health system. In addition, the clinic has been successful in creating models in specific areas, for example care for women experiencing domestic violence, that can be learnt from and extended to other settings.

However, if such efforts to make health facilities women-centred and gender-sensitive need to succeed more completely, RUWSEC clinic's experience gives us an indication of how difficult this is going to be and the multi-pronged efforts that need to be made at different levels. We need to invest in medical education to include an understanding of gender and the politics of health and how this influences access to health care. Structures have to be created, which would ensure that health facilities and providers are accountable and sensitive to patients'/women's needs. The unique doctor needs to become no longer so unique through the creation of a critical mass of young professionals, service providers and programme and policy makers, who imbue health facilities and the health system as a whole, with such values.

Note

1 The Freirean method is based on methods used by the Brazilian educator Paulo Freire. The key features are that education is seen as liberatory and is based on the principles of problem posing, conscientization and linking knowledge to action to enable people to change their own lives.

References

Balasubramanian, P. and T. K. S. Ravindran. 2010. "Promoting Zero Tolerance for Spousal Violence: A Community-Based Intervention in Rural Tamil Nadu, India," *ARROWs for Change*, Supplement 2010 to Vol 11, pp. 1–14.

Boston Women's Health Collective. 1973. *Our Bodies, Ourselves*. New York: Simon & Schuster.

Canadian Women's Health Network. 2009. "The Comprehensive Feminist Approach to Health," *Canadian Women's Health Network Newsletter Fall/Winter 2009/10*, Vol. 12, No. 1. http://www.cwhn.ca/en/node/42064 (accessed 30 March 2016).

Gray Jamieson, G. 2012. *Reaching for Health: The Australian Women's Health Movement and Public Policy*. Canberra: ANU ePress.

Komala, P. and T. K. S. Ravindran. 1991. *A Study of Quality of Reproductive Health Services in Primary Health Centres*. Chengalpattu: Rural Women's Social Education Centre.

Masum. 2016. Programme on Women's Right to Physical and Emotional Health. http://www.masum-india.org.in/health.html (accessed 25 March 2016).

Muraleedharan, V. R., U. Dash and L. Gilson. 2011. "Tamil Nadu 1980s to 2005: A Success Story in India." In D. Balabanova, M. McKee and A. Mills (eds). *Good Health at Low Cost" 25 Years On: What Makes a Successful Health System?* London: London School of Hygiene and Tropical Medicine, pp. 159–192

Ravindran, T. K. S. and P. Balasubramanian. 2007. "Rural Women Take Reproductive Health Matters into Their Own Hands," *ARROWs for Change*, Vol. 13, No. 1, pp. 4–5.

Ruzek, S. B., A. Clarke and V. L. Olesen. 1997. "Social, Biomedical and Feminist Models of Women's Health." In A. Clarke, V. L. Olesen and S. B. Ruzek (eds). *Women's Health: Complexities and Differences*. Columbus: Ohio State University Press.

Saheli. 2000. Reproductive Rights in the Indian Context – An Introduction. https://sites.google.com/site/saheliorgsite/health/reproductive-rights-in-the-indian-context (accessed 2 April 2016).

Subha Sri, B. 2010. "Women's Bodies and the Medical Profession," *Economic and Political Weekly*, Vol. 45, No. 17, pp. 52–57.

World Health Organization. 2007. *Integrating Gender into the Curricula for Health Professionals*. Geneva: WHO.

15 Feminist critical medical anthropology methodologies

Understanding gender and health care in India[1]

Cecilia Van Hollen

1. Introduction

It is difficult for academics to commit to a particular intellectual identity. But when that is demanded, I define myself as a feminist critical medical anthropologist. I have applied this approach to research on women's health issues in India for the past 25 years and I continue to work in this vein. Drawing from my own research experiences, this chapter will explore the methodologies entailed in research as a feminist critical medical anthropologist. I will do this by first unpacking core methodological assumptions behind each component of my disciplinary position, introducing methodologies at each level: socio-cultural anthropology, medical anthropology, critical medical anthropology and finally feminist critical medical anthropology (Section 2). Section 3 will examine how I have operationalized the fusion of these methodological approaches in my own research projects. I conclude by discussing some of the ways in which the findings that have resulted from this feminist critical medical anthropological research have contributed to our understanding of gender and can be useful for improving health care for women.

Since this chapter centres on a reflection on research methodologies, I will not discuss the ethnographic findings of my research projects in depth. It is, nevertheless, important to briefly describe the thrust of my research by way of background to understanding the exploration of methodologies, and I will introduce my studies more in Section 3 of this chapter. My research has focused empirically on social and cultural dimensions of health, medicine, international development and the body in India, and theoretically on globalization and modernity; feminism and gender studies; critical medical anthropology; and social inequality and power. I have been driven by both an anthropological desire to understand human diversity and a dedication to social justice. My projects have been designed with an eye to expanding both the empirical and theoretical horizons of the disciplines of anthropology and South Asia studies at the same time that I aim to provide valuable insights to policy makers, particularly those working in the field of global and public health.[2]

2. Methodological approaches in feminist critical medical anthropology

2.1 Participant observation

In order to appreciate the methodologies of a feminist critical medical anthropologist, it is useful to begin with the foundation of social-cultural anthropology and then add on the layers of accumulative specificity since this a composite approach. Long-term fieldwork and participant observation have remained at the heart of social-cultural anthropological research methodology since the early days of the discipline. What this means in practice varies enormously depending on the research question at hand. At the turn of the 20th century, anthropologists tried to participate in all realms of social activities in relatively small-scale societies in an effort to describe the inner workings of whole societies, often incorrectly treating these societies as if they were virtually isolated from the rest of the world. Social-cultural anthropologists today, on the other hand, typically work in highly complex and often urban social settings and seek to answer more specific questions about communities that are viewed as embedded in multiple scales of relationships, including the global.

Despite these differences, several core methodological assumptions persist. First, it is assumed that there is value gained from understanding the experiences and world views of people who are part of diverse kinds of communities throughout the world and in making those perspectives known through writing. Second, it is assumed that in order to understand those views it is essential to integrate oneself within that community by participating in everyday (and extraordinary) practices. The degree to which one can or ethically wants to participate in social practices, discourses and ideologies, of course, varies significantly. But the goal is nevertheless to understand what the experience feels like and what it means to those who do participate in it, to be empathetic even if not always sympathetic. Third, it is assumed that such participation can enable an anthropologist to gain the trust of members of the communities under study, which in turn facilitates communication and enhances understanding. The establishment of trust is, however, not taken for granted, and today it is acknowledged that these relationships are shot through with complex power dynamics and may be fraught. Fourth, it is assumed that while anthropologists are participating in people's everyday lives, they are simultaneously acting as observers and are analysing practices and ideas through a set of theoretical lenses that they deem useful for explaining the social and cultural phenomenon at hand. Fifth, anthropologists have a holistic view of socio-cultural phenomena and consider it essential to have a broad understanding of how history, language, politics, economics, religion, kinship, the arts and so on intersect to influence the particular topic under examination. Both the research methods and the resulting descriptive and analytical writing are referred to as ethnography.

2.2 Ethnographic interviews

In-depth ethnographic interviews constitute the other main ingredient in a social-cultural anthropologist's toolkit. The aim of such interviews is to understand the perspectives of the people one is studying by soliciting their own narrative accounts of events that pertain to the topic under study. While analysing such narrative accounts, anthropologists must consider how the context of the informants' lives and the context of the interview itself may lead someone to present certain kinds of narratives and certain kinds of facts as truths. Anthropologists may not be concerned about verifying the empirical truth behind such narratives if they are interested only in analysing narratives as insights into the constructed nature of truths. Other anthropologists may, however, try to decipher the empirical reality behind these narrative statements in part through the process of establishing rapport with their informants; in part by situating these accounts in relationship to the anthropologist's knowledge of the social-cultural context; and in part by comparing these narratives to the narratives of other research participants.

While ethnographic interviews have some degree of structure to them in order to address the particular issue at hand and in order to be able to make comparisons and find patterns across the responses, for social-cultural anthropologists the emphasis is on unstructured interviews with open-ended questions that allow respondents to lead the researcher in directions that they consider to be most important to them. If the goal of the anthropologist is to understand the world from varying vantage points, then giving up preconceived notions about what the most salient issues should be and handing the reins over to the informants/collaborators to lead the anthropologist to that viewpoint is crucial. This flexibility is essential to anthropological methodology and anthropologists do not shy away from admitting that much can be gained from embracing the role that serendipity inherently plays in all qualitative social science research. Social-cultural anthropology is somewhat unique among the social sciences because it does not set out to prove or disprove hypotheses per se but rather asks open-ended questions about the human condition and tries to determine and establish optimal research conditions under which to examine these questions from multiple angles.

2.3 Methods in medical anthropology

Medical anthropology is sometimes viewed as a bridge between two subfields of anthropology: social-cultural anthropology and biological anthropology. But in practice, most medical anthropologists approach their research from within one of these major subfields. My medical anthropological training is firmly rooted within social-cultural anthropology, so that is the medical anthropology that I will focus on for the purposes of this chapter. Situated within social-cultural anthropology, the field of medical anthropology examines beliefs, practices, and embodied experiences of illness, health and healing from a comparative socio-cultural perspective to show that illness, health, medicine and the body are shaped by social relationships and cultural values at the level of the individual, the family, the local community and the nation-state, and at regional and global levels. Medical anthropologists today view all medical knowledge systems and practices – including biomedicine – as socio-cultural phenomena.

In terms of methodology, therefore, most medical anthropologists employ the same research techniques that are standard for social-cultural anthropology while focusing on the body–society relationship in health and illness and in the context of healing. While medical anthropological methodologies and research sites are diverse, some commonalities are apparent. Medical anthropologists often observe patient–practitioner interactions in a wide variety of therapeutic encounters, such as in clinical settings (Kleinman 1981). They also elicit and analyse illness narratives from patients and from others involved, such as family members and health care providers (Kleinman 1988, Mattingly and Garro 2000, Mishra and Chatterjee 2013). In some cases, medical anthropologists have provided autobiographical ethnographic accounts of their own experiences with an illness (Jain 2013). Others have engaged in participant observation of medical education in both formal and informal settings (Good and Good 1993, Wendland 2010). Medical anthropologists have conducted ethnographic research in laboratories (Rapp 2000), within public and global health policy or humanitarian aid circles (Justice 1989, Whiteford and Manderson 2000, Redfield 2013) and within medical industries such as pharmaceutical and biomedical research companies (Rajan 2006, Dumit 2012).

2.4 Critical medical anthropology methods

Some medical anthropologists identify themselves as critical medical anthropologists who focus primarily on dynamics of power. Merrill Singer defined critical medical anthropology as an approach that 'understands health issues in light of the larger political and economic forces that pattern human relationships, shape social behavior, and condition collective experience, including forces of institutional, national, and global scale' (Singer 1986: 128). Demonstrating the negative effects of global capitalism and class inequality on health care and health outcomes has been a primary concern of critical medical anthropologists. They have increasingly come to view these negative effects as forms of structural violence and strive to demonstrate the relationships among political economy and health disparities globally and locally (Farmer 2001, Baer, Singer and Susser 2004, Das 2015). Critical medical anthropologists also view identities such as gender, sexuality, ethnicity, race, religion and caste as significant factors in structural violence leading to health disparities. As Paul Farmer writes,

> Their sickness is a result of structural violence: neither culture nor pure individual will is at fault; rather, historically given (and often economically driven) processes and forces conspire to constrain individual agency. Structural violence is visited upon all those whose social status denies them access to the fruits of scientific and social progress.
>
> (Farmer 2001: 79)

Methodologically, critical medical anthropology requires paying attention to both macro- and microstructures of power at multiple levels. It insists on a deep historical perspective to be able to demonstrate how past social processes, such as colonialism and slavery, continue to have profound residual effects on health outcomes today. Following Foucault, many critical medical anthropologists are attuned to dynamics of biopower inherent in and masked by discourses of such things as civilization, modernity, development, freedom and choice which impact health care and shape notions of health, illness and the body (Cohen 2000). In this vein, critical medical anthropologists have found the concepts of (bio)medicalization and pharmaceuticalization to be salient because they show that attributing causes of illness to individual bodies, individual behaviour and individual will alone serves to obscure the social roots of illness, disease and death (Nichter 1989, Scheper-Hughes 1993, Biehl 2005).

2.5 Feminist critical medical anthropology methods

We come now to the feminist critical medical anthropological approach. Feminist anthropology is a broad field with a rich history, and there is not space in this article to discuss this subfield in its entirety. Rather, I will focus on how feminist approaches in anthropology have informed research methods in critical medical anthropology. The second-wave feminist movements emerging in the 1960s in the West moved beyond the first-wave feminist emphasis on legal voting rights to a broader critique of patriarchy within a wide range of social and cultural institutions. One of the key issues of concern was reproduction. Women's roles and responsibilities within the arena of reproduction and reproductive health and rights became a rallying call for feminists at this time. Reproduction also became a primary focus of research for feminist scholars working within the then newly emerging field of medical anthropology, and the study of reproductive processes remains one of the most vibrant areas of inquiry within medical anthropology today.

Feminist critical medical anthropologists initially focused on revealing links between the biomedicalization of reproduction and the control of women's bodies (Martin 1987, Davis-Floyd 1992, Jordan 1993). Emily Martin's (1987) Marxist feminist analysis of medicalized reproduction argued that the biomedical management of women's reproductive health processes (pregnancy, birth, menstruation and menopause) mimicked industrial capitalist models of productivity, efficiency and profit-seeking and stripped women of control over their own bodies by placing that power in the hands of increasingly male medical practitioners, machines and the medical industry. In addition to the critiques of patriarchy inherent in such studies, there was growing concern about the negative health consequences of the highly interventionist approach to medicalized reproduction, chief among these being the skyrocketing rates of caesarean sections. Other feminist medical anthropologists, including myself, began to examine how political economies and other social relations and cultural value systems shaped this process of the biomedicalization of reproduction in varying ways around the globe (Ginsburg and Rapp 1995, Lock 1995, Davis-Floyd and Sargent 1997, Kanaaneh 2002, Sargent and Browner 2011).

Feminist anthropology since the 1990s has highlighted ways that women around the world exert their agency in diverse ways within the constraints of local and global structures of patriarchy (MacLeod 1991, Mankekar 1999, Mahmood 2005). Feminist critical medical anthropologists shifted their attention towards documenting how women actively engage with medical science and technology in complex, context-specific ways (Lock and Kaufert 1998, Rapp 2000, Inhorn and Van Balen 2002). Feminist medical anthropologists studying reproduction at this time began to see the management of reproduction as a site not only for the replication of social-cultural values and relations but as a site of socio-cultural transformation, particularly concerning the construction of gender (Ginsburg and Rapp 1995).

Methodologically, feminist critical medical anthropologists of reproduction have drawn from the approaches discussed earlier, including participant observation in clinical and other settings; ethnographic interviews; illness narratives; discourse analysis of OB/GYN medical textbooks and of global reproductive health policies; and attention to the impact of global, national and more local political–economic relations on health outcomes. They do so with particular attention to core feminist concerns about gender inequality and gender-based discrimination, intersectionality and the politics of representation.

Anthropology's comparative, cross-cultural and cultural relativist orientation dating back to the early 20th century, such Mead's work on *Sex and Temperament* (1935), paved the way for what would develop into the concept of gender as a socially embedded cultural construction as opposed to sex as a biological given. Due to anthropology's holistic approach, feminist anthropologists have been inherently concerned with examining the intersectionality and the co-production of identities (even if they did not always use this terminology) (Abu-Lughod 1990). Influenced by Foucault, feminist anthropologists later began to see 'sex' too as a culturally constructed category (Visweswaran 1997). Feminist critical medical anthropologists have shown how knowledge about the body in varying medical systems is highly gendered, and they have highlighted the role of gender in health disparities. They have done so with an appreciation for the ways in which constructions of gender intersect with other axes of social identities, such as class, race, ethnicity, nationality and sexual orientation.

Feminist anthropology began to flourish in the 1970s at the same time that many anthropologists were engaging in postmodern critiques of master narratives in ethnography and post-colonial critiques of anthropology's role in colonialism and of ongoing orientalist assumptions in anthropological representations (Clifford and Marcus 1986). Feminist anthropologists encouraged such critiques and played an important role in re-configuring ethnographic methodologies, particularly in terms of ethnographic writing (Abu-Lughod 1993, Visweswaran 1997). Reflexive discussions about the impact of the positionality of the ethnographer and of the study participants on the framing of the research questions, on the politics of research interactions and on the research findings and analysis became commonplace in ethnographic writing as a result. A concerted effort to present direct quotes and sometimes long passages of interview dialogues also found its way into ethnographic writing. Both were attempts to recognize that the anthropologist's interpretation was only one possible interpretation, to allow informants to speak more directly to readers and allow readers to come to their own conclusions. These new techniques of ethnographic writing resonated with the broader feminist critique of hierarchy and domination and are reflected in varying degrees in the ethnographic writing styles of critical feminist medical anthropologists today.

3. Researching reproductive health in India

How does one go about putting all of these complex layers of methodologies together in practice? I will attempt to answer this question through the example of my own research on reproductive health in India. Rather than discuss the methodologies at each consecutive layer as I have done earlier, in this section I will show how in practice these elements are highly integrated. First, let me briefly and broadly describe methods used in my research projects.

My first major ethnographic research project on the medicalization of childbirth in India analysed the impact of modernity on the experiences of lower-class women during childbirth (Van Hollen 2003). I showed that although the biomedicalization of birth is part of a global modernizing process, it occurs in unique ways in specific historical, political-economic and socio-cultural contexts. I examined how facets of this specific context impacted choices women made about what kind of care to seek during pregnancy, delivery and the post-partum period. One of the arguments I make in this study is that unlike the middle-class homebirth movement in the United States which has been motivated by a critique of the overuse of technological interventions in a presumed natural process, some lower-class women in south India were rejecting government hospitals and opting to have their deliveries at home not because they were rejecting the new technologies but rather because they were resisting humiliating and frightening forms of class and caste discrimination, and internationally generated, government-mandated pressures to undergo sterilization that they were experiencing at the hands of the medical personnel in the government hospitals. These women did, however, want new medical technologies such as Pitocin drugs to induce labour, and they employed gendered ideas about *sakti* (power derived, in part, through women's reproductive capacity) and modernity to explain why this was important. As a result, they were bringing these medical technologies into their homes without proper recourse to emergency care if needed, a practice that could have unintended negative health consequences for them in the end.

This project entailed ethnographic research carried out for the full year of 1995, one month in 1993 and one month in 1997. The multisite ethnographic research focused primarily on the Nochikuppam neighbourhood in Chennai and on the semi-urban town of Kaanathur-Reddikuppam south of Chennai. Initial contacts with people in these communities were facilitated primarily by two NGOs, the Working Women's Forum and Voluntary

Health Services. I also travelled briefly to six other towns throughout Tamil Nadu and worked in several other low-income communities in Chennai, conducting the same kind of research to confirm that my findings, although unique in some respects, were not anomalies in the Tamil Nadu socio-cultural landscape. I collected data through structured and unstructured interviews with over 70 pregnant and post-partum women and their families in their homes and in public maternity wards. I asked women to describe the social, cultural and physical events of their pregnancies, deliveries and post-partum periods; to comment on how they made decisions regarding where to go and whom to consult for maternal–child health care; and to reflect on the nature of care given in diverse settings. And I observed and videotaped pregnancy and post-partum rituals as well as daily life in the communities. I also interviewed a range of medical practitioners, including doctors, nurses, hospital *ayahs*, multi-purpose health workers and midwives. I observed interactions between the various health care practitioners and women who were their patients in hospitals and homes. I also interviewed government and non-governmental administrators working on women's health policy issues at the state and national levels. Finally, I conducted one month of archival research in the Tamil Nadu state archives to explore colonial policies and programmes for maternal health care in India.

My second major research project chronicled experiences of low-income HIV-positive women in India as they navigated reproductive health decisions (Van Hollen 2013). The Government of India, together with UNICEF, established a public health initiative to prevent HIV transmission from mother to child. While this programme, which targets poor women attending public maternity hospitals, has improved health outcomes for infants, my research also showed that it has sometimes resulted in unintended negative consequences for marginalized mothers because these women were being tested for HIV in far greater numbers than their male spouses and were often blamed and harassed for bringing this highly stigmatized disease into the family. At times, this blame was used as an excuse by in-laws for expelling those women out of the home and denying them access to their inheritance when they became widows after their husbands died of AIDS-related complications.

This research project drew from ethnographic data gathered during six months of fieldwork in Chennai (with brief visits to other parts of Tamil Nadu) in 2004 and one month in both 2002–3 and 2008. Methods used included ethnographic interviews with 70 women living with HIV/AIDS whom I met through HIV-positive 'networks' (community-based organizations run by and for HIV-positive people), through the Y.R. Gaitonde Centre for AIDS Research and Education (YRG Care), through a government maternity hospital; through Zonta Resources (an NGO) and through

Tamil Nadu State AIDS Control Society counsellors' evaluation meetings. I also engaged in participant observation at numerous support group meetings for networks run by and for women living with HIV/AIDS (particularly with the Positive Women's Network) and at other educational and advocacy meetings organized by such groups. Interviews with HIV-positive women focused on how they came to know about their HIV status, how they and others responded to their HIV-positive diagnosis, what role they thought gender played in social responses to people living with HIV/AIDS and their recommendations for improving HIV/AIDS prevention and care. I paid close attention to how women themselves considered gender to matter in relation to the stigma of being HIV-positive. I found that their views of the gendering of this stigma shared much in common with the views of other HIV-positive women around the globe but also differed due to unique socio-cultural factors such as cultural constructions of gendered bodies and of widowhood and widow inheritance rights. Interviews with women who learned of their HIV status through prenatal HIV-testing included discussions about how they made decisions about whether to continue with their pregnancy and delivery after receiving an HIV-positive diagnosis, what their experiences were like during birth, how they made decisions about infant feeding and what they thought about the decisions they had made.

For this project I also interviewed 65 women (of unknown HIV status) during prenatal counselling in government hospitals where the state's Prevention of Parent to Child Transmission programme was being implemented, and I observed prenatal pre-HIV-test counselling sessions in these hospitals. In addition, I met with people working for governmental institutions and NGOs involved in HIV/AIDS prevention and treatment programmes in India and the United States. Finally, I met doctors and counsellors in six government hospitals and at YRG Care. All of these interviews explored assessments of the successes and future needs of HIV/AIDS prevention and care programmes related to mother-to-child transmission.

For both of my research projects, I received informed consent for the interviews with research participants. With consent, interviews were tape-recorded and were later transcribed and translated. Most interviews were conducted in Tamil by me with the assistance of native Tamil-speaking research assistants. Both projects delineate the myriad social, cultural and medical structures which are globally and locally produced and which constrain women's reproductive health choices, while also highlighting how women pragmatically negotiate complex reproductive health terrains. These studies were conducted over several years and entailed a wide range of methods. The description of my research methods earlier only scratches the surface of methodological approaches used. While it is impossible to detail all of the salient issues concerning methods in this short chapter, there are some key overlapping approaches used in these projects that help illustrate the methodological approaches in feminist critical medical anthropology, to which I will now turn.

3.1 Positionality

First, it is important to discuss the issues of positionality in relation to postcolonial and postmodern critiques of representation. My research has always been motivated by an interest in improving health care experiences and outcomes for women from marginalized communities. This means that I often critique problems that call out for policy and programmatic changes and socio-cultural changes globally and locally. As a white American woman, I have to ask myself whether my criticisms of reproductive health policies and practices in India serve to further colonial and post-colonial Orientalist discourses of the negative treatment of women in India, which have been used to legitimate colonial and neocolonial encounters. Methodologically, I try to mitigate this in several ways. First, I choose my research topics following extensive meetings with people involved in women's health programmes and advocacy in India to ask what their concerns are and which topics they feel would benefit from the kind of ethnographic research that I am qualified to undertake. Second, because I use ethnographic research methods to solicit the opinions of research participants and to present their views through ethnographic writing, I feel fairly confident that I am not simply expressing my own preconceived notions. In my writing, I use direct quotes to present people's viewpoints and to represent dialogues between myself and the interviewee or between medical practitioners and patients. When appropriate, I articulate how power dynamics between me and my research subjects (whether they are doctors, policy makers or marginalized women patients) may influence responses they provide. Third, my critiques have been aimed as much at global health policy and global political economic policies as they have been at India's policies or unequal gender relations in India.

My research has been based in the south Indian state of Tamil Nadu, where I have roots going back to my childhood years in the 1970s when my family was living in Sri Lanka for almost four years during which time I visited Tamil Nadu frequently and briefly attended boarding school there. I returned to Tamil Nadu as an undergraduate college student on a full-year, study-abroad programme in Madurai in the mid-1980s. During that year, I was enrolled in an intensive Tamil-language programme at Madurai Kamaraj University, took Bharatanatyam dance classes and conducted ethnographic research on a Mariamman festival in the neighbourhood where

I lived near the Meenakshi temple. In a way, that year in Madurai was like a homecoming for me because it helped me to reconnect with my childhood years in the region, a part of myself that I had found difficult to explain to my American friends. These were wonderful experiences, and I felt an affinity for the people and the cultural practices in Tamil Nadu. In Tamil one never really says 'goodbye' but rather 'having gone, I will come', leaving always the promise of return. And so I have continued to return ever since.

I add these personal reflections by way of commenting on one aspect of my positionality, which cannot be captured by discussions of the complicated identity of either the 'native anthropologist' (Narayan 1993) or the presumed anthropologist as an uninitiated foreigner. It is difficult to articulate why and how these experiences from my youth matter. I have always felt that my regular return visits and ongoing research in the region have allowed me to continue to be myself, more than being an opportunity to understand the 'other'. My life-long connection and commitment to the region; my many years of formal and informal Tamil studies; and my undergraduate and graduate coursework focusing on the history, politics, religion, arts and social and cultural movements of South Asia profoundly shape my understanding of the specific research projects on women's health care that I have undertaken, and my interactions with people over a long time span provide an important historical perspective and an appreciation for continuities as well as dramatic changes over time. Conducting research on health and disease necessitates that one stays up to date on the quickly changing epidemiological, policy and programmatic landscape while also appreciating broader social, political, economic and cultural shifts over time.

Nevertheless, I am keenly aware of the extraordinary privilege that has allowed me to regularly 'go and then come', to access research funds and to write about the lives of those I have met. Given that I have worked primarily with women from low-income, lower-caste communities, the vast differences in our experiences due to socio-economic status serve as an important point of comparison for analysis in my writing. While gender and economic status are constants in my research, I pay attention to variations and to the intersectionality of identities so as not to essentialize the category of 'poor women' or 'Third-World women' (Mohanty 1991). I do this first by asking a set of standardized socio-economic questions to all women I interview (education, employment, household income, marital status, religion and caste) in order to ascertain similarities and differences. Second, by using open-ended, unstructured ethnographic interview techniques, I explore dimensions of women's experiences that they feel are crucial to understanding the health care issues of my study.

3.2 Locations

I find that interviews conducted in people's homes allow for more in-depth discussions on a range of topics compared to interviews conducted in clinical settings because of the privacy afforded in the home setting and a greater comfort level discussing experiences with health care providers. However, in my study on HIV-positive women where there were concerns about family members and neighbours learning about their stigmatized HIV status, sometimes interviews in homes could be stifled or were ruled out from the beginning. Interviews in settings where HIV-positive women met for support group meetings or in a quiet corner of a public park proved to be more conducive to allowing women to open up. Being flexible and allowing participants in the study to choose the time and location to meet is essential. Interviewing the same person on multiple occasions is beneficial since it allows the researcher to reflect on what was said in the first interview and consider it in relation to what others have said about the same issue and to ask for further clarification. Interviews conducted with government officials to understand the public health policy angle of things or with doctors to understand their views required great flexibility as well, and I spent many hours waiting in hallways of the offices of various government ministries and hospitals for meetings. Patience in these circumstances is not simply a virtue but a necessity.

Interviews conducted in clinical settings do offer important insights into the clinical experience of patients and health care practitioners (including *ayahs*, nurses, doctors, lab technicians and counsellors). I have spent substantial time in clinical settings conducting interviews while also observing ongoing activities and interactions. Experiencing medical institutions firsthand – the sights, sounds and smells – provides the medical anthropologist with an enormously valuable embodied awareness of the context for interpreting interview narratives.

Observation has been equally important to my research outside of the clinic. Spending time in homes allowed me to get a feel of the physical and social living environments of women, many of whom shared their one-room government-subsidized apartments with six or seven people in neighbourhoods with unpaved alleyways in between buildings which flooded in the monsoons, making it difficult to navigate on foot. By observing women going about quotidian activities in and around their homes, I gained a sense of the flow of daily life around such activities as cooking, childcare, elderly care, collecting water from municipal water tanks, raising livestock, watching television, going to temples and performing small pujas for goddesses at home. This helped to comprehend concerns women had about lack of access to resources and time required for health care needs and to appreciate how economic and gender inequality impacts women's lives and health. Observations of more extraordinary and ritualized life events helped shed light on important cultural, religious and medical practices and value systems that also shaped women's views on reproductive health care. For example, I attended numerous rituals for women's first pregnancies and bathing rituals for newborns and their mothers.

An important observation component of my research with HIV-positive women involved participating in support group meetings of community-based organizations run by and for people living with HIV/AIDS and participating in advocacy initiatives such as media, legal and human rights forums during which I sometimes served as a scribe. Research with these organizations occasionally put me in prickly situations at the crosshairs of varying groups competing for publicity and funds. Patience and respect were necessities for me in such situations in order to gain the trust needed for my work. Negotiating such tensions as an ethnographer also shed light on relationships between transnational NGOs and local activism, the politics of health care, and the enactment of therapeutic citizenship and fostered an appreciation for the strategies HIV-positive women themselves used to traverse this highly politicized terrain in search of access to treatment and care.

How women navigate multiple structures of constraint and of possibility as they make complex decisions about their reproductive health care is a central question in my work. I articulate what women themselves reported to be key structuring factors while also providing the historical, political, economic, and social context for understanding women's narrative accounts. An understanding of this context comes through inter-disciplinary readings in history and the social sciences; reading reproductive health policy and programming statements and documents; and interviewing health policy makers and planners in India and the United States. From all of this data, I try to elucidate patterns while also showing that these decision-making processes for individual women are often too idiosyncratic for easily generalizable and predictive statements. Anthropology is compelling precisely because it conveys this realistic balance between structured patterns and creative complexity.

4. Conclusion

How have my methodologies as a feminist critical medical anthropologist added to an understanding of gender? This is a question that I have tried to answer in great detail in my previous publications. I cannot replicate all of these ideas here, but, by way of concluding, I will briefly address two major ways my research has contributed to an understanding of gender in India.

The first relates to gender and health care decision-making and the second to reproductive health as a site for the reification and potential transformation of gender.

In my first project on the biomedicalization of childbirth, I delineate key factors contributing to decisions low-income women made about where, how and under whose supervision they wanted to and were able to give birth to their children. This study looked carefully into how women weighed the pros and cons of different kinds of hospital and home births. In my second major research project, I describe a range of factors that went into low-income women's decisions about HIV testing during pregnancy, about whether to continue with a pregnancy after an HIV-positive diagnosis, about where to give birth and about whether to breast-feed or bottle-feed their babies. Both studies showed how factors under consideration in these decisions were linked to global and local political-economic and socio-cultural dynamics. Both tried to draw out the relationship between structures of constraint and women's agency. And both tried to highlight critiques that women had about their constrained options, with an eye to making recommendations for improving reproductive health care.

These studies have helped to further our understanding of the relationships among gender, health care and health in India in ways that could be instructive to people involved in global, national and state reproductive health planning. One of the conclusions brought out through these research projects is that the common global health assumption that poor, lower-caste women in India have little or no control over their reproductive decision-making does not bear out. Evidence that emerges through my feminist critical medical anthropological research methodology shows this assumption to be untenable while simultaneously pointing to the enormous constraints placed on such decisions and also making the point that the consequences of the reproductive decisions that women make may not always be advantages to them in the long run.

The methodological approaches that I have used in my research have also been instructive for understanding gender insofar as they illuminate how the management of reproductive health serves to both reaffirm pre-existing gender norms and provide a space for their potential transformation. The former point will not be surprising to feminist social scientists, particularly the consideration of ways in which gender inequality shapes the management of reproductive health care. Nevertheless, it is imperative that we continue to make such connections apparent in order to change them. Issues of concern in broader feminist movements can and should be leveraged to improve the quality of reproductive health care. The latter point is less obvious but equally important. My methodological attention to both structure and agency in the management of reproductive care helps draw attention to reproduction as a potentially transformative space. For example, as women negotiate the use of medical technologies in diverse ways around the globe within specific political-economic and cultural contexts, they may begin to redefine socio-cultural assumptions about relationships among gender, the body and medical care. Women's reproductive health decision-making can therefore become a powerful site from which to push back against a wide range of gender-based – combined with class- and caste-based – forms of discrimination. When women challenge gender norms implicit in the management of reproductive health, they may become energized to engage in broader forms of political activism around gender equity and social justice issues as a result, as I have witnessed in my research on young HIV-positive widows who became involved in broader social movements to better enforce legal rights to inheritance for widows and movements against widespread taboos against widow remarriage.

I have recently launched a third major study on local perceptions and practices in response to new global health, governmental and NGO screening and treatment programmes for cervical and breast cancer in India. This new project once again employs feminist critical medical anthropological methods and theoretical approaches in order to shed light on women's experiences with illness and health care systems in the hopes of improving health and health care for all. I hope that my reflections on critical feminist medical anthropology methodologies in this chapter will help foster similar much-needed research projects by other scholars in India and around the globe.

Notes

1 This chapter was published in the *Economic and Political Weekly*, Review of Women's Studies, vol. 51, no. 18, 30 April 2016, pp. 72–79. We are grateful to the editor, *EPW*, for permission to republish this chapter in this volume.
2 Research was supported by the Fulbright Foundation, the American Institute for Indian Studies (AIIS), and the Woodrow Wilson Foundation.

References

Abu-Lughod, Lila. 1990. "Can There Be a Feminist Ethnography?" *Women and Performance*, Vol. 5, No. 1, pp. 7–27.
———. 1993. *Women Writing Worlds: Bedouin Stories*. Berkeley: University of California Press.
Baer, Hans, Merill Singer and Ida Susser (eds). 2004. *Medical Anthropology and the World System* (2nd ed.). Westport, CT: Praeger Publishers.
Biehl, João. 2005. *Vita: Life in a Zone of Social Abandonment*. Berkeley: University of California Press.

Clifford, James and George Marcus (eds). 1986. *Writing Culture: The Poetics and Politics of Ethnography*. Berkeley: University of California Press.
Cohen, Lawrence. 2000. *No Aging in India: Alzheimer's, The Bad Family, and Other Modern Things*. Berkeley: University of California Press.
Das, Veena. 2015. *Affliction: Health, Disease and Poverty*. New York: Fordham University Press.
Davis-Floyd, Robbie. 1992. *Birth as an American Rite of Passage*. Berkeley: University of California Press.
Davis-Floyd, Robbie and Carolyn Sargent (eds). 1997. *Childbirth and Authoritative Knowledge: Cross-Cultural Perspectives*. Berkeley: University of California Press.
Dumit, Joseph. 2012. *Drugs for Life: How Pharmaceutical Companies Define Our Health*. Durham, NC: Duke University Press.
Farmer, Paul. 2001. *Infections and Inequalities: The Modern Plagues*. Berkeley: University of California Press.
Ginsburg, Faye and Rayna Rapp (eds). 1995. *Conceiving the New World Order: The Global Politics of Reproduction*. Berkeley: University of California Press.
Good, Byron and Mary-Jo DelVecchio Good. 1993. "'Learning Medicine': The Construction of Medical Knowledge at Harvard Medical School." In S. Lindenbaum and M. Lock (eds). *Knowledge, Power, and Practice*. Berkeley: University of California Press, pp. 81–107.
Inhorn, Marcia and Frank van Balen (eds). 2002. *Infertility around the Globe: New Thinking on Childlessness, Gender, and New Reproductive Technologies*. Berkeley: University of California Press.
Jain, S. Lochlann. 2013. *Malignant: How Cancer Becomes Us*. Berkeley: University of California Press.
Jordan, Brigitte. 1993. *Birth in Four Cultures: A Crosscultural Investigation of Childbirth in Yucatan, Holland, Sweden, and the United States* (4th ed.). Prospect Heights, IL: Waveland Press.
Justice, Judith. 1989. *Policies, Plans and People: Foreign Aid and Health Development*. Berkeley: University of California Press.
Kanaaneh, Rhoda. 2002. *Birthing the Nation: Strategies of Palestinian Women in Israel*. Berkeley: University of California Press.
Kleinman, Arthur. 1981. *Patients and Healers in the Context of Culture: An Exploration of the Borderland between Anthropology, Medicine, and Psychiatry*. Berkeley: University of California Press.
———. 1988. *The Illness Narratives: Suffering, Healing, and the Human Condition*. New York: Basic Books.
Lock, Margaret. 1995. *Encounters with Aging: Mythologies of Menopause in Japan and America*. Berkeley: University of California Press.
Lock, Margaret and Patricia Kaufert (eds). 1998. *Pragmatic Women and Body Politics*. Cambridge: Cambridge University Press.
MacLeod, Arlene. 1991. *Accommodating Protest: Working Women, the New Veiling, and Change in Cairo*. New York: Columbia University Press.
Mahmood, Saba. 2005. *Politics of Piety: The Islamic Revival and the Feminist Subject*. Princeton, NJ: Princeton University Press.

Mankekar, Purnima. 1999. *Screening Culture, Viewing Politics: An Ethnography of Television, Womanhood, and Nation in Postcolonial India*. Durham, NC: Duke University Press.

Martin, Emily. 1987. *The Woman in the Body: A Cultural Analysis of Reproduction*. Boston: Beacon Press.

Mattingly, Cheryl and Linda Garro (eds). 2000. *Narrative and the Cultural Construction of Illness and Healing*. Berkeley: University of California Press.

Mead, Margaret. 1935. *Sex and Temperament: In Three Primitive Societies*. New York: William Morrow & Company.

Mishra, Arima and Suhita Chatterjee (eds). 2013. *Multiple Voices and Stories: Narratives of Health and Illness*. New Delhi: Orient Black Swan.

Mohanty, Chandra Talpade. 1991. "Under Western Eyes: Feminist Scholarship and Colonial Discourses." In Chandra Talpade Mohanty, Ann Russo and Lourdes Torres (eds). *Third World Women and the Politics of Feminism*. Bloomington, IN: Indiana University Press, pp. 51–80.

Narayanan, Kirin. 1993. "How Native Is a Native Anthropologist?" *American Anthropologist*, Vol. 95, pp. 671–686.

Nichter, Mark. 1989. *Anthropology and International Health: South Asian Case Studies*. Dordrecht, The Netherlands: Kluwer Academic Publishers.

Rajan, Kaushik Sunder. 2006. *Biocapital: The Constitution of Postgenomic Life*. Durham, NC: Duke University Press.

Rapp, Rayna. 2000. *Testing Women, Testing the Fetus: The Social Impact of Amniocentesis in America*. New York: Routledge.

Redfield, Peter. 2013. *Life in Crisis: The Ethical Journey of Doctors without Borders*. Berkeley: University of California Press.

Sargent, Carolyn and Carole Browner (eds). 2011. *Reproduction, Globalization, and the State: New Theoretical and Ethnographic Perspectives*. Durham, NC: Duke University Press.

Scheper-Hughes, Nancy. 1993. *Death without Weeping: The Violence of Everyday Life in Brazil*. Berkeley: University of California Press.

Singer, Merill. 1986. "Developing a Critical Perspective in Medical Anthropology," *Medical Anthropology Quarterly*, Vol. 17, No. 5, pp. 128–129.

Van Hollen, Cecilia. 2003. *Birth on the Threshold: Childbirth and Modernity in South India*. Berkeley: University of California Press.

———. 2013. *Birth in the Age of AIDS: Women, Reproduction, and HIV/AIDS in India*. Palo Alto, CA: Stanford University Press.

Visweswaran, Kamala. 1997. "Histories of Feminist Ethnography," *Annual Review of Anthropology*, Vol. 26, pp. 591–621.

Wendland, Claire. 2010. *A Heart for the Work: Journeys through an African Medical School*. Chicago: University of Chicago Press.

Whiteford, Linda and Lenore Manderson (eds). 2000. *Global Health Policy, Local Realities: The Fallacy of the Level Playing Field*. London: Lynne Rienner Publishers.

Index

Page numbers in *italics* indicate table, and those followed by "n" indicate content in notes.

Abdulali, Sohaila 188–9
abrahmani 54, 57–8
academic disciplines 11, 29, 87, 115
actor-network-theory 146
Act XV of 1877 55
Additional District and Sessions v. Judge 'X' Registrar General, High Court of Madhya Pradesh and others 194
Adivasi 68; Koya and Konda Reddi 61; life narratives 57–63
adolescent sexuality 281
affordances 141–2, 152n4; imagined 142
African American 270
Agamben, Giorgio 168–9
Agarwal, Bina 259
agency: description 255; empowerment and 255–9
Agents of Ishq 152n1
The Age of the Poets (Badiou) 164
Agnes, Flavia 171–2
agriculture, feminization of 41–4
Ahangar, Javed Ahmad 66
Ahangar, Parveena 66–7
Akhtar, Azeem 107
alcoholism 59
Aligarh (film) 173–4
Aligarh, U. P. 173
Aligarh Muslim University 173
Ambedkar, B. R. 8, 52–4
American Association of University Women 32

Andhra Pradesh: globalization and 248–63; Koya and Konda Reddi Adivasi 61
animals, sexuality in 121–2
anthropology: medical 332. *see also* critical medical anthropology; subfields of 333
APDP *see* Association of Parents of Disappeared Persons in Kashmir (APDP)
Armed Forces (Special Powers) Act 5
arranged marriage 256
arthi (bier) 101
arts and humanities 165–7
Aryan religion 56
assisted reproductive technology (ART) 19, 123; assessing impact and realities of 303–7; draft bill 305–7; methodological challenges of studies on 300–3; overview 297–9; *see also* surrogacy
Association of Parents of Disappeared Persons in Kashmir (APDP) 66–7
autoethnography 100–1; *see also* real-life methods
Avishai, O. 86
azadi (freedom) 186, 187

Babu, Savitha 282
'backlash' 8; *see also* sexual violence
badaai 64
Badiou, Alain 164
Badrinath, T. 139

Banerjee, Nirmala 208, 209, 211, 212, 213, 226n3
banking sector: class and gender biases 236; defaulters 236; SHG and 233–6
Banks, Jamie 134
bar dancers, ban on, Mumbai 171–2
Baroda 33, 34
Bartky, Sandra 86
Bartlett, Katherine T. 179, 180, 189
Bataille, Georges 172
Baudelaire, Charles 170–1
Baxi, Pratiksha 11, 170
Beard, Mary 138
beef, consumption of 5
Beijing Declaration of 1995 313
belonging, politics of *see* politics of belonging
Benjamin, Walter 101, 170, 171
Berger, John 162–3
Bharatanatyam 340
'Bharat Mata ki Jai' 51
Bihar, government schools in 281
Bilge, Sirma 3, 4
binary frames of gender 1–3
biological determinism 119, 122
biologists 124–5
bionationalism 123
biopolitical power of science 120
Biswas, Ranjita 169
Bivens, Rena 141, 142
Blank Noise project 139
blogosphere 144; *see also* digital media
blogs 144
Bombay High Court 171
Boyle's law 122
Brahminism 56
Brison, Susan J. 185
Brophy, J. E. 134, 151
Butalia, Urvashi 66

Canada 327
castes/caste system 7; Ambedkar and 52–4; arranged marriage 256; consciousness of 62–3; eradicating 277–8; families and 52–4; names and 273; students 276–7
'The Caste System Upside Down or the Not-So-Mysterious-East' (Mencher) 7

Census of India (2011) 41
Central Board of Secondary Examination (CBSE) 271
Centre for Enquiry into Health and Allied Themes (CEHAT) 20, 21
Chan, Anita 147
char-divari (four walls) 101
Chengalpattu 314
childbirth, biomedicalization of 337
child labour 219
child marriage 54; in West Bengal 16
child sexual violence 186
Chowdhry, Prem 66
Chowdhury, Romit 8
civil society groups 139
Clifford, James 94–5
co-educational schools 281
colleges 6
Collins, Patricia Hill 3, 4, 136
colonialism 55
commercial surrogacy *see* surrogacy
Committee of Feminist Economists 207, 208
Committee on the Status of Women in India (CSWI) 214–17
communication, in digital age 131; *see also* digital media
Comparative Education Society of India (CESI) 268
conjugality 58
conjugal rights 55
Connell, Raewyn 1, 252–3
'The Consortium of Pub-Going, Loose and Forward Women' 140
Constitutional Amendment (73rd) 220
content/text, in digital media space 144–5
context, in digital media space *see* medium/context, in digital media space
contextualized affordances 137
contract of surrogacy 309; breach of 309
Couldry, Nick 143, 145
courtroom talk, in America 180
cow slaughter 5
creative economies 247
Crenshaw, Kimberle 3–4, 70n1
criminalization 51

Criminal Law, amendments of 188
critical medical anthropology 334
cross-sex relationships 281
cultural transformation 249
Culture Digitally 146
cultures of science 124–5
cyberfeminism 133; intersectional 151; *see also* digital media
cyberfeminists 9–10, 133–4 *see* digital media
cyberspace, feminism in 139–41
cyborg 133–9
Cyborg Manifesto (Haraway) 9, 133

Dalits: education and 15; food and 5–6; Internet access 136–7; life narratives 57–63; resistance in Una 5; *see also* family/families
Dani, Shantabai Dhanaji 59
Darwinian theory 124–5
Daryaganj 107
Das, Mala 170
Das, Veena 66
DasGupta, Sumona 68
de Certeau, Michel 101–2
Delhi 34; gang rape protests in 11, 186–94; Muslims in 91–108
Democratic Students Union (DSU) 174–5
Department of Sociology at University of Baroda 33
development 12–17; *see also* planned economy/development
Devika, J. 242
Dhanda, Meena 61–2
Dhwan, Nandita 169
Diagnostic and Statistical Manual of Mental Disorders 119
digital Cartesianism 137–8
digital divide 137
digital media 131–52; affordances 141–2; approaches to research 149–50; campaigns and groups on 140–1; context/medium 145–6; countering sexual harassment on 139; material realities 142; problematics and possibilities of 141–3; questions for feminist researchers 143–8; social questions 143; socio-technical assemblages 146–8; text/content 144–5

discrimination 6
disembodiment 134
Dissensus: On Politics and Aesthetics (Rancière) 167
distributed self 134
diversality 138
doli 101
domestic blogs 144
domestic violence 8; RUWSEC's prevention program 320–1
dowry 258–9
draft bill: ART 305–7; surrogacy 306–10

Eapen, Mridul 223–4, 226
Economic and Political Weekly 140
economic liberalization 14; national level 249; policies 248
education 14–15, 17; Dalit selfhood 58; English medium 221; medical 327; *see also* school system
educational investments 248
Education: Domination, Emancipation and Dignity 268
11th Five-Year Plan 222–5
emasculation 63
embodiment 134
emphasized femininity 138
employment: para-teachers 221; in private sector 248, 253–4
empowerment 13; agency and 255–9; multidimensionality of 256
endogamy 51, 53
Engendering Public Policy 223
English Communicative 271
English Course (Communicative) Workbook for class X 273
English medium education 221
entanglements 142
Eroticism (Bataille) 172
ethical feminism 168
ethics: politics and 167; and spirituality 168
ethnographic interviews 332–3
ethnography: as a feminist method 93–5; geographical markers of 97–9
eugenics 119
eunuch *see* transsexual woman *(hijra)*
evolutionary biology 120–1

examination process 283
exogamy 51, 52–3; rules of 53

Facebook 138; online campaigns and groups 140
factish 147
family/families 8; caste and 52–4; contradictory embodiment 63–5; Dalit and Adivasi 57–63; disciplining gender in 63–5; feminist reflections on 49–68; food cultures 6; heterosexual 50–1; Hindutva and 51; home 67–8; institution of 81; neoliberalism and 51; oppression and resistance 54–7; partition and 65–7
Farmer, Paul 334
Feldman, Hannah 185
female infanticide 54, 55
feminism: cyberspace 139–41; Hartsock on 93; Marxism and 95, 105–6
feminist critical medical anthropology 334–7; ethnographic interviews 332–3; methodological approaches 331–7; overview 330–1; participant observation 331–2; reproductive health 337–43
feminist engagements, changing contexts of 6–7
feminist enquiries 93
feminist science and technology studies (FSTS) 116; nature and culture 116; scholars of 121
feminist sociobiology 125
feminization: of agriculture 41–4; of poverty 231
Fernandes, Leela 247
fieldwork, masculinities in 74–88
Fifth Five-Year Plan 216
Fire (film) 173–4
five-year plans 216–17; 11th Five-Year Plan 222–5; Fifth Five-Year Plan 216; Sixth Five-Year Plan 216–17; 12th Five-Year Plan 223–5
food cultures 51; Dalits and 5–6; feminist researcher and 6
Foucault, Michel 158–9, 175n2

Fourth Annual National Men's Rights Meet, Kolkata 77
Fraser, Nancy 230
freedom fighters 34
freedom struggle, women in 35–6
Freire, Paulo 328n1
Freirean methods 314, 328n1
FSTS *see* feminist science and technology studies (FSTS)
Fulbright-Hayes pre-doctoral grant 32

Gajjala, R. 147
Gamergate 135
gaming research 144
gang rape protests, in Delhi 11
Ganguly, D. 136
gay genes 122
gay movement 81
Geetha, V. 5, 56
gender: binary frames 1–3; as a category in law 2; as a category of analysis 2; in science *see* science; sexuality and 278–82; universal characterization 1–2
gendered violence 4–5
'gender galaxy' 2, 22n1
gender identity 63
gender inequality 2
gendering of plans 222–3
Gender Mainstreaming (GM) 206
gender neutrality of rape law 187
gender norms 21; change in 252–3; in marriage 255–9; reproductive health management and 345
gender orders: politics of belonging 50; in social research 2–3, 63
gender policing 80
gender-sensitive care, at RUWSEC clinic 319
genetic code 122
genetic surrogacy 19; legalizing 308; *see also* surrogacy
genomic sovereignty 123
Gerber, L. 86
Ghana, microcredit programme in 240
'ghar wapsi' (returning home) 51
Ghosh, Shohini 170, 173

Girijana Deepika 61
Global Gender Gap Report 2014 260
globalization 246–63; gender norms and 255–9; identities at home and 259–62; middle-class girls 251–3; women as drivers of change 251–5
The God of Small Things (Roy) 174
Goetz, A. M. 235
Goswami, Ajay 81
Goswami, Nirmali 267–8
Gough, Kathleen 32–3
governance, neoliberalism 51
government schools 221, 273–4; in Bihar and Uttar Pradesh 281
Govinda, R. 221
Grameen Bank 237
grassroots leaders/leadership, RUWSEC's clinic 322–3, 326
Group of Feminist Economists 222–5
Gupta, Reena 77–8

haat (a regular local market or fair) 101
Hameed, Syeda 222, 223
Haraway, Donna 9, 99, 116, 133–4
Harding, Sandra 116–17
Hartsock, Nancy 93
Harvey, David 51
hashtag feminism 135–6, 144
health 17–21; reproductive 337–43; RUWSEC clinic 19–20, 313–27; *see also* assisted reproductive technology (ART); surrogacy
Hegde, Radha 145
hegemonic masculinity 81–2, 138
heterosexuality 80–1; homosocial 82–3
heterosexual men, sexual harassment of 81
hidden curriculum 280
higher education 282–3
hijra see transsexual woman *(hijra)*
Hindu, food cultures and 51
Hinduism 56
Hindutva 6, 51, 173–4
HIV/AIDS 338–9
home, families and 67–8

home/family interviews 100; *see also* real-life methods
homophobia 80–2
homosexuality 119
homosocial heterosexuality 82–3
homosociality 82–4
Hopi pottery 186
Horvitz, Lori 270
Human Development Index 220
human evolution 121
humanities 158–77; arts and 165–7; ethical 168; language of literature 162–5; materialist-hedonist 165–8; negation and 164; politics of pleasure, precarity, tragedy and revolution 173–5; social sciences *vs.* 166–7; theory and praxis 161–2
Hunt, Tim 124
Hyderabad 248–63

IDBI Bank 236
identities, at home 259–62
illarikam marriage 61
imagined affordances 142
impunity 5
in-depth interview 83, 147–8
Indian Penal Code (IPC): Section 377 of 2, 80, 173, 187, 189
Indian School Certificate Examination 271
insurance, for surrogate mother 308–9
intercaste marriages 61–2, 189
International Baccalaureate 272
International Conference on Population and Development, Cairo (1994) 313
Internet 9–10; countering sexual harassment on 139–40; feminist campaigns and groups on 140–1; Lister on 131; social researchers and 132; *see also* digital media
interpretive communities 84–7; *see also* masculinities
intersectionality 3–6; Crenshaw on 3–4; social division and 3; as social justice construct 4; violence and 4–5

Intimate Others (Sen, Biswas and Dhawan) 169
intimate relationships: DSU on 174–5; market economy and 169; as sexual anarchy 174

Jaggar, Alison 93
Jahan, Rounaq 244
Jain, Devaki 222, 226n3
Jaising, Indira 189, 194
Jamia Millia Islamia 98
Jamia Nagar 98, 102, 106–8
Jamil, Ghazala 9
Janu, C. K. 60–1, 68
Jawaharlal Nehru University, Delhi 174
Joothan (Valmiki) 6
Jordan, Tim 146–7
Jordan-Young, Rebecca 121–2
Josephine, Y. 221
Joshua, G. 140
Justice Verma Committee (JVC) 187–90

Kaanathur-Reddikuppam, Chennai 337
Kabeer, Naila 231, 237–8
Kamble, Babytai 67
Kannabiran, Kalpana 8, 190, 263n1
Karnataka 139–40
Kasturi, Leela 208, 210–13
Kelkar, Govind 239
Keller, Evelyn Fox 121, 122
Kerala 33–4; Adivasi people of 68; *Kudumbashree* 242; matrilineal inheritance 38–9
khap 66, 189
Khol Do (Manto) 66
Kidwai, Begum Anis 65
Kingdon, Geeta G. 221
knowledge: power and 115, 116; scientific 118
Komarraju, Sai Amulya 10
Konda Reddi 61
Kottakal Kovilakam (palace) 36
Kovilakam, partitioning of 36
Koya Adivasi 61
Krishnan, Kavita 138, 139, 187
Krishnaraj, Maithreyi 208
Kudumbashree 242

Kumari, Ved 190
Kunan Poshpora, Kashmir 4

Lane, Liz 144
Language, Madness, Desire (Foucault) 163
language books 273
language of sex 163
Latour, B. 146, 147
law reform, of rape/sexual violence 186–94
Leach, Fiona 239–40
leaders/leadership, RUWSEC's clinic 322–3, 326
Lee, M. 151
leftist revolutionary thinking 175
legal language, sexism of 194
legislations, gender and 2
Lister, M. 131
literature 162–3
Literature Reader (CBSE) 272–3
Little, Daniel 9, 95
Longino, Helen 121, 123
Lorber, J. 138
'love jihad' 51

Madabhushi, T. 140
Madhusudhan, N. 61, 70
Madurai Kamaraj University 340
Mahajan, Anupama 282
Mahars 59–60
Main Course Book (CBSE) 272
Malabar region 32–3; Gough's thesis 32–3
Malayalam 38
Mallya, Vijay 236
managerial control 237–8
Mandal, Saptarshi 190–1
mandis 101
Mani, Lata 165–7
Manto, Saadat Hasan 66
Mantz, Jeff 263n1
Marcus, George 250, 336
Marcy, Geoff 124
Margulis, Lynn 125
Mariamman festival 340–1
market economy and intimate relationships 169
marriage 256–8; dowry 258–9; endogamy 51, 53; exogamy 51,

52–3; gender norms in 255–9; intercaste 61–2, 189; rules of 53; *see also* family/families
Martin, Emily 335
Marx, Karl 99
Marxism, and feminism 95, 105–6
Marxist feminists 94; analysis of medicalized reproduction 335
masculinities: in fieldwork 74–88; hegemonic 81–2, 138; homophobia 80–2; homosociality 82–4; interpretive communities 84–7; interviews and competing 77–8; overview 74–7; questions threaten men 78–80
Mason, Karen Oppenheim 256
materialist-hedonist humanities 165–8
material realities 142
Mathura Open Letter (Sarkar; Baxi *et al.*) 190
Matoesian, G. M. 180
matrilineal inheritance 38–9
Mazumdar, Vina 39
McChesney, L. S. 185–6
McVeigh-Schulz, Joshua 147
Mead, Margaret 30, 336
media ecology approach 147–8
medical anthropology 333; critical 334; feminist critical 334–7
medical education 327
medical lobby 326
medical profession, RUWSEC clinic and 323–6
medical system 327
medium/context, in digital media space 145–6
Mehta, Aasha Kapur 223–4, 226
Mehta, Deepa 173
Mehta, Hansal 173
Mencher, Joan P. 7
Menon, Lakshmi S. 33
Menon, Nivedita 92, 138, 139, 169–70
Menon, Parappil Madhava 36
men's rights activism 74
men's rights groups 77; annual meeting of 77; gay movement and 81; victimhood 80; women members 77; *see also* masculinities

'The Messy Relationship between Feminisms and Globalizations' (Desai) 246
microcredit programme, in Ghana 240
microfinance 230; overview 229–30; reasons to invest in women 231–2; synergy-based claims 230, 231, 236–7; win–win hypothesis 232–6; *see also* self-help group (SHG)
microfinance institutions 232–3
middle-class girls 251–3
middle-class homebirth movement, United States 337
midnight knock (as metaphor) 68
Mignolo, Walter 138
millennium development goal (MDG) 220–1
Mitra, Avik 83–4
Mittal, Gita 190
mobile phones 137
Mohanty, Chandra 248
Molyneux, M. 242
Monash University in Australia 327
Moon, Meenakshi 58–9
Moreno, E. 184–5
MSM (men who have sex with men) 2
Murphy, Michelle 299
Muslimness 104
Muslims 5; feminist reading of scholarship on 95–7; identity of being 103–5; neighbourhoods/settlements 97–8; segregation of *see* segregation of Muslims

Nader, Laura 181
NAEP *see* National Adult Education Programme (NAEP)
Nagar, Richa 84
Nagy, P. 145
Nairobi International Women's Conference (1985) 238
Nambudiri Brahmin 34
Namjoshi, Suniti 165
Nathan, Dev 239
National Adult Education Programme (NAEP) 314

National Bank for Agriculture and Rural Development (NABARD) 233
National Commission on Self-Employed Women (NCSEW): implications of recommendations 219–21; report and women in informal sector 217–21
nationalized banks 242n1
National Science Foundation (NSF) 37
naturecultures 116, 123–5
Nayar, P. K. 136
Naz Foundation v. Government of India and Anrs 187
Neff, Gina 145, 146–7
Nehru Memorial Museum and Library, New Delhi 283n1
neoliberal capitalism 229, 230
neoliberalism: families and 51; governance 51; sexuality and 167–8
Nights of Labor/Proletarian Nights (Rancière) 169, 172
Niti Ayog 12; *see also* Planning Commission (erstwhile)
Nizamuddin 98, 102, 108
Nochikuppam neighbourhood, Chennai 337
Non-Brahmin Movement 56

OECD *see* Organisation for Economic Co-operation and Development (OECD) countries
Old Delhi 97–8, 102
Omvedt, G. 136
One Billion Rising: 2016 140
online research 10; approaches to *149–50*; questions for 143–8; *see also* digital media
online text 145; *see also* content/text, in digital media space
oppression 8, 49; gender-based forms of 2
Organisation for Economic Co-operation and Development (OECD) countries 213–14
Ott, Notburga 259

The Painter of Modern Life (Baudelaire) 170–1
Pal, Shikha 170
Pandey, A. 185
Panikar, P. G. K. 38
Papacharissi, Zizi 134
Pappu, Rekha 267–8
para-teachers 220, 221
Parpart, Jane 206, 210, 226
partition, and families 65–7
Pasolini, Pier Paolo 164
Patheja, Jasmeen 139
Patna University 274
Patole, Shahu 5–6
Pawar, Urmila 58–9
Pawde, Kumud 62
Pearse, Rebecca 252–3
performance orientation of banks 235–6
Periyar 56
Philips, Susan 180
Phule, Jotiba (Jotirao) 56
Phule, Savitribai 3, 4, 56
Pinjra Tod (Break the Cage!) 170
'Pink Chaddi' campaign 140
Pitocin drugs 337
planned economy/development: CSWI report 214–17; five-year plans 216–17; women's role in 208–14; WRPE 208–9, 210–13
Planning Commission (erstwhile) 12–13; 11th Five-Year Plan 222–5; five-year plans 216–17; role of 207–8; 12th Five-Year Plan 223–5; vision of 208; *see also* Niti Ayog
pleasure, politics of 173–5
poetry 164–5
politics: ethics and 167; Mani on 167; of pleasure, precarity, tragedy and revolution 173–5; Rancière on 167; transgressive 168
politics of belonging 8, 49–50; gender orders 50
positional vulnerability 233
Poster, Mark 131
Potter, Elizabeth 122
poverty 59; feminization of 231; global reassertion of 231
power: biopolitical 120; knowledge and 115, 116
precarity, politics of 173–5
The Predicament of Culture (Clifford) 94–5

private sector 315; employment opportunities in 248, 253–4
Profanations (Agamben) 168–9
Pryse, M. 152
Public Secrets of Law: Rape Trials in India (Baxi) 180, 181
public sector banks 236
punitive rule 51
Punjab, intercaste marriages in 61–2

quality of care, at RUWSEC clinic 318–19
Queen, Mary 135, 142–3, 144

race 22n2; and sex 120–1
Radhakrishnan, Smitha 247
Rahman, Aminur 237
Rajadhyaksha, Ujvala 252
Rajamani, Suresh 81
Ramabai, Pandita 54, 55
Raman, Usha 10
Ramdas, Sagari R. 61, 70
Rancière, Jacques 167, 169
Randles, J. 86
rape: anthropological writings on 184–6; law reform 186–94; medico-legal representations of 183–4; pedagogy and research 190–1; public secret of 179; trial court (1996–98) notes 180–6; women's testimonies to 180; *see also* sexual violence
rape narrative 185
rape survivors 179
RASTA 43
Rastogi, Sooraj 80
Rathod, Sadaf 282
Razavi, Shahra 231, 234
RDS *see* Rural Development Society (RDS)
reactionary gender politics 175
reality: abstraction of 99; conception of 99
real-life methods 9, 99–103; autoethnography 100–1; home/family interviews 100; walking as a research device 101–2; walking interviews 102–3
Recasting Women: Essays in Colonial History (Sangari and Vaid) 54

Regulation of Assisted Reproductive Technologies, India 299
religious orthodoxy 55
Report of the Committee on the Status of Women, India 207
Report of the National Commission on Self-Employed Women and Women in the Informal Sector 207
reproductive health 337–43
Reserve Bank of India (RBI) 233
resident welfare associations (RWAs) 104
Revathi, A. 52, 63–5
revolution, politics of 173–5
rhetorical genealogy 144
Right to Education Act 268
Ritchie, Leon 82
Roughgarden, Joan 125
Roy, Arundhati 174
Roy, Sangeeta 282
Rukhmabai 54–5
Rural Development Society (RDS) 314
Rural Women's Social Education Centre (RUWSEC) 19–20; functional areas 315; overview 313–14; services 315–16
RUWSEC Reproductive Health Clinic 19–20; domestic violence prevention programme 320–1; helping women take charge of their health 321–2; leadership 322–3; medical profession/professionals and 323–6; power inequity 326; principles 317; quality of care 318–19; scope of services 317–18; women-centred, gender-sensitive care 319
Rybas, N. 147

Sagan, Dorian 125
sagotras (same class) 53
Sambhav 46n8
same-sex sexual/romantic intimacy 81
Sangari, Kumkum 163–4
sapindas (blood kin) 53
Saradamoni, K. 39
Sarkar, Lotika 190
Sarvagod, Mukta 59–60
Sassen, Saskia 142

Index

Sathyavathi, Gorre 60, 62, 67
sati 53, 54–5
Satish, Mrinal 190–1
Satyavathi, Kangala 61, 62
savarna (dominant class) 52, 54, 57, 58, 62
Saxena, Jatin 82
Scheppele, K. L. 180
school system 267–83; caste system 277–8; classifying students 272–7; examination process/system 282–3; gender and sexuality 278–82; hidden curriculum 280; overview 267–72
science 115–25; as an institution 123; binary logics of 119; biopolitical power of 120; bodily ontologies 117; colonialism and 117; cultures of 124–5; feminist analyses of 118; gendered worlds of 118–21; history of 119–20; interrogating 121–3; methodology and epistemology 116–18; overview 115–16; Western 117–18
science and technology studies (STS) 115–16
scientific knowledge 118
scientific method 118
scientific methodology 118
scientific objectivity 118
Scott, A. 138
Section 377 of Indian Penal Code (IPC) 2, 80, 173, 187, 189
Seeing Like a Feminist (Menon) 92, 169–70
Seelampur 98, 102, 106
segregation of Muslims 97–108; as counternarratives 105–6; framing research on 97–9; mechanisms driving 108; real estate and 106–8; real-life methods 99–103; self-reflexive account 103–5
self-employment 238
self-help group (SHG): banking and 233–6; description 233; gendered institutional analysis 235; rural women members of 236; women members of 233–4
Semmens, L. 138
Sen, Jhuma 190–1

Sen, Samita 169
Seth, Leila 188
sex, race and 120–1
Sex and Temperament (Mead) 336
'Sex and the Signal-Free Corridor: Towards a New Feminist Imaginary' (Mani) 167
sexism of legal language 194
sex ratio 53
sexual harassment: anthropological writings on 184–6; digital/social media countering 139–40; in the field 184–6; narratives of 191–4; of women protestors 192
sexualities 10, 278–82; leftist revolutionary thinking and 175; neoliberalism and 167–8; work on 169
sexual orientation 121
sexual selection theory 125
sexual violence 4, 5, 179–94; as an object of anthropological research 11; autoethnographies of 184–6; law reform 186–94; overview 179–80; pedagogy and research 190–1; trial court notes 180–6; *see also* rape
sex workers 169–70
Shah, Chayanika 51
Sharma, Nisha 259
Shinde, Tarabai 55–6
Shiv Ram Sene 140
Singai, Chetan 282
Singer, Merrill 334
single-celled organisms 122
Sinha, Mrinalini 1, 2
Sipahimalani-Rao, V. 221
Siras, Shrinivas Ramchandra 173
Sitaram, Shashikala 239–40
Sixth Five-Year Plan 216–17
Slut Walk, Take Back the Night, Why Loiter? 170
Slutwalk campaign 140
Small, Helen 165
Smita, Swati 252
Smithsonian Institution, Washington 46n6
social division 3
social embodiment 138
socially engaged research 205
social media *see* digital media

social sciences 271; *vs.* humanities 166–7
social selection theory 125
sociobiology *vs.* feminist sociobiology 125
socio-technical environments 146–8
socio-technical realities 141–3
Solid: Liquid, a (Trans)national Reproduction Formation (Sangari) 163–4
Sonagachi, Calcutta 170
South Asia 75
Special Economic Zone 230
spirituality, ethics and 168
Spivak, Gayatri 168
Sreenivas, Deepa 283
SRI *see* System of Rice Intensification (SRI)
Srinivas, M. N. 33, 34
Stacey, Judith 93–4
standpoint theory 132
State Bank of India 236
state violence 5
Stepan, Nancy 120
Structural Adjustment Programmes 233
students: classifying 272–7; movement 313; *see also* school system
Subramanium, Gopal 188
Sukumari 45n4
Supreme Court 190; Section 377 and 173
surplus man 53
surplus woman 53
surrogacy 18–19, 163; breach of contract 309; child status 309–10; contract, administration and monitoring of 309; draft bill 306–10; insurance for 308–9; legitimizing 307–10; Ministry of Home Affairs directive 306; overview 297–9; studies on 300
surrogate mother, insurance for 308–9
Susan, Nisha 140
Swaminadhan, Ammu 33–4; family members 34
Swaminathan, Padmini 263n1
Swarup, Aakash 82–3

Sweet, Stephen 255
synergy-based claims 230, 231, 236–7
System of Crop Intensification (SCI) 46n9–10
System of Rice Intensification (SRI) 43–4, 46n8–10

Tacchi, Jo 137
Taj Enclave 98
Tales of the Night Fairies (Ghosh) 170
Tamil Nadu 5, 38–41; reproductive health 337–43; RUWSEC clinic 313–27; SRI 43–4
Tamil Nadu State AIDS Control Society 339
taravads 33–4
Taslitz, A. E. 180, 195n2
teachers 274; para-teachers 220, 221; training workshops 271; *see also* school system
Telangana 249, 263n2
Telugu 249
text *see* content/text, in digital media space
Thampi, Binitha V. 242
Tholakari 61
Tiki, Sabarmatee 46n8
Tiwari, Jignesh 77, 78
'The Traditional Kinship System of the Nayars of Malabar' (Gough) 32–3
tragedy, politics of 173–5
transgressive politics 168
transnational corporations 248
transsexual woman (*hijra*) 2–3, 50; *badaai* 64; law and 63; livelihoods 64; recognition 63; Revathi's account 63–5
Trans-Yamuna cluster 98
trolling 138
The Truth about Me (Revathi) 52, 63–5
12th Five-Year Plan 223–5
Twitter 138; hashtags 144

Ulysses (Joyce) 162–3
Umritzar 55
Una 5
United Nations 206

United States 34; courtroom talk in 180; middle-class homebirth movement 337
universities 6
University Grants Commission 167
University of Baroda, Gujarat, India 32, 33
Unni, K. Raman 38
Unni, Raman 33, 46n5
Upadhya, Carol 247, 250
Uphoff, Norman 46n10
urban women 248
Uttar Pradesh 274
Uttar Pradesh, government schools in 281

Valentine's Day 140
Valmiki, Omprakash 6
Vasavi, A. R. 247, 250
Veerappan 5
Verma, J. S. 187–8
videotaped pregnancy 338
vigilantism 167
villages, in Kerala 39
violence 4–5
Virender v. State of NCT of Delhi 190
Vohra, Paromita 139
Voluntary Health Services 337–8

Wadhwani, Vikaas 79
Wahalang, M. G. T. 140
Wajcman, Judy 142
walking as a research device 101–2
walking interviews 102–3

Wark, Mackenzie 159
Webbed utopia 138
widowhood 53
Willoughby, L. 138
Winkler, Cathy 185
win–win hypothesis 232–6
women: in development programmes 231; as drivers of change 251–5; exclusion from market spaces 240; investment in 231–2; mobile phones and 137; in planned economy/development 205–25; positional vulnerability 233; and racial minorities 121; sciences and *see* science; technology and 137
women-centred care, at RUWSEC clinic 319
women's rights, movements for 8
'Women's Role in Planned Economy' (WRPE) 208–9; report in 1939 210–13
Workbook (CBSE) 272
Working Women's Forum 337
World Bank 263n2; on investment in women 231
World Economic Forum 260

Young, Iris 99
Y.R. Gaitonde Centre for AIDS Research and Education 338

Zakir Nagar 98
Zamorin 36
Zonta Resources 338